THE STAR WHO NEVER
HAD TO SAY "NO"

Lana Turner, Linda Christian, Judy Garland . . . the most beautiful women in the world all loved, and all lost, the most beautiful man. The man to whom nothing was denied, and who never denied himself to anyone — male or female — who desired him . . .

"TELLS THE STORY EXACTLY AS IT HAPPENED!"

—N.Y. POST

Fred Lawrence Guiles, author of *MARION DAVIES* and *NORMA JEAN: The Life of Marilyn Monroe*, teaches at Franklin and Marshall College in Pennsylvania when he is not writing his acclaimed Hollywood biographies.

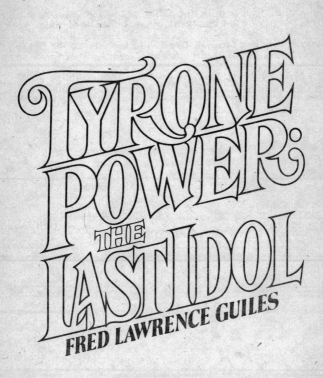

TYRONE POWER: THE LAST IDOL

FRED LAWRENCE GUILES

BERKLEY BOOKS, NEW YORK

Excerpts from *John Brown's Body* by Stephen Vincent Benét from: The Selected Works of Stephen Vincent Benét. Published by Holt, Rinehart & Winston, Inc. Copyright, 1927, 1928 by Stephen Vincent Benét. Copyright renewed 1955, by Rosemary Carr Benét. Reprinted by permission of Brandt & Brandt Literary Agents, Inc.

Interview of Tyrone Power by Harry Gilroy, the New York *Times*, March 8, 1953: © 1953 by The New York Times Company. Reprinted by permission.

Excerpts taken from *Linda: My Own Story* by Linda Christian, © 1962 by Linda Christian Purdom. Used by permission of Crown Publishers, Inc.

Specified excerpt from *You Can't Go Home Again* by Thomas Wolfe. Copyright 1934, 1937, 1938, 1939, 1940, by Maxwell Perkins as Executor; renewed 1968 by Paul Gitlin. Reprinted by permission of Harper & Row, Publishers, Inc.

This Berkley book contains the complete
text of the original hardcover edition.
It has been completely reset in a type face
designed for easy reading, and was printed
from new film.

TYRONE POWER: THE LAST IDOL

A Berkley Book/published by arrangement with
Doubleday & Company, Inc.

PRINTING HISTORY
Doubleday edition published May 1979
Berkley edition / October 1980

ISBN: 0–425–04619–2

A BERKLEY BOOK® TM 757,375
Berkley Books are published by Berkley Publishing Corporation,
200 Madison Avenue, New York, New York 10016.
PRINTED IN THE UNITED STATES OF AMERICA

For Laura Ross,
who has kept a light in her window
for this wandering writer,
and for Larry and Jane.

CONTENTS

viii

AN ACKNOWLEDGMENT

Tyrone Power was as versatile in life as he was on the screen. He was several men, and during the creation of this book I have been fortunate in having the other principal "lead" in each of these lives as an active partner, coming very close at times to the point of collaboration.

His only sister, Anne Power Hardenbergh, has devoted an extraordinary amount of her time, love, and vitality to seeing that Tyrone as a family man, his closeness to his mother and herself, as well as his unwavering respect for their father have been accurately detailed. In an industry where fidelity is considered something of an oddity—and in Tyrone, however briefly, a bit of a miracle—his memory as a lover and husband has been well served by the one woman who understood not only the man but the nature of the enemy that seemed dedicated to destroying their devotion to each other—Annabella Power. As for Tyrone's role as a complex, but always loyal, companion, his closest friend, J. Watson Webb, Jr., has followed this project from its inception with help at every turn, and, in the end, I think, with relief and satisfaction that something of the truth has been caught here.

I want to thank Joshua Logan and Rupert Allan once again for their many kindnesses and for opening significant doors; Tyrone's directors, Henry King, Allan Dwan, Henry Hathaway, and George Sidney, for giving me important background on his work and particular films; George Chasin, Anne Baxter Klee, and Henry Fonda for adding their keen perceptions of the man to this work; and to the following for helping in various ways to bring this portrait to life: Deborah Lawrence, the Marquisa Helena Quintanar, Linda Christian, Taryn Power, Romina Power Carrisi, Leora Dana, Mary Roblee, Robert Webb, Bobby McLean Webb, Mary Loos, Ray Sebastian, André Daven, Maya Van Horn, Sra. Blanca

Welter Alvarez, Robert J. Allen, Michael Steckler, Henry Edw. Lea, Eva Gabor, Cesar Romero, Gertrude Macy, Mrs. Virginia Zanuck, Madelyn Jones, Lothar Wolff, Mrs. Jack O'Rourke, Mrs. Lilian Ruddy, Paul Gregory, and Glenn Ford.

The Library of the Academy of Motion Picture Arts and Sciences has supplied much of the documentary material, without which Tyrone's times could not have been recreated; their staff has my most profound gratitude. Mrs. Felizia Seyd is responsible for much of the text in the Filmography and my thanks to her for her diligence; Mrs. Ursula Fox is due thanks for copying many of the documents and clippings used by the author; and my gratitude goes once more to Carlos Mac-Master for being helpful in so many ways. I am indebted, too, to the staffs of the American Film Institute in Beverly Hills, the Billy Rose Collection at the Lincoln Center Branch of the New York Public Library, Paul Myers, Curator, and the script collection of the Library of the University of California, Los Angeles.

Lancaster County, Pennsylvania   *Fred Lawrence Guiles*

1979

"The secret of charm is bull-shit."

Tyrone Power to friend
Mike Steckler

INTRODUCTION

There are no more idols. No Maurice Costellos. No Valentinos. No Tyrone Powers. Our great male stars today must be of very human clay with the flaws played up instead of down, preferably a mole or two or a pronounced squint, perhaps both; comfortable to sit down with as they chat on a television show; certainly no serious threat to our romantic lives.

The last idol, Tyrone Power, was created by a vast starmaking machine, Twentieth Century–Fox. The star machine was corrupt, but it served to make Hollywood known to the most remote reaches of the earth. The process was dehumanizing, both to the star and to audiences. For a very long time, throughout the great studio period, movies had few admirers for their sake alone. The film language of Griffith or the pathos of Chaplin was seldom discussed. People spoke instead of the grandeur of Pickfair, the Fairbanks-Pickford residence so often shown in Sunday roto sections; the terrible overdose death of handsome Wallace Reid, the sudden death of Valentino, the near-ritualized death of Jean Harlow; Shirley Temple's dramatic powers—"the little Duse"; the size of Garbo's feet and the quality of her plumbing (gold faucets were the much-photographed pride of her rented mansion, a gift from John Gilbert). Shopgirls shed their own identities for something close to Rita Hayworth's or Joan Crawford's. They wrote tons of fan mail and it was answered in due course by corps of secretaries, usually accompanied by autographed photos.

The star machine was at the heart of the studio system. It bore a considerable resemblance to racehorse breeding. The fillies and stallions were carefully groomed for the big race. It is not surprising that many studio heads, Darryl F. Zanuck and Louis B. Mayer among them, acquired stables of fine horseflesh, Zanuck for polo, which was his other passion, and Mayer for racing, which was his.

Most stars were tractable, but a few had fits of rebellion and temperament. In the beginning, Tyrone was docile, the ideal star who would do anything assigned him, with the great advantage of not looking any particular way except exceedingly handsome. His adaptability and versatility would damage him with critics more than any number of mediocre films. He would be overused by Zanuck because Tyrone could do a competent job with nearly everything assigned him, but to do a *brilliant* job, he had to have the right role. There was not nearly enough care taken by Zanuck and others in shaping his career. He became a tool for the studio rather than a prized gem.

All of this concern about the handling of stars became academic with the collapse of the studio system in the middle 1950s. Already, since television had begun enticing audiences away from the neighborhood moviehouses, moviegoers had become far more selective. Films themselves had to be sold on their merits or star power as separate attractions by this time, following the breakup of the moviehouse chains once owned by the film companies. Cast adrift over the next decade were Greer Garson, Alice Faye, Rita Hayworth, Glenn Ford, Kim Novak, Ava Gardner, Dan Dailey, Gene Kelly, Alan Ladd, Ginger Rogers, Robert Taylor, Lana Turner, and Clark Gable. With one or two exceptions, their careers foundered. After all, the studios had made most of them into the images seen on the screen. The collective studio mind was behind each and every career. A mindless star can only trace an erratic course.

Tyrone Power had just managed to break his bonds before the final dissolution. But his roles for Zanuck, with perhaps three or four exceptions, all had fallen into three categories: swashbucklers in the athletic tradition of the first Douglas Fairbanks; film-idol turns with the heavily scented feeling of all the Valentino vehicles; and breezy comedies of the sort that William Haines had made his own province until his premature retirement from the screen. We are not quibbling over comparisons. Tyrone was far more romantic than Fairbanks, a much better actor than Valentino, and less brash and cocky than Haines. But he had been assigned really strong properties on only a handful of occasions. Pleasing and holding the loyalty of vast numbers of fans who cared little about the nuances of fine acting held first priority at Twentieth Century-Fox. Tyrone had been held in check by box-office concerns. There was a delicate line in every dramatic exchange he could not cross on the screen. Rage could only go so far; passion had to be bridled after a point; sarcasm had to be projected fleetingly since any hint that it was ingrained in the Power character would alienate the audience.

So he had not made the final leap from thoroughly professional leading man to great actor. He was not invited, as Olivier had been, to skip from Dreiser's *Sister Carrie* to his own version of *Richard III* and then to John Osborne's *The Entertainer* (the latter a film of the successful play which Tyrone had seen before his death). Archie Rice was a character Tyrone felt he could play well. Olivier was *his* idol, someone who had reached heights he aspired to and in whose presence (in London and occasionally in California) Tyrone felt both humble and exalted.

Tyrone would have liked to become the American Olivier. He had the craft, the dash, the voice. That would have been his natural place in the American theatre as heir to a name that went back to the earliest years of the nineteenth century. But try as he would, he could not turn his back on the idol business, and all those years of being charming on screen and off had drained away some of the passion that was a prerequisite for greatness. He only came close to Olivier's screen stature three or four times during his long career.

What he did have besides almost incredible handsomeness was his voice. It was without qualification the finest romantic voice of this century. For Tyrone, as he matured as an actor, that was a crippling affliction. For his producers, it was an instrument worth millions at the box office.

Because of that voice and those looks, Twentieth Century-Fox used all of the superhype they could contrive to churn up the fans. Tyrone called this "the monster," and that button-tearing, hair-ripping creature trailed after him everywhere, even in the last years of his life when his private and career affairs began going awry. He had hated the servitude impelled by his several long-term contracts with the studio, but they had sustained him through two marriages and divorces. His past follies were costing him more than his present, and that huge studio salary kept him extremely comfortable—the only way he could live finally—through it all.

What was it like to be mobbed by screaming women at every airport, in front of every hotel? Tyrone Power "handled" it. He was the coolest member of his party wherever he went. It was something his studio bosses had seen in him from the very beginning. "Here is a young man who knows where he is going."

We were only allowed to come close to the complexities of his private self once on the screen and that was in *Nightmare Alley*, a film he insisted upon doing against the advice of his employer and nearly everyone else on his home lot. Tyrone felt that there was a great deal of hypocrisy in being a film star, an *idol* if you will; it was a con game, and he wasn't very happy having to play that role day after day. In *Nightmare Alley*, he played a monstrous hypocrite, a con artist, and the honesty of that portrayal thrilled him. What was the public to make of it? Well, few moviegoers got to see it. It was sneaked out for one-week runs at Fox's theatres. No massive promotions. No personal appearances. It was an indulgence on Zanuck's part—Darryl F. Zanuck, head of Twentieth Century-Fox and the man who took all of the credit for creating the most popular leading man his studio ever would have.

There are few villains in this book. Tyrone Power was admired and loved by nearly everyone in the film colony. He had no enemies, except himself, and even that came late in his life. He genuinely liked people and wanted their affection in return. He went to great lengths to achieve that. There were few displays of temperament. He was always up in his lines, always on time on the set. He was proud of his craft, wanting to be as successful as the two famous Tyrone Powers before him, his father and great-grandfather.

But Tyrone was no paragon. A man who seemed to get his highs from falling in love, he had more affairs than any leading man in recent memory and, consequently, littered the Hollywood landscape with more broken hearts. Like a number of men, he seemed far more loyal to his male friendships than to the more tormented liaisons with the ladies. A loyal son and brother, he was generous, loving, and responsible to his family. He was also a changeling, given to wild, spontaneous hijinks. He could toss aside his mature mien with a roguish smile, and the free spirit within him was liberated. He was a man of profound complexities.

I

THE STAR MACHINE

Forget the schedule. You put as much time as you need in on this boy.

> *Darryl F. Zanuck to*
> *Henry King*

HENRY KING was more than the fair-haired boy at the newly merged Twentieth Century-Fox Studios; he was a man whose particular interests in films paralleled those of his employer, Darryl F. Zanuck, almost exactly. They both loved Americana and exploited it shamelessly, for entertainment's sake. They respected screenwriters and were able to get the best from them. They had identical sentimental streaks concerning children, the elderly, motherhood, and the working man. As a veteran director—by 1936 he had been in the movie business nearly twenty years—King was more expert with crowds and mobs than anyone in Hollywood, and he could explain a piece of business to an insecure film star like Alice Faye, whose background had been entirely in a chorus line and in front of a dance band, so that she could moved an audience to total empathy.

In the summer of 1936, he was in his office in the executive building at his studio making plans for the release of his latest picture, *Ramona*, from Helen Hunt Jackson's Indian romance, starring one of his favorite contract stars, Don Ameche, and Loretta Young. *Ramona* was the first Western to be shot entirely in Technicolor, although not the first outdoor film in that process, that honor going to *Trail of the Lonesome Pine*, which had come out in February. At that moment, King was very pleased with the way he had taken a "B" picture assigned to him by Zanuck's producer of programmers, Sol Wurtzel, and by telling all of the Jackson story and casting it properly had brought the picture up to an "A" level, and at no increase in the budget.

King's secretary interrupted to tell him that a young man

would like to see him. "A Mr. Tyrone Power. He wanted just to say hello."

King thought that the boy's late father may have suggested that he contact him sometime because Tyrone, Sr., had worked on at least one picture with King. It was around 1930 and the picture was *Hell Harbor*. "We went to sea for sixteen days," King recalled, "and we had no radio. Everything was done by hand. It was a sailing ship. In those days, the director made up all the dialogue. There was no dialogue written in the script, only business. . . . I laid out a great big scene for Mr. Power to do, told him what to say. We rehearsed it a couple of times and in the middle of a take, he leaned toward me and out of the side of his mouth said, 'Throw me the line! Throw me the line!' Like they do in the theatre many times. I just looked at him. When the scene was over, I said, 'That's very good, boys. Thank you. I'm going to make do.' But Mr. Power was unhappy. He said, 'Well, if you'd have thrown me the line, it would have been a darned sight better.' I told him, 'Mr. Power, I don't mean that. The scene stinks. It's awful. But the greatest piece of acting I've ever seen was when you came over and said, "Throw me the line." There was a man in distress, wanting something more than anything on earth. It so impressed me, I couldn't speak. That's what goes over in pictures.' "

Then suddenly there was young Tyrone Power smiling in front of his desk, "This dashing young man," as King described him, "not twenty-one yet." Tyrone told King he had signed a stock contract in New York. "Mr. Moskowitz signed me up, and I want to do something. I don't want to just sit around. I know you have this big picture, *Lloyds of London*, and if there's something in it I could do, I'd just love to do it." King was impressed by the young actor's self-possession, the crisp sense of knowing exactly what he wanted and where he should go to get it. The director was just completing a test of Don Ameche through five different periods in the picture. He said nothing to young Power about that. He sat there for a few minutes, chatting idly and evaluating the boy, his attitude, his personality, his walk, his obvious sensitivity, which seemed thoroughly masculine, without thinking of anything specific in the way of parts.

King completed the Ameche test and then began noticing

that actor's shortcomings. He was not nearly as handsome as Tyrone Power. He had a big Adam's apple. Yet Tyrone's looks had been refashioned in part by the studio. Mrs. Darryl Zanuck remembers sitting with her husband in a projection room while he screened tests made back in New York, and Tyrone's test came on. "My husband gave his okay to many of the actors he saw that night, but turned Ty down. The boy was very young, had beautiful eyes but his eyebrows were very thick and came across his forehead, which made him look like a monkey. I asked my husband to please have another test made, pluck eyebrows, leaving a space. . . . He did, and the result was startling!"

King liked Ameche personally and that admiration would help ensure the actor a long career as a leading man at Fox. Now King phoned Zanuck and told him the tests on *Lloyds of London* were ready. He phoned his chief cutter, Barbara McLean, known to everyone as "Bobby," and told her to take the footage to "big room one" at two o'clock. That afternoon, Zanuck came into the big projection room with five or six men with him. They were his "yes" men but all had learned not to say even that much until the screening was over. Zanuck hated to be interrupted while any rushes or tests were being run.

A small, nervous man who, according to Gene Fowler, carried a long cigar as though it were a polo mallet, Zanuck was a mogul who rarely seemed to sleep. At three in the morning he was usually in a projection room at the studio viewing rushes from the dozen films in production at any one time. He maintained a small bedroom behind his office where he would catch a few hours' sleep before another frantic studio day began.

After the Ameche test was run off, everyone around Zanuck exclaimed that the star was "just great." They were convinced that their boss was deeply loyal to Ameche. "Oh, he's perfect!" someone said. "He's it!" said another. Zanuck then turned to King and asked, "Henry, how do you feel about it?"

"I like him," King said, but Zanuck, of course, already knew that. "But I just finished with Don in another picture, and I'd like to make one more test. Test someone else to use as comparison."

Zanuck's loyalty to King went far deeper than his feelings for Ameche. "Why, sure, Henry. Make as many tests as you want."

The remark annoyed King. He had been with Zanuck long enough to feel perfectly free to be candid with him, as most others were not. "I only make tests when they're going to be taken seriously," King said. "These tests are expensive. It costs money to make them and they're no fun. Worse than making a picture. It's harder work."

Zanuck was unruffled. King was such an extension of himself, he probably looked upon this outburst as akin to a mild attack of indigestion. "That's perfectly all right. Who did you want to test?"

"There's a boy who came up to my office, Tyrone Power. I'd just like to make a test of that young fellow. Same test as Ameche."

Zanuck got to his feet and the other men followed. They were giving one another astonished looks. King hadn't been informed that only a week earlier Tyrone Power had been fired by director Sidney Lanfield from the musical, *Sing, Baby, Sing,* an Alice Faye vehicle loosely based upon the John Barrymore—Elaine Barry headlined romance. Lanfield considered him weak in the role of Ted Blake, a newspaper reporter with redemptive Orphan Annie impulses to salvage others' lives, and a week or two into production, the director had given the role to Michael Whalen, an Arrow-collar type who had played Shirley Temple's father a couple of times. The firing was especially upsetting to Miss Faye, who had seen promise in Tyrone and had urged Zanuck to cast him.

Zanuck chewed on his cigar, studying King for a moment or two. King was a shrewder judge of talent than Lanfield. "Sure," Zanuck said finally. "Go ahead and make it."

King got the same cast together, about five players in all. Tyrone came up to his office, eager but surprisingly not terribly nervous. They discussed what he should project. And then very quickly, they shot it.

Zanuck was again called and the big screening room was made ready. The studio boss came in with the same five or six men. Afterward, Zanuck sat in silence for several moments. Then he turned and asked his aides, "Which boy do you say? This boy or Don Ameche?" To a man they said, "Don

Ameche." Inscrutable as always behind the dark glasses, he then glanced at King, and the director told him that he preferred Power.

"Why?" Zanuck asked.

"This boy has the makings of a better actor. He's better-looking. He's young. *He's romantic.* And another thing. In three years, this fellow will be the Maurice Costello of our time. We need talent because God knows we don't have much."

"Put him in it before I change my mind."

After Zanuck and his men had left, King asked cutter Bobby McLean whom she preferred. "Tyrone Power," she said without any hesitation. "He looks better in the costumes."

Nearly everyone at the studio was sorry to learn that Don Ameche was out of *Lloyds of London.* The film was slated to be Zanuck's prestige picture of the season, something he felt compelled to do once or twice a year as homage to Griffith and Thalberg, the already legendary Metro production chief who died while *Lloyds* was in production. Zanuck, the great popularizer of history and apocrypha, liked the challenge of a carefully chosen risk, and *Lloyds of London,* the house built on risks, was certainly that.

It was a heady beginning for a twenty-two-year-old actor just out from New York. Two small parts in *Girls' Dormitory* (with Simone Simon in her American debut) and *Ladies in Love* (as Loretta Young's aristocratic young love) and Tyrone was cast in the male lead of the studio's most ambitious film of the year. By going straight to director King, it was Tyrone himself who had engineered that masterstroke and not audience reaction to his brief appearances in the earlier pictures, even though preview-goers were considerably impressed by his walk-on in the Simon movie with his one line: "Could I have this dance?"

With *Lloyds,* Tyrone was launched on a long waltz through history and fable, changing his aspect frequently but never missing a beat, fifteen years of the Zanuck waltz.

On the set of the huge production, there was some concern about the reaction of their leading lady, Madeleine Carroll, who had replaced Loretta Young. Miss Young had taken

Ameche's sudden and enforced withdrawal from the film with considerable anger and annoyance. But Miss Carroll's star was on the rise. She had come to the studio fresh from her international success in Alfred Hitchcock's *The Thirty-nine Steps* (1935) and was about to be even more celebrated that fall in *The General Died at Dawn*, in which she had played opposite Gary Cooper. A great, classic beauty with cameo features, Miss Carroll had something of a temperament, not so much that of a prima donna as that of a schoolmarm, which she had been before entering pictures. But she had heard of the first Tyrone Power, an important name in London's theatrical history, so she allowed that heritage to override her concern about her leading man's relative inexperience. She was being paid many times what Tyrone was receiving each week, the salary for all stock players at the studio being fixed at a modest $75.00 a week. But that sort of imbalance was not unusual in the days of huge stables of players. Marilyn Monroe was paid $750.00 a week for a very long time opposite leading men (who invariably were rendered invisible by her effacing glow) who were paid several times that. The way Tyrone looked at it, Miss Carroll had arrived and he had not. But he was determined to see that he did. One of the most remarkable things about Tyrone in his professional career is that no one ever saw him stumble.

Tyrone was not alone in his determination. Equally aroused to a near passion for him to succeed were Henry King, Darryl F. Zanuck, and film editor Bobby McLean. And it was not simply the huge studio investment involved. Tyrone had a gift for invoking affection and loyalty in others. Rather a strange quality in one so urbanely detached in manner.

When Bobby McLean realized that King was favoring Tyrone in every possible way, she began ordering closeups in almost reckless profusion. It became a kind of private joke between them. Madeleine Carroll, who was used to being so favored herself, although never with such intensity as this, must have been bewildered by the rushes (the daily scenes screened every night for Zanuck, King, and others). She knew her leading man was just another member of the studio stock company despite his illustrious name. But there he was, or rather there his face was on the screen, often just from the hairline to the chin, getting the sort of lingering camera attention only a few stars on the level of Garbo received.

Tyrone responded instinctively to this loving camera attention. It was a though he expected it, although probably not so soon. His later leading lady Anne Baxter described his on-camera quality: "He was the most beautiful man I ever saw. No question. They would be lighting us for a closeup . . . and just watching him, studying his face, it was really a panoply of gorgeousness. The eyes were glorious, the shape of the face, the perfection of the mouth, profile, and he had a charm, an unforced charm. . . . "

Absolutely nothing was left to chance. King remembered getting a note on the set from Zanuck asking him to drop by his office when he finished one night. "Henry," Zanuck said, "I've been watching the rushes. This boy is doing great. He's doing fine. But I just want you to know that had we put Fredric March or somebody else of that calibre in the picture, we would have paid two or three hundred thousand dollars for them. This boy is working for peanuts. . . . I want you to spend that extra money if you feel it necessary. I don't want you to be hurried. Take all the time you need with that boy because if you can keep him all the way through the picture as he is up to now, he'll be a star."

King did not need to be told. In the more than thirty major features he had directed since 1920, including *Tol'able David, The White Sister, Stella Dallas,* and *State Fair,* he had never lavished more time and money on one production before. In fact, *Lloyds of London* would set a new standard of costliness and perfection of detail for King from which there would be no retreat. King looked upon this development not so much as a promotion for himself as an example of Zanuck's fair-mindedness. "Many people thought he was tough and hard," King said of his employer, "but he was not."

Lloyds of London was a considerable commercial success. It played the Roxy in New York, flagship of the Fox circuit of plush moviehouses, where it was held over. The critical consensus was that it was dubious as history but that the ladies would respond to Tyrone Power. Critics were on the whole generous to Tyrone, although the New York *Times* said that "he is required by the frequently lofty script to utter occasional passages which seem addressed to a hearkening posterity. . . . " As Jonathan Blake, he is a party to the founding of the insurance syndicate which was to become known as Lloyds. He is also an old friend of Lord Nelson and, in typical movie hero fashion, helps bring about Nelson's victory. Tyrone looked splendid as Jonathan, his dark brown hair covered by a blond wig for the role, and just this side of beautiful, saving him by a hairsbreadth the abuse heaped on male beauty by the press and public which Robert Taylor had to endure. It could not be expected that he would burst upon the cinematic scene fully developed as a leading actor. Color and dash and emotion were kept within certain modest limits in his part. His voice was that of a perfect leading man for radio, with lovely tones and inflections. He moved with great grace and seemed to have an uncanny instinct for always being where the camera lens could frame him best. Some of the trouble may have resided in the script. The part was not a profound one, not one a fine actor could act from the guts outward. Such roles were a long way off, such a long way, in fact, one wonders if Zanuck was afraid that Tyrone Power was a handsome young leading man who could never be in the same league with Fredric March or Henry Fonda.

But real acting talent was beside the point in the days of the great studios. Dozens of stars were created by the various star-makers—Mayer, Zanuck, Goldwyn, the Warners—stars whose principal qualification was being photogenic. Katharine Hepburn was already in films on terms precisely like those that would bring Tyrone to fame. Instead of being beautiful, she was striking. Her voice was arrogant and unusual. She moved and behaved in an eccentric fashion. Bette Davis was all of this with the added dimension of spite or malice lurking somewhere behind the eyes. But they were not ladies who could command the stage with sheer acting talent. Both would try, and Hepburn would even seem to succeed, but audiences were going to see Hepburn the star, not Hepburn the actress.

Zanuck was seldom wrong about such hunches. He knew just as soon as the film was assembled and he sat through the rough cut that he had more than simply another prestige re-creation of "history." Here was a young man almost unconsciously sexy. If Gable was sexual king of the outdoors, Zanuck would make Tyrone Power his equivalent in the boudoir. For that reason, Tyrone's next few pictures would require him to behave badly, and then repent at the end—a blood brother to Rhett Butler, whose screen incarnation by Gable was only two years away. Zanuck, as a veteran showman, knew that nothing drew women fans to a male star more certainly than the cad reformed or redeemed.

Women fans responded as anticipated, and it was an international turnout. Tyrone's weekly salary shot up first to $250, then $350. He moved his mother, Patia, to a more comfortable apartment on Franklin Avenue in Hollywood. Sister Anne Power was then living with her first husband in Honolulu. Within less than a year, Tyrone had rented a medium-sized "California colonial" on Perugia Way in Beverly Hills with a view of Catalina (on a clear day) from the huge window wall in its L-shaped living room. Mother Patia moved in to run the household. There was a sense now in Tyrone's life of everything being possible. It seemed that with each new picture (and they were coming out every three months), Zanuck behaved in a more fatherly way toward him. It was understood that anything he needed, *anything*, or wanted, all he had to do was ask. Metro's most romantic leading man, Robert Taylor, was being handled in much the same way. Louis B. Mayer had told him that he was the son he had always wanted. Both young men (Taylor was three years older than Tyrone) could not avoid being spoiled a little.

The publicity department took him in hand after each film was wrapped up and sent him on personal appearances. Zanuck had the final okay on these itineraries. Tyrone's earlier stage experience had made him relaxed in front of audiences, but then he had been in small roles and largely unknown. Now, just his appearances touched off cheers and applauses, the sort of ovation Maurice Evans got at the end of *Hamlet*, the difference being that Tyrone had no need to perform. All he had to do was smile and wave. Of course, when he spoke in that suave, seductive voice of his—"I'm so happy to be with my friends in Detroit"—a collective moan from the ladies out front could be clearly heard. On those tours, his accommodations were far more luxurious than anything he knew back in California. In New York, the studio reserved for him a suite in the Waldorf Towers.

At the end of the first big tour, Tyrone needed to catch his breath. On December 20, 1936, he flew to Cincinnati, where he had been born and where his beloved grandmother "Mudgey" Réaume still lived, as well as Aunt Madeline and Uncle Charlie Réaume and his wife Hortense. It was a joyous reunion and it was a relief for him to be reduced to normal scale again.

Leading lady Loretta Young held a special niche at Twentieth Century-Fox. Along with Constance Bennett, she was the only other female star to be taken along from Twentieth Century Pictures as an asset by Zanuck when the merger with Fox took place. But Connie Bennett seemed only at home (on the screen) in stories about the rich, and in those mid-Depression years, such stories were no longer terribly fashionable. Loretta Young emanated a deep curiosity and sympathy in any setting. It was something about her enormous, nearly bovine eyes. Her presence in a film guaranteed an air of decency. She seemed not so much to have leaped over the wall of some convent as to have floated over. Miss Young had a nimbus and Zanuck knew that it brought money into the box offices.

Loretta already seemed "ageless," but she was only a year older than Tyrone, if one is to believe her studio biography, yet already a screen veteran, a graduate of the silents in which she had made her debut as a child actress at five, in a film starring the equally ageless Fannie Ward (*The Only Way,* 1918). Three years later, she appeared briefly in Rudolph Valentino's *The Sheik*, and at fifteen she had reached at least her novitiate on the path to cinema sainthood when just her glance in closeup in Lon Chaney's *Laugh, Clown, Laugh* (1928) was clearly inspirational. Her two sisters, Polly Ann Young and Sally (screen name—Blane), were both in pictures, although Polly Ann was about to retire and Sally's star was in eelipse.

Loretta was an evangelical Catholic who kept a collection box for the poor near her on the set of all of her pictures. It was called a "cuss box" by her colleagues, and when anyone used profanity within her hearing, he or she had to put a quarter in the box. Cameraman Leon Shamroy angrily stuffed a five-dollar-bill in her box when she approached, chiding him, and told her, "that should hold me till noon."

Divorced from actor Grant Withers in 1931, Loretta had a

reputation for being a not very gay divorcée. A brief affair with Clark Gable during the filming of *Call of the Wild* (1935)* had been followed by a long period of seclusion. But she seemed terribly interested to learn that the studio's handsomest new leading man was also a Catholic. She decided to make amends for having backed out of *Lloyds of London* when Don Ameche was replaced. She told Zanuck that she really would not mind appearing with Tyrone Power, and he generously gave her Tyrone's services as co-star in three films, one after the other, in 1937: *Love Is News, Café Metropole* and *Second Honeymoon*. They were all successful and equally forgettable movies. *Café Metropole* had been written by Zanuck's "court jester" Gregory ("Grisha") Ratoff, whose gossip and tears (Grisha could get very emotional) amused the studio head. Grisha was always *on*, and all that expenditure of emotion stimulated Zanuck. Grisha had made a career of playing variations of himself on the screen, most frequently Jewish producers mangling English more extravagantly than Goldwyn, puffing away at a cigarette in a holder as long as his arm and often wearing a beret to show he was a genuine cosmopolite. The slight story he had written was not very fresh, but considerable style had gone into the dialogue. It concerned a rich American family much impressed by foreign aristocracy excited by the prospect of daughter Loretta snagging a Russian prince (Tyrone), who is actually an American impostor very nearly on the skids. Graham Greene, the British novelist and for nearly five years a film critic, admired the script and the performances, but thought it was very nearly spoiled by dull direction. American reviewers were more charitable, but Greene's quibble rankled in Zanuck. That same year, Greene had suggested that Shirley Temple's appeal was sexual and made a comparison between Miss Temple and Marlene Dietrich. Zanuck sued Greene for libel and later won nearly ten thousand dollars. The director-culprit was Edward H. Griffith, whose most prestigious films

* One of several successes Darryl F. Zanuck had as head of Twentieth Century Pictures, which during a two-year span produced, among others, *The Bowery* (1933), *The House of Rothschild*, *Bulldog Drummond Strikes Back* and *The Mighty Barnum* (all 1934), and *Clive of India* and *Les Misérables* (both 1935). Released through United Artists, their uniform high quality and box-office success paved the way for Zanuck's merger with the Fox Company in mid-1935.

had been *The Animal Kingdom* (1932) and *Another Language* (1933). He would not direct Tyrone again. Zanuck saw to that, and Mr. Griffith soon moved on to another studio.

Loretta and Tyrone began to be seen together around town, doubtless encouraged by the press agents at the studio. "Ty," Anne Baxter recalls, "was an extraordinary combination of gentleman and actor, who wanted to be taken very seriously. . . . I don't believe he was a user ever." Under the circumstances, a beautiful woman alone such as Loretta must have been profoundly impressed by all of that. His manners were impeccable. He had no intention of advancing his career through her. Indeed, her boss seemed to be managing that far better than she ever could.

Zanuck could not have been pleased by Loretta's seriousness over Tyrone. He had an extensive investment in both of them. And doubtless he was aware by now that Tyrone's charm affected everyone, men and women alike. It was dangerous because it was so natural, so instinctual. Nothing would be gained by breaking Loretta's heart. Tyrone had to be taken in hand like his own son and persuaded to use a little caution with the ladies.

Loretta may have been warned, too. Veteran screen star that she was, she took the gossip columnists to task for reporting her hand-holding with Tyrone. "A woman may go with whomever she pleases in any other town but Hollywood," she complained. "If an actress is seen dining with a man, it means she is romantically interested in him. If she is seen twice, she is engaged to him. If three times, she is probably secretly married. If she goes places with a boyfriend a few times and then stops, the gossips say that they have had a spat. And if a few weeks elapse before she is seen with him again, the rumor manufacturers blandly announce that the two have quarreled and are now reconciled."

A near-familial tie developed between Tyrone and the Zanucks. Eminently logical. You take a young man, your own employee, aside one day and tell him not to be so generous with his intense attractiveness, develop a little distance between himself and others, especially if they're lonely and vulnerable. Save most of it for the screen. Zanuck had been and was still, quite often, a writer. Writers who go around talking out all of their ideas frequently have trouble repeating themselves on paper. Tyrone's charm might be bottomless, but who knew? Zanuck already saw Tyrone as a great romantic star in the tradition of Valentino, but with a difference. Valentino was sensual and impassive. Tyrone was sensual as well as vigorous and vital.

Whatever Zanuck may have advised Tyrone to do, there was a change in Tyrone at about this time. While it may have led Loretta Young into a temporary state of despair, she seemed to recover quickly and became one of his most vocal admirers on the lot. Zanuck, the not so gray eminence, was pulling what strings he could to end the liaison. He had Tyrone sent to Chicago and then New York for personal appearances.

It was still winter in mid-March when Tyrone arrived by air. There was snow on the rooftops of the buildings surrounding the Waldorf-Astoria. He settled in for a ten-day stay, but on the weekend, a cable came from Zanuck ordering him back by Monday to start on a new picture. Tyrone had been cast opposite the skating star Sonja Henie.

The "romance" with Loretta was officially over when Sonja linked her arm possessively through Tyrone's and accompanied him to the first of a succession of nights on the town. Tyrone's friendship with Sonja, who was about as unlikely a candidate for movie stardom as one could find with her chubby body and appealing but undeniably peasant features, was an almost identical reprise of the Loretta Young entanglement. With one difference. Sonja made everyone aware that Tyrone had won her heart. Privately, Tyrone was of two minds about that. He was like a great, regal butterfly, which is dazzling to behold on one's arm for a fleeting moment but can be destroyed by a possessive cupped hand. Sonja's hurt and bewilderment were yet to come. Now they were swept up in a dizzying round of publicity-engineered affairs.

It was difficult in the Hollywood of that day to tell the real from the fake, even among some of Tyrone's friends. A few thought that he was "serious" about the Norwegian star. A larger number, including director Henry Hathaway, believed that Sonja was "crazy" about Tyrone. And the couple did not clarify matters when they bought identical Cord convertibles, hers completely white to match her all-while outfits, which she favored; Tyrone's black. Some of their friends thought Sonja had paid for both cars, since her salary was more than his. Whoever paid for the Cord, Sonja was headed for a major disillusionment. Tyrone was a congenial, attentive escort in whom love seemed to have no existence.

Snub-nosed, merry-eyed, and adorable Sonja and Tyrone were to make two films together, *Thin Ice* with Tyrone as a young prince in love with a peasant girl (Sonja), and, long after their close relationship was behind them, *Second Fiddle* (1939), in which Sonja played a schoolmarm from Minnesota who goes to Hollywood, where she meets Tyrone, a press agent hired to promote an affair between a singer (Rudy Vallee) and the girl from the hinterlands.

It would be a mistake to assume that because Sonja Henie was unbeautiful and about as self-conscious in a dramatic scene as the most ungifted amateur, she was not enormously popular. She typified the kind of non-actor Zanuck seemed to enjoy promoting to stardom. First there had been Rin-Tin-Tin, the war-orphan police dog found on a German airfield following World War I, and for whom Zanuck had written a long series of successful scripts; then the Dionne Quintuplets, nonprofessional *Wunderkinder* made so by nature and the headlines of the day; and also in 1936, that dyspeptic bullfrog, Irvin S. Cobb, who it was hoped could fill the shoes of Will Rogers—Rogers having died the previous year in a plane crash. Only Cobb was a misfire and failed to connect with the vast movie audiences of that day. Perhaps there was something just a shade too misanthropic about him.

Zanuck had helped build the Warner Brothers stock company of players, that hard-working lot that included Joan Blondell, Dick Powell, Glenda Farrell, Ruby Keeler, Bette Davis, Humphrey Bogart, and ubiquitous Frank McHugh, who seemed to be in everything. Now he was doing the same thing for his own company, putting together a stable of performers so that any desirable property (bestselling book, hit play, story, or original screenplay) could be case competently, if not brilliantly, without going outside. He had no real hope then of rivaling Metro with its policy of maintaining its "strength through depth," by keeping on salary the most sought-after stars in films and backing them up with the finest supporting actors around, and then ranged behind them a whole phalanx of starlets and young leading men or juveniles being groomed for possible stardom. Henry Fonda kept resisting any long-term contracts, but Zanuck had Tyrone locked into a seven-year deal and was already on such intimate terms with him, he expected that to be renewed indefinitely. Zanuck now considered Tyrone on a par with Dick Powell, who had come to Warners while Zanuck was there, and fast approaching the popularity of the rather sullenly beautiful Robert Taylor over at Metro. Of course, Powell was able to carry a tune rather nicely, but Tyrone was more credibly spirited and romantic. As a rival to Taylor, Tyrone projected a slightly impudent *savoir-faire* that made him seem something less than a real threat to Metro's idol for several years.

Some of Tyrone's success derived from his voice. Taylor's, probably in an effort to sustain a masculine "unemotional" level, tended to be monotonous. But Tyrone's was shaded to match the mood and circumstance of the moment, and, in the presence of his leading ladies, altogether too seductive for its own good. Much of his facility in this area was traceable to his two years in radio back in Chicago, where he had first met and worked with Don Ameche, another "voice-leaner." Tyrone's reliance upon his vocal instrument rather than his whole persona would make director Henry Hathaway goad him into reaching for color and nuances in his speech that were more riveting than lyrical. And it was not just his voice. He moved through any action or piece of business too effortlessly. He may well have been a born actor; it was certainly an inheritance. But it was a curse, too, since it forced him to contrive challenges. Directors were too quick when Tyrone was on camera to say "Print it!" Whenever a movie critic would write of one of his performances: "Tyrone Power is Tyrone Power," he would grit his teeth and agree with them.

Tyrone's cool self-assurance presented the slick fan magazines with a tantalizing subject. Being a slick article himself, Tyrone provoked reams of purple prose. "Member of the lost generation," a *Photoplay* series read, "in good standing. . . . They're your children, or your friend's children; they were born to War, reared to the Jazz Age, matured in Depression. . . . They speak a mongrel tongue, a composite of forthright slang, old proverbs used satirically, and Noel Coward. . . . Their code is simple: Get wherever you're going before someone else does, and stay there. Create something that will make money, lots of it, *quick*. Don't be sentimental. Take a cab if you're too tight to drive, and hurry, hurry, hurry—because anything might happen.''

Some of these Hollywood journalists had the perception to see the more obvious traits of Tyrone. He did have a knack for tossing off witty ripostes over which even Mr. Coward might well have chuckled. He had a relentless sense of humor about anything to do with his ripening stardom. On the surface at least he tried to laugh off what was most consistently threatening in his life—a movie failure, an unflattering review, or any assumption that he was where he was because he was Zanuck's or King's protégé. He would have been far too sensitive, too thin-skinned to survive for very long if he hadn't developed the defenses of humor, a kind of exaggerated courtliness, and a closeness to his family with whom he was still the young man he had been before the superhype at Twentieth Century–Fox had engulfed him.

Tyrone was now a frequent visitor at the Zanuck oceanfront home in Santa Monica. He often practiced polo at the Zanuck ranch, Ric-Su-Dar, in the San Fernando Valley, never once giving away the secret that he really didn't like to ride.

Mrs. Zanuck, formerly Virginia Fox and a film ingenue some years earlier, liked to fix him Sunday brunch. Consciously or otherwise, the Zanucks attempted to keep to a minimum Tyrone's weekend carousing. He had met both David Niven, then working for Sam Goldwyn, and Errol Flynn, his counterpart at Warner Brothers, who had shot to fame as *Captain Blood* much the way Tyrone had in *Lloyds*. This trio boozed heavily, knew a variety of young women, and exploited "starlets" far more mercilessly than any producers who might conceivably have done the girls' careers some good. At least in Flynn, there was a profound contempt for women. Flynn's example was not a good one for an impressionable young leading man to follow. As it turned out, the difference between the two men was that in Flynn, gallantry was almost entirely surface. It was "darling" to their faces, and "bitch" behind their backs. With Tyrone, gallantry was inbred.

Then, too, there was the influence of a new friend who had come into his life in 1936, a Cuban-born actor brought to Twentieth Century–Fox from Universal, Cesar Romero.

Romero, too, had come from Broadway, and he had starred on the stage in *Strictly Dishonorable* (1929) and *Dinner at Eight* (1932). A suave womanizer on the screen, away from the camera, "Butch," as he was known, was quite different. He was extravagantly kind to the ladies and had numerous women friends, but he almost never got involved. He was their pal and confidant.

Romero liked Tyrone enormously when they first met at a party thrown by agent Maynard Morris. It must have bothered Romero to learn that Tyrone was running with a small group of actors who prided themselves on their female conquests. Sensitive Tyrone seemed very out of place, but he was very much his own man and he had to make his own mistakes and pay for them as well. Romero's friendship would survive all the coming triumphs and disasters in Tyrone's life. Romero and Tyrone, among other things, shared a loyalty to Zanuck that would do their careers no harm.

Gradually, Tyrone felt less and less need to prove himself irresistible to the ladies. A romantic by nature, he needed one relationship with a woman, not a fresh one every Saturday night. He drifted away from Flynn and sought some stability in his love life.

In 1937, diminutive Janet Gaynor was suddenly the toast of the film colony all over again, just as she had been a decade earlier. But her new success had come away from her old studio, which was now Tyrone's. She had made *A Star Is Born* (1937) for David O. Selznick and while she lost out in the Academy Awards to Luise Rainer (for *The Good Earth*), she was certainly the most talked-about actress of the season. Everyone had thought her career was nearly over and there she was on top again.

Janet was seven years older than Tyrone, but he did not know the exact number or care. He preferred slightly older women on a steady basis. They were less silly, for one thing, and they generally knew what they wanted even if they had trouble finding it. The age difference between himself and Janet Gaynor had allowed him to become infatuated, a teenage crush, in 1929, when he was ushering at the Walnut Hills Orpheum in Cincinnati on evenings and weekends. He had seen her musical, *Sunny Side Up*, innumerable times, always on the job. He was intoxicated with the songs and the sound of the Gaynor voice, which had an occasional human crack in it. When they were on the Fox lot at the same time over a year earlier, she seemed unattainable. But now through nothing less than a miracle, he was her peer and he didn't hesitate to get in touch.

Tyrone began inundating Janet with roses, and within weeks they were, by chance perhaps, in New York at the same time. They were together almost constantly during that holiday. Then back in California, Tyrone began spending a great many hours in her Beverly Hills home. She had been divorced for some time and seemed amused and diverted by Tyrone's intense admiration. He discovered that she was literate and bright and they could discuss books and read aloud together from classic plays like *Private Lives* and *She Stoops to Conquer*. She met his family, mother Patia and sister Anne. Anne said years later that she liked Janet very much.

II

ANNABELLA IN THE WINGS, WHILE THEY BURN CHICAGO DOWN AND "ALEXANDER" IS REBORN

Ty was not guileless. . . . He knew how to handle himself with men and women.

Anne Baxter

ZANUCK had not yet become a Francophile, although Paris would one day be his second home. In 1936, he had begun moving in that direction. He introduced Simone Simon to American moviegoers with considerable success. Now he was handed another French actress named Annabella, a discovery in the late twenties of the great director René Clair. She had come into the company through Sydney Kent, then president of Twentieth Century–Fox and, as Annabella describes him, "a real gentleman."

Annabella was born Suzanne Charpentier in Paris to a magazine publisher and his wife. When she was four, they moved about forty miles away to the village of La Varenne-Saint-Hilaire, a favorite spot for Parisians seeking a country estate. After she had played a small, "silly" (her word) role as the vivandière in Abel Gance's *Napoleon* (1926), René Clair began grooming her as a potential star and in 1931 cast her as the heroine of his magnificent *Le Million*. Clair's hunch was right. The public and critics alike welcomed her to the ranks of Danielle Darrieux and Simone Simon, and the older Madeleine Renaud, Françoise Rosay, and Arletty. She had a marvelous face, the planes more severe than in Garbo's; it was a strong face, suggesting a woman with a will, but with a radiant, redemptive smile that turned all of that severity into pliant femininity.

Annabella was the mother of a growing young girl, Annie, but was separated from actor Jean Murat, who was about to make his most celebrated film for Jacques Feyder, *La Kermesse Héroïque*. She needed a change, and she was happy to be making films at last for an American company, and even happier to learn that these films would be shot in London.

Her sudden eminence in European films had given her a measure of independence, and she had told her friend, Mr. Kent, that she wanted no part of Hollywood.

Finally, the studio had a script which they would like her to consider for her English-speaking debut, *Wings of the Morning*, adapted from a currently popular romantic novel. Annabella's English was not good, and for some weeks a language tutor visited her daily, but by late 1936, or shortly after the release of Tyrone's *Lloyds of London*, Annabella was in London, where *Wings of the Morning* was to be filmed.

The man Zanuck most respected as an actor but who, he knew, privately despised him, Henry Fonda, was sent over to be her leading man. During their first week before the cameras, the director became hopelessly bogged down in technical problems attendant upon the movie being shot entirely in Technicolor, the very first color production made in England. The actors were definitely a second consideration and very soon rebelled, neither one suffering fools silently. Zanuck then sent over one of his best editors, Harold Schuster, promoting him to director, and the shooting resumed.

Rushes were viewed in blue only, since three negatives were shot simultaneously in those early color days. Yet despite all the difficulties, including Schuster's inexperience and Annabella's trouble with the language, the movie was a glorious, eye-filling romance. Remembering the look of *Becky Sharp*, which had color of the postcard variety, Schuster asked the cameraman to tone down everything. The British fog helped. And the movie had an elegiac feeling about it, not unlike that of the Swedish film made thirty years later, *Elvira Madigan* (1967). The story may have been a partial inspiration for *National Velvet* (1944), since there is an identical theme of a girl dedicated to her racehorse and her successful efforts to conceal her gender.

The international success of *Wings of the Morning* (it was a huge success in Europe) convinced Zanuck that he might have another Garbo. Like Garbo, in *Queen Christina*, Annabella was required to dress as a boy through much of the action. She made a beautiful boy, and it convinced Zanuck of her considerable range as an actress. The film also sold him on color for many of his major future productions wherein its use would not dissipate the drama. For many years after *Wings*, it was believed by Zanuck, Cohn, Goldwyn and nearly every major figure in the film industry that color inevitably detracted from a dramatic narrative. *Wings of the Morning* had been a color *tour de force*, a fortuitous conjunction of rigid color control, misty English weather, and a romance that could not suffer from being even slightly distracting in its pictorial beauty.

Tyrone saw *Wings of the Morning* at a studio screening. He said he thought it was beautiful, but he had no special comment about Annabella. He seemed more struck with the intense romanticism projected by Henry Fonda, who was now his friend, and possibly wondered if he had a rival there. Still, Fonda was continuing to turn down every term contract Zanuck offered him.

Meanwhile, in Anita Loos's *San Francisco* over at Metro, Jeanette MacDonald had sung at the top of her lungs the rousing theme song among the ruins after part of the back lot had been laid waste by the "earthquake of 1906," during which she was reunited with her brawling lover, Clark Gable. It was one of the most successful pictures of 1936, and it was certain to lead to a cycle of "musical" or dramatic re-creations of disasters. As soon as its huge grosses were made public, Zanuck began discussing another legendary American catastrophe, the burning of Chicago.

Mrs. O'Leary and her cow, who had kicked over the lantern that had started the conflagration, according to popular (and erroneous) history, were to be featured prominently. Henry King would have to direct it, naturally, since he was the studio's specialist in American history. In their first conferences about the project, the two men began talking less of Mrs. O'Leary's cow and more about her sons. There would be one generous-minded, civic-spirited son, who quickly acquired definition as *Don's* (Ameche) *role*. For dramatic conflict, there would be an errant son who ran with the wrong crowd, the boy who thought only of himself but would, in a grave crisis, show his true O'Leary colors by putting his life on the line. Zanuck could think only of Clark Gable for this latter part, since that kind of character was a specialty of Gable's and he had done just such a turn in *San Francisco*. The studio head made a deal immediately to borrow Gable in exchange for Metro's choice of Twentieth Century-Fox stars.

Gable and Harlow were then a very hot team at the box office, having done four pictures together, and were involved at
the moment in the production of a fifth, *Saratoga*. Zanuck
decided to borrow Harlow as well.

Henry King always went off with the script of a major picture to be by himself for two or three weeks. This time, he
chose Honolulu, but his timing was unfortunate, for there
was a ship strike called almost as soon as he landed and he was
stuck there. Zanuck finally cabled him to get back just as soon
as he possibly could. "We're postponing *Mrs. O'Leary's
Cow*. Will you please read *Heidi*?"

King knew that Zanuck was thinking of the children's
classic as a vehicle for Shirley Temple and he was vaguely
miffed. He had nothing against little Miss Temple (not so
little any more, since she was approaching her tenth year), but
there were half a dozen directors under contract who could
handle such an assignment over their shoulders. King decided
that the best way to confront Zanuck with the word that he
had no intention of directing *Heidi* was in person, so he
caught a Japanese ship to San Francisco.

"I sent Zanuck a cable," King recalled, "and told him I'd
be there as soon as I could. He sent an aeroplane to San
Francisco to pick me up." He desperately wanted to know
why Zanuck was not doing the movie after all the preparation
that had gone into it.

"We can't get Clark Gable."

"What in the hell do we want with Clark Gable? . . . The
way that this character (Dion) treats his mother. With her
doing washing, taking down shirts to iron them and then him
wearing them, and with Dion's age at the end of the picture
when he crawls up to his mother's knee, a hardened criminal.
Believe me, the audience should all want her to kiss him right
under the chin." King knew how to channel his own sentiment
so that he could erode Zanuck's determination on almost any
matter under discussion.

But this time Zanuck stood firm. "Henry," he said,
"you're crazy. Gable did *San Francisco*."

"Does he have to play in every picture there's a fire in?"

Zanuck saw through King, but he seemed to enjoy these
"showdowns." "So you really don't want to do *Heidi*?"

"No, I don't. What I'd really like to do is take a nice, clean young fellow like Tyrone Power. He's young enough to be doing all the crazy, idiotic things Dion does, and when at the end he goes up and breaks down in front of his mother and is sorry, people are going to believe him."

Zanuck said nothing, but a week or so later, King got a call to go down to Zanuck's office. There were a couple of producers there, and no one seemed to know what the meeting was about. Once inside Zanuck's inner sanctum, Zanuck began to pace the floor, swinging about a club which he used to strengthen his wrist for polo. "About a week ago," he began, "Henry came back from Honolulu and came in here with the most cockeyed story I ever heard. I just couldn't believe it. But after giving it some thought, I think he's exactly right and I want you all to start *In Old Chicago* (fortunately, they had given the script a new title) and go right ahead with it."

The staff producers were still at sea, since they had recently learned through Metro's Eddie Mannix that Jean Harlow was very ill and could never make another film. She died very soon afterward, and her terminal illness, the producers felt, had put the quietus on the project.

Seeing their bewilderment, Zanuck repeated what King had told him a week earlier. "The cockeyed idea is that Henry wants to put Tyrone Power in the role of Dion because he says Clark Gable is too old and they'd hate him and his mother scene would be wrong."

Production began. King decided that Alice Faye should replace the dying Harlow in the role of Belle Fawcett. Zanuck, who was extremely careful about casting matters except in his growing conviction that Tyrone could play anything, asked King if he had ever worked with Alice Faye. He said, "She can't remember from here to there."

King felt that Miss Faye's problem was insecurity. She had worked with Lanfield and a couple of other directors who had yelled at her, and she was extremely sensitive. Just to satisfy Zanuck, King made a test of her with Tyrone. It was a neat reversal of roles for Tyrone and Miss Faye. Just as she had gone out on a limb for him (to little avail) on *Sing, Baby, Sing,* now he was able to oblige her on *In Old Chicago.* He patiently filled her in on how he was projecting Dion's character. He was nearly all guile with just enough surface charm to get by with it. For the test, Miss Faye was sitting at a vanity table and had to look up in the mirror and see Dion's image there. Despising him at that moment, she was to turn and throw a jar of cold cream at him. Miss Faye was convincingly angry, and no one questioned her ability to act again. In fact, as she slipped deeper into her role, she was so competent, Zanuck began bragging that the company had a "new actress" on the lot. By the end of production, she was so warm, appealing and convincing as Belle, she and her leading men, Tyrone and Don Ameche, began informal discussions on doing *Alexander's Ragtime Band* together some weeks before *In Old Chicago* was even finished.

Alice Faye was pure Hollywood star. She had a vast following, in no way the result of her acting skills, which despite her small successes in parts of limited range rarely allowed her to stray very far from her own personality. Basically, this was an innocent, blond, wronged woman who nearly always forgave the heels in her films and came back to them, often trailing a little glory she had acquired in her abandonment. Her tremulous, throaty voice in song became the most successful vocal instrument of American films. She introduced more new popular songs than Al Jolson, Eddie Cantor, and Judy Garland combined.

On screen, she was rarely defiant (which she tried to be as Belle Fawcett), and there was seldom any hint in her screen presence that there was an independent mind behind the innocent facade. She could be buffeted by the ill winds of the screenwriters and ring perfectly true.

Her background had been mostly in *George White's Scandals* and as a radio singer with Rudy Vallee's band. All of her acting technique was learned at the Fox lot, either with coaches or on the set with a number of Zanuck's most skillful directors. She was given a variety of young women to play, including Lillian Russell, and she turned them all into demure, appealing ,and, quite often, smiling Alice Fayes. Solemnity or heavy drama made her self-conscious. She could not play a murderess, an adulteress (except in her heart, bless her), or a hedonist. Any role along those lines would have bewildered her millions of devoted fans and prompted angry letters.

Tyrone and Alice Faye appeared in three films together, two of them outstanding by any measure. He was continuing to grow as an actor, and the same audiences that came to see

Alice Faye as herself began in a limited way to appreciate Tyrone's skills as a performer. The two stars had one thing in common beyond their mutual success. Their birthdays were the same, although she was born in 1915, making her exactly a year younger.

And what was it Tyrone Power projected with this eighth film for Twentieth Century-Fox? Like Miss Faye, he was becoming famous for his smile, but it was far more versatile than hers. It could be delighted, seductive, ironic, and even menacing. But he was fine without it, for then he worked almost entirely with his eyes. They could flash with sudden anger, melt with adoration, flirt outrageously, and, half-closed, send young women in the audience into ecstasies. His six-foot body was not being overlooked either. He had fencing lessons regularly and he played tennis often with David Niven and others. Zanuck was continuing to teach him the rudiments of polo, although he was far too valuable to play in a match. A bad bruise or break might delay a picture. Zanuck breathed much easier when Tyrone was playing croquet on the large, flat greensward fronting the Zanuck desert house at Palm Springs.

Tyrone had become one of a handful of Fox stars of interest to other studios, the others being Shirley Temple, Don Ameche, Alice Faye, Loretta Young, and Simone Simon. Hunt Stromberg, a major producer at Metro-Goldwyn-Mayer, was already holding preliminary discussions with Zanuck to borrow Tyrone to play opposite Norma Shearer in his spectacular production, *Marie Antoinette*, the script for which had been prepared under the aegis of Irving Thalberg before his death in 1936. Later, it would be said that it had been at Miss Shearer's suggestion, so clearly Tyrone had caught the eye of numerous actresses beyond the walls of the Fox lot.

Alice Brady, who played Mrs. O'Leary in *In Old Chicago*, had been in films, with occasional sorties on the stage, since 1915. The daughter of famed Broadway producer William Brady, she had a reputation off-screen for playing more than for working. She was droll, once sending a pair of dueling pistols to comedian Stan Laurel when he and his wife at the time were involved in what appeared to be a non-stop quarrel; she was impish and bawdy. She liked her scotch and handled it well. Her irrepressible presence on the Hollywood social scene eventually led filmmakers to cast her to type as her off-screen self, and in nearly all stills from her films from *The Gay Divorcée* (1934) on, Miss Brady had a cocktail in her hand.

Not so as Mrs. O'Leary. Here she projected a patient endurance, a bit of Mother Courage combined with Whistler's Mother and Marie Dressler. She became a treasured friend to Tyrone and went to the local pound to fetch him a dog when she discovered that he was (horrors!) dogless. She named the mutt "Pickles" rather than the more common "Heinz," and Tyrone loved the ragged beast.

Miss Brady's career turnabout enchanted the critics and turned the Oscar race for best supporting actress into a real competition between her and sprightly Dame May Whitty, who had the advantage of having repeated her stage *tour de force* as the crotchety invalid who meets a murderer in *Night Must Fall*. Miss Brady won, as did assistant director Robert Webb, who had handled much of the mob action during the burning of the city. *In Old Chicago* was nominated as Best Picture, but that Oscar had gone to *The Life of Emile Zola*. 1937 was a great movie year. Other nominees were *The Awful Truth, Captains Courageous, Dead End, The Good Earth, Lost Horizon, Stage Door* and *A Star Is Born*. Such vintage films coming one after the other makes one wonder what has happened to the movies. It was a year when Hollywood had gathered behind its studio walls much of the finest acting, directorial, writing, and technical talent in the world.

Henry King, who had a fatherly interest in Tyrone, evoked a stronger response in the young star than Zanuck, because he didn't always play it safe. King was a passionate flier and kept a single-wing Waco at the Metropolitan Airport in the San Fernando Valley. Soon after *In Old Chicago* was wrapped up, he took Tyrone up and began to show him how to handle the plane himself.

Zanuck was not especially happy to learn that King's enthusiasm had infected Tyrone and that he was beginning to take flying lessons. When he went up on his first solo flight, "Pickles" was on the field and, once Tyrone figured out how to secure him in the two-seater plane, a passenger.

From then on, Tyrone always flew whenever he could, both commercially and privately. In that early time, flying gave him a little distance in which to find himself again, just as later it would help exorcise the demons that were crippling him.

Popular music in American was swept by a wave of change as the nineteenth century ended. In 1899, Scott Joplin, a Negro pianist in New Orleans bordellos who had taught himself to read music and compose, wrote "The Maple Leaf Rag." Ragtime was the first formalized attempt to set down the exhilarating, liberating rhythms of Negro jazz. But rags were a special sort of jazz. They did not have the long-sustained wailing notes of the blues, not the martial percussiveness of such later jazz as "The King Porter Stomp." Ragtime had a frenetic, restless lilt of its own with very few pauses. It was music with a high blood pressure and it admirably lent itself to saloon piano music, to early jazz combos from New Orleans to Chicago, and even to the calliopes of merry-go-rounds. If a singer had the lung power to meet its demands, rags began to be sung in cabarets and vaudeville.

Joplin was to write dozens of ragtime pieces, including the later famous "The Entertainer" (theme music for the movie *The Sting*, 1974). He was even to compose a black opera, filled with ragtime arias. But the most popular rag of them all would be written by a white man. In 1911, America went ragtime crazy with Irving Berlin's "Alexander's Ragtime Band." Berlin actually had written the tune earlier as "Alexander and His Clarinet," but that year a celebrated vaudevillian, Emma Carus, sang the new version in her customary raucous style (Emma was a belter) during a Chicago engagement. Within days, the theatre was packed and by the end of her first week, all Chicago was humming, whistling, and even attempting to sing snatches of a song that came close to putting as much strain on an ordinary voice as "The Star-Spangled Banner."

"Alexander" became the biggest popular music craze of the twentieth century. It popularized social dancing because it could be danced to a modified fox trot. Country clubs and cabarets now had to install dance floors. Hotels began holding tea dances in late afternoons. Dancing to the piano or gramophone record even invaded the parlor. In 1913, someone wrote in the London *Times* that only in America could ragtime have been born. "It is the music of the hustler and of the feverishly active speculator.''

Along with W. C. Handy's "The St. Louis Blues" and a handful of other popular tunes, "Alexander's Ragtime Band" went into the social history books as among the most significant and influential music of our time. So when Darryl F. Zanuck invited Irving Berlin to come to Hollywood in early 1938, twenty-seven years after "Alexander" was composed, he came planning to remain until "a film cavalcade" of his great tunes had been put together by him with the help of Richard Sherman, a studio scenarist. Finally, a screenplay was written by Lamar Trotti and Kathryn Scola with Zanuck contributing ideas constantly.

Zanuck had brought screenwriter Lamar Trotti out of the Motion Picture Code Authority Office (Will Hays's province in that day), where Trotti had been so shrewd in helping producers out of Code difficulties that he seemed more writer than code-enforcer. He was a man who knew what would play on screen and what would not, although occasionally (*Wilson*, 1944), enthusiasms for his subject could carry him to excess. He had written *In Old Chicago*, contriving the screenplay from old fables rather than historical truth. Now Zanuck was asking him to do much the same for Irving Berlin, but in reverse; turn a man (Berlin) into a legend. The script was to be tailored to the requirements of the same trio of stars: Tyrone, Alice Faye, and Don Ameche. Trotti knew without being told that Tyrone's character had to have a touch of the bounder in it, but in *Alexander*, it was considerably modified. He played a man more obsessed with ambition to succeed as leader of "the bes' band in the land" than with the charms of his blond singer, who quietly carried a torch.

Tyrone was told of the project even before Berlin's arrival. He knew that the popular composer had done the scores of two of Fred Astaire and Ginger Rogers' biggest hits (*Top Hat*, 1935, and *Follow the Fleet*, 1936.) Berlin also had done a score for Zanuck the previous year (*One the Avenue*, starring Dick Powell, Alice Faye, and Madeleine Carroll) from which a standard had survived, "I've Got My Love to Keep Me Warm." Tyrone had no qualms at being cast in a musical even though he had had no training as a singer. Berlin wrote one new number, "Now It Can Be Told," with the most limited vocal range of any song he ever composed, and it is conceivable that Tyrone might have done it competently but, in production, first Don Ameche sang the ballad and then Alice Faye in her liquid, slightly tremulous style, and it became another Berlin hit.

The film was set in 1915, and Tyrone played Roger Grant, as in *Grant Street*, a young San Francisco scion who disappoints his family by declaring his allegiance to ragtime and giving up his studies of the classical violin.

Roger manages to pull together a small jazz group, consisting of two trumpets, a drummer, a pianist (played by Don Ameche) and himself on violin. Their first gig is in a Barbary Coast saloon where they persuade a coarse, befeathered saloon singer (Alice Faye) to join them, especially since she has a lively tune in her repertoire, "Alexander's Ragtime Band," which she acquired in a bar during her knockabout career. She is quickly transformed by the elegant Roger into a natural, well-groomed beauty.

The New York producer Charles Dillingham—the name, incidentally of an actual person active in Broadway production at the time—hears the band and Stella, but decides to take only Stella to New York. Stella, emotionally tied to Roger, is reluctant to leave, but pianist Charlie, despite his own love for her, tells her she would be a fool to let this offer go by. Roger, thinking only of furthering his band, is angered by her decision to go East.

World War I intervenes, and Roger enlists. He is asked to pull together a band for the troops, and he and his army band are appearing briefly on Broadway when the call comes to leave for overseas. The soldiers, led by Roger, march out of the theatre to the waiting boat, to the snappy, marching beat of a Berlin song, while a stricken Stella looks on from the audience.

Stella marries Charlie during the war, but her heart is still Roger's, and Charlie allows her to divorce him. (Ameche was to play the part of the loser in a triangular situation so often just his name in the cast gave away the plot.) Meanwhile, the war over, Roger hires Jerry (Ethel Merman) who sings so loudly and lustily, she helps make the band just right for the post-war jazz fever. They eventually wind up playing Carnegie Hall, which is where lonely Stella sees them, watching from the wings until Roger sees her and pulls her on-stage to sing once again the song that brought them so much fame (and heartache).

Somewhere in this colorful saga is a clue to Zanuck's huge
success as a barometer of public taste. Give an audience a
dash of honky-tonk, a bitter *soupçon* of failure or difficulty,
either financial or romantic or both, and then an exhilarating
flood of success. The simple plot-line allowed musical breaks
in almost machine-gun bursts, including "Oh, How I Hate to
Get Up in the Morning," "Blue Skies," "All Alone (by the
Telephone)," and more than twenty others. In the wake of
the film's promotion, "Alexander's Ragtime Band" became
the most popular song in the nation all over again. Music was
moving into the swing era and Benny Goodman and his im-
mortal group of bandsmen recorded it. The recording became
one of Tyrone's lasting favorites.

The film itself, despite its banal story line, was lifted by
Henry King into an entertainment that is as beguiling today as
when it was first made. It made the best-ten list of nearly all
film critics in 1938 and appears on an astonishing number of
"best films of all time," including that of the International Motion Picture Almanac. In retrospect, it is a much
better movie than the film that won the Oscar that year,
You Can't Take It with You. The informality of *Alexander*,
its easy looseness and casual weaving of conventional story
and song make it seem unimportant, but it was a perfect
meshing of studio talent and Broadway's (Berlin) with no new
star to promote, no message to espouse, and no disaster to
outmatch from another studio. No film in the years ahead
would approach its enduring popularity among Tyrone's entire body of work. Its maker, Henry King, was to call it the
movie he personally enjoyed the most of all of his sixty-five
features.

Beginning with this film and lasting nearly a decade,
Tyrone would be handled by Zanuck as an old-style movie
star, playing everything from remakes of old Fairbanks and
Valentino films to Jesse James. Tyrone never once protested.
He respected Zanuck and there was a deep well of gratitude in
him for what his boss was doing for him. He was given a
chauffeured limousine, although unless he was too tired, he
preferred driving himself. He was given access to the executive
steam room, almost the only actor so honored. It became
clear to everyone at Twentieth Century–Fox that just as
Nunnally Johnson was Zanuck's most-favored writer and
Henry King his most-favored director, Tyrone Power was
now indisputably his most-favored star.

The fan mail began pouring in, and at first Tyrone was assigned a woman secretary. But he was seldom comfortable around her. He had to watch his language. One of his favorite put-downs of anyone was "ass-hole," and it didn't matter that the woman told him that the word was perfectly agreeable to her ears, Tyrone got rid of her and hired a rangy Canadian a dozen years older than himself named Bill Gallagher. Bill was a nephew to "Uncle Frank" Adams, who had been Tyrone's father's lawyer, and was now handling the son's business affairs for a hefty commission. Bill Gallagher was as plain in face and figure as Tyrone was attractive. That was as it should be, and around Bill, Tyrone was more open and more truly himself than with anyone else on the lot. Bill became a permanent fixture in Tyrone's life, traveling with him and generally looking after him until he died.

Norma Shearer was a recent widow when production on *Marie Antionette* began. She and her late husband, the mythic and yet too mortal Irving Thalberg, had been the most golden of couples. He had made her into one of the talking screen's favorite leading ladies. Even though nearly half a million dollars had been poured by Thalberg into the development of the screen property *Marie Antoinette*, including the purchase price of the Stefan Zweig biography, Norma's first declaration was that she was planning to retire from the screen. For the sake of her acting reputation, it is a pity that she did not. She would have only two truly praiseworthy films in the years ahead (*Idiot's Delight* and *The Women*, both 1939).

It had indeed been Miss Shearer's notion to borrow Tyrone Power to play the young Count, who is in love with Marie. She had seen all of his pictures and thought he had more appeal than her own studio's Robert Taylor. In fact, Taylor's woodenness would help bury her in her last film (*Her Cardboard Lover*, 1942).

Zanuck was pleased that his faith in Tyrone had been so justified by the industry, although there were a few billing problems. John Barrymore had been cast as King Louis XV with Robert Morley as Louis XVI. As released, only Tyrone and Norma Shearer were billed above the title. There was also a strong emphasis on mob scenes, since the budget on this "sweeping panorama" of the French Revolution was one of the highest in Metro's history. Despite director W.S. (Woody) Van Dyke's rapport with Tyrone, who was every bit as professional if not as capable as Robert Morley, Tyrone seemed even more callow than he had in *Lloyds*.

Working with John Barrymore was a great disappointment to him. This idol of his earliest years as a juvenile could not remember even the simplest of lines and had them chalked on huge blackboards out of camera range. He was often drunk on the set or missing altogether. Upon seeing this wreck of what had once seemed so fine, Tyrone resolved to be the most disciplined leading man ever.

When the reviews were in, after its opening in August, 1939, Tyrone was utterly demoralized. They read very much like those routinely received by Taylor—"Tyrone Power is handsome in the role of the Count," or, more discerningly, "Tyrone Power is wasted in the role of the Count." Fortunately, *Alexander's Ragtime Band*, which had been made in far less time than *Marie*, opened just a week before the Shearer film, so it was easy for Tyrone to shake off the blues. *Alexander* was still running long after *Marie* had made its pedestrian rounds. As for Zanuck, he determined never to loan out Tyrone again, thus depriving Tyrone of two prize screen roles that would have advanced his career as an actor immeasurably, *Golden Boy*, the Clifford Odets play that made William Holden a great star in 1939 in a part for which Columbia's head Harry Cohn believed Tyrone ideally suited, and then again in 1942 when Warner's Hal Wallis tried to get Tyrone for the role in *Kings Row* that eventually went to Robert Cummings.

While Tyrone's star was rising so spectacularly, his sister Anne's marriage was deteriorating. In late 1937, she returned from Honolulu to the mainland, going briefly to Las Vegas for a divorce and then moving in temporarily with Tyrone and mother Patia on Perugia Way. Sad as Tyrone was to see his sister's life so upset, he was relieved to know that someone now would be with Patia more of the time. Within weeks, he helped get Anne a job at his studio as an assistant reader in the story department. The pay was so low, Anne and several other employees who had been given jobs on the strength of a family association with the studio called their table in the commissary "the Bureau of Poor Relations."

Tyrone always kept Patia informed of what was happening

in his life, but he was in no way tied to her. When she occasionally disapproved of something he was doing, he would try to convince her that she was mistaken, but he rarely declined to do it.

Patia Réaume Power had been forced by circumstance to be both father and mother to the children. Tyrone Sr. and Patia had separated when young Tyrone and Anne were toddlers, and he had married another actress, Bertha Knight. But Patia had been no ordinary parent. She had instilled in both children a respect for the acting profession, the Theatre, making it seem much the noblest available to man. This, despite their actor father's desertion of them all; and, it must be said, she sustained a respect in them for him, too, never failing to point out his achievements and reminding them often of his place in the theatrical firmament. Patia felt strongly that in their partial abandonment, there was a danger her children might be damaged in self-esteem. She taught them both to be terribly proper, assuring them that actors (and she never let them forget that she was an actress) were classless and should be equipped to move freely on any level of society. Good manners became as unconsciously implanted in them as the ability to walk. Patia Power was a one-woman finishing school in many ways, her sense of discipline strong but rarely harsh, and her imprint would be visible throughout the lives of Tyrone and Anne. She also taught them to enjoy and reverence life, to appreciate all the little and large things, or, as Tyrone himself listed them on one occasion: " . . . sights, smells, feelings, loves, hates, successes, disappointments, illnesses, and moments of supreme bliss."

Patia was in no sense Tyrone's partner or companion, as Clifton Webb's mother Maybelle was to him. She had command of the house on Perugia Way but not of his life. At about this time, Tyrone invited Eve Abbott, an actress with whom he had become involved during the run of Katharine Cornell's *Saint Joan*, to stay at Perugia Way when she came to California. The relationship between them had cooled to a platonic level, and Tyrone was getting more deeply involved with Janet Gaynor by the day—but not under the same roof with his mother. Out of respect for Patia, their trysts were occurring at inns in the desert or the mountains. There was an immediate clash of temperaments between the women—Evie, a jazz baby born about ten years too late for the flapper years, wearing flaming red ensembles, eager to try everything at least once and appealing to *that* side of Tyrone, and Patia, reserved, forever proper, fitting everything into its place. At Tyrone's suggestion, Evie returned to New York.

Patia would surrender control of the Perugia Way house at just the right moment—when Tyrone was about to marry. She often made mistakes in her life; the seas around her could be stormy; but she always reached port intact. So, too, did Tyrone. And there was a bond between them beyond that. When Tyrone phoned his mother once or twice a week and, occasionally, every day, it was not because he was being dutiful. She was as much responsible for his success as Zanuck was. She had helped mold something rare in the theatre and even rarer in Hollywood—an actor who was also a thorough gentleman.

Still smarting from Metro's misuse of Tyrone's talents, Zanuck sought a vehicle for him that would be very nearly as significant historically as the French Revolution but in which Tyrone would have the pivotal role. It occurred to Zanuck that one of the great engineering achievements of all time had been overlooked as screen material—the building of the Suez Canal.

Scenarist Sam Duncan was deep in researching the life of Ferdinand de Lesseps, the man who masterminded the entire idea of the Canal and its construction, to be played by Tyrone, of course, when Zanuck asked him to write in an appealing role for Annabella. *Suez*, as the screen project came to be called, was not just to be a solo vehicle.

In the fall of 1937, Zanuck decided that Annabella should be given the full treatment accorded his greatest stars by his publicity department. The buildup began with far more intensity than Mayer's promotion of Garbo back in 1926. Annabella was interviewed by all of the film magazines. Essentially a very private person, she was firm with the studio in insisting that, while she was not being uncooperative, her after-studio hours would be her own.

Edith "Edie" Goetz, Louis B. Mayer's second daughter, who was married to Zanuck's second-in-command, William Goetz, threw an enormous party in Annabella's honor, soon after her arrival. It was crowded with directors, producers, and stars who were curious to see the latest Zanuck import.

Few knew that he had nothing to do with putting her under contract, but nearly everyone had heard that she was being paid $75,000 per picture, which was then a sum that commanded respect. Edie Goetz, who had met Annabella in Paris, thoughtfully had seen to it that there were several members of Hollywood's French colony in attendance, including stars Simone Simon, Charles Boyer, and Danielle Darrieux, and directors Julien Duvivier and Anatole Litvak ("Tola" was really Russian, but he had made his reputation in French films and had come to Hollywood that year). Annabella had worked with Boyer in three pictures—the French version of a German film, *Barcarolle d'Amour* (1929), the French version of an American film, *Caravan*, and *La Bataille* (both 1934). That evening at the Goetzes, she met once again Boyer's British-born wife Pat Patterson, and discovered that the Boyers looked with some amusement at the highly chauvinistic French community and were doing their best to become thoroughly Americanized. Annabella found that attitude very close to her own. She had come to love American food, California, *Americans*. While most of her compatriots spoke longingly of Paris, their precious *pommes de terres frites, biftecks,* Hermès calendars, and Paris dailies, she delighted in the ugly sprawl of Los Angeles, hamburger stands, backyard swimming pools, and the breathtaking views of sea and mountains. To their horror, she admitted publicly that she had fallen in love with America. Backs began to be turned.

When Annabella had arrived to do *The Baroness and the Butler* opposite William Powell, she had taken a bungalow at the Beverly Hills Hotel with her mother, her daughter, her English secretary, Violet Wright, and Pierre, her younger brother, as well as two dogs. That situation had proved too inconvenient and costly almost immediately and she moved to a furnished house on Chalon Road in Bel Air. Annabella was overwhelmed by the beauty of the houses in that exclusive neighborhood. Since she always rented furnished places, she moved a lot, whenever a new house struck her fancy. By spring 1938, she was living in her third American home on St. Pierre Road.

In Europe, Germany had occupied the Rhineland, and civil war was still raging in Spain. Germany would soon annex Austria, and the French government was foolishly proclaiming the Maginot Line, an underground maze of fortifications along the Alsatian border, as impregnable. Annabella's father, Paul Charpentier, knew better, and he had remained behind to look after their two homes at St. Cloud and Le Pilat.

There was an even more foolish air of unreality within Hollywood. Annabella thought the town was totally out of touch with what was happening in the world. But she didn't mind that. In fact, she welcomed it with relief.

Annabella's husband, actor Jean Murat, came for a month's visit between pictures, and they regretted that their screen careers seemed to be keeping them apart for increasingly longer periods. Murat, twenty-two years older than Annabella, had told her when they were first married that any time she wanted her freedom, she could have it. He would prove to be a man of his word.

The activity at her studio, Twentieth Century-Fox, struck Annabella as both a little ridiculous (so many "yes" men around Mr. Zanuck!) and terribly efficient. Shirley Temple and Alice Faye were the reigning princess and queen, and Tyrone Power was indisputably the studio's king and darling. The Charpentiers called him *le petit cheri* because of his incredible male beauty. Only Annabella had seen him, and that was at a big party at Jack Warner's. Then Tyrone had been surrounded by noisy admirers at the bar. He was laughing when she caught her first glimpse of him. Then he saw her and came over to her corner. "I hear we are going to work together," he said, adding that he was much looking forward to it. She thanked him and left almost immediately. She was in the midst of shooting a film with Bill Powell and had to get up at five-thirty.

When the pre-production phase on *Suez* began, Annabella and Tyrone had to go through the routine of tests on makeup, hairstyling, and costumes. She was terribly impressed by the care that went into an American film. No one in France had seemed to worry about how the lights struck her coiffure before the cameras rolled. She thought Tyrone was very considerate and patient throughout all of that. She went home and told her family, "I don't want to hear another word or a laugh about *le petit cheri*. He is a gentleman. Very unpretentious. And he's the kind of actor like Henry Fonda or Jean Gabin who, if you have to do a scene by yourself, is behind the camera helping you and doesn't rely on the script girl.'' She considered such thoughtfulness both refreshing and wonderful.

The story of *Suez*, which Duncan contrived and which was then fashioned into a screenplay by Philip Dunne, whose work on *The Last of the Mohicans* had greatly impressed Zanuck, moved on two levels—the genesis of and attempts to build the canal; and the frustrated emotional life of De Lesseps, torn between two impossible loves. One was an almost entirely hidden passion between De Lesseps and Countess Eugénie, to be played by Loretta Young, her last co-starring role with Tyrone. The other, from the lowest class, the illegitimate daughter of a French legionnaire, and little more than a camel girl, was to be Annabella's part. Eugénie had more ambitious plans than DeLesseps and eventually became Napoleon's empress. Annabella, illiterate and hopelessly outclassed, could never hope to remain close to her beloved, despite his strong feelings for her.

When production began, Annabella was a bit intimidated by Loretta Young's aura of glamour. Loretta had a great air of authority; all heads turned when she entered the sound stage; and the weight of it encouraged Annabella to stay in her dressing room at lunchtime, where she had sandwiches and coffee.

Early in the film, Tyrone and Annabella had a scene together in De Lesseps's study. Tyrone is seated by the fireplace, fretting over his inability to move forward with the construction of the canal and Annabella is at his feet, equally upset by her failure to console him.

Annabella was unaware that earlier that morning, the studio management had posted a notice on the wall of the makeup department announcing that a former studio executive had died and that they wanted everyone on the lot to share a minute of silence in his memory at 11 A.M. Then in the midst of shooting Annabella's impassioned speech to Tyrone in which she tried in vain to reassure him, all of the lights went down. In the semi-darkness, she glanced at Tyrone and wondered why he had such a sad expression so she stood regarding him for a moment, then began to laugh, and with rather broad Gallic gestures, said, ''Listen! It's nothing! Don't worry. The lights will come back. In France, it happens all the time." She didn't stop there, but began giggling, thinking how ridiculous it was for all of these people to be plunged into such gloom by a technical failure.

The lights came back and Tyrone, finding her callousness nearly incredible, asked sternly, "You don't know that we had a minute of silence for Mr. So-and-So, who has just died?" His words pierced Annabella like a knife. Her eyes widened in horror at her own stupidity. She thought, "Oh, migod! I love my part. I love the people around me. I love America. And they are giong to think here is a silly little actress from Paris, the French frog with no feelings!" From laughter, she abruptly swung into a fit of weeping. Her mascara started to run, her breath coming in short convulsive gasps.

Director Allan Dwan, apprised of what had happened, came up to his stars and put up a warning hand. "Stop, stop everybody! It's 11:15 now. We'll have an early lunch and Annabella can get some new makeup." She ran off, her hand covering her offending mouth, toward her dressing room. Two of the crew intercepted her in an attempt to calm her down. "Don't worry," one of them said, "he wasn't so nice. Everybody knows you didn't know what you were doing." She moaned in reply and continued running.

Tyrone's secretary, Bill Gallagher, knocked on Annabella's dressing-room door and told her that Tyrone and Mr. Dwan would like her to join them for lunch at the Cafe de Paris, which was the studio commissary. She hesitated, and Bill smiled and said, "I don't think you have any choice but to go. You're expected."

So Annabella cleaned the black streaks from her cheeks and went off to the commissary. Dwan and Tyrone had a glass of port waiting for her to perk her up.

At the end of that day's shooting, Tyrone asked Annabella if she had ever seen a radio show being done. She said that she had not. "I'm doing a show for the Theatre Guild on the Air, and I have to go right from the lot to the radio station. Come along. We'll have a bite. It's quite interesting." And that was the simple beginning of their friendship. She was wearing her hair short because of the wig required for her part, a plain blue suit, anklets and flat shoes—so unglamorous, in fact, that her mother, Mama Lily, was appalled.

Tyrone seemed intent upon showing her everything about

the radio studio, what the engineers did, as well as the director. He noticed that Annabella was not like most of the other leading ladies he had met. She listened. She rarely spoke about herself. She had a broader grasp of events and personalities than he had, but this quality only slipped out. She was shy to let him see it. Her sly wit punctured every inflated ego in sight and this delighted him. And she had a gamine beauty and a strength of will that were magnetic.

If queenly ambitions and different social stations kept Eugénie and De Lesseps apart in the movie, on the set the thing that *really* kept them apart was Annabella and Tyrone's obvious delight in her. Allan Dwan seized upon this at once and in the final shooting script, he got it onto the screen. Loretta was dismayed and rendered terribly insecure because of all this. She told Dwan that she was afraid she wasn't getting her emotions across. The film must have been an ordeal for her, but she had a great deal of respect for director Dwan. He had produced and had a hand in casting her in her very first feature picture, a silent made by First National entitled *The Whip Woman*. She knew that he had worked under Griffith and had done the best films of both Gloria Swanson and Douglas Fairbanks. Dwan assured her that she was fine, but she may have been seeking an ally in him, someone in whom she could confide. Unfortunately, Dwan made it a rule never to get close to his actors. In this, he was very much like his mentor, Griffith, a man whom even Lillian Gish called "Mr. Griffith."

Tyrone was worried, too, chiefly about the characterization of himself and Eugénie. Dwan, who had much admired Tyrone in his previous films and felt he was a born actor, tried to reassure him. Dwan always went more for conviction than for perfection. "I never did many takes," he said. "If you get a well-worked-out, well-rehearsed scene, the spontaneity is there. After that, it's stale. You begin to think it out and it's not as good. Sometimes an actor will tell me, 'I didn't mean to do that,' but the very fact that it was done in just that way made it fine. It was a natural thing. The way Tyrone would take hold of a lady's arm, just that little touch meant, 'I like this person.'"

Tyrone told Dwan, "I don't think I should touch her (Eugénie). After all, she's going to be the empress." But

Dwan said, "The hell with that! You're a man, and she's a woman. The people who bought the tickets are looking at you and Loretta, not at kings and queens. They're only human. They'd like to see you grab her and kiss her, and that's what you want to do. That's what she wants you to do. There'll be a helluva round of applause, so if you feel like it, do it!"

Tyrone never did know how little Darryl Zanuck respected Dwan. He asked Dwan after the sneak preview if Zanuck had said anything about it, and Dwan quoted the studio head as saying "Nice picture." This was almost a grudging compliment to Dwan. During his seven-year stay at Twentieth Century–Fox, he had worked mostly under Sol M. Wurtzel, who was in charge of all of the company's lesser films or programmers. Zanuck had not hired him in the first place; he was a carry-over from the old Fox Company. But after he had turned *Heidi* (which Henry King had declined) into a glorious triumph for Shirley Temple and revived her career, Zanuck was briefly grateful, and *Suez* was a part of that gratitude. Overall, Dwan described his years at the studio as chiefly marked by "Zanuck's complete indifference."

Suez turned out to be an epic drama with a very modern look about it. It has no happy ending, and its drama's building blocks are frustrations, both external and emotional. Loretta's role as Eugénie was more glamorous than anything she had done before, and there was heavy promotion for the Empress Eugénie hat, which she wore throughout the movie. It was a felt or velvet affair with a feather, resembling Robin Hood's headgear more than a little. Such hats were popular throughout the western world upon the film's release and became, like Joan Crawford's shoulder pads, another case of the cinema changing public fashion.

The climax of the film comes when a wind and sand storm blows up, destroying much of De Lesseps' creation. Dwan lined up a number of wind machines, and Tyrone and Annabella are supposed to race hand-in-hand through this natural disaster, Tyrone being knocked unconscious en route to safety. Annabella then ties him to a post so he can't be blown away and a great gust lifts her bodily into the air and blows *her* away. They find her broken body later and that resolves the problem of social differences between the lovers, heaven being an egalitarian plane.

Technically, this scene posed problems. Dwan used a stunt-girl in a harness on a flying rig secured to a derrick boom, but on the first take she was blown by the enormous gusts into a brick wall. Not seriously injured, the woman received an extra check for the accident. Then there was the problem with the sand. Ordinary desert sand tended to cut the skin from the actors, Annabella protesting loudly. It also made their eyes red and swollen. Breakfast cereal, purchased in huge truckloads. was substituted and photographed like the genuine particle.

Before Dwan discovered the cereal, however, Metro held the premiere of *Marie Antoinette* at the Carthay Circle Theatre. It was expected that Tyrone would attend and escort leading lady Norma Shearer inside. This was done, without complications, and Annabella, by prearrangement, came late and sat on the other side of Tyrone. Neither she nor Tyrone saw the movie clearly, their vision impaired somewhat by the effects of the sandstorm. Miss Shearer seemed very pleased with the picture as she stood surrounded by well-wishers at an after-premiere party at the Trocadero. When she saw Tyrone and Annabella with eyes redder than anyone else's, she said, "Oh! You've been so moved!" They agreed that they were, but had to disappear quickly to rid themselves of their pent-up laughter. Then they spent the rest of the evening dancing, their first public appearance socially. The following day, the ninth of July, he pressed her again to marry him. Annabella immediately wrote Jean Murat asking for her freedom.

Some months after the European release of *Suez*, the De Lesseps family went into a French court and sued Allan Dwan and the studio for suggesting that their honorable ancestor Ferdinand ever had entertained lustful notions concerning the Empress Eugénie. The French judge ran the picture, and the following day declared: "This picture does so much honor to France that under no circumstances could any family or any member of a family interfere with it in any manner," and the case was thrown out.

When Annabella first went to visit at Tyrone's house on Perugia Way, Janet Gaynor was there. She seemed to Annabella like a member of the family. "They were holding each other about the neck," she recalled, but she didn't know anything about their earlier relationship. She didn't read

American movie magazines, or fan articles in newspapers. She thought they just seemed terribly friendly, *simpatico*. Janet's intelligence impressed her most of all, and Tyrone was very much excited about some records of Hawaiian music which Janet had heard in the Islands. He played them on a phonograph in a playroom over the garage which he had set up for his relaxed moments. Janet had given Tyrone a novel to read—*Forever,* by Mildred Cram, about the transmigration of souls or something close to that. He discussed it with Annabella, who tried not to disparage it, since Janet seemed to think it so interesting, but it ran counter to everything she had been taught during her Catholic school days.

Tyrone's mother, Patia, pleasant but reserved around Annabella, was warm and motherly toward Janet. Apparently, Patia felt that Tyrone's interest in Annabella was transitory, that she was just his leading lady; she remembered all of the leading ladies of the past, some from her son's pictures, some not, but all from the Fox lot (he was very loyal there!)—Arlene Whelan, Sonja Henie, and Loretta Young. When the film *Suez* was well out of the way, perhaps their relationship would fade. It was simply a question of Janet "hanging in there" until this happened.

But in the weeks and months ahead, the relationship grew stronger. Although Janet Gaynor had come close, Annabella had done something which no other woman had succeeded in doing. She had broken through that reserve of good breeding in Tyrone and found underneath as much zest for life as she had herself. Vivacity is a quality traditionally French, and it could have been something tightly bottled up in the Réaume side of his family in his mother's time. Certainly Patia had helped cap the bottle. But it had bubbled to the surface in his grandmother Mudgey, whom Tyrone adored.

By the time *Suez* was completed, Tyrone had taken all the stops out of his romantic opera. He was not terribly original as a suitor, but what he lacked in freshness, he made up for in dash and impetuosity. Every day, there was a new bouquet of cut flowers either on the front patio of the Charpentier home or on the front seat of Annabella's car, left there as Tyrone drove to work. When the rest of the family was out, Tyrone would bring in a trio of musicians to serenade his new love beneath a wrought-iron balcony off her bedroom. On occasional nights, he would climb over the low wall surrounding the house, after parking on a nearby street, and athletically climb up and over the balcony rail into her room to make cautious love. During one such attempt, he suddenly saw the patio door open and Annabella's secretary, Miss Wright, step out to smoke a last cigarette before bedtime. He knelt out of sight, counting the endless seconds of that unexpected interruption.

Annabella's family saw how serious it was with her. Her father, Paul Charpentier, had come for a short visit, and he had seen and sensed how devoted Tyrone was to his daughter. Naturally he worried about the possibility that such a handsome man might break her heart, but that was a risk she would have to take. Charpentier fell in love with Los Angeles, and sat for hours in the back garden each evening looking at the galaxy of lights going on in the city below their house in Bel Air.

One Saturday, Tyrone drove Annabella to a castlelike restaurant in Riverside, where they had a splendid view of desert and mountains while they dined. She thought, for once, he was more involved in writing notes to himself on the menu than in concentrating all of his attention upon her. "Perhaps it's a note on some script or other," she thought. Then he handed her the menu, and he had written:

> T'would be my greatest happiness,
> My fondest dream come true
> Could I but see
> How I could be;
> More in love with you.
>   *June 20, 1938*

When they got back to town, he brought her a copy of Housman's *A Shropshire Lad*, which he had rebound in leather, and he had copied his doggerel on the flyleaf.

Before summer was over, Tyrone had bought a gold-plated charm in the shape of a heart, had jeweler Joseph in Los Angeles slice it into two halves, and had a chain made for each half. They shared that heart throughout their years together.

Once Tyrone began taking Annabella everywhere, including to the Zanucks, Zanuck seemed threatened. Studio heads frequently interfered with their stars' lives. They aborted marriages and romances and afforded them privacy only within the severe limits imposed by themselves. In Annabella, Zanuck had an adversary every bit as strong-willed as he was.

Over the Fourth of July weekend, Tyrone and Annabella went to Ensenada for the holiday. They were four, although Tyrone always dutifully informed the studio of wherever he was going, and they obliged him this time by sending ace photographer George Hurrell to take several shots of the group on the beach. The others in the party were Evie Abbott and Cincinnati ice cream entrepreneur Wil Wright, who had brought his recipe and equipment—looking like a large laundry tub—to Hollywood at Tyrone's suggestion and had made a great success. The ladies shared a room and Annabella thought that Evie was gay and charming. It was only when Evie appeared with disarming casualness in the years ahead with other candidates for Tyrone that Annabella saw a pattern emerging.

Tyrone and Annabella walked alone together along the beach there at Ensenada, and he told her, "I don't know where. I don't know when. But I want you to be my wife." There were only the sea and sky as witnesses, and so it would be in the future whenever he had something of critical importance to tell her. They flew back to Los Angeles that night and, as Annabella recalls, "Everywhere we looked, it was fireworks. So we had stars in the sky and stars on the ground and we were flying in the middle of them."

Zanuck now took steps to block any matrimonial plans. He lined up a series of pictures for Annabella, all to be made in London. She balked, but he was insistent. She then refused to go abroad to do the first of the films when it was scheduled and she was put on suspension. When she routinely turned down London-based productions, so Tyrone's agent Charles Feldman told her later, she was black-listed and unable to work for anyone in pictures for a very long period of time. She would have to wait nearly ten years for another fine script to come her way and then it was at the insistence of a personal friend, director Henry Hathaway (*13 Rue Madeleine*, 1947).

In truth, Annabella had lost much of her ambition for a great American success when she met Tyrone. The money, the glory of stardom, had seemed the equivalent of happiness to her for several years, but then, in 1938, her goals changed.

"Nothing compares with that kind of happiness," she said of her love for Tyrone.

Failing to remove Annabella from the scene, Zanuck put Tyrone into a new production, which was to be filmed on location farther from Hollywood than any film up to that time in an American setting (Missouri) and on a schedule longer than any of Tyrone's previous pictures. Jesse James only robbed banks. Zanuck's movie, based on the desperado's life, would rob Tyrone of his girl.

III

THE MAKING OF
JESSE JAMES

In Noel or Pineville at a certain time of day already publicized, we sat up on the tailboard of a truck and we signed thousands of autographs. You couldn't do 'em all, but you did it for an hour. It was an experience I didn't enjoy. Ty, perhaps because he was more used to it, knew how to handle it. I was always impressed by the way he could handle it. He kept pleasant. I'd get terribly angry.

Henry Fonda

THE EDITOR and publisher of the Sedalia, Missouri, *Gazette*, back in 1870, had published a running account of the criminal escapades of bank-robber Jesse James, who rode that part of northern Missouri with his brother Frank and a band of local boys turned desperadoes. The Sedalia articles were highly favorable to Jesse, suggesting that his motives were closer to those of Robin Hood than to an early-day Dillinger, that Jesse's mother's farm had been expropriated unlawfully and for a pittance by the railway trust for a right-of-way, and that the railways and the banks were in league together against the oppressed and downtrodden farmers.

Zanuck's favorite screenwriter, Nunnally Johnson, had got copies of these old papers and had fashioned a screenplay from them. The studio head was so excited about its prospects, he immediately sent a copy to Henry King, who had first rejection on nearly every major property.

King was equally enthusiastic, but he thought at once that it should be done outside the studio. Perhaps, away from the major cities such as Kansas City, there was country approximating that of Jesse's day there in northern Missouri. That weekend, after thoroughly studying Johnson's script, King got into his Waco and flew to Kearney, Missouri, where he rented a car and drove out to what had once been the James farm. Robert James, Frank James's son, was living there. The old James house still stood with a rather decrepit and swayback barn behind it. Jesse's tombstone was there in the backyard, although the stone itself had been chipped away by sightseers to about half its original height.

King spent nearly a week at the James farm, coming back from his hotel room in Kearney every day for several hours of conversation with Robert James. He made copious notes, some of them finding their way into Johnson's final shooting script, and he made notes to himself, so that he would not forget, about bits of action he felt should be in the movie, some of them in the interest of historical accuracy, although drama always took precedence over fact in any Hollywood production, on location or in the studio. The director was immediately aware, however, that none of the countryside resembled the very rural landscape of Jesse's time. An electrified railway, an interurban, cut through the farmland; paved roads were everywhere; and wherever there was space for it, a billboard blocked the view of hills and streams and even was painted over the handsome weathered barnsides. When he discussed his location problems back at the hotel, one of the guests told him of a place in the Ozarks called Pineville, far to the south, which had remained virtually untouched by the twentieth century.

King asked assistant director Bob Webb to join him during his second week in Missouri, and they flew down to the heart of the Ozarks in the southwestern corner of the state. From the air, it seemed clear that it did come close to the look of the 1870 Missouri farmland between Liberty and Kearney. They made several passes over local farms searching for a place that could approximate the James place. Then on the ground, they took off in a rented car prowling the back roads. Pineville itself seemed fine as a substitute for Liberty. It was a rough-looking older town, the buildings mostly of clapboard with peeling paint. They had recently paved the dirt streets, but King knew that could be remedied with several tons of hauled-in dirt.

A plain old farmstead, known as the Crowder farm was finally located between Pineville and Noel. They pulled up near the house and made Mrs. Florence Crowder a handsome offer to rent her place for several months. It was more than she could possibly earn from the farm in several years of operation, but it did give them the right to make any changes deemed necessary for the production. A wire fence around the home was torn down and a picket fence put up. A split-rail fence was erected near the barn. Out back, the studio crew was brought in later to duplicate a section of the farmhouse with a fireplace and stairway just as it appeared inside but with the fourth wall missing, giving them the advantages of a studio set where the camera could track in freely and pan without architectural limitations.

The most controversial aspect of the local production was the studio's casual carnage of local livestock. Mrs. Crowder had several hundred prize guineas, kept in a pen some distance from the house. When their uproar spoiled a take, the production manager ordered them killed and the company fed on Mrs. Crowder's prize guineas for a week or so. Later, during a thrilling chase scene in which Jesse, Frank and others are being pursued by a posse, three of them plunge on horseback from a cliff into a river. Several horses were killed trying to get a perfect take. Eric H. Hansen, then an executive of the American Humane Society attacked the movie *Jesse James* "as being one of the most bare-faced wanton episodes of cruelty to animals in the past few years." He said that more than six hundred anti-cruelty societies in the United States were going to protest to Will Hays, president of the Motion Picture Producers and Distributors of America. In actual fact, the James film was not exceptionally cruel when considered in the context of a less humane time. During the filming of every Western during the 1930s and even into the 1940s, horses were routinely thrown to the ground during ambush or shoot-out scenes through the use of a trip-wire. It was customary to lose a horse or two during any film. There were some directors still using such cruel devices, against all the humane rules then in force and with the SPCA policing nearly all production as late as the mid-1960s. Since childhood, Tyrone had felt an extraordinary compassion for all dumb creatures. It was not a weakness in him; curiously, it was one of the strongest aspects of his character. Curious, because he was not audibly a "bleeding heart," and you had to know him very well to sense this trait. He was upset by the accident at the cliff, but he did not blame director King or assistant director Bob Webb. Instead, he blamed the industry. The insensitivity of the studios eventually would sicken him.

The extreme heat of that summer of 1938 brought sudden prosperity to one of Mrs. Crowder's sons when Henry King suggested that he sell cold soda pop on the lawn of the Crowder place to the hundreds of sightseers who stood behind the security ropes. The first day, he ordered thirty cases and sold them in an hour. The next day, he ordered as many cases as the local supplier could truck in and that evening told King that he had sold over three hundred cases of pop.

The mayor of Pineville and the local Chamber of Commerce worked closely with King, seeing that their town was kept as raw and "unmodern" as it had been throughout most of its life. The only masonry building in town was the old red brick courthouse, which King knew would photograph beautifully in the color film he had mapped out.

Tyrone, as Jesse, was to share star billing with Henry Fonda as brother Frank. Tyrone saw the fakery in the script immediately, the efforts to win the audience to empathize with outlaw Jesse through purity of motive, mother love, and, finally, a harsh death at the hands of Jack Ford, one of his most trusted friends. It reminded him more than a little of the way Metro's writing staff had taken a stab at rendering Marie Antoinette pitiable. But at least Nunnally Johnson had based his work on original sources, even though they were prejudiced in Jesse's favor, and there might just be a grain of truth in some of it.

Tyrone was still, about most things, naïve and terribly innocent, his familiarity with literature and music still to come, even though mother Patia had instilled in him an appreciation of Shakespeare and the classical theatre. His high school years at Dayton and then at Purcell Catholic High in Cincinnati had given him only a rough handle on history. His dizzying rise at Zanuck's studio had not given him time to recover from a sort of "Gee whiz!" wonder about it all. In an informal diary he kept of that long location trip, he wrote:

> "What a day! (*August 26, 1938*) And what a trip! Not my first location trip, but one that promises to be as exciting as the picture I'm going to make. Director Henry King is, like myself, air-minded. We left Hollywood this morning in his streamlined Waco cabin cruiser, one of the swankiest I've ever seen, and here we are, right over the green-swept Ozarks. . . . Reached the airport at Neosho, Missouri . . . and we roped the plane down to a barbed wire fence. . . . Nice country with beautiful unexpected views."

The natives of McDonald County, especially those in Pineville and in the neighboring resort town of Noel, had welcomed the film people despite the temporary upheaval in their lives. Historian Bruce Catton took note of the interesting collision between Hollywood and rural America in a newspaper column:

> That Hollywood movie company that went to a small town in Missouri to make a picture seems to have learned something. Fresh from the land of make-believe, where everybody acts a part off-stage as well as on and where the sorry old rule that it's every man for himself is followed right up to the hilt, these movie people spent a couple of weeks or so in a place of complete unworldly innocence. . . .
>
> But somehow these back country Missourians didn't see all of this as a grand opportunity to gouge the rich folks. . . . The movie people actually had to argue, and argue hard, to get their hosts to take money for their rooms. The restaurant-keepers never thought of boosting their prices, but went right on selling chicken dinners for 50 cents.

The film became an obsessional topic of conversation and interest for everyone in the area. There were few Ozarkians in that corner of the mountains who did not contribute something. Nearly everyone in McDonald County was drawn into the production in some fashion, either as an extra or the lessor of a guest house or simply the owner of a farm over which the James gang could gallop. Many local men grew beards so that they would be more "in character." Young women, especially the prettier ones, were drawn to the movie location as though the rainbow ended there. Most brought pictures to prove their photogenic quality, and these were screened by makeup chief Ray Sebastian, who referred a number of them to assistant director Webb for extra work.

Ray had a reputation as a lothario, and his pursuit of women and frequent successes were the subject of an ongoing, raunchy discourse with Tyrone whenever he was being made up or they were drinking together. Tyrone rarely discussed his amorous affairs with anyone, but it was not unusual for Ray to "set up a date" for Tyrone on the strength of his prior knowledge of the girl. Once, he glanced at a row of photographs of Fox contract actresses on the wall of the makeup department at the studio and, laughing, told Tyrone,

"We've had them all, haven't we?" It was only a slight exaggeration.

A number of old buggies and other horse-drawn vehicles were taken out of barns and polished up for possible use in the movie. One buckboard, bought in the 1890s, was to be used to carry the body of Jesse James to the graveyard behind his farm home.

It was decided that most of the shooting would be done in Pineville and living accommodations would be in Noel, which already was used to catering to tourists. Fonda, villain Brian Donlevy, John Carradine, leading lady Nancy Kelly, Randolph Scott, Slim Summerville, J. Edward Bromberg and "mother" Jane Darwell went eastward by special train to the Ozark location along with the crew, comprising nearly a hundred in all. There was a great deal of heavy equipment aboard, four baggage cars full, including the cumbersome Technicolor cameras.

The chief press aide was treated to a beer in the bar car by Henry Fonda, in all innocence, and didn't stop until he had passed out. He was sent home within a week and the studio's chief publicist, Jim Denton, came to the location. Denton had been planning to come anyway because the Ozark location had begun to be covered by the wire services. On the day of the arrival of the special train, more than five thousand people had jammed into Noel "to see the stars." Henry Fonda recalled that "they came from Chicago, from Tennessee, from Oklahoma, they converged, like 'Let's go!' on us. They got into their family car or trailer or truck or by pogo stick. There were thousands. Now, I have never experienced anything like that in my life and I hope I never will again. We were never not watched doing everything from peeing to eating to working. You were watched constantly. You couldn't avoid it." One morning at breakfast, Fonda called to a young girl who was standing with several dozen others watching raptly and said, "Young lady, some day I'm going to come over to your house and watch you eat breakfast."

Publicist Denton became another fixture in Tyrone's life. As the studio's most important star—and with *Jesse James*'s success, he would shoot ahead of Shirley Temple—Denton accompanied Tyrone on nearly all of his promotional junkets, most of his locations, and became nearly as close to him as secretary-companion Bill Gallagher.

Tyrone missed Annabella terribly, but life, wherever he happened to be, continued to go on and he with it, all atingle to embrace each new experience. In late August, he wrote Annabella in Paris, where she had gone during his absence to divorce actor Jean Murat:

> The picture is going along well, but these 5:30 calls are killing me. We even work on Sunday, and that is not very much fun. It has been terribly hot and it usually rains sometime during the day, so all in all it's not too pleasant. I'm afraid "Suez" spoiled me, it was all so lovely and peaceful and great fun. I talked to Mr. MacFadden who came on from the studio yesterday and he said he had seen it again the night before he left, and they are all raving about it. I only hope I'll be back in time to see the preview, in about three weeks. That is going to be the *great* night of my life; and I'll be so proud of you, my darling, and just to think that I won't be able to let anyone know just how happy I am for another month. But *then* EVERYONE will know that my sweetheart is the best damn actress in the world. (Oh! I love you so much.)
>
> Coming home this evening through the moonlight, I dreamed up a little something, which you'll find at the bottom. Just to let you know that I am thinking of you every moment. Everything I see, everything I do, is all wrapped up in you.
>
> Please write soon, my angel, and let me know how everything is, and what the temperature is in Paris. Know that I'm thinking of you and praying for you always and that you have the heart, the soul and all the love of
>
> Your
T.
>
> *I've seen the ecstatic beauty*
> *of moonlit nights in May*
> *and watched the dawn with its golden touch*
> *Color a coral bay.*
>
> *But all the wonders I've ever seen*
> *all the nights and the dawns that I knew*
> *I would gladly trade or give them away*
> *For one fleeting glimpse of you.*
>
> *T.*

• • •

His letters were written in the late evening, his "quiet hour."
When his day began at dawn, he moved about the location
with controlled excitement, interested not only in his part and
his scenes, but in everything that was happening. He was
eager to get to know the natives, and one day when he was not
needed "on the set" at the Crowder farm, he spent the
morning chatting with a neighboring farmer, E. B. Barker,
who had been hired as a security guard to keep an eye on
equipment. While his facade was beautiful, he cut through all
of that shining surface with a genuine interest in other people.
Later, Barker said, "That Power boy, a finer boy never set
foot in this county. He slipped away from the crowd one time
and spent half a day talking to me. Of course, there are a few
people who are a bit snooty."

Tyrone was installed in the summer cottage of Mrs. F.W.
Baughman, whose home was of two stories and was one of the
few buildings in that part of the Ozarks that had air-
conditioning. It was situated on a bluff overlooking the town
of Noel. Although he and Bill Gallagher had the house to
themselves, with a cook-housekeeper coming in every
morning, Tyrone wrote in his diary that "I found a room in a
private home on the outskirts of Noel . . . eleven miles away
from Pineville by pavement, eight miles by gravel. . . . Director Henry King has a nice room in a beautiful white house
commanding a grand view of the little town and the majestic
hills. (They're called mountains down here, but I mustn't take
the word too seriously.)" He neglects to mention that he had
other rooms beyond "a room" as well as his own "majestic"
view of the resort community. Some of his friends would call
this modesty, but it more closely resembles guilt and it was a
trait that would persist in Tyrone as accommodations
everywhere became grander, more opulent.

The privacy afforded by the Baughman house made it easy
to quietly enjoy a roll in the hay with some of the local girls
who were lucky enough to have been hired as full-time extras.
One in particular, possibly recommended by Ray Sebastian,
interested Tyrone enough to become his "girlfriend" for
several nights running. Bill Gallagher, as was his custom,
made himself invisible in another part of the house.

Whether by accident or otherwise, the girl succeeded in
getting herself pregnant, although Tyrone did not discover

this until word reached him in California the following summer. Then he learned, just before embarking on a wedding trip with Annabella, that he was the father of a son, born in Missouri in June 1939.

The young woman, of an old Ozarkian mountain family, made no claims upon him and eventually married, but the infant was put up for adoption immediately after his birth. Tyrone was elated by the news and despondent when he found that there was no way of tracing the child. Adoption procedures in 1939 were very different from today's. Few records were kept and there was a conspiracy of anonymity swallowing up each adopted child. Natural parents rarely located their offspring when they had a change of heart. Tyrone never did find his lost son, his first-born, despite months of search with the considerable assistance of those in his confidence. Somewhere today, probably in the Midwest, a man moving into his forties does not know that his father was Tyrone Power.

By the time they were ready to shoot, Pineville had become a raw cluster of buildings clearly on the edge of empty western hill country. The Dixie Belle Saloon had gone up, the sheriff's headquarters, and the printing plant of the old Liberty newspaper, where character actor Henry Hull would re-enact the James partisan publisher. Power lines had been removed. And the townspeople of nearby Noel had nearly all been cheerfully evicted from their homes, moving in with relatives in the backwoods. The movie production was a historic distraction in their lives as well as an economic lifesaver. Before the "Jesse James" company left, nearly a quarter of a million dollars would be spent locally. The back of the great Depression had been broken in that corner of the world by Darryl F. Zanuck, who was so pleased by the treatment of his company, he had another film shot there (*Belle Starr*, 1941) three years later.

But there were few amenities of the sort most Hollywoodians are used to. The cast and crew ate their evening meal at a restaurant in an Ozark "resort" on the Elk River called Shadow Lake, which was little more than a swimming hole with a diving board and a raft and with a ramshackle pavilion beside it where meals were served and dancing was permitted on Saturday night. Its custom was mainly rangy, mountain blue-collar types who still chewed tobacco and wore sleeve garters, a few obviously lonely women, and couples who had no other place to go. Flanking these regulars were the hundreds of gawkers who were everywhere, like a plague of locusts, and their number remained constant throughout the twelve weeks of the production.

"Shadow Lake tonight!" would ring through the company every day as they wound up the day's shooting, the words shouted in ironic resignation, of course. Dreadful as it was, the place was the only faint sign of life for many miles around. Tyrone took a shine to it and often danced on Saturday night, his partners invariably attractive young ladies from the ranks of tourists, the girls being only semi-conscious at the time, clearly in a half swoon of ecstasy.

The long distance location (1,550 miles from Hollywood) was something new for a Hollywood studio to attempt, and Zanuck's press department was exploiting that fact for all it was worth. Soon, most of the weekly magazines, then including *Newsweek, Time, Life, Collier's, Liberty* and *The Saturday Evening Post*, sent writers to do a piece about it. *Life* sent its brilliant photographer Alfred Eisenstadt along with a writer to do a photo essay. It became a publicity bonanza.

Character actor Henry Hull was not needed during the first week of shooting, and he arrived in the dead of night, carried in a drunken stupor to his room in Noel. Hull's drinking was as mythically prodigious as Barrymore's, Although he never permitted it to affect a performance. Actually, he was more worried about what the gallons of coffee might do to him as King's aides helped get him ready for shooting each morning, and pneumonia was next on the list because of all the cold showers he had to endure.

Hull awoke with his usual hangover in his ground-floor suite in Noel and stared incredulously at the crowd of sightseers pressed three and four deep against his bedroom windowpane. He threw them quickly into shock by pretending they weren't there and getting out of his pajamas as fast as he could, strutting about the room in the nude. A few older women began to reel away in a near faint.

Eventually, Shadow Lake had to be roped off and sheriff's deputies along with studio security people posted to keep the crowds behind barricades during mealtimes. Fonda, who was essentially a very shy man who "considered acting the best therapy in the world to overcome it," continued getting angry as the mobs stared at his every bite. Tyrone took it smilingly as nothing particularly unusual. He seemed to accept such attention as part of his role as star, which at that point he obviously enjoyed. He often waved a greeting to the crowd and seemed to thrive on this adulation, much as Marilyn Monroe would do nearly two decades later. Perhaps both being essentially fatherless made them peculiarly responsive to the affection of hordes of people.

Much of the sightseers' attention, of course, was centered upon Tyrone. Very possibly, if this had been a movie being made with Henry Fonda and Nancy Kelly alone, many of those who had driven five or six hundred miles to get to Noel and Pineville would not have made the effort. But with Tyrone as the initial attraction, the scene had fed upon itself and news stories now were covering the extraordinary crowds that had converged on that remote corner of the Ozarks. Crowds attracted crowds, as always. Alfred Eisenstadt took a remarkable photo of Tyrone and Fonda sitting on top of what appears to be a railway car, handing down autographed pieces of paper to the hundreds of gawkers gathered below.

It was Zanuck's trademark to open a film having a historic background with a printed legend superimposed over the opening shot. *Jesse James*, purporting to be a factual account of the exploits of the most famous of American bank robbers, was no exception. Nunnally Johnson wrote:

After the tragic war between the States, the eager, ambitious mind of America turned to the winning of the West. The symbol of this era was the building of the transcontinental railroads; they represented the heart and soul of the national industrial plan and engaged the whole people between 1865 and 1873.

But the advance of the railroads was, in some cases, predatory and unscrupulous. It brought with it the confiscation of the lands and property, and took away the homes and livelihoods of many. Whole communities of simple, hardy pioneers found themselves victimized by an ever-growing ogre—the Iron Horse (*and we see such a black monster coming at us behind the legend.*)

It was this uncertain and lawless age that gave to the world, for good or ill, its most famous outlaws, the brothers Frank and Jesse James.

The James brothers were not co-equals outside the law. In the flyers sent about and tacked on trees and fence posts, a thousand dollars was offered for Jesse "dead or alive" but only five hundred dollars for Frank. In the filming, Frank, as played by Fonda, began very early in production to seem more convincing and thus more interesting to audiences. Tyrone was acting the role of Jesse with spirit and total professionalism. His every mood was right, as written and directed, but Fonda, through some genius for timing or, more probably, a longer career in the legitimate theatre, came through as a human being.

Still, Tyrone was ideally cast. Jesse is described as being about twenty-one when the movie opens and Tyrone was twenty-four but looked younger. As Jesse, he is "a good young man, not aggressive but without any fear whatever. Let alone, he probably would have developed into nothing worse than a tough, young farmer." But he was not let alone. When his mother, played by Jane Darwell, refuses to turn over her land for a pittance to the thugs representing the railroad trust, Jesse tries to organize other farmers in a resistance movement and tells them they must get a good St. Louis lawyer. During his last encounter with the railroads' strong-arm men, Jesse has nicked their leader in the hand with a bullet. A warrant for the arrest of Jesse and Frank throws a monkey wrench into their farmers' revolt and, at his mother's urging, they leave the farm to go into hiding. But the thugs refuse to believe the boys are gone and, fearful for their lives, they toss a fire bomb into the James house, killing the boys' mother. Tyrone wrote of that day's eventful shooting:

> Mrs. Crowder's two grown-up sons went to work for us today as bit players. For a sequence in the film we had to toss a bomb into a big rambling farm house and set it afire. It became the duty of the Crowder boys to help us form an old-fashioned bucket brigade to put out the fire in their own home. . . .

This terrible incident ignites something in Jesse and he is

from then on a killer bandit and a deadly enemy of the railway trust. Jesse tells his band of farmer-brigands: "We'll tear up every tie it lays down—and every rail it brings into Missouri—and we'll make 'em pay for every acre of land it swindled us out of."

Jesse holds up the first train out of St. Louis at night. Luck was again with director King, for as Tyrone wrote in his diary:

> Henry King has an uncanny ability to discover and uncover things. Imagine finding a ten-mile stretch of railroad on the old Frisco line near Southwest City—eight miles from Noel! It was here he decided to film the great train robbery. He also discovered an old engine and three passenger cars that had been used in the time of the James boys. They were all reworked, repainted and put in top condition for the filming.

Jesse, Frank and the others in the James gang are masked as they frisk the passengers of their cash. Screenwriter Johnson had considerable respect for Fonda as an actor and had fashioned the role of Frank James carefully to the actor's measure, describing him as "a few years older than Jesse, a deceptively mild-looking country boy, drawling and laconic in speech, with a dry sense of humor . . . a slow starter but a buzz saw finisher.

Tyrone was on the phone with Patia several times a week, and he was careful not to say too much about Annabella. He knew that his mother was unhappy about his involvement with a (slightly) older, much worldlier woman. Actually, Annabella had been married twice, but it is doubtful that Patia knew about that brief first marriage to French writer Albert Sorré.

Because of the disapproval of Patia and Zanuck, who were his "parents" in this connection—his real mother and the father-figure in his life, Tyrone and Annabella had made elaborate plans to keep their forthcoming marriage a secret until the very last moment. This was not a thing which Tyrone did with any enthusiasm, as Patia always had shared everything in his life before.

Meanwhile, Annabella was attempting to keep her mission in Paris out of the newspapers, but it was impossible to keep the news from Zanuck, since the studio had a Paris office very much in touch with the film world. In the French capital, Annabella was not simply waiting for the legalities regarding her divorce to be taken care of. She had an old commitment to do a film for director Marcel Carné, who asked her to star opposite Jean-Pierre Aumont in *Hotel du Nord*, a story of two star-crossed lovers whose suicide pact fails when the young man shoots his sweetheart, then loses his nerve before he kills himself. The girl survives and the youth is thrown into prison for attempted murder of the only person who means anything to him—a neat conceit. Annabella played the girl with an inward sadness that was really her longing to be close to Tyrone again.

On September 16, Tyrone wrote:

We're on our way back to Hollywood with most of the scenes we wanted safely in the can. Throughout out stay we worked every day except for the one I got off to go to Tulsa. We were up every morning at 4:30 or 5:00, had breakfast, make up, donned our costumes and were on the set at Pineville or the Crowder farm 11 miles away by 8 A.M. We worked straight through until six or seven every night, depending upon the sun. It was grand fun, every minute of it, for all of us. In the end we left because the crowds, though very sensible and reasonable, just got too big. Traffic was tied up, business was at a stand-still, and standing crops were getting trampled. . . .

Throughout much of October, while waiting for Annabella to return, Tyrone hung around the cutting department at the studio waiting for rushes of *Jesse James* to be shown. It was in the corridor outside one of the several projection rooms that he met one of the "messenger boys," who worked in the receiving room of the cutting department, J. Watson Webb, Jr., a young New York scion, two years his junior, a Vanderbilt on his father's side and a Havemeyer (the founder of the "sugar trust" in America) on his mother's, a millionaire by inheritance who wanted to learn movie-making "from the ground up." Watson recalls that there were "always warm, friendly 'vibrations' between us. Then one night when I was on the 'night shift,' Tyrone happened to walk through the receiving room on his way to the car, having just viewed some film. He stopped and chatted with me for a few minutes, asking me a few questions about myself. When he found out I had only come out to California six weeks before, and was living alone in a small apartment in Beverly Hills, he said to me: 'Well, one night when I get through running film, maybe you'd like to come back and have dinner with me at my house. I'm living in a rented house with my mother in Bel Air.'' Tyrone knew that this tall, rather patrician-looking young man was someone Patia would respect, not least for his good manners. When they had their first dinner together a few nights later, as Watson remembers: "By the time that evening in October was over, I felt as if Tyrone and I had been friends for years, and he later told me that he had felt the same way."

Patia encouraged the friendship, not that it needed any encouragement. She may have felt that Watson Webb could distract Tyrone from his obsession with Annabella, which she hoped might burn itself out.

But when Tyrone eventually introduced Watson to Annabella, she felt the same warm rapport that Tyrone had. Watson and Annabella instantly became close friends. To a woman less secure than Annabella, Watson's obvious profound regard for Tyrone could have been unsettling. Rosalind Russell once said that when Tyrone entered a room, it was like a light turning on. Clearly, that light had turned on in Watson's life and was much the brightest thing he had ever encountered. He had turned his back on the social scene in the East and now was slowly making friends in California, nearly all within the film industry. When he met Tyrone, suddenly he realized that here was a man as much in love with films—and life—as he was. Watson, to a large degree, abandoned his innate shyness around Tyrone and with his ear-grabbing Vermont accent, moved from enthusiasm to enthusiasm. The two men seemed never to run out of material for conversation. For his part, Watson reeled off some vivid description of a mutually known personality, a piece of brilliant direction or editing he had just seen, a carefully detailed genealogy of someone's family (he knew even aunts, uncles, and cousins of many American families), cackling over an eccentric he admired or a come-on he had observed, or, occasionally, succinctly putting down an overrated industry icon.

In the years ahead, among Tyrone's male friends, only Watson became truly his confidant. Tyrone must have sensed, too, a loyalty in Watson that was rare in the movie world. Watson would remain loyal to Tyrone and to his memory literally forever, and, in his turn, Tyrone protected his friendship for Watson with silence when called for and avowals when necessary.

Of Tyrone's three wives, only one, Linda Christian, warned him that his devotion to her must push Watson to the sidelines. Annabella welcomed Watson as both an ally and as the necessary male companion Tyrone needed to keep the drives within him in balance.

In early December, Tyrone and Annabella conspired by mail and phone to steal a few days together far from Hollywood and their family complications. Tyrone and secretary Bill Gallagher took off on a month-long vacation tour through South and Central America by air. That much was officially announced and it was handled by the press department at the studio. The trip was even to be financed by the film company.

Ever since the pressures of stardom had become severe and it was nearly impossible to escape them, Tyrone had dreamed of having an isolated retreat to which he could fly with Annabella, in his own plane, and renew his energies. During that vacation, he took a lease on an island off Mazatlán, Mexico. He even brought out a contractor and a carpenter to show them what he wanted by way of "a shack." There was an old well on the site and Tyrone was delighted to know that one of the building problems already was solved.

He and Bill fished and climbed hills, enjoying the views of water glimpsed through jungle growth. They slept like babes each night, physically exhausted. Somehow, Tyrone became more "himself" on such excursions. His language became more vulgar and all the layers of propriety so carefully woven into his persona by Patia fell away.

In Mexico City, they needed a police escort to get them to their hotel, and finally in Buenos Aires on November 21, despite a heavy rain, over four hundred women broke through a police cordon at Moron Airport and smashed windows in their effort to reach and touch Tyrone. He and Bill escaped by sneaking through a back door of the airport administration building. The women, many of them in their teens, wept in frustration and anger. Then at Santiago, Chile, there was a tense moment as several hundred women surrounded the plane after it touched down and the two rather frightened Americans had to wait as the local constabulary literally shoved the mob aside, beating a path to the plane's ramp for them.

Annabella's agent was trying to patch things up with her studio. All would be forgiven if she would go from Paris to London to do a new picture for Zanuck. But she had a slight cold that day and she managed to magnify her illness into such a crippling case of laryngitis, the agent had difficulty understanding what she was trying to say. The plan was to meet Tyrone during the first week of December in Rio de Janeiro. They naïvely believed that no one would know anything about it.

In Lisbon, someone recognized Annabella on the deck of the liner bound for Argentina. The word traveled rapidly, for in the headlines of a Rio newspaper that very evening was the announcement that Annabella, "one of the greatest stars of France," was on her way. When the ship arrived, the pier was black with crowds awaiting her arrival, including all of the local reporters and writers for the wire services.

Tyrone fumed silently in his suite at the Copacabana Hotel. Everything was going wrong. By the next morning, a long telegram would arrive from Patia pleading with him not to marry this "older woman" and ruin his life. It seemed that Zanuck had spoken with his publicity chief, Harry Brand, who had phoned Mrs. Power and told her all the terrible things that would happen to poor young Tyrone if he made this mistake. Patia's clincher was that he would be throwing away his career.

Annabella was pursued to *her* suite in the Copacabana—on another floor from Tyrone's—by the press, and finally agreed to a press conference. Their little joke on everybody had exploded in their faces. It very nearly made her laugh, since it had turned out to be everything they sought to avoid. And some of her comment was indeed funny. She said first of all that she had agreed to act as starter for the main race of the midget cars on Saturday evening; she denied that there was anything mysterious about her visit to Rio and that her sole reason for coming was to visit her cousin, who was married to an Argentine gentleman. About Tyrone, she said that they

were just good friends. Then Annabella did sound a little like
Garbo by getting a bit nettled, telling an insistent reporter that
she did not like publicity about her private affairs.

Cables from the studio followed Patia's, and Tyrone was
visibly shaken by the time he and Annabella finally got
together. One thing had become clear to both of them; there
was no way they could have a secret romance.

Tyrone needed some peace and time to himself, so he sailed
back to New York. Upon their return, by separate planes, to
Hollywood, Tyrone had become open about his feelings for
Annabella. To a friendly reporter, he called her "a miracle of
a woman. She made me aware of things in myself I could
never have found myself."

It was Hollywood at its zenith by the end of 1938, the last
great flowering of the studio period before the oncoming war
in Europe began to shrink foreign revenues. During the
months ahead, movie goers would see the first truly mature
Western in John Ford's *Stagecoach*, the most famous movie
ever made in *Gone with the Wind*, the most enduring musical
in *The Wizard of Oz*, the most critically acclaimed version of
a classic in *Wuthering Heights*, Garbo's last great performance in *Ninotchka*, and a new, natural kind of beauty in
Ingrid Bergman (*Intermezzo*).

Zanuck seemed too involved with product and quantity to
seriously study the trends and portents. Twentieth Century-
Fox was now a vast, successful film company with strings of
moviehouses, a large stock company of players, and several
house directors whose box-office records were impressive.
Although he would acquire *The Grapes of Wrath* that year for
filming later, he was still deeply committed to the tried and
profitable—backstage musicals, historical adventure, chiefly
American in locale, and Shirley Temple. Tyrone fitted ideally
into Zanuck's scheme, and in mid-December, when he began
work on *Rose of Washington Square*, because of his immense
popularity, he was able to sustain his employer's belief that
star vehicles nearly always brought in the greatest revenue.
Fox people knew that they were in the business of entertaining
the public, not educating them or uplifting them. A great
many of them, former burlesque, cabaret, radio, and
vaudeville people, didn't mind at all. In time, Tyrone would
mind very much.

Although the last Sonja Henie–Tyrone Power musical would follow *Rose*, Zanuck already had purchased a major best-seller for Tyrone, Louis Bromfield's *The Rains Came*. The production would cost more than two million and, despite its setting in India, would be shot in its entirety within the studio walls. Tyrone already had arrived on the list of the top-grossing Box Office Ten.

His rise had turned out exactly as Henry King had predicted. Within three years of his advent into the ranks of Hollywood leading men, the mantle of Valentino, which everyone had believed had fallen on Robert Taylor's shoulders, really had dropped onto those of Tyrone Power, where it would remain until the idol business was finally of no significance.

IV

THE THREE POWERS

. . . I have a Patron, the only one I ever sought, but whose favour has well repaid my pains and solicitation. . . . I allude to . . . my Public, much courted, much abused, and commonly accused of either being coldly neglectful or capriciously forgetful of all sorts of merit. To me . . . you have proved most kind, and hitherto most constant. . . . Yes, my Public, throughout my humble career, I have at all times of doubt or despondency invariably turned to you, and never have I been coldly received. I have leaned heavily upon you, yet have never found your aid withdrawn.

Tyrone Power the Elder, 1836

THE MOST literate of the three acting Tyrone Powers was the first, known at Tyrone Power the Elder, grandfather of the second Tyrone (a generation was skipped during which no member of the Power family became successfully involved with the theatre*). Less handsome than his celebrated descendant namesakes, he was inclined to stoutness, fair-skinned with light hair, and was the very essence of working-class Irishman. He was born in the country of Waterford on November 2, 1795. His father died while he was a small boy and his mother moved the family to Wales, near Cardiff.

Tyrone the Elder first appeared on the stage in Monmouth, Wales, as Orlando in *As You Like It,* with a strolling company. He said later that he remained with them chiefly because he was much taken with the actress playing Rosalind. It was to become a family weakness, this habit of falling in love with leading ladies, that would seriously disrupt the lives of all three Tyrones.

A theatrical historian next has Tyrone appearing as Alonzo in a small-scaled historical forerunner of the present-day *Royal Hunt of the Sun* called *Pizarro* on the Isle of Wight in 1815. But he had not yet found his niche in the theatre, and the following year, he accepted a post in the British Commissariat Service in South Africa, where he remained for more than a year. He tried to make a go of office work in the colonial service, but he was bored beyond description. He had

---

* Maurice Power, son of Tyrone the Elder, went on the stage but he was largely unknown and died in obscurity at Bath in 1849. His brother Harold with his wife Ethel toured in what they called "An Entertainment," a comedy turn performed in lecture halls and written by Harold in collaboration with William S. Gilbert.

an enormous curiosity to see new places and experience all
that life could offer, possibilities that were realizable as an
actor. These urges were so strong, they appear to have passed
into his genes and would reassert themselves in both his
grandson and in the last Tyrone when he succeeded in films.

The frustrated civil servant determined that he had to get
back to England and into the theatre on a permanent basis.
Returning to the British Isles, he joined a repertory company
and attempted, in quick succession, the Shakespearean roles
of Mercutio and Benedick, and that of Charles Surface in *The
School for Scandal*. He was not very convincing in any of
them. Tyrone the Elder had mastered projection and many of
the mechanics of acting but it was all "surface" with little
feeling and credibility.

Still, he persisted. Tyrone the Elder was a stubborn Irishman, and he moved to Dublin, then a hub of theatrical activity, where he played both Romeo and Jeremy Diddler. He
was gaining confidence as an actor but persuasiveness still
eluded him. No one could blame Dublin theatregoers for
rejecting a stout Romeo, but the parts thinned out to the point
where his tenacity became a serious threat to the welfare of his
wife and children. So in 1818, he retired from the stage, doing
a variety of "civilian jobs" to sustain himself and his family.

But the dream of great success on the stage never left him,
and in 1822 he made his debut in London at the Olympic
Theatre, followed quickly by appearances at the Lyceum,
the Adelphi, and finally Covent Garden, where he played
Rolando in *The Honeymoon*. For the next five years, he
jobbed around London and the Midlands making himself a
familiar and eventually an accomplished and sought-after actor, considerably in demand. Then in 1827 came the role that
changed his life. He was asked to play O'Shaughnessy in
Peake's farce, *The 100 Pound Note*, and he performed the
gusty, roaring, blathering Irishman with such skill and
authenticity, fame came "overnight" to the long-struggling
Tyrone.

What is especially interesting is that each of the Tyrone
Powers became celebrated for one particular theatrical genre:
Tyrone the Elder as the supreme Hibernian, always asked first
to play any major Irish role on the London stage; Tyrone, Sr.,
his grandson, as a great Shakespearean actor in America; and

Tyrone of the movies in pseudo-historical derring-do with sword in hand and *en garde*.

Tyrone I soon became the rage of two continents, bringing his repertoire of Irish comedies to Philadelphia, New York, and other American cities. He especially loved Philadelphia, where he stayed at an elegant old hotel on Chestnut Street and enjoyed walking down to Front Street and the Delaware River. He kept a travel diary and eventually, in expanded form, those notes became the basis for a travel book in two volumes entitled *Impressions of America*, a mild best-seller in its day. With a genuine affection for Americans, he carefully recorded all of America's virtues and practically none of her faults. He was at his best in describing places, giving the reader detailed accounts of villages, mountains, rivers and lakes, as well as accurate rundowns of just how Philadelphia differed from Pittsburgh, or New York from Chicago.

He became an inveterate transatlantic traveler, almost always alone or with a male companion, since his wife had a brood of eight children, four boys and four girls, to look after back in England. On March 9, 1841, he closed a run of several weeks as Gerald Pepper in *The White Horse of the Peppers* at the Park Theatre with a curtain raiser he himself had written, *How to Pay the Rent*. Two days later, together with an intimate young friend, Lord Fitzroy George Charles Lennox, he sailed from New York Harbor aboard the steamer *President*, bound for Liverpool.

During a farewell party just prior to sailing given by several of his actor friends in Manhattan, the tragedian Edwin Forrest, who was frequently Tyrone the Elder's companion around New York, told his friend that he had "a bad feeling" about the *President*, and urged him to delay his departure and take another ship. But Tyrone simply smiled at this presentiment and patted his friend's arm, thanking him for his concern. He could not imagine a more seaworthy vessel than the *President*. It already had made three crossings; it was 273 feet long. More to the point, Lennox was overdue in London and had postponed his own return trip so that he might accompany Tyrone back to England.

Just beyond Nantucket Shoals and some hours after blasting a greeting ("spoken" in nautical jargon) to the ship *Orpheus* on the morning of the twelfth, the *President* went

down in heavy seas. All 123 passengers and crew perished.
Tyrone the Elder was forty-five years old, or less than a year
older than the last Tyrone when he died just as suddenly mid-
career. His sailing companion, Lennox, was only twenty-one,
the second son of the Duke of Richmond and a descendant of
King Charles II. The grief-stricken Duke, knowing how close
his son was to the actor, told Tyrone's widow that he would
do anything humanly possible to help her fatherless children,
some of whom were nearly grown. As a direct result of that
offer, eldest son William Tyrone was given a commission in
the Army by the Prime Minister, and he served with such
distinction that he was knighted by Queen Victoria.

Unlike the last Tyrone, who was brought up by his mother
to be an actor, his father, Frederick Tyrone Power (he never
used his first name professionally) met every conceivable op-
position from his family. The stage was considered by
Tyrone, Sr.'s father Harold to be so declassé that he had used
the name Harold Page for many years when he was working
in the theatre.

"You would have thought," Power told a theatrical
historian, "that I had tried to do a murder when I said I
wanted to be an actor. My uncle, Sir William, once asked me,
while I was on a visit to him, in Ireland, what I meant to be
when I grew up, and when I answered 'An actor!' he was
mightily miffed. 'Don't ever let your Uncle Fred (we were
supposed to have great expectations from Uncle Frederick,
who was very wealthy)—'Don't ever let your Uncle Fred hear
you say so,—or your father, either!' Both of them *did* hear
me say so, however, and I was immediately taken from
school, at Dulwich College (that's where I got all the
education I ever had), and packed off to Florida, to work on a
ranch and learn the business of growing oranges." The
foreman of the orange ranch was a savage, drunken lout who
got his kicks by having Tyrone bound hand and foot and
forcing liquor down him until he got staggeringly drunk when
he would be freed to career about crazily and amuse the
foreman and his crude gang. He wrote pleading letters to his
father begging for the fare home, but Harold Power *never
opened them*. He would tell his wife, "They're only from
Fred [one can see why Tyrone came to hate his first name]
wanting to come home and be an actor." One of these letters

fell into the hands of the ranch foreman and he threatened to kill Tyrone. "I was frightened," Tyrone said, "and I ran away, to the nearest town." There, the foreman caught up with him and attacked him with a black-snake whip, but Tyrone was more agile and the monster fell into the ocean (the orange ranch was on the eastern shore of Florida). Tyrone took those precious minutes while his assailant saved himself to clear out, walking to St. Augustine.

It was in that oldest city in the New World that young Tyrone first appeared upon the stage. He was engaged by Ralph Bell, manager of the Genovar Opera House where straight plays were frequently staged, in the role of Gibson in *The Private Secretary*. That was in 1886, when he was seventeen years old. (He had been born in London on May 2, 1869.) He was not paid, but was given food and lodging.

While he was gaining experience in one small role after another, he began reading "the trades" (theatrical publications) assiduously. In one of them, there was a classified ad seeking a "Young Man to play Leading Juvenile; Good Looker, on and off; Must have Square Cut." He may have been given pause by that "good looker . . . off" since that could mean just about anything; but he wrote the manager who signed the ad in Philadelphia, and shortly received a request to come at once. Tyrone had little knowledge of America's geography and thought he might walk it, but he was shown a map and quickly disabused of this notion. Friends of his, many of them in the army post at St. Augustine, made up a purse to pay his fare North, and he arrived in Philadelphia in mid-winter in his summer suit with a straw hat. Dengue fever, which had become chronic with him during his stay in Florida, gave him a gaunt and yellow look. When he rang the manager's bell, that gentleman took one look, said "Too young!" and slammed the door in his face.

The St. George Society saved him, quite literally. This was an organization set up in the United States to look after Englishmen who might need help. Tyrone recalled later that "They gave me a blue ticket, for a meal, and a red one, for a lodging, and sent me off to an address about half a mile away. When I got there and presented my blue and red tickets they took me in, but before I could get a meal or a bed I must take a bath, in a public bathroom, in turn with a lot of other unfortunate chaps,—pretty queer, down-and-out sort of lot they were, poor things! It was about the most humiliating of all my experiences. I was a good deal more than glad to get the meal, though. I shall never forget the ghastly-looking green-kalsomined room in which they herded us. Then a young parson came in and talked to us; a fine fellow he was! He looked at me a good deal, and after his talk he took me aside, into a corner. 'Who are you?' he asked, 'and how do you come to be *here*?' I told him. 'But *you* can't stay here; come along with me,' and led me to his own quarters. . . . The parson gave me a little wine and soon pumped my whole story out of me, and then he made me take his own bed for the night, and slept on a sofa in his study. Next day he rigged me up with some decent clothes and loaned me money enough to get over to New York and keep going for a bit. I never forgot him or his kindness.''

Beginning with the wretched "amusement" area of the Bowery, Tyrone then began working steadily on the stage, moving into a repertory company touring New England, Pennsylvania, and New York. He was still so poor that the seat of his trousers had worn through so he "took care to let the other members of the company precede me from the train and station." There followed a long period of barnstorming the East. Finally, back in New York, he offered himself as a "first old man," which was a principal part. The agency handling the transaction complained that he was "nothing but a boy!" The young man dismissed this, telling them, "Never mind that. I'm Tyrone Power, and I can play any part you give me." It could have been his own son speaking fifty years later.

Mademoiselle Fanny Janauschek was considered one of the finest actresses of her time with a considerable range. She played high comedy as well as *Medea*. It was 1888, and Mademoiselle had her own company presently playing an engagement in Brooklyn at the Amphion Theatre. Then in her fifties, she was in decline financially and artistically, but she refused to give up her sovereignty as an actress-manager. She was the first to see that Tyrone had a great natural dramatic talent. She began instructing him in detail and he absorbed all of the stage business and nuances of characterization Mademoiselle had acquired during her long career. She paid well, for that day, and Tyrone earned thirty-five dollars a week.

That was the turning point in his stage career. That fall, in his twentieth year, Tyrone played the old man in *Dominie*

Sampson in Montreal. Mademoiselle was amazed. "Never have I seen such an assumption of age by one so young. Et ees wonderful . . . marvelous!" The last Tyrone would attempt the same thing in his thirty-ninth year (playing a beloved old man at the end of the film *The Long Gray Line*), but that was very different from attempting it at half that age. Mademoiselle gave him two cardinal rules for an actor: "Everything worth doing is worth doing well" and "In acting, always take all the time you need." Tyrone attempted to abide by those precepts for the rest of his life.

Mademoiselle Janauschek is important in this chronicle for another reason. Her personality was so strong and Tyrone was at such an impressionable age, her imprint on his character and his own personality was lasting. He, in his turn, when he was coaching his son in the rudiments of acting, passed along this same feeling to him. For one thing, she had a keen sensibility; her mind, however, ruled her emotions. Her imagination was vivid, but in acting she left nothing to chance. She had a remarkable facility at impersonation, and her voice was resonant and deep, projecting to the farthest reaches of any theatre. That voice could be harsh or gentle, sweet or strident. She had enormous authority and she dominated the stage whenever she was on.

Tyrone was with Mademoiselle for three years, after which she retired "temporarily" because of financial problems. Several years later, she would reappear, but in a "trashy" drama for sensation-seekers and Tyrone went backstage to pay his respects. Then she wept because of her "degradation."

He was only idle a few weeks. The actress Ellen Terry sent him from London a letter of introduction to Augustin Daly. One of Daly's older actors was seriously ill and shortly died, and Tyrone was again playing old men; but the Daly Company was one of the finest in America. Tyrone opened as Sir Oliver Surface in *The School for Scandal* at the Chestnut Street Opera House in Philadelphia. By the end of that week, he was playing Holofernes in *Love's Labour's Lost*. Despite his advancement artistically, Daly was not known for prodigality and Tyrone was paid only $20.00 a week.

Augustin Daly had cold eyes, the air of a martinet, and no compassion whatever. After satisfactorily performing leads during his first week, Tyrone was demoted to minor parts, not because Daly was displeased but because Daly wanted everyone in his company, especially those newly arrived, to know what it was to struggle. Still Tyrone was taken with the Daly Company on their tour of England in 1893, and while there, he left Daly, and with some money he had saved and considerably more he borrowed, he produced a play he had written, *The Texan*, starring in it himself, at the Princess Theatre in London. The critics dismissed it and it closed the first week, leaving Tyrone in debt for the first time. The great pride he felt when he told his parents of the venture was dashed overnight, and he avoided visiting them afterward because he knew his father would ask him how he proposed paying back that fortune he owed.

Tyrone jobbed around England throughout that year, working briefly for Herbert Beerbohm-Tree, touring in *The Red Lamp* as General Zouroff and eventually appearing in that role before Queen Victoria at Balmoral.

Back in New York, Daly once again hired him, this time for more important roles, and he remained with him more or less steadily until 1896, when he joined a western repertory company managed by T. Daniel Frawley. That was an exciting time for Tyrone since there were two brilliant actresses with Frawley, Maxine Elliott and Blanche Bates, and together they toured Hawaii, then known as the Sandwich Islands.

Tyrone was a passionate man from his youth, yet another trait he passed on to his son. He had a great deal of difficulty extricating himself from backstage affairs when his ardor had cooled. Finally, in 1898, while he was appearing with Augustin Daly's company but this time in leading roles, Tyrone fell in love with an actress then playing in New York, Edith Crane, and they were married. Tyrone and Edith became an important husband-and-wife team and began their first tour in Australia in November. They performed *Tess of the D'Urbervilles, Trilby*, and finally *The Taming of the Shrew*. But the stage partnership and the marriage were short-lived. He was too much in demand and far too handsome. Edith could not cope with it, and they separated within a few years.

Daly was among those impressed by Tyrone's enormous development as an actor, and in 1897 he signed him to play Caliban in his production of *The Tempest*. The bestial wretch was strikingly projected by Tyrone. He felt that it was the greatest challenge he had yet had in the theatre. With this role, he could submerge his good looks and be something less than human with a dragging gait and, animal strength. Tyrone was almost painful to watch, he was so true to Shakespeare's intentions. Fifty years later, his son would attempt a similar subhuman part with equal critical success in *Nightmare Alley*.

In London, Henry Irving engaged Tyrone to play Bassanio in *The Merchant of Venice*. With him as Shylock and Portia were Irving himself and the beautiful Ellen Terry, who earlier had interceded in his behalf. Tyrone was then thirty-three years old and at the peak of his abilities. Word of his great talent crossed the Atlantic and while Irving was planning even more significant work for him, an offer came from Mrs. Minnie Maddern Fiske in New York. Mrs. Fiske was putting on a production of the story of Magdalen and needed a powerful actor to portray Judas. Irving was disappointed, but told Tyrone: "*Judas*?—ah, great part—ought to be—like to play it myself—great opportunity—mustn't miss it—shall be sorry to lose you—*need* you—but better take it!"

Mary of Magdala opened in Milwaukee on October 23, 1902. It then moved to Chicago for two weeks and opened in New York at the Manhattan Theatre on November 19. Tyrone's performance electrified both critics and audiences and Judas placed him overnight in the front rank of world actors.

Tyrone was not a prosperous actor who could be choosy about what he played. In between engagements, he began going up to the wilds of Canada, where he fished at a lodge on the Richelieu River. Around 1905, he bought a small parcel of woodland on the river and built a cottage there, which he called Two Elms. It was primitive, but it became the first home he had ever had and the one to which he would always return throughout his life. He fished on its banks and took up oils and painted scenes surrounding his "cabin."

While he was there, he received an offer to appear with Mrs. Fiske again in *Becky Sharp*, an adaptation of the Thackeray work, *Vanity Fair*, as the Marquis of Steyne. The Marquis is described by Thackeray as being a short man and Tyrone was over six feet (almost exactly the same height as his son). Tyrone made audiences forget the disparity by emphasizing his character's elegant air, his nonchalance while steeped in evil and his deep-dyed cynicism, which was made to seem as the only possible behavior for a gentleman of his standing.

Tyrone's place in the American theatre in the first two decades of the twentieth century was unvaryingly at the very top. There were *Ulysses* (1903), *The Servant in the House*, in which he co-starred with Walter Hampden (1908), *Thaïs* with Constance Collier (1911), and the lavish musical *Chu, Chin, Chow* with Florence Reed (1917).

The death of his first wife, Edith, in 1912, even though they had been separated for years, reminded him of his mortality. He had had far too many affairs and dalliances. He was forty-three years old and as yet had no family. In 1911, he had gone to Cincinnati to play a week in a tour of *Thaïs* and during one of the social get-togethers of the touring company and local theatrical people, he met a drama teacher and Shakespearean actress, Helen Emma Réaume, known professionally as Patia Réaume. She was half French, and her dark hair and brown eyes gave her a Latin look which appealed very much to Tyrone. When, in 1912, he learned that Edith Crane Power had died, and he was legally free, he hurried to Cincinnati to propose to Patia. She accepted, knowing very well that he would be away from home much of the time. But perhaps she could become a part of his world. She had been involved with the theatre since she was a very young girl and teaching for her Aunt Helen (Schuster-Martin) since she was fifteen. She thought she could handle that.

Tyrone was between engagements and persuaded Patia that they should get married at the border town of Rouse's Point, New York, about forty miles from Île-aux-Noix, which was the site on the Richelieu River of his spiritual home, Two Elms, in the wilds of Quebec. There they would spend their honeymoon.

Patia saw another Tyrone at Two Elms. In his beloved retreat, he dressed like "a brigand," wearing his oldest clothes and declining to shave. One of the things that had struck Patia most forcibly when they first met was his elegance: pearl-gray spats, stickpin, and an immaculately pressed suit. But at Two Elms, he was "himself," and that was a side of him Patia looked upon with considerable relief. He was far from the admiring ladies here, and he knew it.

Road tours proved more threatening than the wilderness.

When Tyrone was wanted for a new play, Patia went along. She traveled with him for a while. But that was getting too close to the man he had become through twenty-five years of trouping. Tyrone had become such an inveterate ladies' man that he could not refrain from all the instinctual vibrations he projected whenever there was an attractive woman around. Patia was sophisticated about the theatre and its ways, but she was not terribly pliant. She had very set ideas about how a husband should behave. Romantic he may have been, but now he had to curb that drive. Strains were felt.

Several months pregnant, Patia returned to Cincinnati, which she had convinced Tyrone should be their home and not New York, where most of his ladies resided, or Two Elms, where he had his roots, because of its isolation. Patia began to see that there would rarely be any middle ground where Tyrone was concerned.

And it was in Cincinnati on May 5, 1914, that their son, christened Tyrone Edmund, was born. He was a tiny, frail baby and was a delicate child throughout his early years.

The movies were beckoning Tyrone, Sr., and had been for some time. As winter approached, he signed a contract to do two silent pictures, and on the advice of their family doctor, who thought that baby Tyrone might fare better in a warmer climate, the Power family moved to California, taking an apartment in the Hollywood area.

Patia was soon pregnant again, and in August 1915, a daughter was born, whom they named Anne. Unlike Tyrone, she was vigorous and weighed nearly ten pounds at birth. In the early 1916, when Anne was barely six months old, the second of the features was being filmed and, needing an infant, she appeared briefly with her father in *Where Are Our Children*?

Later that year, a second crisis occurred in the Power marriage. They were casting a huge musical in New York, *Chu, Chin, Chow*, which was roughly based on *Ali Baba and the Forty Thieves*. They wanted Tyrone to play the lead opposite Florence Reed. *Where Are Our Children*? had been so successful, Tyrone could have become an important film star, and Patia was well aware of that. For Tyrone, the musical was an exit from a deteriorating relationship. Patia was firm, with a very clear notion of what she wanted for her family and herself. Tyrone was used to his freedom; marriage was an unnatural state, a cage really, and he was obviously overjoyed when the opportunity came to skip.

Patia hated irresolution. Either she was a married woman or she was not. Before Tyrone left, she began discussing divorce. During the very long run of *Chu, Chin, Chow* (in which a young Marion Davies had a small role), Tyrone and Patia were divorced.

Patia and the two children lived briefly in San Diego, but then she rented a bungalow in Alhambra, which was within sight of snow-capped Mount Baldy. They were just twenty minutes away from San Gabriel, which was the site of one of the first missions founded in California by Father Junipero Serra. There was a museum there which portrayed details of Father Serra's life, with a theatre, where a Mission Play written by John Steven McGroarty was performed daily with several evening performances a week. Patia secured the leading role and was away from home much of the day, but by that time, they had discovered a jewel of a nurse-housekeeper by the name of Frieda Tracy, whom the children and Patia called "Pet."

Pet Tracy became a kind of second mother to Tyrone and Anne. She was an ample-bosomed lady with dark brown hair severely tied back in a bun. While the Powers were not very active Catholics, Pet was a Christian Scientist. The children had been raised by their mother with rather firm discipline (but never severe) and their backsides were often paddled. Pet followed Patia's rules on child care just as though the mother were there. But there were some joyous moments quite often. On Saturdays, sometimes she took them by interurban to Redondo Beach, where they would have a picnic and spend the day.

When Tyrone was six and in the first grade, sister Anne enrolled in kindergarten, and they attended the same public school. Kindergarten was only until noon and when it was over, Anne would sit at her brother's desk and wait to be taken home. Tyrone was extremely protective around his sister and once, at seven, brought her into the house and told Patia and Pet that Anne was not to be allowed to play with a certain neighbor boy anymore because he had used horrible words in her presence. This protectiveness would continue throughout their lives until his death. Anne thought that he might be sharing some of the father role with his mother, quite unconsciously.

Tyrone never became a vigorous, roughhousing type of boy, but he did outgrow his delicate health. While in maturity he became something of a loner; as a boy he liked to play with other boys on their block, and in rainy weather, he and Anne would create their own theatre with whatever props they could find. Once, they did the entire *Robin Hood* story, playing all the parts, and performed it for Pet without flubbing a line or a cue. They both had been schooled in memory retention by Patia.

The children also grew up with Shakespeare as something living and an everyday part of their lives, and not, as with most children, a dull text forced upon them at school. Patia drilled them in breath control (diaphragmatic breathing), tongue exercises, and voice projection.

They were kept very much aware of their father and there were occasional, but not frequent, visits. Tyrone, Sr., was not very good at remembering their birthdays. He was not a man to routinely send off cards and presents on such occasions. But he would see something that was "just the thing" for little Anne or a scarf for Tyrone that might become him and off they were mailed.

When Tyrone was in the second grade and Anne in the first, they were taken out of school for three months and went to Grandmother "Mudgey" Réaume's house in Cincinnati, while Patia resumed her teaching at the Schuster-Martin School. Their grandmother was a devout Catholic, and it was during that stay Tyrone and Anne had their first catechism training. Despite their mother's involvement with the Brothers of the San Gabriel Mission, it was much too far away from their California home for the children to attend. There in Cincinnati, they made their first Communion at a midnight mass, which was an exciting and impressive experience for both of them, and quite dramatic.

Back in California, eventually Tyrone and Anne were again at school together—the St. Ursula Academy, which took boys up to and including the sixth grade. Pet Tracy had left them by this time. The children never understood just why, but Anne thought it was some private matter in Pet's family. They did not lose touch with her, however, and sometimes Pet would come on a Saturday and again take the children to

Redondo Beach for an outing as in the old days.

When Tyrone was seven, he made his first "professional" appearance on a stage as Pablo, the neophyte of the Franciscans. He had one line, which he later said was frequently drowned out by the roar of a passing train. But acting was not just a diversion to him. He took it very seriously. Father Tyrone was then starring as a street preacher in a D. W. Griffith film, *Dream Street* (1921), made in the Griffith eastern studios, and the critics had praised him. Patia had taken the children to see the film in downtown Los Angeles.

After five seasons in the Mission Play, Patia began to consider returning to Cincinnati to live. A brief friendship with a California man, Clarence T. Arper, had led to a disastrous marriage. He did not get along well with the children. So late in 1922, once again divorced, Patia took her little family back home.

As Anne was growing up, Patia began to feel that her daughter needed more spiritual guidance than she was getting. Anne then was sent off to the first of a series of boarding schools, all Catholic, while Tyrone spent his first year of high school (1927) with the Jesuits in downtown Cincinnati, where one of the priests, Father Flynn, took a great interest in Tyrone. Even though he was with the brothers there for just a year, Tyrone remembered Father Flynn all of his life and considered him a positive influence on his life.

The following year, 1928, brought Tyrone, Sr., back into their lives. He was starring in a tremendous success, *Diplomacy*, an old Sardou comedy first presented in 1878, which in an earlier revival (1901) had made a great star of William Faversham. Now Tyrone had joined Faversham and Jacob Ben-Ami and leading ladies Helen Gahagan and Frances Starr in a brilliant new production. There was a post-Broadway tour that had brought them to Cincinnati for a week. Patia, Tyrone, and Anne went downtown to the Clinton Hotel to greet their father in his room and then be taken down to the dining room for dinner before the show. Relations between Tyrone, Sr., and Patia were stiff and quite formal, but young Tyrone was in a quiet glow of delight.

That year, too, Tyrone had gone off to St. Mary's, a Jesuit prep school later a part of the University of Dayton. He was there for a year, and during his first summer at home, he took a job at the Walnut Hills Orpheum, the moviehouse in their part of town, as an usher. His interest in films and acting by now had become an obsession, and he kept a notebook in which he commented on each movie he saw while on the job. Since he was able to see it repeatedly, he thought he could tell how it was put together and he made notes on the movie's structure. He analyzed the stars' performances and those comments went into his notebook.

In the afternoon, he worked as a soda-jerk in a drugstore near the moviehouse. By the time he was ready to go back to Dayton for his junior year of high school, he had saved enough to buy himself a decent wardrobe. The Powers were not very well off and suddenly he had begun to notice that he was not "smartly" dressed. From then on, he was.

At the last moment, however, Tyrone decided that he did not want to attend boarding school any more. He had met two local boys, Wil Wright and Bill Walsh, who went to a Cincinnati Catholic high school named Purcell, and he told Patia that he wanted to go there, too.

The young men became inseparable and frequently double-dated on Saturday nights, going to dances and student parties. Tyrone became much more independent of Patia, and his late hours on the weekends must have been agonizing for her. Still, he respected her and her attitudes generally. She had told both children often enough, "There is no life; there is no death. There is only experience." And now he was trying to soak up all the experience he could get.

At Purcell, Tyrone met Brother Bill Schroeder of the coaching staff. Although Tyrone was interested in drama nearly to the exclusion of all else, Brother Bill became the dominant male figure in his life at that crucial moment when he felt that he had to decide whether he could survive as an actor. His instincts told him that he could and Brother Bill backed those feelings totally. In time of self-doubt in the years ahead, he would remember Brother Bill and his faith in his eventual success. They never lost touch, and Tyrone would return to Cincinnati as a world-famous film star especially to visit his old counselor and friend.

It was understood by all the family that Tyrone would make his bid in the theatre just as soon as he finished high school. Patia had ingrained in both children a faith that they could attempt just about anything, but Tyrone felt that at sixteen, he needed all the help he could get to reach his goal, which was, he confessed, film stardom.

Tyrone had recorded in his notebook enough about inex-

perienced actors to convince him that he must develop
dramatic skills before attempting the Hollywood scene. He
told Patia that he wanted to spend some time with his father,
if he would take him. A letter sent to Tyrone on Fox Studio
stationery and dated April 12, 1930, had stayed in his mind
throughout his last year at Purcell High School. His father
had written:

Dearest Bingo:
. . . I am thinking about your ambition to become a
Screen Actor, and wondering how I could assist you. You
will not be able to do anything for year, is that so? You
must remain at school. May I suggest a course for you to
take up which will lay the groundwork for your future in
acting.
   Take Singing Lessons
   Take Dancing Lessons
   Take General Calisthenics
   Study Enunciation
   Declaim aloud once a day
   Study your face, and the emotions that pass over it in
the mirror
   Learn to control your entire body so that it may
respond gracefully and truly to your intelligent direction.
   How to listen intelligently to what another character is
saying.
I would wish to impress upon you the importance of
singing, speech, breathing, and it would be of great service to learn at least the rudiments of music, to be able to
read at sight, and play the piano. . . . Acting is work,
hard, hard work.
You are fortunate in having such an accomplished
mother. She will instruct you, and she will agree with me
that the more accomplishments you possess the more
valuable you will be as a player.
The talking picture opens up illimitable opportunities. In
a very short time all the great artists will be brought under its spell, and the Theatre, as I have known it, will
only exist in a Metropolitan Center. . . .
Exteriorally you possess everything. The rest is for you to
develop. Try for beauty and truth in all you attempt.
Nothing is 'just good enough' on the screen. One acts un-

der a magnifying glass. So you may imagine how vital it is to exercise the most meticulous care and judgement. Things that we have done, and do with great effect upon the stage, are crude when exposed to the searching eye of the Camera.

I tell you all this to try to show to you the necessity of intensive study on your part. There is no "hit and miss." To get an effect you must study the cause that promotes that effect. I hope you have the gift of imagination. Pay strict attention to your physical health, the body in the best of condition. Keep your mind alert, ready to seize and hold and transmit. Read noble books. See noble pictures, paintings. Though indeed we are wonderful today, do not be blind to the fact that great and beautiful souls have lived in all ages. . . . "After me cometh a builder, tell him I too have known."

I mustn't bore you dear boy. I have neither the power nor the desire to insist upon what you should or should not do. I merely wish to indicate what my experience teaches me is necessary to a full development of whatever talents you may possess. If you do go on the screen, I want you as you do yourself, to get to the TOP. I want you to take the place I have missed. And you shall. Remember you bear a highly revered name in the history of the stage. Your great grandfather, whose name we both bear, was one of the great lights of the theatre. Not even at this late day is it forgotten. It is a banner in your grasp to carry to greater heights.

So dear Bingo, understand in your heart that I am entirely in sympathy with you, and whatever I can do to help you, to encourage you, to inspire you, to the very best of my ability I will do. But as I told you, Bingo, all the money in the world, all the love, can get you nowhere, everything depends solely, unconditionally upon yourself. You are in command of your ship, you shape its course, you alone know its port, and only by your own skill and knowledge shall you weather the storms and stress of the voyage. Think of me, to continue the metaphor, sent out on the sea of life with a weak craft, without a rudder or compass. . . .

> Your affectionate father,
> TYRONE POWER

• • •

Two months later, a second letter followed to his son, called "Bingo," after a wide-eyed comic strip character, this one mailed form the location for *The Big Trail* (1930), an epic western that was to launch John Wayne on his career:

> . . . I am not much of a one to give advice, and I do not see wherein you need any. It is perfectly right and proper for you to seek enjoyment, and to go out and meet friends. In Hamlet you may read the advice given by Polonius to his son, Laertes, with profit. I doubt whether any modern father can improve upon it. Read it.
>
> So now you have your holidays. Fill every hour with joy and store up pleasant memories to carry with you through the serious hours of work ahead. I congratulate you upon being a senior.
>
> The picture is coming along, and I do believe is even now considered by the experts in the studio to be a marvel. I am fortunate to be associated with such a fine type of screenplay. I find that the work has but very little to do with stage acting, as I know it. The scenes are strikingly brief, and take hours to *shoot*. The episodes do not follow each other, and sometimes I do not comprehend where we are. I am willing to leave the problem to the expert hands of our director, Raoul Walsh, who is by all opinion, a master. Well, one day you will see it, and see what an infernal blackguard your father is, and hear him growl and roar over the plains and mountains. My ever fond love, dear Bingo.

Through further letters and phone calls, it was agreed that Tyrone, Sr., would meet his son in New York upon the boy's graduation from Purcell and take him for a few weeks up to Île-aux-Noix so they could get reacquainted. They had not spent any appreciable time together since Tyrone's infancy, of which Tyrone remembered nothing.

Patia and Anne saw Tyrone off on the train in mid-June 1931. Patia must have sensed that she was losing her boy, not to his father but to the world. She believed even then in his eventual success—that was something she shared with her ex-husband—and this was but the first step. Then there would be a second step and a third, all leading away from her. Yet, she knew, too, that he would never abandon them, that he had a great love for her and Anne. She had taught him to be an independent spirit, but she had almost against her will allowed him to perform in many ways a father role, especially with Anne. That was something that distance and time could not erase.

Father and son continued on up to Quebec, where they were to remain for six weeks. Tyrone was nearly as tall as his father now and had a grave handsomeness and a penetrating glance that seemed ever on the lookout for the booby traps in life. They were his mother's eyes.

Tyrone had no old clothes, since he had outgrown everything "old," so his father lent him some of his. They roamed the river banks, fished for their dinner, prepared their own meals back at Two Elms and constantly talked theatre. Tyrone, Sr., told him about the hard, early years, and he undoubtedly felt some apprehension about young Tyrone. If this closeness only had come a few years earlier. Now, Tyrone, Sr., knew that he was past his prime, even though he was only sixty-one, and suited for character roles, not leading men. His clout with theatrical managers had lessened within the past five years.

But he could help Tyrone with his equipment, his technique. Even if his name might open a door, the talent had to be there or nothing significant would happen. He wanted to know what his son had learned from Patia, and Tyrone explained about the breathing, the tongue exercises and all the rest. As they stood on the bank of the Richelieu River, Tyrone, Sr., asked young Tyrone to deliver the line, "A fool thou art!" so that anyone on the opposite bank could hear it. Tyrone shouted across the river, and his father shook his head.

Then Tyrone, Sr., without perceptibly raising his voice, projected the line easily across the river and back into the woods beyond. Young Tyrone was much impressed and practiced until he could do the same. So it was with the extended help of mother Patia over the years and the concentrated effort of his father for more than a year that the remarkable voice of Tyrone Power took on resonance and flexibility.

Tyrone, Sr., had to go to Chicago in August, where he was to do a season with the Chicago Civic Theatre. The trial period together at Île-aux-Noix had gone even better than he thought it would. He was alone now. His last wife, Bertha Knight, had died in 1927, and he welcomed young Tyrone's company. Beyond that, there is no question that he loved his son, had grown to love him very much there in the Canadian wilderness. There he had shown his boy something of his other great passion in life, his art. There were now dozens of marine and landscape paintings stacked against the walls of Two Elms; there were portfolios bulging with delicate pastels of river scenes and the sea. Tyrone was far too untutored and preoccupied with acting to make even a stab at drawing, but he was bowled over by the talent his father had, especially in capturing those eerie moments in the moonlight when trees and grass are silvered by it. Many years later, when he heard that his father's cottage was still as he had left it, though he had been dead for nearly ten years, Tyrone would go to Île-aux-Noix and collect all of the art works and bring them back to California.

The two Tyrones took a train from Montreal to Chicago and within three days, Tyrone, Sr., went into rehearsal as Shylock in Fritz Lieber's production of *The Merchant of Venice*. Tyrone went on as a supernumerary, clad in the robes of a Venetian merchant. His presence onstage went entirely unnoticed until one night during mid-run, while his father was sharpening the knife preparatory to taking "his pound of flesh," the knife suddenly flipped out of Tyrone, Sr.'s hand, flew through the air in the direction of Tyrone, who ducked, and struck the woodwork behind the young man's head.

Following the Chicago repertory season, Tyrone, Sr., accepted a Hollywood offer, and the two Powers trained west on the Super Chief, settling into the Hollywood Athletic Club upon their arrival. The Power name no longer brought in a large salary, but it was enough to support them comfortably, and one supporting role followed another. Tyrone, Jr., tried to get work as an extra, but failed.

Finally, an important role came along for Tyrone, Sr. It was the title part in *The Miracle Man* over at Paramount. While not the leading role—the stars were Chester Morris and Sylvia Sidney—it was much the most important talking-picture part he had been given and he worked all through November and up to the Christmas holidays, 1931.

On December 23, Tyrone had come to his father's room, dressed for an evening with some of his father's friends. But

Tyrone, Sr., was not yet ready. He complained of feeling unwell. Young Tyrone had a keen sense of another's well-being. He would give someone he knew well a look and say, "You all right?" Now that sense told him his father was very ill indeed. He picked up the phone and called a doctor.

But it was too late. His father called out to him and Tyrone sat on the edge of the bed, cradling the elder Tyrone in his arms. Then this man he had really only come to know and love within the past eighteen months slumped against his chest and died of a massive heart attack.

Tyrone, Sr., had had a lawyer in Los Angeles, who acted as his agent-manager. His name was Frank Adams and he came from New Brunswick, Canada. Now Adams stepped in *in loco parentis*, helping young Tyrone with all the necessary details. His father, Adams said, had requested cremation, which was performed; the ashes were sent to Patia. On Tyrone's next trip home, he and Patia took the ashes up to the Richelieu River and scattered them there.

Tyrone remained at the Hollywood Athletic Club until he could find a cheaper room. He made the rounds of casting directors and always got an interview because of his basic attractiveness and his name. But when he told them of his background in the theatre (limited) and movies (zero), they inevitably told him they "would keep him in mind."

In March 1932, his persistence finally paid off. William Wyler was directing *Tom Brown of Culver* starring (who else?) Tom Brown and Richard Cromwell. He needed one more cadet, and Tyrone was hired for two days, his first screen experience. It was shot at Universal Studios, and, interestingly, Tyrone would return there twenty years later for his first independent production, *Mississippi Gambler* (1953).

Tyrone believed that he should hang around Hollywood until *Tom Brown* was released in July. Surely then someone would see him on the screen and it would lead to a movie career. But the movie opened that summer, was a mild success, and disappeared almost without a trace even though the New York *Times* said, "the boys act like boys instead of like road company Hamlets" and it was made in Wyler's meticulous fashion, detailing the tyranny of older boys against the "plebes."

Tyrone did not even consider returning to Cincinnati. Patia

had told him and Anne all of their lives, "There is no place you cannot go; there is nothing you cannot do." Well, he had gone to Hollywood, and he had seen that several thousand others had done the same and, of them, only a few hundred were working steadily enough to support themselves. He had never seen so much despair in his life.

He headed back for Chicago. In the few months they had been there, he had made more friends than he had in a year in Hollywood. Actor-manager Fritz Lieber was especially fond of him, and Tyrone thought that he might get some small roles during the fall rep season.

Tyrone failed in that, but he did land a job with a Chicago radio station reading the funnies on Sunday morning. His voice had got him the job and not his looks, something of an irony after all the hopes he had riding on his screen appearance in *Tom Brown*. Also on the "funnies" show was another young actor named Don Ameche. They were too different ever to be intimates, but they formed an association that lasted through all the vicissitudes of their careers.

The radio show paid him just enough to survive on, and when the Chicago World's Fair opened in the spring of 1933, Tyrone rushed to the fairgrounds to see if he could find some supplementary job. He did, and throughout that first season of the Chicago Fair, he was pushing people around in rolling wicker chairs.

Then in late summer, one of his Hollywood friends wrote that producer Leonard Sillman was putting together a revue, which opened in August as *Low and Behold*, starring Eve Arden. Tyrone was a straight man in one of the sketches, but he was so delighted to be working on a stage in a speaking part and *in Hollywood*, he wrote Patia and Anne to *please* come out and see him. He did not tell them that he had been surviving on avocados from a tree near the window of his boardinghouse room and frequent and welcome dinners with some old family friends, the Franzen sisters, Nell and Mary, spinsters who had a small bungalow in Hollywood. Patia had met them during World War I when they worked together at the Hollywood branch of Women's War Relief. The Franzens' income apparently came from a family trust, although they both had appeared in silent films.

The Powers were reunited in early September. Patia and Anne decided to remain in California, and they lived for a while in San Diego, where Patia played in a stock company and Anne, who had had much the same training as Tyrone, went on a local radio show. Meanwhile, Tyrone's run in *Low and Behold* had ended and he had moved north to Santa Barbara, where a handsome little playhouse named Lo Barro was the center of theatrical interest. He found work there as an assistant stage manager and in small parts.

Tyrone jobbed around California, even becoming a chauffeur for several months to a writer named Arthur Caesar, who had a beachhouse at Laguna Beach. It was while he was with Caesar that he took a day off to work in a bit part as a West Point cadet. (One can imagine the interview with the casting director. "Have you had any screen experience?" "Yes, as a cadet in *Tom Brown of Culver*." "You're hired!") The Warner Brothers film was the Dick Powell–Ruby Keeler musical *Flirtation Walk* (1934).

In the summer of 1934, the Chicago World's Fair reopened for its second season. Tyrone again returned to the midwestern city, where he obtained work as an actor in an exhibit on Hollywood moviemaking, encountering there his old friend from radio Don Ameche, who also was appearing in "the production" in front of the movie cameras (without film).

His first real acting break came that September when he was hired by Mrs. Bror Dahlberg, a wealthy Chicagoan whose husband ran Celotex, for her stock company. One of his father's leading ladies with the Fritz Lieber repertory, Helen Menken, had recommended him to Gilda Dahlberg, and following the run of *The Green Bay Tree*, on which he had been assistant stage manager, he was given the role of Freddy in Edward Sheldon's *Romance*. For the role of the matriarch, Mrs. Dahlberg had imported that *grande dame* of the theatre, Eugénie Leontovich. The company played the Blackstone Theatre, and Tyrone was with them for over two months.

Also in the Dahlberg company was an eccentric young man named Robin Thomas, who was John Barrymore's stepson and whose mother was Michael Strange. Robin was openly homosexual, which was not unusual backstage, and he took a great fancy to Tyrone. His personality offstage was far more intriguing and successful than any role he assumed for Mrs. Dahlberg. He seemed to have endless rolls of bills in his pockets and he was profligate while escorting Tyrone and others in the company whom he found acceptable to gourmet restaurants and the "in" nightclubs.

Tyrone was flattered by all the attention Robin was paying him. Robin already was part of the company when he arrived, and it was apparent almost immediately that there was considerable admiration and respect for anyone Robin singled out, since he was terribly choosy. He could afford to be on two counts—he was rich, and he was handsome. He had the faunlike looks of a youthful Nijinsky, but with blond hair, and luminous, intense blue eyes.

Tyrone told Robin that he preferred girls. The wording was carefully chosen, as always, in articulating his feelings. But Robin did not appear to be dismayed. Robin told his half sister, Diana Blythe (later *Barrymore*, when she went on the stage), that Tyrone was "divine," and that he was planning to bring him to New York. He phoned his mother, Michael Strange, to whom he was her protected darling, and said that Tyrone Power was coming East with him to "take Broadway by storm" and would be staying with them. Miss Strange told her son that, of course, young Power would be welcome to stay as long as he liked, and she would help him all she could. Fifteen-year-old Diana wrote Tyrone to be sure and bring along a photograph of himself, which he could inscribe to her, and said that she knew why he looked so familiar in the photo Robin had shown her—"You are Adonis come to life."

Michael Strange was then living at 10 Gracie Square in an oversized, old-fashioned apartment with a huge salon and a balcony overlooking the East River. She was at once both fiercely private, maintaining a disheveled studio where she wrote obscure verse and plays as she reclined in a hammock brooding and gathering her thoughts, and terribly social. Her parties were sparkling events where the more adventurous socialities met Bohemia, and in Miss Strange's hands, the mix was fine. Not the least interesting of thes salon habituées was the hostess herself. She wore heavy mascara and covered her face with rice powder rather like a geisha. She preferred to wear severely tailored men's suits, and while she was married to John Barrymore, they appeared in matching outfits, usually made of velvet and satin, with silk shirts topped by collars with long pointed tips known as "the Barrymore collar" and flowing black string ties. They also matched their affairs—her young poet-lover against his latest conquest—so that there would be all-night-long, tempestuous rows over them, loud enough to wake the children, Diana and her half brothers, Leonard, who was eldest, and Robin.

It was hard not to admire her determination to fashion her own destiny. She had been raised Blanche Oelrichs, the pampered daughter of a rich, venerable New York couple, married Leonard Thomas, who was even richer, and then, following the birth of her second son, she rebelled. She banished Blanche Oelrichs Thomas and invented Michael Strange, forbidding her own children to call her anything but "Miss Strange." She set out to offend all of her peers among New York's best families by smoking cigarettes incessantly, marching down Fifth Avenue with the suffragettes, bobbing her hair, and creating her own milieu instead of fitting herself into the established one. At fever-pitch of revolt, while husband Leonard was overseas during World War I, she had a torrid affair with the leading matinee idol of the day, John Barrymore. He was almost equally manic, an alcoholic long before he made his great leap to stage stardom. They were two explosive devices attached to the same fuse and it was anyone's guess as to who would blow up first.

Then, in the mid-twenties, John's stage success took him to Hollywood. Distance made him see how tortured their relationship really was. He began to look seriously about him at the women swooning at his feet and decided that Dolores Costello, who had a saintly mien and porcelain-figurine body and features, was pliant enough to become the third Mrs. Barrymore (his first marriage had been brief).

Michael Strange's powerful narcissism and iron will had a devastating effect upon her children. Diana, dressed in hand-me-downs from her mother throughout her adolescence and early womanhood, had her father's love of gaiety and, even before she reached her majority, his incurable attachment to alcohol. Robin, deprived of his father and smothered by his mother's indulgence and affection, utilized the vast trust funds set up for him by his father to lead a life as eccentric as his mother's while, at the same time, attempting to succeed on the stage. He failed in the latter and eventually gave it up, retiring with his lover to a country estate because, as he told Diana, he couldn't stand living under the same roof with his mother.

So flamboyant was Robin that Tyrone later screened out Robin from his "official biography" as prepared by his movie studio. There was a curious double standard regarding homosexuality within the film industry, which prevailed throughout the great studio period (from the 1920s through the 1950s) and hangs on among the old studio hands.

Tyrone at nineteen already saw a dualism in his own nature. Patia's influence on him had been almost as great as Michael Strange's on Robin, but Patia rarely indulged Tyrone. Years later, he said with a touch of pride that she never spoiled him. Yet fate had dealt him the kind of excessive handsomeness that disarmed everyone and, on top of that, he had his father's flirtatiousness. It was the drama of his life and he was on a tightrope most of his adult life.

Tyrone reached Gracie Square before Robin. By pre-arrangement, they had come East on separate trains. Robin was very shrewd about human relationships and wanted Tyrone to win over his mother completely on his own. At this time, she had become Mrs. Harrison Tweed, yet another millionaire, but was still "Miss Strange" to everyone, including Tyrone.

He arrived in New York a week before Christmas. He met his host, "Harry" Tweed and Diana at breakfast, dressed for a day of "making rounds" of producers' offices in a dark blue pin-striped suit. Diana stared at him and told him that he was "even more beautiful than your picture." Harry Tweed warned her not to embarrass Tyrone. Then, that evening, Diana found him in the sitting room standing disconsolately in front of the fireplace. "Did you get your job?" she asked, and he told her that he had had no luck. "You know," he added, "there's a Depression still on. It isn't easy. I don't expect to find one right away."

And he did not. But Robin saw that he was circulating among theatrical people who counted. There was some possibility that Robin would introduce Tyrone to Noël Coward, but he did not succeed in this until Coward was in New York to launch his short-lived *Point Valaine*, and by then Tyrone already was firmly set on a different course under staider but no less glamorous auspices. Tyrone's friendship for Coward then proved more durable than Tyrone's with Robin. When he was around Coward, he could be absolutely himself. Around Robin, he was a showpiece to be admired.

Tyrone enjoyed Michael Strange's company in limited

doses. She was sincere in her eccentricity and he couldn't abide pretension or phoniness. He was expected to be around whenever there was one of her salons, and by late January he was becoming such a permanent fixture, he told Robin that he was a little embarrassed about it. Robin tried to persuade his friend, Ted Peckham, who ran an escort service for women who needed a date for the evening, to hire Tyrone. Unfortunately, Peckham wanted only Ivy League types and Tyrone had only a high school diploma.

But there was an unexpected breakthrough. A middle-aged socialite at one of the salon gatherings was enchanted with Tyrone. It was often his custom at a party to single out someone and turn on all the charm he possessed. It was one of the ways he dealt with his father's rejection of his mother—and, indirectly, of himself. The lady was overwhelmed and told him that he was wasting his time making the rounds of production offices and agents. "Anyone as attractive as you are should go right to the top management and show them what you have to offer," she said. Then when he seemed to demur—he had visited every theatrical management firm in town and couldn't get inside the manager's office—she said that she would write a letter the very next day to the office of producer-director Guthrie McClintic, who was married to and staged all the plays for Katharine Cornell. "The McClintics are very old and dear friends of mine." Of course, Tyrone had heard that one before, in that very room, in fact, and because this was cocktail-party conversation, he put it out of his mind.

But later that week, a call came in for Tyrone from the McClintic office. It was Gertrude Macy, production manager for McClintic, asking when he could come in for a chat. As calmly as he could, Tyrone wondered if the next day would be too soon.

Miss Macy was used to seeing handsome actors walking through the office doorway, but still she was enormously impressed by Tyrone's appearance. "He really was adorable," she recalled. "So I took him in to Mr. McClintic and said, 'Here's a boy I'd love you to meet so we can remember him when and if something comes up.'"

Katharine Cornell was about to go into rehearsal with Burgess Meredith in an anti-war play by John van Druten, *Flowers of the Forest*. When work on the production began,

Miss Macy remembered Tyrone after all the roles had been cast. But they needed an assistant stage manager who could also understudy. She told McClintic, "This Power boy will do anything and work for minimum. He wants to learn about the theatre and he'll play any part, and that would get him to understudy at rehearsals with the stage manager." McClintic agreed and Tyrone was signed at the minimum of fifty dollars a week.

Tyrone was very ambitious and eager, and so attractive in his earnestness, the stage manager became infatuated with him almost from the first understudy rehearsal. During his three years of jobbing around the country in the theatre, Tyrone had become very sophisticated about sex. Word of his close friendship with Robin Thomas could scarcely be kept a secret within the theatrical fraternity. Yet Tyrone never felt compelled as do so many young men to clarify his sexual preferences. Nor was he ever heard to put Robin or his kind down. He seemed not to care what people thought in this department, and this did nothing to lessen his popularity among his peers in show business. It also must have occurred to him that his friendships with men almost never got him into serious difficulty while those with the handsomely endowed women he preferred caused him no end of grief. Beautiful women and handsome men would weave their way through the rest of his life—the women in the center ring each for her season, with the men mostly on the perimeter.

Tyrone really was not interested in the stage manager in any physical way and he had far too much at stake with this production to get involved with anyone. Everyone in the company, including Miss Cornell, knew what had happened, but they loved and respected the stage manager very much and they were beginning to be very fond of Tyrone. So Tyrone went on about his business, was always respectful and all-business around the stage manager, and the episode was forgotten.

Flowers of the Forest had a brief run, losing some money for its investors. To recoup, Miss Cornell planned a revival of *Romeo and Juliet* with Maurice Evans as Romeo. Tyrone was given the small role of Balthazar, and then after getting good notices and pleasing Miss Cornell, he was promoted to the role of Tybalt. Orson Welles, exactly a year younger than

Tyrone and recently back from a year with the Abbey Theatre in Dublin, was signed on as Mercutio.

As Tybalt, Tyrone had to be a kind of menace, but wily and athletic. He projected all of this and looked darkly handsome in black velvet. He had a fencing scene and took lessons daily. He worked harder than anyone in the company, studying lines, taking French lessons, eating properly to keep his strength up. The trip was strenuous. They played seventy-seven cities in thirty-nine weeks, including San Francisco and Los Angeles on the West Coast.

When they were playing Los Angeles, a talent scout for Universal (where Tyrone had done *Tom Brown of Culver*) came backstage and told Tyrone the studio was interested in him and proposed a seven-year contract at two hundred dollars a week the first year, then three hundred fifty dollars, and ending up at five hundred dollars a week. That was a great deal of money in the middle of the Depression in 1935. It would be a forty-week-a-year paying contract, and the studio would give him lessons in drama, dance, and fencing while he was on salary. Tyrone had no agent at his elbow urging him to take it, and he badly needed sound advice. He went to Maurice Evans and asked what he thought he should do. Evans said, "Take it," But Miss Cornell took a very different view. She and her husband saw a great deal of promise in Tyrone, and she warned him that he hadn't enough to offer the movies yet. "If you let them buy you," she told him, "you're going to miss very valuable background you will need." Tyrone listened to her and turned down the Universal offer.

It was the policy of the McClintics to tour until a show was really ready before bringing it into New York so that a pre-Broadway junket might last months. They regularly excluded from their tour cities like Philadelphia, Washington, and Hartford because they were too accessible to the New York critics. They decided that *Romeo and Juliet* was not ready for Broadway and began changing all the parts around.

Maurice Evans remained as Romeo, but Orson Welles was demoted from Mercutio to Tybalt, which Tyrone had been playing. Naturally, Tyrone was devastated, but he recovered quickly when he realized that Miss Cornell still believed in him. He was cast as Benvolio, and for Mercutio, the Mc-Clintics brought Ralph Richardson over from London. It was a powerhouse cast and the production won rave notices.

Romeo and Juliet ran for an entire season in New York, and Tyrone took his own tiny apartment, which eventually he shared. He had moved out of Michael Strange's residence a few weeks before the first tour because the partying was interfering with his acting studies. Still, he remained in touch with her and Robin for years, although with great success finally his, he was less and less inclined to mention them.

Then in the fall of 1935, Miss Cornell, who seemed to prefer classic drama, decided to revive Shaw's *Saint Joan*. Tyrone at last had a showy part, that of Bertrand de Poulengey, and he was in the opening scene, which he did exceedingly well. It turned out to be one of the finest Cornell productions in her entire career.

Hollywood talent scouts are not, as rumored, akin to bolts of lightning striking attractive young men and women at random. They are much more like fox-hunters, relentless in pursuit of their quarry and out to win, fair or foul. There was another long break in tour for *Saint Joan*, and while they were in Los Angeles, an attorney for Twentieth Century–Fox named Alfred Wright, who was a personal friend of production manager Gertrude Macy, came backstage and told her that his company was interested in Tyrone. He said that if it would be disastrous to Miss Cornell to lose him, they would hold off for a while. Miss Macy said that it would not be disastrous to lose Tyrone, even though everyone in the company had tremendous affection for him, but it was decided that he should be allowed to open in New York since the production was sure to be a hit and that could only be good for Twentieth Century–Fox in promoting him.

After *Saint Joan* had run for several weeks, the film studio's New York manager, Joe Moskowitz, came backstage and spoke with Tyrone. Tyrone knew it was coming and this time, he had Miss Cornell's blessing.

There was a farewell dinner party in Tyrone's honor on the evening before his departure for California given by the McClintics. They were all genuinely sorry to lose him. He had not yet reached his full potential as an actor; he was, in fact, a considerable distance from that. But he had won all of their hearts, and he would be sorely missed.

V

THE RIGHT WOMAN,
AND
THE WAR BEGINS

IN THE middle of October, 1938, Tyrone flew with Bill Gallagher to New York for the opening at the Roxy of *Suez* on the fourteenth. When he ran into Simone Simon there, on a brief stopover before she flew on to Paris, he asked her to be a courier and sent a long, love-sick letter to Annabella.

The movie got generally good notices, Annabella faring even better than Tyrone or Loretta Young. Word of their interest in each other had now reached the gossip columns and Tyrone, when asked about her, said "Fantastic! We are merely good friends." It was one of his weaker performances and no one was deceived. Annabella, in Paris, was not about to have her divorce derailed by a possible countersuit. She glanced determinedly at the press and said, "Tyrone Power? He is a nice boy. But that is all."

To Annabella, Tyrone wrote: "At least here (*in New York*), I feel that I'm a *little* closer to you, but Hollywood seems so far away. Darling you must hurry back soon. I don't know what I'll do for the next two and a half months. It's going to be terrible." Then he surprised and delighted her by revealing that he was still a practicing Catholic (she was afraid he had lapsed). ". . . guess what I did!" he continued, describing a visit to St. Patrick's. "Twelve little candles, angel, the one extra one is for the star that I love better than anything in the world. It was so peaceful, so quiet in there, I had a wonderful talk with you, the best I've had since you flew away. I must have more of them."

Rose of Washington Square was Tyrone's last picture with Alice Faye, and shooting began while he was waiting for Annabella's return. He was asked once again to play a con

artist and lady-killer, but it was Zanuck's idea to "fic-
tionalize" the life of Fanny Brice and her relationship with
con-man Nicky Arnstein. Nunnally Johnson, who did the
screenplay, carried the parallels so far, he even had Miss Faye
singing "My Man," with a broken heart, of course. Despite a
disclaimer at the beginning of the picture that "any resemblance to any persons, living or dead, is entirely coin-
cidental," Fanny Brice sued Twentieth Century-Fox, and it
was settled out of court before the picture's release. Later, the
same basic story would appear in a Broadway musical and
film authorized by the late Fanny's daughter—*Funny Girl*, in-
troducing Barbra Streisand to screen audiences.

Tyrone worked hard on *Rose of Washington Square*,
allowing some of his happiness to seep into his role of con-
man Bart Clinton, although it came out as suave charm,
which was exactly right. He was counting the days until
Annabella would be back with him. In late November, he
wrote:

> . . . to think that in 4 more weeks we will be together.
>   Oh Angel, I do love you so much, and the longer we
> are apart, and the more I see of other people the more
> wonderful I think you are, and the deeper you go into my
> heart, or what's left of it. Maybe we are sent these things
> to test our love; just to see how great it is. But I do know
> that it is the biggest thing in my life, and always will be.

And in a number of ways, that remained true.

Tyrone and Annabella were married on April 23, 1939, in
the living room of her home on St. Pierre Road in Bel Air.
They made several attempts to convince the Los Angeles
diocese that it would be proper for them to have a church
wedding, but they failed. Because of that, Annabella had
created a kind of altar around the fireplace, or perhaps *bower*
is a better word. Flowers surrounded that side of the room,
and the words of the officiating justice, the Hon. William J.
Palmer of the California Superior Court, had as much weight
behind them as any intoned by a priest:

> ". . . and in the presence of God, whose blessing we now
> invoke upon this joyful, yet sacred service.

"Whatever may be the customs, the attitudes and the whims of a people passing through the changing forms of its civilization, marriage remains, and ever will remain, a romantic, beautiful and significant event. . . ."

Judge Palmer concluded by citing the responsibilities involved, especially "Kindness, with its many little acts of thoughtfulness, in order that the romance of marriage may be kept alive and fresh . . ." and "Care, with its noble deeds and sacrifice, in order that the beauty of marriage may be preserved. . . ."

Pat Patterson Boyer was matron of honor and that perennial loser in a triangle, Don Ameche, made this performance conform to all the film dramas he and Tyrone had done together by seeming perfectly cast as best man. Patia had softened her attitude toward Annabella. It was the beginning of a closeness between them. The Charpentiers were gone, their American holiday over. Mama Lily had returned to France with son Pierre to be with her husband Paul and her other boy, Jean. With them went Annie, who had become very close to her grandmother.

But Tyrone's sister Anne was there, a delighted witness. The Zanucks were among the missing. The sudden wedding plans had taken the studio by surprise. Still, there were cameramen from the news services waiting out in the garden, and only the whirr of their motion-picture cameras and the long cords trailing after them marred the reception on the patio afterward. A radiance, and the glow could nearly be seen, emanated from the bride and groom. It made tolerable the carnival mood imposed upon the al fresco gathering by the media.

Then they were off in Tyrone's Pontiac coupe, vaguely hinting to the press that they were headed for Santa Barbara. They drove around the mountainous roads of the canyons near Malibu until they found a small backwoods inn kept by an old couple who had never been to the movies. While they had their wedding supper of fried eggs, they overheard the couple's radio blaring the news of the wedding and describing them in such detail the woman came back to the table and asked, "Are you the two people from Hollywood who just got married?" With that, their much-sought privacy vanished and they came back to St. Pierre Road in the dead of night. All the guests had gone, and they were alone finally as husband and wife.

Tyrone had to work the next day. There were no toasts drunk to Tyrone and Annabella's future around the Fox lot. When his current picture was finished, they would have a brief honeymoon flying around the Grand Canyon and the Southwest, abbreviated by retakes required for a foolish trifle he was making with Sonja Henie, *Second Fiddle*. When they flew along the bottom of the Canyon, Annabella said that she was terrified. But truly Annabella Power had as much daring as her husband. She had been toughened as a small girl when she was unofficially a member of the French boy scouts. This had come about because her father, formerly a magazine publisher, was also head and founder of the scouts in France, and little Zetto, as she was known, invariably attended their camp-outs, usually sleeping on straw. Younger brother Pierre was not very strong, so she had done all the things he could not—swimming in rough waters, riding, and skiing.

The couple settled into their handsome new modified Georgian mansion built by but never lived in by diva Grace Moore. Negro architect Paul Williams had designed it. Both Annabella and Tyrone had fallen in love with it on first sight because "every window was a french window. We were in and out . . . on the balcony, on the terrace."

It was Grace Moore's dream house, designed especially for her while she was basking in the great success of her early films (*One Night of Love,* et al.). But she had disliked her last film, *Louise,* so much that she had put the house on the market before shooting was completed, and Tyrone and Annabella were the first prospects who looked at it. They bought it before anyone else had a chance to see it. It had pink satin walls in the master suite and the initials "P" for Perreira (Miss Moore's married name) etched into the numerous mirrors around the place. It could stand for "Power," of course, but Annabella thought it was pretentious. She insisted that the monogrammed mirrors and the pink satin be removed, although much of the expensive carpeting remained. It also had a marvelous garden, planted months before the house went up and known in Brentwood as "Grace Moore's botanical garden" on three acres of land. There were orange and pepper trees, and a rose garden.

For nearly a month, while they waited for a collection of fine old French Provincial pieces to arrive, a gift from Annabella's parents, the couple managed with just a bed, some wrought-iron patio furniture, and a pinball machine, which Tyrone considered an essential. Once all the rooms were furnished, however, they lived quite differently. Tyrone had his own bedroom suite with a small bathroom and dressing room, and Annabella had hers. For Christmas, Annabella had a steam room or sauna installed in his suite, since she seemed to feel it necessary to be next to parboiled every working day after coming from the studio (before that, Zanuck had given him access to his own steam room at Fox and, unconsciously perhaps, Annabella did what she could to discourage that camaraderie.)

The Rains Came by Louis Bromfield had become a best-seller, a book-club selection much sought after in circulating libraries. It was a potboiler involving a natural diaster that would take any film production budget immediately into the stratosphere. It was warmed-over Maugham without the first-hand insight, wry comment, and experience of the British teller of tales. It would be difficult to market such hokum today since it was not published as trashy fiction, for which there is always an audience. In it, an Indian, Major Rama Safti (Tyrone), takes his internship at Johns Hopkins and returns to Ranchipur, India, where he sets up a clinic for the natives, who are of the lowest caste. At the time the book was purchased, Tyrone was number two at the box office, trailing Hollywood's "Andy Hardy," Mickey Rooney, by the smallest of margins. The morally rotten British colonials are represented by Lady Esketh (Zanuck borrowed the most popular leading lady of the day, Metro's Myrna Loy, for this role) and an old lover of hers, Tom Ransome (played by Warner Brothers' George Brent). When the rains begin at Ranchipur, they never stop, and soon there is a great flood, during which much of the movie was turned over to the special-effects department.

When retakes were finished on *The Rains Came*, Tyrone and Annabella were at last free to embark on their much-delayed wedding trip. Before leaving California, he instructed secretary Bill Gallagher to contact him at once if he turned up any leads on his son, whose birth he had just learned about. No word would be forthcoming.

The Powers flew first to New York, where Watson had made arrangements for them to stay at his parents' seventeen-room apartment on Park Avenue. It was by far the most elegant living space Tyrone ever had seen with its boudoir in antique boiserie removed from Wenvoe Castle in Glamorgan and the walls of that room (Watson's mother's) enhanced by painting an epoch apart in style and feeling but oddly compatible—a Goya and a Mary Cassatt, the latter painter once the intimate friend of Electra "Ma" Webb's. In the oversized living room were paintings by Degas, Rembrandt, Manet, and Corot, but the ambience was not that of a millionaire's Park Avenue residence, but rather the quiet comfort and unobtrusive distinction that seemed bred into the Havemeyer side of the family and which Watson had inherited. This oasis of great charm and separateness from the outside world on upper Park Avenue would be "home" to both Powers on several occasions to come. Annabella and Ma Webb embraced warmly, kindred spirits that they were. Electra Havemeyer Webb, too, had enjoyed a happy, love-supported childhood. She collected old things, Americana in particular, and her collection would outgrow numerous stables and storage areas, and require an extensive museum (at Shelburne, Vermont) to hold it all. Even more impressive in Annabella's eyes was Ma Webb's remarkable hospitality. There was always an extra place set at the table for some (usually missing) last-minute guest. If they were six at dinner, a seventh place would be set.

Then the Powers boarded the *Rex*, which would take them to Naples to begin a leisurely tour of Europe. The very first night out, Tyrone sent off a batch of cables, part of a film star's ritual, and then grabbed a blank and scribbled the following:

MARCONIGRAMMA

Urgent!!!!!

Annabella P.

It doesn't matter where

I love you
,,   ,,   ,,
,,   ,,   ,,
,,   ,,   ,,
,,   ,,   ,,
,,   ,,   ,,
,,   ,,   ,,   very much

T.

They did not seclude themselves; they were highly visible. There was something in both of them that wanted the world to see their joy in being together. Annabella thought then that "we were at the top of our happiness."

A press representative from the Paris Office of Twentieth Century–Fox came aboard the liner as they were getting ready to disembark at Naples. He was a jovial, big-boned American who told them that he had planned everything on their wedding trip down to the last detail. Then he followed them down the gangplank and joined them for lunch, where he gave them the details of the press conference he had set up for later that afternoon. Tyrone nodded as though this were merely the price of fame, but Annabella was appalled. Still, she said nothing and charmed all of the newspapermen at the press conference in her usual fashion, giving them a piquant but surface glimpse of her great love for Tyrone. Then Mr. Press Bureau joined them for dinner, and Annabella simply couldn't believe it. But her happiness was so deep, she said nothing that night. On the following day, the trio went to Pompeii and again were together for lunch and dinner. As Annabella recalls it, "He said that he had fixed up everything to go to Venice and he had ordered a Hispano-Suiza and we (*the trio again*) would leave the following day at two in the afternoon. We would meet with the press before and he had made reservations for us all at Florence. We were going to stop on the way and everything was perfect and nice, etc. I told Tyrone that a honeymoon was for two people, not three. And that's where the sweetness of Tyrone was beginning to be his enemy. He said, 'But the man came especially from Paris!' I said, 'Of course he did. He was from the office in Paris. He had two days in Naples and he came ahead of us and he had a wonderful time. He can go back to Paris or stay in Naples or do whatever he wants, but he's not coming with us.' "

Then Tyrone asked me, 'Do you think we can do that?' "
Annabella had to remind herself that here was a young man
who had not matured in the outside world, but in a
Hollywood studio. His values were theirs; he had much to
learn. And in the years ahead, he would have in Annabella an
infinitely wise professor.

This was a Tyrone who did not know the meaning of
rebellion or assertion of self. He only knew that he already
had offended his employer gravely by marrying Annabella,
and since he had been for more than three years entirely in the
studio's hands, his every move either ordered by them or
reported to them, he could not imagine dismissing Zanuck's
press representative. Theirs had been the most romantic
marriage in Hollywood in many years, and even if it was in
defiance of Zanuck (a major element in the world's absorption in their romance), in Tyrone's mind they owed Fox
at least this courtesy—allowing one polite gentleman to be
always in the background keeping the world informed of their
progress as they moved about the Old World on their blissful
journey.

Annabella told him that such an idea was "idiotic." "We
don't need their Hispano-Suiza. We can get a car of our
own," and she suggested that they go at that very moment and
see what they might buy in the way of a little car. She did not
see herself as in any way "bossy." She was just insisting that
Tyrone assert himself, something she would do often in the
years ahead. Their friends began to see Annabella and her
strong sense of her own identity, formed not in the studios but
within the bosom of her family in France, as the bedrock of
that marriage. Tyrone certainly had not found himself until
stardom had caught up with him at the comparatively early
age of twenty-two. In that youth was a flock of redeeming
qualities—romanticism, affection, dedication to his work,
loyalty and an abiding curiosity about all of life that were
ingrained in him—but the man had been shaped by Henry
King, by Darryl Zanuck, and by a host of other specialists at
Twentieth Century-Fox.

They bought a Fiat and said nothing to anyone. On the
following morning, shortly after dawn, Tyrone wrote a little
note of thanks and apology to the press aide from Paris and
left it at the lobby desk, and then he and Annabella took off in

their new car. It was done in such haste, they failed to learn all the mechanical details of their vehicle, and when they drove off and encountered their first traffic jam, they couldn't find the horn. So they drove through crowds of pedestrians at about three kilometers an hour because they didn't want to run over anyone. They had no reservations anywhere; all of that had been abandoned along with the press man. Neither of them knew any Italian, but they managed and it was much the most joyful lark of their lives.

In Rome, they met up with Count Freddi Rossi, who had been a fellow passenger on the *Rex*. He was close to someone at the Vatican and arranged an audience with Pope Pius XII. Annabella had not brought a black dress, so she borrowed one from their maid at the Excelsior Hotel, and Count Rossi gave her a black lace mantilla to cover her head and a pair of black stockings. The Pope gave them his blessing and both of them felt that it very nearly made up for their inability to be married in church back in Los Angeles.

Wherever they moved, people looked upon them as a symbol of happiness. Some stranger would come up to them and say, "Oh, let me touch you. You are so happy!" And once someone thrust a rosary in Tyrone's hands so that his happiness would bless it.

In Venice, after a gondola ride in the Grand Canal, they climbed out of the craft to find Cary Grant and his girlfriend Phyllis Brooks waiting for them at the landing area. Then they drove through the south of France across to Le Pilat, on the Atlantic, the seaside home of the Charpentiers. Along the way, Tyrone asked Annabella to teach him all the old French lullabies she could remember her mother singing to her. He said that he wanted to give her mother "a present." Then at Le Pilat, he knelt on the living-room floor next to Mama Lily's chair, took her hand in his and sang all the French baby songs Annabella had taught him. Mama Lily broke down and wept, she was so moved, and Annabella was touched again by his innate sweetness.

They spent a month at Le Pilat, swimming, playing tennis on the family court right next to the sea, fishing, and having a glorious time in the sunshine that seemed never-ending.

France and Great Britain had declared war on Germany on September 3, 1939, following the Nazi invasion of Poland.

Tyrone and Annabella were en route home from their wedding trip aboard a seaplane, the *Dixie Clipper*, which they had boarded in Lisbon, and were stopped in the Azores refueling when the news came over the ship's radio. A chill seized Annabella. She thought of her family whom they had just seen at Le Pilat. She worried most of all about her daughter and brother Pierre.

No more than a month after their return, Annabella felt compelled to go back to Europe to see what could be done about getting her family out of France. Some of her friends told her she was crazy even to set foot in her native land because "they might not let you back out again." She told them, "If I don't try to help my family and bring back my daughter, I would die of shame. If I cannot come back to Tyrone, I will die of despair. I have no choice but to try and do my best." Her parents said that they planned to shut down the house at St. Cloud and settle at Le Pilat for the rest of the war in what would soon become "Vichy France." Her brother, Pierre, could not leave France because the French government would not give a young man of seventeen a passport. Annabella even thought of dressing him as a girl and smuggling him out, but Pierre balked at that, so she brought only her daughter, Anne, back with her.

The Power home at 139 North Saltair in Brentwood was surrounded by the estates of other film people. The Gary Coopers, their favorite neighbors, were across the street. The Powers and the Coopers took dancing lessons together when the rhumba was wildly popular, their instructor a diminutive Mexican just a bit over five feet tall. Tyrone rolled on the floor with laughter as "Coop," a terrible dancer, solemnly "made the square" of the rhumba movement while dancing with the little Mexican.

Fred MacMurray and his wife lived on several acres on the corner lot nearby, and Cesar Romero bought a home a little over a block away. There were streets behind them that were still unpaved, where Annie, Annabella's daughter, would ride the white horse Tyrone had given her without fear of traffic. Annie and "Moonlight" became a familiar sight on those back roads.

Everybody loved Tyrone. Even the grips and the other

workers at Fox thought he was "a regular guy." Their home began to attract a fair-sized crowd every Sunday almost from the moment Annabella returned from her urgent family business abroad. Scotch and vodka flowed freely, and every parlor game that came along was played with gusto. This Sunday "salon" was international in flavor. Among the regulars were the Rex Harrisons (she was Lilli Palmer); Anatole Litvak; Claudette Colbert and her doctor husband, Dr. Jack Pressman; Bill and Edie Goetz; Douglas, Jr., and Mary Lee Fairbanks; Ernst Lubitsch; David Niven; Pat and Charles Boyer; Clifton Webb; Cary Grant and his wife at the time, Barbara Hutton, together with her prankish cousin Jimmy Donahue; Ceasar Romero; and, later, the Garson Kanins (she was actress and writer Ruth Gordon).

Ruth Gordon had come to Hollywood in 1942 to spend a fortnight with her friends the René Clairs (Clair had been brought to America to direct, and his great filmmaking period ended in commercialism). Ruth came to the Powers' Saltair house to spend a quiet Sunday by the pool. Although she was then forty-six years old, she told Annabella and Tyrone that she was "crazy" about Garson, sixteen years her junior. Annabella recalled that she bubbled like a teen-ager and had her face suddenly blossomed with acne, no one would have been surprised. She told Annabella and Tyrone that she wasn't sure it would be wise to marry so much younger a person, but in the next breath she was describing her trip West on the Twentieth Century Limited, which was for her a blissful journey with the thought of Garson constant. "We stopped at Albuquerque for fifteen minutes and I went for a walk," she said. "Life was so wonderful at that moment. The air smelled of sage and the first stars were coming out. I saw two little red lights getting smaller and smaller on the horizon. *They were the tail lights of my train!*" Tyrone interrupted her, saying, "Ruth darling, what the hell are you doing here? You want to marry Garson. He wants to marry you. Get the hell back to New York and do it!"

The Zanucks were not a part of this party group, but they always invited the Powers to their functions. They still dearly loved Tyrone, and Zanuck was quite polite to Annabella socially. Formal dinners were elaborately prepared on Saltair to reciprocate, and at one such affair, Tyrone overheard a

visiting New York woman remark with some disdain, "You
never know what to expect from these Hollywood people."
Tyrone immediately went into the kitchen and instructed
Henry Shields, their butler, to see that one of the pet goldfish
from the formal garden go on temporary duty in the lady's
finger bowl. When it was served, he deadpanned his way
through a long monologue on California missions as the
guests stared in shocked wonder into the bowl. Shields was
cracking up in the kitchen, but Tyrone made sure that the lady
got more than a momentary surprise.

Watson had become very nearly a member of the
household. The Powers had an extra key made for him so that
he could drop in even if they weren't home. When he and
Tyrone had influenza at the same time, Annabella insisted
that he leave his own house and she fetched him herself. He
stayed with them until he had recovered and she nursed both
of them. He was the brother Tyrone had never had.

Watson had begun to rise in the cutting department at Fox.
He was beginning to make friends in the film colony. Zanuck,
Henry Hathaway, and Joe Mankiewicz, among others, soon
would respect him for what he had achieved on his own, while
at the same time finding him a fascinating enigma. He knew
very important people within the film colony, yet he never
pressed anyone for a favor. Like Tyrone, he had a near impeccable integrity. When Zanuck began inviting him to Ric-
Su-Dar Ranch in the desert, he may have been the first
assistant film cutter so honored, but it was not his friendship
with Tyrone that had brought it about; Watson was born a
Havemeyer, a Vanderbilt, and a Webb, and had been around
and been courted by people of consequence all of his life.
Movie moguls, nearly to a man, had been born poor boys,
and nothing pleased them more than being on intimate terms
with a member of entrenched society. The irony for Watson
was that he had abandoned that society to start his career in
films at the bottom. So the Hollywood crowd certainly knew
of Watson Webb's existence.

Without either Tyrone or Watson knowing it was happening, a legend began to grow around the friends as a latter-
day Damon and Pythias. The true essentials of their relationship probably foreshadowed those between Ratso (Watson)
and Joe Buck, the Midnight Cowboy (Tyrone), with the men

at the top level of the social stratum instead of the bottom as in James Leo Herlihy's book.

The legend grew for specific reasons. In 1941, Watson began building on a ten-acre parcel of land on Crescenda Street, less than a block from the Powers. His early American "farmhouse" was to be an unpretentious place suitable for a bachelor with a considerable collection of American antiques. Since Watson was working long hours at the studio, Annabella was deputized to oversee the progress of the work done on the Webb house. Checking on it every day, she thought it was moving so slowly, she bought a miniature workbench about six inches high with a complete set of tiny tools and gave the curio to Watson with a note saying that if he expected his house to be finished "by 1985," he had better get to work himself.

To some, it seemed a little like *Design for Living* with Tyrone as the focal point of the troika. But Annabella knew differently. She and Tyrone were "madly in love." Perhaps such a profound passion needed a witness, and Watson often found himself in that role. He had to be infinitely adaptable.

Tyrone's life was now structured around Annabella. Watson had to fit himself into that life plan. What Annabella respected in Watson throughout the years was his unassailable loyalty to them, especially to Tyrone, and Watson's distaste for phoniness. In Tyrone's words, Watson was "a realie" and so was Annabella.

In early 1940, the three of them flew to New York together. The overnight flight took more than twelve hours in those days, and the commercial airliner left Los Angeles a few hours before dark and was due in New York early the following morning. Before dinner in the cabin, they played a French card game called belote, which Annabella had taught the men. (When her brother Jean heard that she had been someone's teacher of the rules of the game, he asked, "How could you dare?" since she was a notoriously poor player.) Tyrone and Watson asked Annabella to keep score, and she jotted down their initials, TWA. Then Tyrone giggled, looking up in some surprise, and said, "You know we happen to be flying TWA, but do you realize the three of us are TWA, too?" Thus they became a solid triumvirate, especially in times of adversity or during the holidays. At family get-togethers, they all would troop off ensemble—Christmases, New Year's Eves, reunions of every kind. Watson was drawn into the Power family. On the East Coast, the reverse held true. The Powers became part of the Webb family.

Annabella had tried very hard to become pregnant, because Tyrone wanted a son so badly. So did she, and she went to two different gynecologists in Los Angeles to seek advice and help. Finally, Irene Mayer Selznick suggested that she try a Dr. Salmon in New York's Mount Sinai Hospital, and Annabella went East in mid-July, 1940, for surgery.

She decided upon the operation at an especially chaotic time for her. Zanuck was insisting that she do a film in London on loan-out and the agent in London who had negotiated the deal saw his 10 per cent (of $75,000) disappearing when she refused even to discuss such a project. He was furious and thought that celebrated Annabella had changed from a sophisticated, responsible actress into a love-sick idiot.

A process server entered her hospital room without knocking. Annabella was half naked, and her private nurse could not prevent the man from approaching the bed and throwing the papers at her. She then lost all control and began screaming in rage and humiliation. Finally, she calmed down enough to phone Tyrone in California. She had tried to keep any word of her dispute with Zanuck from her husband until that moment. Tyrone called the surgeon, and "raised hell," but one must note that he failed to call Zanuck and do likewise. That night, he wrote her:

> . . . It takes me a long time to get the Irish up but when it does it fairs attention. If it costs me every cent I have, if it takes me to my dying day, I'll find the bastard who served those papers. I've already called Walter Winchell *(the most successful of the syndicated gossip columnists, who was a personal friend and had appeared in two films for Fox)* and he was horrified; he thought I ought to have guards put outside your room. I get so God-damn mad just thinking of it. . . .

It would not have occurred to Tyrone to challenge his employer. Studio heads were gods and one simply did not face down Supreme Beings. But he phoned Watson, who was staying at his family's estate on Lake Champlain in Shelburne, Vermont, and told him of the trauma. Without a moment's hesitation, Watson said he would leave for New York "first thing in the morning" and he stayed in the city, visiting Annabella for hours and having rare, very private conversations. They developed a rapport that nothing could destroy. It would survive her divorce from Tyrone and his eventual death.

On Christmas Eve 1940, Tyrone, Annabella, and Watson were going to Patia's for the evening. It had become their custom, beginning in 1939, to spend Christmas Eve with Tyrone's mother and then have open house all day on Christmas at Saltair. But on this, their second Christmas together, they had a little detour to make in Beverly Hills. Only a week earlier, on his Jell-O radio show, Jack Benny had told his audience that he was planning a huge Christmas party. "Tyrone and Annabella will come," he said, "Barbara Stanwyck and her husband what's-his-name. And Clark Gable. It will be fantastic! And, of course, I'll treat all of them to some numbers on my violin."

So TWA drove up to the impressive Benny mansion, dressed as always for Patia on such occasions to the nines, and wearing big smiles, they rang the bell. Jack opened the door, and Annabella remembers that he had "no tie, just slippers, and bewildered, and Tyrone said, 'Hello. We're a little early but we've come for the party.' And, of course, I didn't dare to open my mouth. Watson was shy as always. Tyrone had this smile, and we all went in. And we arrived in the living room and Jack had all of the family that he never had generally, family we didn't know, old grandmothers and aunties, and everybody was amazed. Mary Benny turned white and she looked at Jack and she tried a big smile. She whispered, 'What are we going to do?' And for fifteen minutes Tyrone didn't stop saying how wonderful it was and saying, 'Jack, what are you going to play for us?' making a joke about the great violin player and so on. Then I saw Mary say something to someone to rush to the kitchen. And Tyrone went right on with his big act. He was having a helluva good time. And after fifteen or twenty minutes, he said, 'Okay children, it was all a big gag. But be careful of what you say on the radio next time or otherwise we'll be back again.' And we left."

•   •   •

Most American women would have seen Watson as a rival
and made scenes about him. Annabella had made of him the
closest friend she had other than Tyrone in America. She
knew where the real threat to their marriage lay and she had
caught a glimpse of it before they were married.

It was a belated birthday party in the middle of May, 1938,
and a typical Hollywood party had been given in Tyrone's
honor. At any such gathering, whether in his honor or not,
Tyrone always was surrounded by women. Being naturally
flirtatious, he did little to discourage it, and on those few
occasions when he was too bored with it and wanted it to stop,
found that there was simply no way to discourage them.
Annabella, as his date, was not particularly delighted by this.
In fact, she was not very comfortable among ordinary
Hollywood folk in their outlandish dress, with their overloud
voices, speaking of the most trivial matters or repeating
foolish gossip. When she looked at Tyrone surrounded by
these women, she felt he was cheapening himself and that he
did not belong there. *Her* Tyrone was so much better than
that. Her strong image of Tyrone would bring out the very
finest in the man; he would become as mature as he ever
would get as he tried to measure up; but in the end, he would
lose her because he would fall back to earth among such
creatures as Annabella saw surrounding him that night. She
managed to make her way up to him and said, "I think I have
to go."

Tyrone was disappointed. Had he expected her to accept
this, she wondered. "But the party was given for me," he
said.

Annabella was always direct about important matters. "I
can't stand it anymore. It's like seeing a beautiful black swan
surrounded by geese. I don't want to see you anymore that
way."

Annabella did not yet feel endangered or vulnerable. At
that early point in their romance, she felt safe in declaring herself on certain delicate matters.

Well into their marriage and several compromises and un-
derstandings later, they seemed to have accepted one another.
On several levels, their marriage was working.

As a girl in France, Annabella always had been able to get

out into the country. La Varenne outside of Paris was semirural, and she believed that anyone who could live in the country was blessed. Throughout her childhood, there were edible things growing around her and often wildlife. She recalled that there was a little snake in the strawberry patch near her family home, or perhaps she invented the snake. Having only a few companions living close enough to play with, she developed a rich imagination as she was growing up. Her father encouraged her in this and often inquired about how she had spent her day with her "friend," a playmate who was entirely made up. And she would tell him.

Tyrone's only experience in country life had been during his youth when he had joined his father in the Canadian wilderness. But he was so profoundly in love with Annabella—that love was, he felt, the most important thing that had happened to him in his entire life—he wanted to please her. So the three acres at 139 North Saltair became a miniature farm. The two horses had come first, including Moonlight, Annie's horse. Annabella's daughter and Tyrone would remain in close contact until his death. Sometimes, Annabella would take the other mount out; she enjoyed riding far more than Tyrone did.

They bought about two dozen Rhode Island Red laying hens, and Tyrone had an elaborate brooder-house built after one on the Louis Bromfield farm. The novelist had told Tyrone that chickens were far more productive and less prone to disease if they were not allowed to run about the yard, so the Bromfield chickens were housed in small cages that sat like penthouses atop a chute or an incline down which their eggs would drop—into straw or some other cushioning agent. Although Annabella had some misgivings, she said nothing as a replica was put together in their back yard at considerable expense.

But one day several weeks after the Rhode Island Reds had been caged, Annabella suddenly felt an urge to let them run. She thought that it was nearly criminal to "jail" them like that on such a beautiful day. So one at a time, she removed them and placed them on the ground. To her horror, she found that they could not walk. The weeks of confinement had paralyzed them. It was several hours before even one of them could stand and wobble around.

She and Tyrone always had their time for "secrets" after

they had gone to bed and turned out the light. Now in their secret hour, she said, "I think it's so sad for those poor hens over there. They have no fun and the garden is so beautiful." She didn't want to make too strong a case for freedom; she was moving slowly since Tyrone had spent a great deal of money having the Bromfield brooder-house built and he always showed it off to friends. Tyrone said nothing; she thought he was half asleep.

The following morning, Tyrone had to get up at dawn to go to the studio. At about seven, before he went for his car, he said, "Come on. I have something to do and you need to help me. Put something on your shoulders." Annabella put a wrap about her and he took her by the hand. They went down to the garden and he told her: "Let's take out those goddamned chickens. They're too unhappy there." Then one after another, they liberated the chickens. He noticed with the same alarm she had the day before how they fell over and couldn't walk, but he had to leave for work. At lunchtime, the phone rang and it was Tyrone. "How are your chickens?" he asked. "Can they move?" Happily, Annabella was able to say, "It's okay now. It's good." The Rhode Island Reds had regained their mobility and were scratching about the garden in freedom. The expensive brooder-house was scrapped.

They sometimes lost count of the dog population on Saltair. After Pickles, Tyrone had acquired a beautiful German shepherd bitch whom he called "Lady." She often went on trips with them and was on location in Utah during the shooting of *Brigham Young* (1940). Then there was a mixed Labrador named "Princess," who had a litter of eight puppies. For a very brief time, there was a goat, given to Annie by their dentist, and it was a fine pet for a few months. But when the goat reached maturity, they discovered that it was a billygoat, and a rather bellicose billy who butted every moving biped or quadruped, broke everything he could ram his head into or kick, and gave off a most offensive odor which no amount of bathing could eliminate. The billy was taken away, and apparently met an untimely end.

Henry Hathaway had moved over from Paramount Studios to Twentieth Century–Fox in 1940. He had been a writer first, but since the early 1930s, he had been directing and had moved up from programmer Westerns to specialize in making pictures with major leading men. At Paramount, he had become Gary Cooper's favorite director, and he began at Fox, knowing that he would be directing their top male star, Tyrone Power.

For Hathaway, the move meant considerably more money, since the offer from Zanuck was most attractive, and a quasi-independent status. He had as much authority on his pictures as Henry King did on his. For Tyrone, in a subtle way, this meant he was taking a healthy step away from the pervasive control of Zanuck. That, as much as anything, was the impetus behind his instantaneous and enduring friendship with the director and his wife, Bianca, known to her friends as "Skip". Beyond that, Skip and Annabella discovered they had a great many common interests. They were both sophisticated women with an enthusiasm for good conversation that was not Hollywood-parochial.

The first Hathaway–Power production was Tyrone's only attempt to play a gangster role, although he played a great many rogues. *Johnny Apollo* told the story of young Bob Cain, who has been embittered by his millionaire father's imprisonment for embezzlement. Trying to go straight himself, he finds backs are turned when he seeks a job following his father's jailing, and he throws his lot in with the underworld. Dorothy Lamour, who was the leading sex queen on the Paramount lot when Hathaway was there, was borrowed to play a moll-type, "Lucky Dubarry," and to sing "This Is the Beginning of the End," which became rather popular that year.

As an actor, Tyrone impressed Hathaway with his professionalism. Here was no mere "re-actor" as were so many of the big-league leading men the director had known. There was a cool intellect at work behind his questions about what he was supposed to project. The lines had been mastered the night before, and it was only his voice that bothered Hathaway. It was *too* skillful; it did most of the work. They had a brief discussion about that, and Tyrone quickly agreed that he relied far too much on it. Despite the thinness of the story and its gimcrack melodrama, a new Tyrone Power was emerging in *Johnny Apollo*. Here are the first hints of the surprising range of the leading man who would rock critics with *Nightmare Alley* and *Witness for the Prosecution*. The film did well upon its release. No film with Tyrone could do otherwise, since he was then indisputably king of the box office, according to a New York *Daily News* polls and the figures coming into the trade papers. Writing in the old New York *Sun*, reviewer Eileen Creelman wrote: "It's been quite a while since Twentieth Century-Fox ventured into the Warner's fields and took a crack at a gangster story. These underworld thrillers take a certain knack—a knack that sometimes seems to consist mainly of speed and still more speed. 'Johnny Apollo,' now at the Roxy, does not maintain a particularly racing pace." But it did not matter; the crowds came anyway and the matinees were packed with Tyrone's female admirers.

Star and director (Hathaway) moved almost immediately into production of a Western epic to which Zanuck felt drawn, the story of the founder in Utah of the Mormon Church, Brigham Young. The title role was to be played by Dean Jagger, a skillful character actor who had made several films going back to the earliest talkies but who had failed to achieve stardom. Zanuck felt that as Brigham Young, Jagger could make it finally in the rather rare mould of character leading man. There had been several in the past: Emil Jannings, Lon Chaney, George Bancroft, and, at that time, Spencer Tracy and Humphrey Bogart. Jagger would be valuable to the studio if he could carry a film as these other men had, but in *Brigham Young*, he needed help. So Tyrone was called in, and his role is a curious one, almost incidental to the main theme of the struggle of Young to establish his followers on the western frontier. Tyrone hated his role as scout for the Mormon Migration. In every way except billing, he was a supporting player. But at Zanuck's urging and with his great new friend Hathaway directing, he went along with it. Hathaway proposed that Tyrone bring Annabella along to the Utah location and the director brought his wife, Skip. The Powers and the Hathaways attempted to take the edge off a monumentally boring assignment by treating the location trip as a prolonged cookout. A number of critics were surprised to find Tyrone in such a small role and some suggested that his fans were being cheated. But the Hollywood moguls were used to such criticism and shrugged it off. In the years ahead, Tyrone would become bitter whenever the picture was mentioned.

The Powers' home and poolside had become an elite social spa on the Hollywood scene. The group had grown to include

Gene Tierney, Mary Anita Loos, Van Johnson, John Loder, and agent Charles Feldman. If Annabella secretly smiled at the irony of her own home being turned into a Hollywood playpen when she had tried so hard earlier to pull Tyrone away from *that*, her Gallic charm never faltered. In a way, it was a needed distraction for her as the Nazis occupied all of France and in June 1940 set up the Pétain government at Vichy. All word from her parents ceased before the Red Cross could set up temporary and inadequate lines of communication.

Watson knew how desolated Annabella was by that, and his mother, Ma Webb, phoned Annabella to tell her that she was now her "sixth child." To memorialize this, Tyrone bought her a gold-plated charm in the shape of the number *six*. Both Tyrone and Watson were great believers in charms to commemorate all significant occasions. A great many of them would be bought in the years ahead.

The Nazis had domiciled their officers in the villa at St. Cloud, to which the Charpentiers had moved in 1935, and in their retreat some four years later would remove everything, including Annabella's Count Volpi, an award given her in Venice for the finest acting of the year in *Sacrifice d'Honneur*. Since it was a rather horrid-looking object with a heavy marble base, she was not heartbroken. She remembered that when she went to pick it up, it practically broke her back.

Hovering in the background throughout the first months of their marriage was "business manager" Frank Adams, a holdover from Tyrone, Sr.'s affairs. He was routinely skimming off 25 per cent of Tyrone's wages as his staggering commission. Documents such as tax forms were handed Tyrone and he signed them without reading even the large print. He trusted "Uncle Frank" (who really was secretary Bill Gallagher's uncle) because he preferred to trust people. Life was easier that way.

But Annabella's Gallic suspicions were aroused when she noticed that under "personal expenditures" were ten pairs of shoes for her, when she had bought only one. It was true that ten pairs had been sent over from Saks for her selection, but she had kept just one. Then, when their 1939 income-tax forms were thrust under their noses and it called for a substantial check from Annabella to Uncle Frank's office to cover her taxes on her films released that year, she balked.

"But," she told Uncle Frank, "don't you remember? I had to pay my taxes before we could leave on our wedding trip? As a French citizen, I couldn't leave the country until they were paid." Tyrone flared at this challenge and ordered her never even to hint to Uncle Frank that he was not trusted.

So for the next several weeks, Annabella, together with Bill Gallagher, who volunteered to help nail his uncle, for whom he had no great affection, sifted through all the documents they could find. For more than three years, Tyrone's income had been tapped again and again by Uncle Frank. Adams then decided that the only way by which he could save himself was to become Tyrone's stepfather, and he very nearly convinced Patia Power to become Mrs. Adams. But Grandmother Mudgey Réaume, who was now staying with Patia, discovered the plot quite by accident and had someone drive her up to Adams' home in the San Fernando Valley, where the marriage plans were aborted at the eleventh hour.

Nearly all of Tyrone's savings, and by then they should have totaled a considerable fortune, had been siphoned off. It would take him several years to recover from this betrayal of trust. His financial affairs were placed in the hands of the firm of Morgan Maree, who represented about half of the stars and filmmakers in Hollywood.

Charges could have been brought against Frank Adams, but though Tyrone now saw Adams' perfidy clearly, he still failed to seek legal redress. Adams had spent the money, he reasoned. What good would putting him in jail do? And he was profoundly embarrassed by the incident. It made him seem incredibly naïve and vulnerable, which in a number of ways he was, but he didn't want that broadcast to the world.

Tyrone's relationships with his directors, like his affairs in the years just ahead, followed a predictable pattern. He would be assigned a new director, enjoy the experience, and almost immediately propose the man to Zanuck for his next production. And follow that with someone else. It was not fickleness, but he seemed to move from one enthusiasm to another, directors, actresses, books, plays, dogs. Of course, there were constants. Annabella was one, and Watson, and his mother Patia and sister Anne, and now Annie, whom he wanted to adopt.

Zanuck had refused to loan Tyrone to Columbia to do *Golden Boy* (1939), which, had he made it, would have been the most important film of his career up to that time, so in a moment of contrition, Zanuck signed *Golden Boy's* director, Rouben Mamoulian, to direct Tyrone's next picture, *The Mark of Zorro*.

Zorro, which had been one of Douglas Fairbanks, Sr.'s greatest successes, was an inspired piece of resurrection by Zanuck. Oddly, it allowed much of the wry, sardonic off-screen Tyrone to be seen finally on the screen and win a vaster legion of fans than ever. Movie audiences' tolerance for satire had been underestimated by most of the Hollywood film-makers, as the grosses for *Zorro* proved. And Tyrone loved everything about the film. His foppish Don Diego Vega (by day) and his masked Zorro who strikes terror into the tyran-nical Spanish colonial rulers of early California by night were equally exciting. Tyrone by now was able to handle the dueling scenes without using a double. But satire was the thing, and public acceptance of this new Tyrone was so strong, future essays by him into swashbuckling adventure which were intended as serious romantic adventures would be haunted by the ghost of Zorro so that audiences waited for laugh cues that never came, except occasionally unin-tentionally.

A close friendship developed between Mamoulian and the Powers. He came frequently to Saltair and they talked theatre until the wee hours; Tyrone told him that he and Annabella would like to do a play together and asked if he would be in-terested in staging it. A property was found, *Turn Again Home*, one of the few attempts at drama by the Canadian novelist Morley Callaghan. The Theatre Guild got involved at some point and it appeared that it might really get on the stage.

But Zanuck clearly would not tolerate such a thing. Although the project had all the earmarks of an ambitious en-deavor that would lose every penny, Zanuck announced that Tyrone's next film would be a remake of one of the most suc-cessful of Rudolph Valentino's pictures, *Blood and Sand*, that Mamoulian would again direct, and that the great (but mostly unemployed) Alla Nazimova would play Tyrone's mother. The studio had a deal with Columbia to borrow Rita Hay-worth as the feminine lead.

Turn Again Home was shelved, and Mamoulian threw all of his considerable resources as a filmmaker into making *Blood and Sand* better than the original. He worked closely with art directors Richard Day and Joseph C. Wright in creating dramatic contrasts through color and chiaroscuro so that the look of the film would be as exciting as the drama.

Tyrone and Annabella went to Mexico City at Mamoulian's suggestion to see several bullfights, and to observe the elaborate ritual surrounding the matador on the eve of the fight. The leading bullfighter in Mexico at that time was Armellita, and he graciously allowed them to watch his wife at her prayers in their home and observe at close hand the fears of those closest to him. On the following day, in Armellita's bedroom, Tyrone was invited to stand by as the matador's dresser laid out the elegant, braid-encrusted "suit of lights" and waistband, and then encased him in them. Tyrone and Annabella with a press representative from the studio were given the notables' box at the ring, and there was polite applause as Tyrone accepted the matador's hat when the bullfight was dedicated to him.

While she did not enjoy bullfighting and was a very long distance from being an aficionada, Annabella had attended fights in Spain and tolerated them when necessary. Much later in her life, she would become an intimate friend of bullfighter Luis Miguel Dominguin. Tyrone, however, was a novice. He was very excited about everything and even had gone below to take a long look at the strongest bull in the pen before they had entered the box. By the time of the main event, following the preliminary corridas, he had turned green, and he leaned against Annabella a moment to whisper, "I feel terrible. I'm going to be sick." Annabella became panicky for a few seconds. She thought, "Migod! He's a big star from Hollywood! The fight is dedicated to him *What can we do?*" So she took out her handkerchief and put her head down into it, and the publicity man turned and said, "What's the matter?"

"I think we will have to go," Tyrone managed to say. "Annabella doesn't feel well." They left as spectators' heads turned momentarily to watch the two men helping sensitive Mrs. Power out of the ring. No one seemed to notice that Tyrone's head was lolling on her shoulder. Then as soon as they were in the car, which had been allowed behind the arena, Tyrone fainted. Annabella opened his collar as the publicity man looked on in stupefaction.

Blood and Sand was as handsome to behold as Annabella's

Wings of the Morning had been four years earlier. With its central spectacle of animals being killed for the entertainment of the public, it probably would not be produced in today's heightened consciousness. Its melodramatic story by Blasco Ibáñez was on the primitive side and screenwriter Jo Swerling's attempt to make it more literate did not help. But Tyrone as the lowly peon turned matador was not only convincing, he was as strikingly handsome as any film actor before or since. The presence of both Rita Hayworth as an alluring vamp and Linda Darnell as his childhood sweetheart paled whenever he was on the screen. It was a little like Clark Gable or Laurence Olivier attempting to compete for visual attention with Marilyn Monroe. In the wake of its great success, every studio in Hollywood was begging Zanuck for the loan of his services, but the answer was invariably the same: "Tyrone Power is not available for loan-out."

Zanuck's policy of exclusivity with Tyrone had a bit earlier terminated his radio career. The intense romanticism of his voice was nearly half of his appeal, making him a natural for radio versions of screen successes. These were half or full hour adaptations of films that had made the rounds of the moviehouses much earlier. Tyrone appeared regularly on the Campbell Playhouse, the Lux Radio Theatre, the Jack Benny and Louella Parsons shows. Radio was every bit as popular as television is today and dramatic shows were covered routinely by the daily papers. In November 1937, the Brooklyn *Daily Eagle* reviewer wrote: "Tyrone Power rates three loud, lusty cheers for the surprisingly competent job he's doing in the Sunday night 'Hollywood Playhouse' series. He's one of the few movie men who are just as much at home on the air as they are in front of the camera."

So successful were these and other dramatic radio shows, studio heads, including and especially Zanuck, were infuriated. They blamed falling box-office receipts on the hundreds of thousands of moviegoers who were staying home to *listen* to the movie. Zanuck called in Tyrone and told him that he was not to appear on radio again *ever*.

Louella Parsons was thrown into a state of agitation. She was getting nearly all of her guest stars for next to nothing in a game of lighthearted blackmail. When Stan Laurel asked five thousand dollars for an appearance on her show, she was struck dumb with shock but rallied to do Laurel and Hardy discreet damage in their final screen years. Led by Louella and an unlikely ally, Jack Benny, a rebellion was organized. Jack's comedy show regularly featured stellar appearances that read like the cast for *Dinner at Eight* and many of the stars were his personal friends. As an accommodation of sorts, they were paid by Jack's sponsors something more than a token fee. The stars remained on the air waves, although their numbers diminished for a time. Tyrone, however, never appeared commercially on radio again.

The studio's possessiveness with Tyrone would cripple him seriously when many years later he sought greater freedom and they were quick to give it to him—all of it, at the end of his second seven-year contract. They had denied him radio celebrity and continuity; they had denied him the range as an actor given Olivier and Dirk Bogarde abroad and Cary Grant, Burt Lancaster, Edward G. Robinson, and Henry Fonda, to name just a handful, in America, who had worked for or whose films had been distributed by nearly all the major studios. That Tyrone was able to lift himself up when freedom came and survive on the same level as the stars mentioned above is an indication of his strength of will and resources as an actor.

With only a brief respite, Tyrone was rushed into his first film dealing with the ever-widening war. It was Zanuck's notion to do a film on the aerial warfare that had become so critical to Great Britain's survival. He dictated a story outline about a pilot in the R.A.F., "a fellow like Tyrone Power played in *In Old Chicago*. He is a cocksure, know-it-all, a breezy, brash young guy" and in that first rough scenario, he is killed during the initial aerial assault by the Nazis designed to bring the British quickly to their knees. The finished first draft was called *The Eagle Flies Again*. As Zanuck became more excited by the film's potential, he brought in the finest talent his studio had at the time. Betty Grable had threatened to topple the reigning queen of the studio, Alice Faye, in *Moon Over Miami* (1941), and when Henry King was brought in as director of *The Eagle Flies Again*, both men agreed that Miss Grable should be teamed with Tyrone. "What a team they made!" King recalled years later.

In January 1941, after a script had been dispatched to the

public relations arm of the R.A.F., they gave their blessing to the production but suggested that the pilot live. The title was changed to *A Yank in the R.A.F.* and Leo Robin and Ralph Rainger were brought in to supply a couple of songs for Miss Grable. Tyrone had looked upon the part of pilot Tim Baker as his first chance ever to play a real-life character, and the musical interludes disturbed him. But Henry King convinced him that the public expected Betty Grable to either sing or dance or both. And when the picture was released in September, the critics agreed with Tyrone that a chance to capture a significant moment of the current war on film had been compromised by Hollywood convention. Still, the studio was proved right when the public flocked to it in droves.

Ever since Tyrone and Annabella's involvement with the Theatre Guild in trying to mount the Morley Callaghan play, the couple had, in their shop talk, spoken of little else but getting onto a live stage together. If Lunt and Fontanne could do it, why not Power and Annabella? In late spring, 1941, they got in touch with producer John C. Wilson, who was a friend, and asked for his help in realizing this dream. Jack Wilson had got close to them during their earlier stage attempt and when the Callaghan project failed, proposed that they revive Ferenc Molnar's *Liliom* at the Westport Country Playhouse with which he was affiliated. Zanuck had turned down Tyrone's request to be allowed to appear with his wife then. The studio head's feelings against Annabella were still far too strong, but Tyrone could not guess that there was any bitterness in Zanuck for his wife. He simply believed that the studio did not want him to appear before a live audience at that time.

But with his new film "in the can," Tyrone again asked his boss about doing a play in the summer theatre, and, this time, Zanuck, flushed with a sense of triumph over *A Yank in the R.A.F.*, agreed.

Liliom is a rough-mannered, love-sick carnival barker who returns from fifteen years in purgatory to his wife Julie whom he has beaten regularly and the little girl he has deserted. Lee Strasberg came up from New York to direct the play, and it was scheduled to be performed for two weeks beginning on August 16, 1941. The engagement was sold out almost immediately.

Doubtless word of the enormous interest in Tyrone and Annabella as a stage team thoroughly alarmed Zanuck. Tyrone received a phone call on Friday before the Monday premiere giving him orders to return immediately to Hollywood for retakes on *A Yank in the R.A.F.* He was heartsick, and Annabella suspected a plot. With her encouragement and Lawrence Langner's (head of the Theatre Guild), Tyrone told Zanuck the retakes would have to wait.

Legal noises began to be heard from the Coast, so Langner himself phoned the studio and told them that he had an Equity contract with Tyrone which the studio had okayed weeks ago. "That was only a gentlemen's agreement," Fox business aide Lew Schreiber told Langner. It took Langner awhile to learn that he was not dealing with gentlemen.

Then the theatre management sought legal counsel and their lawyer, Ken Bradley, told Langner that under an old Connecticut law, one could stop a person from leaving the state if by so doing he or she broke a contract. The Bridgeport sheriff was called in and introduced to Tyrone, who thought now that challenging Zanuck was great sport. There were jokes all around, Tyrone grinning and saying to the sheriff, "You mean I am *forced* by law to stay in Connecticut until I open in the play?" The studio was forced to back down and said they would wait for him until the middle of the week.

The critics were unanimous in praising both Tyrone and Annabella, one writing, "There was no doubt left in anyone's mind last night but that the film star could turn to the medium of the stage at any time and command the respect of his contemporaries. . . ." Of Annabella, *PM* said that she "fits admirably into the quiet emotional role of Julie. . . ."

Their opening-night audience was about half made up of friends and a roster of their names reveals something of the wide-ranging social life the Powers had adopted. From the French colony had come Jean-Pierre Aumont, who escorted Simone Simon; from the Continent, too, had come the Duc di Verdura and Baron de Gunsborg. From the theatre were Gilbert Miller, George Abbott, and Leonore Corbett. Clifton Webb had come East especially to attend, and there was Elsa Maxwell, who considered Tyrone "the most beautiful man in the world."

Appearing several times during the course of the play in small walk-ons was a tall young actor by the name of Zachary

Scott, who would not be discovered by Hollywood's scouts for another two and a half years.

Adding an element of persuasion to the dramatic proceedings was the obviousness of the stage couple's love for each other. It affected everyone and was enchanting. When it happens on the screen, as it did during the Garbo films with John Gilbert, it does not strike audiences as especially touching. It is so easy to fake such profound rapport through slick camera work, eyes meeting eyes, etc. But it is very rare for lovers to play out a dramatist's variation of that relationship on the stage. What Tyrone and Annabella really felt for each other was very private, but in *Liliom*, they were able to infuse their roles with real romance. For many in the audience, that was a magic moment to be cherished in the perilous years just ahead.

After only two performances, Tyrone flew back to Hollywood for the retakes on his last picuture. He promised that he would return and asked that only the rest of that week's performance be canceled. He did return that Sunday and the run was completed.

Annabella was able to touch a sensitive nerve in her audiences with the closing line in the play, "It is possible, dear—that someone may beat you and beat you—and not hurt you at all. . . . " In her life off-stage and off-secreen with Tyrone, a subtle transposition of that line was taking place. Word was beginning to come to Annabella on the swift wings of gossip, as it always does, that Tyrone was having affairs at the studio with his leading ladies. In the summer, it was with Betty Grable. That fall, he happened to be working with both Frances Farmer and Gene Tierney in *Son of Fury*, which must have kept him busy not only in the hay but in directing traffic as well. Miss Tierney was an old friend who came regularly as the Powers' guest to the Saltair house.

Annabella knew that Tyrone was unable to say *no* to anyone. She had got close to Veronica ("Rocky") Cooper, Gary's wife, and Rocky had weathered a long, long succession of such episodes. And then, too, there is something in the psyche of French women that enables most of them to cope with infidelity and avoid confrontations. There was also a naïve side to Annabella; at least it was a quality she often projected very convincingly. She chose to remain innocent and to shut her mind to such stories, and by so doing managed to remain by Tyrone's side longer than anyone else in his life. Tyrone would disclaim ownership of his misbehaving self. "That wasn't me," he would tell her, and she knew what he meant.

That summer of 1941, Annabella heard through her French friends that her old compatriot and now famed author, Antoine de Saint-Exupéry, had been taken to the hospital in Los Angeles. She knew that he was in town, since she was in constant touch with director Jean Renoir and his wife, and Saint-Exupéry was staying in their home. During her first free moment, after getting the news, she drove to the hospital.

She had met him years earlier, in 1935, when she was starring in *Anne-Marie* with Jean Murat, then her husband, and Saint-Exupéry would come in occasionally to help in the production, since he had written the screenplay. The film was mainly concerned with aviation and nearly all the conversation on the set was about flying. She had felt a little lost and they had not got close.

When they met in his hospital room, Annabella remembered that he seemed very happy to see a French face, "above all to speak French, for it must be said that in spite of all his qualities, he never had a gift for languages." He had a book of Andersen's fairy tales by his bedside and Annabella picked it up and began reading "The Little Mermaid," then closed it and recited the rest of the text from memory. This so impressed Saint-Exupéry, whose passion, other than aviation and a cosmic sense of the world gained perhaps from seeing things from a very high altitude, was fantasy or fairy tales, that the two became close friends and accomplices.

After his discharge from the hospital, Saint-Exupéry took a modest, nondescript little apartment on the edge of Los Angeles. Annabella would leave the Saltair house with a basket of food to visit him. She would find him convalescing on a sofa; she would sit on the floor in a sunny corner and lay out their "picnic." Mentally, they would leave the anonymous room and move deeply into a dream country which Saint-Exupéry made up as they went along.

When he was well enough, Saint-Exupéry visited Saltair, where Tyrone came to appreciate not only his passion for flying but his talent as a magician. Tyrone's playful, often childlike temperament was matched by Saint-Exupéry's. They seemed born to understand each other even though neither had mastered the other's native tongue. Tyrone would watch the sleight-of-hand and the card tricks open-mouthed, often asking his friend to repeat a trick so that he might learn how it was done. Then he would try it himself, the props usually falling on the floor.

Tyrone and Saint-Exupéry clowned around the house. They could have been ten years old. On one level, the years had not touched either of them. When they got onto the subject of their respective planes, it was a conversation that might last half the night. Saint-Exupéry was surprised and delighted to find a film star so little involved with himself and so much in love with life. He inscribed a copy of his book on the mystical quality of flying, *Wind, Sand and Stars*:

> *For Annabella and Tyrone*
> *with my deep and definitive friendship.*
>
> *In memory of the oasis that their home was for me*
> *in a melancholy period when friendship had no*
>   *price.*
> *To thank them for contributing so much to make*
>   *this planet habitable.*
>   *A. de St.-Ex.*

Annabella observed a schism in the Saint-Exupéry personality. The imaginary flights into fairytale land, the sleight-of-hand, the clowning were reserved for a very small number of intimates. Tyrone had been honored. When Saint-Exupéry was with more than five people, he resumed his normal man-of-affairs mien, a little sad and distant, speaking of scientific problems, of serious literature, and of the war. That war soon would draw him back to his countrymen, and his brilliance as a pilot would be dedicated to the rescue of his beloved France. But there was one more remarkable thing he would share with Tyrone; both men would die at the age of forty-four.

Annabella and Tyrone were at home on Saltair when the attack on Pearl Harbor began that Sunday in December 1941. They both wept tears of anger and frustration. Annabella had a sick dread that the war, now global, was going to hurt her very badly. She was prescient about a number of things, and her apprehension was nearly palpable for weeks.

The Japanese bombs appeared to have shaken several latent incendiaries in Hollywood. Darryl F. Zanuck, for one, threatened to go off at any moment. He dispatched a cable to General George C. Marshall, Chief of Staff, offering his services, and he began alerting key executives that he might be gone for as long as it would take to defeat the Axis. All of his key people were stunned. Zanuck *was* the studio. Then the order came through from Marshall making Zanuck a full colonel, and he was assigned to supervise training films in England. At least he would be subjected only to aerial bombardment there, but no, that did not satisfy this scrappy bantam, and he got permission to make a documentary movie *under fire* of the North African campaign. There was some fear for his survival, and the identification being so strong, for *the studio's* survival.

Tyrone's admiration for Zanuck, which had been so high throughout his rise to stardom, had been seriously eroded by Zanuck's occasional "spankings." Immediately upon the Powers' return from their wedding trip in 1939, Zanuck had rushed Tyrone into a programmer that seemed to have been fashioned from leftover scraps of Jean Harlow's *Wife vs. Secretary* (1936, Metro), although the picture, *Daytime Wife*, had a rather low-voltage substitute for Harlow in Linda Darnell. At seventy-one minutes, the "comedy" could only be intended as half of a double feature, the conventional moviechain program at the time. Tyrone protested to Zanuck, and there were assurances given that Tyrone would be "protected." Pev Marley, one of Tyrone's special friends on the lot and someone whose work he admired very much, would be manning the camera. Zanuck's crony, Gregory Ratoff, would direct, so there was no complaining about that. Ratoff was competent, but not on a level with Hathaway, King, Brown, or Mamoulian.

On Christmas night 1941, despite the war, friends were invited to join the Power family in a celebration of such warmth, producer André Daven said later, that it stayed "in my heart like a great bonfire." Daven, who worked for Zanuck, came with his wife, Danielle, along with René and Bronia Clair, all "a little strange so far from home . . . and you wanted us to be gay and happy as you were gay and happy." Tyrone, remembering how much Annabella's French friends valued their Hermès day books, which were now unattainable because of the war, had asked Annabella to have some of them made up, and she had run all over Los Angeles to find a printer and binder. Daven kept his Hermès day book through the years and said, "it is one of the testaments to your graciousness."

A huge tree stood on the south end of the formal living room engarlanded with blue, white, and red ribbons of the French tricolor. A mountain of gifts was heaped about it; logs blazed in the fireplace; champagne flowed freely. Annabella saw that all of the tables were decked with flowers from the garden.

Often, when Tyrone was a little high on booze, he would declaim or take over in some fashion. Now he stood on a chair, impersonating a professor of philosophy conducting a course in ethics. He declared to his students, "The things that I love most in life are alas immoral or illegal or grossly unvirtuous. Then what should I do?" Each of them in turn developed his or her point of view, attempting to outshock the last speaker in flouting morality. Before the last of them had done his bit, the night had slipped away and Annabella interrupted "the class." "That will have to do," she told them. "It's time for all of us to go to the kitchen and throw together a solid breakfast." Daven recalled that sunrise in their garden as "the sun of the king, the Magi, and we were happy."

In Zanuck's absence, beginning in early 1942, William Goetz was to run the studio. Tyrone, along with everyone else, wondered what that meant for him. The Powers were frequent guests at the Goetzes' home. Even though Edie was something of a social lionhunter, and Annabella was rapidly becoming more informal in her entertaining, the Goetzes and the Powers remained very close.

Goetz began making changes almost at once. Zanuck's steam room was changed from Zanuck green to another color. Some of Zanuck's trusted top people such as chief editor Barbara "Bobby" McLean began to be nudged aside by newcomers on top pictures.

When Zanuck departed, Tyrone was in the midst of his second picture about wartime England, this time playing an English soldier, Clive Briggs, a man from the lower class who has become self-educated to the point where his reason tells him it is madness to fight and die for middle- and upper-class values, and he deserts. Tyrone made no effort to attempt a British accent, prompting David O. Selznick to write Buddy Adler (who succeeded Zanuck for a time at Fox) a dozen years later: "I know that Twentieth Century Studio customarily disregards these things, and that they have not the slightest compunctions about having Tyrone Power or any other actor play English roles—or for that matter even English nobility and royalty!—with the same accent that he plays Texans or Kansans." Eric Knight's *This Above All* had been a mild best-seller because it aired in print all of the doubts some had about why the war against Hitler was a just war. It is important to point out that Eric Knight had written his novel when the war was in its early phases. World War II has been called, rightly I think, a just war, if there is such a thing, because near the end as the Americans and British from the West and the Russians from the East began liberating the death camps, the Holocaust itself emerged with shocking clarity. Yet during most of the fighting throughout that war, men were in action because they were ordered to be there; there were officers whose sole role in the war was "orientation," telling the men why they were fighting and trying to convince them. The Nazis had done a most efficient job of keeping the massive scale of their atrocities a secret, since there were so many loyal Germans surrounding the crematoria with a solid wall of silence and blindness. The point Knight finally makes through this tale of Briggs, who deserts from the Army after Dunkirk, is that "The age of reason in you says you don't want to fight in such a warped and ill-defined war. The age of faith in you says you must fight so that Britain won't lose. Brain and emotion, deadlocked in a struggle—your body the battle ground." He says this to an attractive WAAF whom he has encountered while absent without leave, and they have had several days and nights of a ragtag affair, in haystacks, inns, and boardinghouses. Prue, played by Joan Fontaine, is from the upper classes, but even her faith in dying for Britain is shaken while they make love and talk and talk. In her memoirs, Miss Fontaine writes the Tyrone was very much under Annabella's thumb, and he could do no more with her (Miss Fontaine) in their dressing rooms than play cards. She possibly did not know that affairs with his leading ladies had become temporary obstacles which Annabella already had overcome through tolerance and not making an issue of them. Despite Miss Fontaine's great, aristocratic beauty and keen intellect, Tyrone seemed not to have been attracted to her. The vibes were wrong.

Annabella's old friend and director from her days in the French cinema, Anatole Litvak, directed *This Above All*, and the critics were unanimous in citing Tyrone's growth as an actor. Yet there was always among them someone with a needling bringdown. *Time* magazine said "Although Tyrone Power gives the performance of his cinematic career . . . it is not good enough," and gave him low marks for being too handsome. He would be as underrated in his time as Cary Grant, Edward G. Robinson, Tony Curtis, and James Cagney (until his *Yankee Doodle Dandy* later that year—1942). For the same reasons that kept Marilyn Monroe from even being nominated for an Oscar throughout her screen career despite *Bus Stop, Some Like It Hot,* and *The Misfits*, Tyrone was forever kept from the list of critics' darlings and often paid grudging, fainthearted praise.

Early in 1942, the greatest French film star, Jean Gabin, was enticed to Hollywood in an abortive attempt to make him as popular in America as he was abroad. Gabin quickly settled into a modest bungalow in Beverly Hills and resumed an old, close relationship with Marlene Dietrich. Zanuck producer André Daven phoned Tyrone, and said that he and his wife, Danielle, were going for dinner to Gabin's, and he knew that Tyrone and Annabella would be most welcome to come along. Annabella had made two pictures with Gabin in France.

The two couples arrived at the tiny cottage, which was about the size of the gardener's hut on Saltair. They had to ring the bell a couple of times, and Tyrone wondered if André had the date right. Then the door was opened by a slightly out-of-breath Marlene, in an apron but looking exquisite. "Oh, hello," she told them, "excuse me, I am cooking a ragout for *mon Jean* and I must stay in the kitchen."

Marlene then disappeared, but there was a blazing fire going, taking some of the edge off the cramped look of the place. In one corner, there was a table set for four with a red-and-white-checked tablecloth very much like those seen every day in Left-Bank cafés. After five minutes, Tyrone said that he could use a drink, and thought with relief that he had been

overheard, for at that moment, Marlene came running into
the room. She rushed past them to the front door, looking
distracted and peering out into the night. Tyrone whispered to
André, "She looks like the fisherman's wife waiting for her
man to come safe to port through the storm." The foursome
suppressed a giggle and that was the way the evening went,
always on the edge of laughter, which civility forbade.

Finally, a chauffeured car arrived, and Gabin came into his
house, smiling, very warm and full of Gallic charm for
Annabella as someone fondly remembered for about one
minute, since Marlene waited for her moment. Then the
lovers hurled themselves at each other and there was a
passionate love scene played out in front of their gaping
guests, and taking longer than would be required to finish a
double scotch. It was Gabin who remembered their guests and
glanced toward the kitchen, which was an alcove in one
corner. "Smells awfully good in there."

"Oh, I hope you'll like it, *mon Jean*," and Marlene again
seemed altogether concerned about his approval. "I was
worried. You came *so* late!" The Fox Studio, which had
brought him over for his American debut, was only fifteen
minutes from the cottage. Gabin had no explanation, but now
he did offer some hospitality. He told his guests to fix themselves a drink.

Tyrone had a bottle of scotch in his hand and it remained
there as he watched Marlene go to her knees in front of Gabin,
take slippers from under the couch and remove his shoes. She
massaged his feet for several minutes, during which, for lack
of a glass, Tyrone began drinking from the bottle. Annabella
could not help staring at this little scene of domestic bliss, and
Gabin glanced in her direction and winked as if to say he was
helpless, a victim of Marlene's adoration.

The dinner, prepared by Marlene, was well worth waiting
for, and it was served by her. After liqueurs, Gabin suggested
to Marlene that the guests might enjoy a little music. She
demurred, but he insisted, so she finally disappeared and
came back with a musical saw. Seated on one arm of the
couch, with her fabulous legs crossed, she began to play. The
Powers and the Davens were astonished, but impressed. She
played it well. During the light applause, Marlene told Gabin
that it was his turn. So he left them briefly and returned with
an enormous accordion of mother-of-pearl with finely tooled

leather. Before he could begin, Marlene rushed out and fetched a worker's cap and a small scarf, which she put just so on his head and around his neck. It was a little tableau from the Place Pigalle.

Gabin only knew one tune, which was, not surprisingly, *Dark Eyes*, but Marlene listened raptly. Tyrone and André were ready to fall apart with laughter at this point, but Marlene's rapture kept them in line. When they were finally outside, Tyrone told the others, "It must be an awfully good show in the bedroom!"

On July 26, 1942, Tyrone and Annabella opened their spacious grounds on Saltair to the public for the benefit of the Free French Relief Committee. Booths were set up— sometimes just a card table and a lawn umbrella—and it was Tyrone's idea that the stars should come and auction off things that they owned. The most successful saleslady was Joan Crawford, who sold some of her lined lingerie for an outrageous sum. Neighbor Fred MacMurray came over with hunting equipment. Annabella recalls, "We made quite a lot of money. I've forgotten now the amount because we were not taking care of that. There was a special business lady from the French consulate. We just did the work, and we were very happy. The only thing [*and she laughs at the memory*] was we had no garden left. There were thousands of people. We were dead in the evening. But we had done something."

For *The Black Swan* (1942), Tyrone had to grow a mandarin mustache in the role of Jamie Waring, an adventurer on the high seas. Henry King had insisted on the mustache against the wishes of the studio hierarchy. He wanted to accommodate Tyrone, who was aching to do some real acting and break free from the idol mold. King remembers that *The Black Swan* achieved that. It "gave Ty a great sense of satisfaction. It's the first time he'd had comedy and drama and melodrama all in one heap (not to mention the satiric edge he gave to all of it). You know, he hit the woman [Maureen O'Hara] in the mouth and slapped her, pretty near knocked her out and put her over his shoulder. He had a great flair for all this. His great downfall was that he would get with directors who would want him to be 'strong,' and Ty would force strength. It's like playing golf . . . If you force it, you can't eat your hat. That was the weakest thing about him. When he would stand firm, he was as strong as the rock of Gibraltar.''

When the film was done, Tyrone attempted to relax for a few days at the Saltair house, but he felt depressed every time he listened to the war bulletins. By this time, even the most remote islands in the Pacific had fallen to the Japanese. He was intense in his feelings about his country; his affection went deep, although he was no jingoist. He had mixed feelings about the Russians as America's ally, but he was not a political animal and rarely had much to say about it. As much as any film star, he was an internationalist. Patia had given him the manners to fit in anywhere, and Annabella had given him the friends from everywhere, and they loved him. His politics were not very involved or profound.

Tyrone and Watson had bought motorcycles, Tyrone a Harley-Davidson and Watson an Indian, before Pearl Harbor. It was a liberating agent for both of them—and after Pearl Harbor, a way of beating the gas-rationing problem. Sometimes they rode together, but often it was alone, back and forth between their homes or off on errands around Brentwood or Los Angeles. For a while, Tyrone rode his to the studio until the management told him to stop because of the risk. Once or twice, Annabella was given a ride, behind Tyrone, and she thought it was a great lark. She recalls one trip all the way to Santa Barbara on it. Neighbor Keenan Wynn caught the fever and bought one, and occasionally the three of them rode together, the Brentwood version of Hell's Angels, complete with leather jackets and dark glasses.

Once America was in the war, an air-raid warning system was set up. Japanese attacks on the Pacific coastal cities and bases were considered to be in imminent peril. Tyrone and Watson were assigned air-raid warden duty two nights a week, their headquarters being a small real estate office at the corner of Sunset Boulevard and Thurston Drive. Between patrols, they sat in the blacked-out building and spoke far more intimately of their lives and their friendship than they ever had before. They discovered that they both had longed for the close companionship of their fathers, but Watson's had been severe and unloving and Tyrone's had been away until it was almost too late to do his character any good. And Tyrone professed an affection for Watson that cut deeper than any "pal" relationship. He opened up to Watson in a way he had never done before. It had taken a war to bring them to talk to one another so personally about themselves, but once they had, an understanding began that nothing could touch. It was a small miracle that it had happened at all, since men are notoriously close-mouthed about their innermost thoughts.

Watson was enormously pleased that this had come about, but he wondered what it had meant to Tyrone. A month or so later, Watson had to go to New York for a couple of weeks to straighten out some complicated family finances, and Tyrone wrote him:

June 1, 1942

. . . Believe me Watson, the things you say in your letter about friendship, and ours especially, I say 1000 times. For you are, after all, the only close one I have. But after our nights on watch together, you should know that. . . . I don't have to tell you all those things that you know.

Things are going along here at the same pace. The Colonel [Zanuck] is still in Europe; you've read about Hedy [Lamarr] & George [Sanders], & the picture [*The Black Swan*] drags along. Having Annabella home again is divine, of course, & we spent the two holidays [Memorial Day weekend] in the sun by the pool, & (*she*) wished you could have been there to join us. Will be leaving in about another 5 weeks.

It seems such a damn shame that just when the studio is becoming pleasant to work in, that I have to leave. . . .

As the Japanese advanced and the war blues got worse with Tyrone, he told Annabella that the only cure for his depression was to get involved in the war. When he wrote Watson that he would be leaving home within five weeks, he was referring to entering the Navy. In April, he had enlisted in the United States Naval Reserve and was told that he probably would be taken into the morale and recreational division as a chief petty officer.

That spring, Annabella had been persuaded to tour in a national company of Noël Coward's *Blithe Spirit* as the dead Elvira. She toured the Midwest and the East, finally settling in Chicago, where they played for nearly six months. Tyrone caught Annabella's show in Chicago, and later she joined him in the East, where his film company was doing location shooting at the Naval Submarine Base in New London, Connecticut. In July, studio head Goetz began preproduction work on "a propaganda film" starring Tyrone. *Crash Dive* was being produced by Milton Sperling and was meant to show audiences *and* potential recruits something of the lives of the men on the dangerous submarine patrols around our coastal waters.

While Tyrone worked, Annabella studied with a speech coach to rid herself of her strong accent. Another stage offer had come in for her to star in Franz Werfel's *Jacobowsky and the Colonel*.

Saint-Exupéry was in New York, on his way to North Africa where he would join the Free French. He invited Annabella to go to Central Park and set out once again for one of his "never never lands," but she had to decline because of her speech lessons. Chiding her for this, he said that he couldn't understand why she would sacrifice hours to a project of refining her English, which project he seemed to look upon as somehow disloyal, when she could employ her time far better by going with him to the park and feeding the squirrels. "What a catastrophe!" he told her.

Sensing a plot to keep him from military activity and on the screen, Tyrone, on an impulse, went to the Naval Recruiting Office in downtown Manhattan to enlist. He informed them of his Naval Reserve status.

But there was a slip-up somewhere. No one at the Naval Recruiting Office knew anything about the Navy wanting him in morale or entertainment. He told them that he had a pilot's license, but they did not seem interested in that either. The officious Navy man seemed to have something against film stars and Tyrone was turned down as "unqualified," and told that he could enter the Navy as an ordinary seaman or, possibly, he might be right for a specialist's assignment, which was just below a commission. Tyrone naïvely applied for that and, after an interminable all-afternoon wait, was informed that he was unqualified for that, too.

Tyrone left downtown Manhattan angry and with a sudden determination to forget any work in "morale." He felt that he had been conned into that anyway by the studio. He would get into the war in his own way. It was with enormous relief that he boarded a plane accompanied by Annabella to fly back to the Coast, where the principal photography of the new movie was to be shot.

The week of their return, the U. S. Marines were launching a massive, bloody attack on the Solomon Islands in the South Pacific, the first large-scale offensive action of the war by the Americans. Successful beachheads were secured, and the Japanese were pushed back into jungle infested by cannibals and crocodiles. The fighting was mostly hand-to-hand with Marine scout bombers overhead blasting a path for the Americans. Fighting had been especially fierce on volcanic Guadalcanal Island, where a Japanese air base was captured. That single battle would not be decisively won until February 1943.

When he got home each night, Tyrone flicked on the radio to follow the news of the Marines' fate. His interest seemed obsessive, but was probably no more all-consuming than his earlier fervor over a director, a book, or an affair. This was, of course, more important. Then when he heard how vital the Marine bomber scouts had been to the action, he finally knew where he could be most useful in the war. He would fly one of those small bombers.

Jo Swerling's shooting script got into Tyrone's hands in mid-August and he realized that *Crash Dive* was not a significant contribution to the war effort. Anne Baxter gives us a clue as to how "important" it was, recalling that it was "my first picture with Ty. He played a handsome, dashing naval officer with a very rich grandmother named Bert. Dame May Whitty played it. I was just the love interest, between Ty and Dana (Andrews) . . . the eternal triangle. I was a teacher in a girls' school and supposedly engaged to Dana. Ty pursued me and won, thereby creating a bone of contention between himself and Dana under submarine circumstances. . . ." Upon its release, Bosley Crowther writing in the New York *Times* articulated Tyrone's views on the film: "More of that Hollywood warfare, which looks like nothing at all but the unbridled fancies of scriptwriters worked out through special effects. . . . no more sense of reality about this war than a popular song. . . . It leaves one wondering blankly whether Hollywood knows that we're at war."

Some of his earlier rebelliousness still moving him, Tyrone

decided on a course of action to abort the production—at
least his part in it—and not be damned in the eyes of the absent Zanuck, who was at that moment at a desk in London,
itching to get a closer look at the war against the Nazis.
Earlier that week, a contingent of American Rangers had participated in a raid of Dieppe. On August 24, 1942, Tyrone
enlisted in the Marine Corps as a private.

The war machinery was about to make Tyrone a mere mortal again, a "buck-ass private" to be given basic training at
Camp Pendleton, when the outrage in Goetz's office subsided
enough to allow wheels on high levels to begin turning. A
Marine officer called Tyrone into his office and explained that
he had just received orders to release Private Power for four
months back to "civilian duty" at his film company to resume
production on a picture which the government felt was a
useful propaganda piece. Tyrone wondered if anyone in the
higher levels of command had read the script.

The production of *Crash Dive* moved ponderously forward. For a contrived bit of unimaginative melodrama, it set
some sort of record with its final shooting schedule of four
months plus the additional time spent at New London the
previous summer. Now there seemed to be no doubt. There
was a studio conspiracy to keep Tyrone out of the war as long
as possible. Was this another of Zanuck's conundrums?
Seeking desperately to risk his own neck while putting in a
word to keep his favorite young star from the front lines? The
man who was happier when Tyrone was on the croquet green
rather than the polo field?

By mid-October, Tyrone was restless and bored. Bored with
his career, bored even with the staleness of life at Saltair.
More than three years of life as an elegant suburban squire in
one of the poshest suburbs in the world with the same
exquisite, enchanting wife had finally gotten to him. If the
war, which seemed far more exciting in every way and at every
level, had not happened, this malaise would have been
delayed. But, in Tyrone, it was inevitable. The best life, after
a thousand days of it, became the dullest. It was a little like a
man with a sweet tooth drowning in molasses. Yet, once it was
lost to him when the war caught him up and swirled him
away, he would miss all that like the very devil.

On October 16, he and Annabella saw an early screening of
For Me and My Gal, starring Judy Garland and Gene Kelly.

Annabella enjoyed it, and they talked about it afterward. Tyrone couldn't stop talking about it. He was astonished by Judy's sudden emergence as a dramatic actress. She was no longer a sweet teenager naïvely moving through life and as yet unfulfilled as a woman. She even *looked* different. He told Watson how impressed he was but, with him, he was less reserved in his enthusiasm.

A week or so later, Annabella had to fly East for four or five days to see Tony Muto, a friend on the Washington staff of Fox Movie-tone News. Muto had offered to help her make contact with her mother in Occupied France. Since her stay took in the weekend, Annabella was not home to attend a party at their neighbors', the Keenan Wynns. The Wynns (she was Tyrone's old New York girlfriend Evie Abbott) lived near the Gary Coopers on Saltair. Tyrone went to the Wynns's party alone, and met Judy there. He told her that her performance in *For Me and My Gal* was "beautiful."

Judy was a shambling bundle of insecurities at that moment. Recently divorced from composer David Rose, in her nineteenth year, and just stepping into womanhood, she found it hard to believe that *Tyrone Power*, the most beautiful man in the world, was standing there like any ordinary human being, and telling her that anything about her was beautiful. One of her many insecurities was that she believed herself homely and about as sexy as Zasu Pitts. And one of her ways of dealing with that was by making herself available to the most attractive men she could find and taking them to bed. She had had a long string of affairs in that endeavor, which were nearly always successful at the beginning because she was in reality extraordinarily attractive in bed and out of it. Her pursuit of sex to prove her point was just the opposite of Tyrone's. He, nearly always being pursued, couldn't fail to know how attractive he was, and having been rendered slightly neurotic by his unorthodox upbringing, was utterly unable ever to deny the gift of himself to any presentable and charming person who sought it, the only prerequisite being that the person please him. It would have shocked him, had anyone ever called him promiscuous. His random sexual encounters were always one at a time, with a little space between them, never leading anywhere.

Annabella was worldly in the best, the truest sense. She was not as yet disillusioned. It was not in her nature to be. Around

Tyrone and many others, she still projected a sense of near-naïveté. She discounted the tales gossips brought her.

Judy Garland was equally blind, but in a different way. She *wanted* Tyrone to be perfect, and so he was going to be. When friends who knew of Tyrone's long trail of broken hearts (but little of the man) tried to tell her, Judy refused to listen. From their first tryst at Judy's Sunset Boulevard apartment and then at her home in Bel Air until the affair withered months later, she was euphoric. Just as Tyrone seemed pure in spirit through all of this transitory involvement, so Judy was the naïf she had played in a dozen films whenever in his company. But she was free and he wasn't. Within weeks of their meeting, Judy was asking Tyrone to seek a divorce. He told her that Annabella was not quite her old vivacious self; she had too many burdens with the war—her parents and brothers temporarily lost to her in France, her career, which had been brilliant, sacrificed because of him. Judy was not a very patient young woman.

As lovers, they were perfectly matched. Judy seemed able to satisfy Tyrone as few women had. Annabella was disadvantaged by a rival who was becoming something more than an infatuation. For the first time in their marriage, he had to lie to her. Things were strained in the bedroom. She found him cool and unresponsive. He would phone to tell her that they were shooting late on the foolish production in which he was mired, and dinners were missed.

The reckless abandon in the Garland bedroom was not the greatest threat to his marriage to Annabella, however. He could find that release outside from time to time and always with someone he could trust. The real threat resided in Judy's appeal. Tyrone gravitated to children and animals. Mature and even something of an intellectual around Saint-Exupéry or Rouben Mamoulian, he always felt a warm response toward naïve creatures. He could communicate with children on their level and they always loved it. His sister Anne recalls seeing him frolicking often in the pool at Saltair with half a dozen neighbor children clinging to him. David Niven writes of a Christmas Eve when Tyrone was chosen to play Santa Claus to the stars' children even though, with the help of a great deal of Niven's scotch, he was "loaded in every sense of the word" when he arrived in their midst. Judy appealed to that instinct in Tyrone. He was drawn to childlike waifs—to the screen image of Janet Gaynor, the unexpected helplessness of little Annabella crying her eyes out because of a gaucherie during a tribute to a dead executive, and now vulnerable Judy, playing the innocent with all the dramatic skill she had been acquiring since childhood.

Secretive with Annabella, he was open about Judy at the studio. She even was invited to the Café de Paris, the studio commissary, for lunch, smiling and clinging to Tyrone's arm. He discussed the possibility of their doing a film together and gave her the Mildred Cram novel *Forever*, to which he had been introduced by Janet Gaynor and which he had passed along to Annabella. Tyrone clearly was not faithful to the women in his life, but for many years he was faithful to this book.

Judy could not have been more ecstatic. Wherever she went, on the set of *Presenting Lily Mars* and off, she spoke of little but Tyrone. The idyllic phase, however, was short-lived.

Tyrone's movie was wrapped up finally in mid-December. As the holidays approached, some sort of truce had to be worked out because it would be his last holiday before going off to the war. He was due to report at Camp Pendleton for boot camp on January 2, 1943.

On New Year's Eve, the Powers went with Watson to the Walter Langs. Lang had directed for both Tyrone (in *Second Honeymoon*) and Annabella (in *The Baroness and the Butler*). Mrs. Lang was "Fieldsie," secretary and pal to Carole Lombard, who had been killed a year earlier in a plane crash while on a bond tour similar to one Annabella was about to undertake. The Langs were especially dear friends to the Powers, but Watson never had met them before. It was a farewell to Tyrone and to their neighbor Glenn Ford, who also was entering the Marines.

The day after New Year's, Watson drove Tyrone to San Diego to the gates of Camp Pendleton and watched his friend as he walked toward the headquarters of the walled encampment. Tyrone was cheerful. It was as though a great burden had been lifted from him.

There is ample evidence that Tyrone welcomed the tough new discipline that had been imposed upon him once he was in uniform, that it helped shut the lid on some of the devils pursuing him, and that it was an exciting new life experience. There are dozens of photographs surviving of the new recruit

lined up for inspection, doing his own laundry, cleaning his
rifle, getting an injection, having chow, asking for seconds,
and "shooting the breeze" with his barracks mates. The only
question, and it must have been in the minds of the other
Marines, is just how odd it was to have a photographer snap-
ping away at Tyrone during each phase of this monotonous
routine of basic training. But the fact was that a still or movie
camera was far more ordinary to Tyrone than the imple-
ments of war. He paid no attention to the presence of the
photographer, who was from the public relations arm of the
Marines. Soon, as he was caught up in and made part of the
American fighting machine, there would be no trace of a
camera and thus no record on film of his battle activity.

Tyrone was not just a quick study with lines; he mastered
nearly everything required of him thoroughly and expertly in
very short order. For *Alexander's Ragtime Band*, he mastered
the fingering of a violin; for half a dozen other films, the
sword, and no fencing expert doubled for him. Now at Camp
Pendleton, he became so expert with his rifle that he was
awarded a medal and scroll for marksmanship within two
weeks after beginning his training on the rifle range. In a
photograph taken of the ceremony, there is a fierce and
humble pride in his eyes and the set of his mouth. Among his
mates at the boot camp, this was the way they always saw
him. The truth seemed to be that Tyrone had very little vanity
about him, not to be confused with awareness of being exceptionally handsome and talented. He sent Annabella a letter
from camp the day after this ceremony:

Wednesday, Jan. 20, 1943

My darling,
    Last evening I sent you some photos of the ceremony
yesterday morning when I got the scroll, and had the
thing pinned on me by the Colonel. Thought you would
like to see them, and as for the paper, would you have it
framed, or something? It might be nice to keep.
    It was really very impressive though. I had to come out
in front of all the boys, and the old man shook my hand,
and everything. I was nervous as hell, and it was at about
8 o'clock A.M. and colder than cold. But I played the
whole thing to the hilt. Why, I couldn't have been

prouder if it was the navy cross he was pinning on me. It even made the papers down here. . . . My darling, I am sorry that you felt so depressed. But I know just what you meant. It did seem like only an instant I saw you. And Saturday seems like a whole week ago.

I'm glad Annie liked my letter. Give her my love, and a big kiss. Tell her to be a good girl, and study hard.

I hope that [sister] Anne is resting comfortably. Please tell her that I think of her so often, but that I just don't seem to find the time to write.

Bobby Lewis [a prominent New York director and a co-founder of the Actors Studio] wrote me a letter. Please call him, and tell him that my gratitude is unbounded. It was so gay, and amusing, and so like him. A million thanks, and tell him when I have a minute, I'll try to answer him.

Good night, my darling. Just know I think of you, and pray for you, and love you with all my heart. And thank you again for everything, and most especially for just being you.

Love,

Tyrone

Anne Power Hardenbergh, pregnant and alone in her country home in Marin County, California, had come down to the Saltair house to stay with Annabella. "We were like sisters," Anne recalled, and they remained so permanently. Anne had an artistic bent, but she was not a dilettante. She had nearly equal interests in both painting and musical composition. During and just before the war, she was deeply committed to art and had studied with John Hubbard Rich, Aloys Bohnen, and John Garth. Being the sister of an internationally famous film star had made Anne withdrawn and rather moody. The heat generated by Tyrone's celebrity might have reduced her to a cinder, but after studying with Rich for a short time, in her own words, "He realized that something *glorious* was happening to me." She stepped out of Tyrone's long shadow and became her own person again, as she had been throughout their years of growing up together.

During those first weeks of boot camp, Tyrone felt it necessary to hold his home together. It was really all that he had. It was damnably hard for him to imagine a home life with Judy. He would drive home to Saltair each weekend, and, quite often, if there weren't guests, get into civilian clothes. His Saturday night absences from Judy's bedside did not go unnoticed. He had asked Watson to buy her some flowers for Valentine's Day and enclose a personal note from him, but they were not acknowledged for some time. On that sentimental holiday, which fell on a weekend, he chose to stay near the base with Henry Fonda, who was a naval lieutenant. They caroused in San Diego, and Tyrone wrote Watson: "I don't believe I ever have seen him more affable." Fonda was known to have unpredictable moods. In that same letter, he said that Judy "told me the most flattering things about you the other day. They [Judy and her friend from Metro, Betty Asher, whom she later denounced as a studio spy] really adore you. And I'm so glad. I just knew that it would be like that." In reality, Watson hadn't liked Miss Asher at all.

For nearly a month after that, Judy refused to see him. She had given him an ultimatum in January about Annabella. She, too, had seen his weakness—his inability to act if by that act others were hurt. Either he would ask Annabella for a separation and divorce, or he would lose Judy. Her impatience, growing in part from the pressure of Tyrone's critics among her friends, was to spoil her future chances for happiness with other men. She never would love anyone again as deeply as she had Tyrone. She would settle for something less in every case.

It seemed a simple matter for Tyrone to become involved in family matters again. Annabella pretended that nothing had happened, and some of the tension eased. The birth of eight puppies to Princess helped. The little furry creatures delighted him, and whenever he was in the yard or by the pool, he had one of them in his hand, usually nuzzling it against his cheek.

The stork remained close to the Saltair house. In March 1943, Anne Hardenbergh gave birth to a daughter, Neeltje, a Dutch name long in her husband's family. She was nicknamed "Pixie" almost at once. Peter Hardenbergh, the baby's father, was with the Army somewhere in the Pacific. Following the return of Anne and the baby from the hospital, Patia and Grandmother Mudgey came for the weekend to welcome Anne and the only Power grandchild. The house overflowed with women, which seemed not the least bit peculiar to Tyrone, who had been around them almost exclusively since infancy.

The weekend following Pixie's arrival, there was a reception and cocktail party being held at the Ambassador Hotel in Los Angeles in honor Mme. Chiang Kai-shek. Her husband's prestige was then at its crest and otherwise sound-thinking people by the millions around the world confidently believed that Chiang would be ruling China following the war with Japan. It was certainly part of General MacArthur's grand strategy. So nearly everyone at the party believed that they were in the presence of a significant First Lady, and nearly everyone in the film colony who was not a committed liberal was there. Since it was on the weekend, Tyrone, resplendent in his dress Marine uniform, escorted Annabella. He was, for Tyrone, slightly overweight, having taken too many seconds in the mess hall at Camp Pendleton, where he spoke of the food as being of excellent quality. But they were a radiant, beautiful couple, and Annabella, in furs against the March chill, was careful to look cheerful and unconcerned while at the same time peeking behind the curious stares they were getting. Among the guests was Louella Parsons, who had been generous in her column to both of them and who now told Tyrone, as he leaned over to kiss her cheek, that she hoped that this meant that all was well in his home. "Just wonderful," he replied, with a tight smile.

Afterward, Tyrone and Annabella crossed the street to Perino's Restaurant for dinner. Once they were alone together there, conversation was strained. Tyrone had felt Annabella's discomfort in that cocktail crowd. It was obvious that nearly everyone knew that something was wrong between them. Annabella, in a sick dread, felt that the only way back for them was by getting it all out in the open. "What's wrong?" she asked. "What's troubling you?"

"I'm in love with somebody else," he said.

"Yes, I know," she told him. She would like to have broken a few pieces of china, but this semipublic drama called for absolute control.

Tyrone seemed surprised. "How could you? I know Watson didn't tell you."

"No, he didn't, but give me a pencil and I will write the name."

Tyrone handed her a pencil, protesting that there was no way she could possibly know. No one around *him* down at the boot camp knew anything about it, and he and Judy had been reasonably discreet, or so he must have thought. But Annabella lifted up the tablecloth and on the pad underneath wrote out "Judy Garland."

The exigencies of wartime saved Tyrone for the moment. He had to hurry back early the next day to Camp Pendleton. How many marriages and relationships were saved during the war by just such military urgencies? Annabella, sick at heart, convinced herself that she would leave him. "It is over," she told herself. "Dead."

Tyrone could not bring himself to go further than that declaration to Annabella, but calamity had happened. Judy was pregnant with his child. She was, of course, terrified. Tyrone had been shocked into action. He told Judy that he would tell Annabella "everything," and that she would have to give him a divorce. With his gift for improvisation, a whole new future was mapped out by him. He and Judy would marry the moment he was free. Watson would be best man.

Then suddenly Tyrone was selected for officer's training school at Quantico, Virginia. Now he felt that Annabella had to know *why* he and Judy must marry, and he told her. She was chilled by the news, said little, but when pressed, told him that she would never agree to a divorce. He found it difficult to tell Judy the news and fudged the cold truth a little; she was despairing and near suicidal. All of his last weekends were spent with her. He would leave camp and go straight to Watson's, where he kept his gear. When he left with other Marines during the first week of April, a fog of doubt and uncertainty had enveloped his life. For three days and nights he was traveling under the most primitive circumstances. He wrote Watson en route:

If you have never ridden across country on a troop train, you have never really lived. It is not air-conditioned, so they leave the windows open day and night. . . . I know I don't have to tell you what I would give to be at 152 Glenroy [Judy's house] right now. God—sometimes I don't think I can stand it. I do love her so. Maybe this is all good for one, I don't know. But I do know that from now on my life is going to be different.

Judy was sustained emotionally for several weeks by those last nights with Tyrone. She believed that somehow Annabella would be moved to compassion for their dilemma, for Tyrone if not for her. Tyrone's argument with Annabella finally was that *he wanted this child*. He hadn't wanted it this way, but now that it had happened, he really wanted it.

In early April, at her request, Watson escorted Judy to a party held by Decca Records, for whom she recorded, honoring Leonard Bernstein. Watson knew everything and gave her all the support he could manage, which was considerable. He was no mere "beard." His sweet gallantry touched her, and it was good to have him at her elbow. There were so many manipulators around her, it was refreshing to be with someone so determined to be accepted for what he was—a film cutter and friend, who wanted nothing from her.

Tyrone's training occupied his days. A good part of his growing skill as a Marine came from his efforts to push aside temporarily all of his irresolution and doubts about the future through hard work and application. It may even have been that he always had done that since early manhood. He never had been free of one problem or another, usually involved with his affections, and he worked harder on the stage and on the sound stages than anyone. Both Katharine Cornell and Henry King could attest to that.

Annabella, a very determined lady, had resolved to save their marriage. While Tyrone—and Judy—waited for word from Chicago, where the tour of *Blithe Spirit* was winding up, Annabella was making plans to go to Washington for as long as it would take to make Tyrone see reason. Later, Annabella would concede that only she and Judy had loved Tyrone purely for himself, but now she was fighting to save her future. As Tyrone stewed, his only confidante was Watson and he wrote him that he was

terribly depressed at times. I just can't see ahead at all. Everything seems so futile, and pointless, and we all appear to be like those squirrels in a cage. Running like hell, and never getting anyplace. I just don't understand anything any more. The moment I think I have all the nasty corners of my life tucked in and neat and orderly, then something just scatters them all, and I have to start all over again. . . . What I wouldn't give for one evening with you at 1170 [Crescenda Street] with just the fire, some music, and a couple of drinks. Maybe I could get squared away again. I'm really sure that you are the only friend I have in the world. And I don't say that feeling sorry for myself. But I say it with a great deal of pride, and an infinite amount of gratitude. It isn't everyone that can even boast of that.

Annabella arrived in Washington, near the Marine base, full of qualms. She was desperate to save their marriage, but at that moment, Tyrone seemed bent on destroying it. On the day of her arrival, Tyrone was writing Watson asking him to give Judy his love and tell her that he hoped that she would come East to see him.

Annabella arrived on the weekend and Tyrone came in that Saturday. The confrontation took them nowhere. Tyrone pleaded, and Annabella was resolute. He said that if he did not marry Judy, she would have to have an abortion. Still no concession came from Annabella. Tyrone wrote Watson that he was

at a loss to know exactly what the set-up was. I tried to bring up the subject of the friend in N.Y. [Judy, beside herself, had flown there to await the news of the showdown.] But every time I did, I got no place. The conversation would just die. Time will tell though, I guess. On that subject I received a couple of very strange letters from 20th men in N.Y. which I never could decipher. I'll tell you about it later.

A week later, Tyrone still had not been able to fulfill his promise to Judy to stand up to Annabella and "tell her I want out. I want Judy and I want my child."* Perhaps, Judy must have thought Tyrone was as irresolute as some of her friends said he was. She certainly believed that Annabella had an iron will, and, disgusted and disheartened, she returned to Hollywood.

* Annabella denies that she knew of Judy Garland's pregnancy and that Power asked her for a divorce at the time of the Garland affair.

Those "friends" around Judy who sought to protect her now moved in for the kill. All of their charges against Tyrone could not now be refuted by his exciting and loving presence. She was going from *Lily Mars* into *Girl Crazy*, with only a short break in between. A Mexican abortion was arranged and carried out literally overnight. When word of that reached Tyrone, he sagged in defeat. There was no chance with Judy now. Waiting in the wings was dynamic and gifted Joe Mankiewicz, the writer-director and producer. Mankiewicz was an imperious man who could have stepped into Napoleon's boots during the retreat from Moscow and very possibly turned a monumental defeat into a triumphant victory. He was not merely persuasive. He brooked no disagreement, striking terror into the hearts of normally insensitive studio executives. It was like Judy to turn to someone who was Tyrone's complete opposite. No one could blame her. She needed someone strong—like Joe M.—to sustain and protect her. The emotional scars of that abortion never would leave her. Yet, in the back of her mind, and for many years to come, her memory would flick on some tender moment with Tyrone and she would tell whoever was close to her at the time, "It really was different between Tyrone and me. It was no small affair."

As for Annabella, she took the train to New York on a Monday following these uncomfortable meetings. Once there, she began dating as many men as she could find time for. Her beaux included a pilot in the Air Force, a noted British actor of sophisticated comedies, a writer who was between marriages, and a member of an old New York family. She only used her suite at the Hotel Pierre for sleep and an occasional small social gathering.

On Sunday evening, June 5, 1943, Annabella had about eight friends in her suite, including the writer, who was apparently serious about her. Tyrone had received his commission as a second lieutenant on Thursday, June 2, and he was very proud of his new uniform and bars. He went up to New York Saturday afternoon, unannounced. It was his notion to walk in and surprise her. He came into the suite, froze for a moment, regained his poise, and then chatted with everyone for a few minutes before leaving.

That Monday, he wrote Annabella the most difficult letter he ever would compose:

Monday, June 6, 1943

My only darling:

   You have received many letters from me over the years since our hearts first met, but this is going to be the longest on record. As a matter of fact, this letter is in two parts. Entirely seperate of (sic) each other. The only similarity being that they both deal with you and me. I don't rightly know which part should come first, but we have to start some place.

   What can I say? Or rather, how can I say all that's in my heart tonight? To try to explain my actions of the past few months would be not only futile but ridiculous. I have been like a sick person, and I have been *so* sick. I have felt the last few days that I am getting a *little* better. I'm regaining a little of my equilibrium. But everything that I touch & everything that I eat still tastes of gall & wormwood.

   The only time lately that I have been even remotely happy was when I have seen you. Oh please believe me, you must believe me! That's the only thing I have left. Just to see you, & be with you helped *so* much to quell the nausea in my soul. I have looked forward to these week-ends as someone who is in prison looks to be taken out into the sunlight once a week. I don't believe you will ever know what it means to me to open the door of that apt. on Saturday evening & see you there. It's so bright & gay & you look so lovely—it's the most precious moment of my week. Then when we are together I can forget for a few hours the leprous state my soul is in. It stinks to high heaven! And it cries to you for help. That is the rub. To come to you after all, & say here I am, what is left of me. Can you do anything with it? Or is it even worth while doing anything with?

   And then came last Sunday.

   Not that I deserve anything, but if you had only tipped me off a *little bit*. I would have been prepared, and I wouldn't have felt *quite* so much a fool. It's funny, but I felt it the moment I walked into the house. I knew I shouldn't be there. What a sigh of relief must have wafted itself over the congregation when I took my leave. I knew it existed of course, because we had talked about it. But I didn't know it had gone quite so far. It is really over between us, isn't it? My darling, my darling! What a blind, idiotic, stupid fool I've been. How I have taken the most precious gift any man was ever given & dashed it to the floor. I am walking over it now, in my bare feet, & every cut is a million years of agony. . . .

I really feel like a man in a dream. All this is not happening to us. It couldn't! Weren't we the ones who had the whole thing licked? Didn't we know all the answers? I just didn't stop to think. That's all, no more no less. . . . And God damn it I love you so. I love you so very *very* much. I only love you, my darling. How I've wanted to tell you that, so many times. And I always will. I know there will never be anyone but you for me. There just *never* could be. . . .

And in the second part of this longest letter of his life, he recalls their happy moments:

a mosaic of such happiness . . . Riding up to Anacapri in a bright red fiacre . . . a picnic lunch we had on the little sand spit in the bay at Le Pilat. . . . the look in your eyes that first night we tentatively fingered the caviar on the Rex. And how we laughed. . . . why stupid, *stupid* ass that I am, did I have to burn the house to find I had diamonds in the cellar, all the time?

He said he believed that other people "cluttering up" their lives had led them to this precipice.

Isn't that true? Whenever we had any words at all it was always because of what someone else was, or had said, or had done. I know I'm a little late in making these observations, but I wanted you to know.

Annabella wept when she read the letter. Tyrone wanted so desperately to be pure, and while something in her knew that he always would fail on the surface, she tried to believe that the spirit within was untarnished. Very possibly, this was the case. He struck many people as someone who seemed untouched by the sordidness of some of his involvements and encounters. Many years later, long after his death, his youngest daughter, Taryn, would make a wise observation about this

side of her father, whom, she confessed, she could not recall
from her childhood. "I grew up basically with this
superhuman idea of him," she said, "because everyone
always said only how wonderful he was. But as I got older, I
found out some things that could be flaws or would be considered weaknesses, and in a sense I was glad to hear some of
this because it proved that at least he was human. . . .
everyone has flaws. I learned from Cesar Romero that he
really was a dedicated actor and that he loved his public. He
put everything else, anything that would destroy that image,
aside, and he would rather suffer personally. . . ."

Annabella phoned him that evening and said that they both
had made mistakes. Several weekends followed in New York
and they became lovers again. [He wrote Watson:]

These last few weeks have been wonderful in New York
with Annabella, I don't know what it is, but it seems as
though everything was starting out all over again. It may
not be the same ever for her but that's the way it is with
me. So *many* things have been ironed out, and I have
learned many lessons and have been shown much. Only
really *great* things are born out of pain I'm afraid. It's
maddening that life has to be that way, but it seems to be
so. I am really happier and more at peace than I have
been for about a year and a half. And I may add that it's
a *wonderful* feeling too. I don't know what happened in
the other department. Not a word—no answer to my last
wire two weeks ago—nothing! [Tyrone had asked Judy if
he should come to meet her in New York, but that was
not what she had proposed. Tyrone's resilient affections
are remarkable: When Judy slammed the door, he suddenly saw what "an ass" he had been.]

Annabella was not so easily healed. For her, the scar tissue
from the Judy involvement would be there always. It had differed from his previous dalliances with leading ladies because
it had been discussed; it had caused a breach between herself
and Tyrone. There was nothing shadowy about it. Then after
one long cry of anguish to Watson as late as July, Tyrone
manfully attempted to put it out of his mind. At least to him,
it was scarcely the "brief affair" many of Judy's biographers

have assumed. Tyrone's affections had been diverted for
nearly a year.

There was one other great problem in Tyrone's life con-
current with his wayward emotions. The matter of his contract with Fox had to be settled one way or another. The first
seven-year period was up, and renewal was expected by the
studio with no complications from Tyrone. But he had had a
great deal of time to think about his servitude there since he
had entered the Marines, and he wanted certain rights defined
and guaranteed. He wanted the right to do at least one outside
picture a year; he insisted upon his freedom to do a Broadway
play when he was between pictures; and he was limiting his
film activity for his home studio to only one production a
year. Fox resisted right down the line. They wanted Tyrone
exclusively or not at all. They told his agent, Charlie Feldman,
that there was nothing to discuss. But Tyrone said that the
company owed him at least a little dialogue after all the years
and the millions he had brought into the box office. If Zanuck
were there, he asserted, Fox would have presented Feldman
with *its* terms. There would have been some kind of compromise. But Feldman had encountered a stone wall in Goetz,
business manager Lew Schreiber, and others in the Fox
hierarchy.

Annabella had gone back to California when Tyrone finally
had been given his first assignment as an officer, temporary
duty on the instruction staff at Quantico. It was not what
Tyrone had wanted. He was aching to get into flight school.
So far, the only war he had got involved with was the one he
was waging against Fox. He wrote Annabella:

What a stinking bunch of sons-of-bitches all those
bastards are out there. Why I wouldn't re-sign with Fox
now for a half interest in the Goddamn company. But I'll
bide my time. I haven't heard from them yet. Maybe they
were just bluffing again, about wiring me [a wire to the
effect that because of his "unhappiness," they would
assume he would not be renewing his contract with them
and they would consider the matter closed]. But they
won't get anything out of me, you can bet. We'll just
have to play it a bit close to the vest for a while, but we'll

make out all right. Just know I love you more than anything else in the world, and how can we lose?

Annabella could not resist that. The last of her defenses dissolved. It was she and Tyrone against the world or, more particularly, against her *bête-noire*, Twentieth Century-Fox. The dispute had bound them together again.

She was bolstered, too, by frequent calls from Saint-Exupéry in New York, where he said he thought he was stalled, still unable to get the proper clearance to fly with the Free French. He was writing a fairy tale for grownups to read to their children, *The Little Prince*, and he read her passages from the manuscript over the phone. She knew that he was not rich, but his phone bills must have been astronomical. Of course, she was delighted. Later, the galleys would arrive when she was visiting Tyrone near his Marine base and he would read the last chapter to her. They both wept shamelessly. In this passage, the Little Prince has encountered a golden snake, during his travels on the planet earth (the boy is a celestial voyager from a very tiny asteroid). The snake would like to be kind to him rather than lethal, and the reader is left to ponder on the motive behind this kindness when he bites the little fellow on the ankle and the Little Prince falls . . . as gently as a tree falls. "There was not even any sound. . . ."

The tale is told by a pilot whose plane has come down in the desert, but where, from out of nowhere, he encounters the Little Prince. The mutual joy in the fairy tale shared by Annabella and Tyrone was sparked by Saint-Exupéry's reduction of mankind's weaknesses to simply understood riddles. Under the disillusion is a zest for living all three of them had in abundance.

Tyrone may have been helped to clearsightedness about his fellow man's foibles through reading *The Little Prince*; he had come to his unhappy conclusions about his studio on his own simply through the objectivity the Marines had granted him by taking him a continent away from Hollywood. His conviction now was that his old status as a trained seal for Zanuck or Goetz was intolerable. He badly needed Annabella's strength at that moment. He had to tap it by phone and letter. Even with her support, he still had some doubts:

. . . I have been doing a hell of a lot of thinking of late, and of course as usual, I'm still going around in circles. It all has to do with the business of the Studio, and all that merde. I talked to Charlie [Feldman] this afternoon, and he told me just what I thought he would. That the studio would not listen for a minute to my offer. Well, I asked him what they had in mind, and he told me that they had made no counter proposition. So I said that I wouldn't say anything more until they came back with something. It all has to do, of course, with the fact that they want me exclusively, and the one picture a year frightened them. When I said that if they didn't want that, they might not get me for any, he as much as said that they would take their chances. And also let me know that there was a war going on (this information relayed to a newly commissioned Marine in 1943!), and that the business was going on at the same time, and that they were spending a lot of money and time developing *NEW PEOPLE!* [Emphasis Tyrone's] So that's the way the wind blows. They just slightly hinted, just slightly, mind you, that they might not want me, when this was all over. How do you like those apples?

But this is what I have been thinking, honey. I don't mind the struggling, and the fighting that we are going to have to go through, if I don't accept. I can do it. But I can't do it without you. And therein comes the rub. I don't know whether I want to ask you to do it. It might not be very pretty and we can't tell how long it will last. And it isn't the way I had meant things to be at all. Do you follow me?

It would be so easy, just to pick up the phone and say, yes. Then there would be no worries, no troubles, no dark nights. Everything would be taken care of, and we would never have to worry again. But could we live with that big, black ugly thing that I would have inside? That wanted to come up and choke me, at every turn. I am just trying to see this whole thing from every side. I don't want to be guilty of neglect, or to say that I didn't think of something, when we make the final decision.

Then too, I think of what's happened to me. There is something that has happened to me, you know. I don't quite know how to explain it, nor really what it is, myself. But this is the only way I can express it. A few years ago I wouldn't have hesitated a moment. I know what my answer would be. And it wouldn't be printable. But now . . . what is it that makes me cautious? When that thought came to me last night driving home, for the first time, I felt old! I really felt that I was 30. And that maybe 7 years of ease have told. Could it be that my fighting days are over? I don't believe it. I just want you to know that I don't believe it. And I also wanted you to know from how many different angles I had considered this thing. It's a hell of a big thing that WE have to decide upon.

My God, but I have gone on tonight! I won't say any more right now. Think of what I have said, and let me know what you have to add. It will probably be the key. . . .

Tyrone wanted Annabella to urge him to stand up to the studio because in that freedom lay their salvation. With Zanuck keeping her off the screen, they would return to the stage together. The Saltair house was paid for; she had put up half and he the other. There was no mortgage over their heads.

Beyond that, asking her to share the burden of coming to such an important decision was an indirect way of declaring himself through with Judy. Or so he thought at the time.

It could not be an easy decision. There *were* responsibilities. Tyrone having forbidden Patia to accept any money for the work that she did, his mother depended upon his support altogether. Annabella was blacklisted, and young Annie was in private school. Sister Anne and her new daughter were guests at Saltair, and there was the small household staff, who got a good salary.

Feldman was known as a tough negotiator in money terms but he crumbled like a soggy biscuit over demands for any sort of independence for his clients. A decade later, he would have trouble with Zanuck when Marilyn Monroe insisted upon similar rights. He told Tyrone that Fox had new stars like Dana Andrews, who were not in uniform and were being groomed to take over. There the matter rested for some weeks.

While Tyrone was training Marines at the Command School for combat, presumably in the South Pacific, Annabella was asked to join a war bond selling tour. It was grueling, with no time to recuperate between stops, but she was physically strong despite her small size. There were three servicemen with her, one from each of the fighting arms, and all of them wounded. As a kind of backup chorus, a trio of beauties posed prettily and assisted in the sales.

At each stop, Annabella would make a rousing little speech, and there were six or seven such stops each day. They traveled by private plane, and they picked out some crowded spot in each city where their little carnival would be set up—post offices, factories, large insurance buildings. Once, they were sent to a dry state (Kansas), and the wounded sailor thought that very inconsiderate of their sponsor, the U. S. Treasury Department. But another member of the party said that he had provisions, and a bottle was magically produced, and when that was gone, another. Annabella recalls: "We were lost along the way that day because we never appeared." It was their only such lapse. By the time they reached the East Coast, Annabella was a wreck, in spite of her rugged constitution.

One of the things Annabella missed on that trip was her quiet hour. She had no chance at solitude. "I was never alone," she remembers. "Always with people, even at lunch. I need to be alone from time to time." She began to feel rundown, and her last stops were made in near-freezing temperatures, many of them out of doors. By the time she reached New England, it was late September and that part of the country had moved early into autumn. She had gone East from a fast trip through the South, which she had hoped would take her into Texas.

During Annabella's long tour, Tyrone had been shipped to a Marine air base at Corpus Christi, where he was to receive flight training and attend ground school before an assignment in the Pacific. He did not know then that he would be kept there throughout the winter of 1943-44. Were wheels at high levels moving again?

Whatever future Tyrone now had he was pinning on a life with Annabella. She was not nearly so sure. It was not just her zealousness in helping with the war effort that was keeping her on the move. From now on, until the end of the war, she would spend very little time in the Saltair house. In early 1944, at her suggestion, the house would be rented furnished to a doctor's family, and Anne Hardenbergh and her infant daughter moved to a rented cottage on Point Loma in San Diego, a place she had loved as a child. Patia was already back in her own apartment and deeply involved as an assistant to a woman physician who worked with electrotherapy. Tyrone spent the last half of the war with no home to go back to, even if the war had ended suddenly and he had the chance. He blamed himself for that.

When it was announced in the Corpus Christi papers that Annabella and her bond-selling troop would be coming in, Tyrone said "I was so excited. . . . I had a room all set for us at the hotel and left a note for you, and the car, the night before. It is needless to add that my disappointment was complete. . . ." For companionship, he had turned to a "very nice boy. I know you will like him. A Lt. Tabelling from Jacksonville. It was his mother who sent him the clipping that told me you had been there. I immediately called the theatre there, and they said you had gone to Birmingham, and there I lost the trail. . . . it's really horrible not knowing where you are. . . ."

He knew that she would be ending her tour in New York and told her, "I would be very careful in New York. Try not to spend *too* much.

"I am madly jealous of your going to New York, of course. And when you see *Oklahoma* again, look at it for me too. . . ."

When Annabella reached New York, she was emotionally and physically exhausted, and certainly not up to seeing *Oklahoma* or anything else. She was feverish, and the doctor told her she had double pneumonia.

Annabella didn't want to worry Tyrone with her illness, and kept the news from him for several days. He wrote her again from Corpus Christi:

> Went up to Dallas at the crack of dawn [4:45] Saturday and got back yesterday afternoon. It was, as you know too well, hectic as hell, but we did succeed in selling quite a few bonds. There was Bob Taylor, Bob Sterling, Bill Holden, Jack Holt and myself. We did a radio sketch from the stage of a theatre. It was very nice, and very short. But we did have a few laughs.

Now I'm back to work again. I flew this morning, and now to ground school this afternoon. All the planes have been flown back in again, and the danger has passed [a hurricane warning]. Everything is normal. Although right now it does look like it might rain later today. . . .

How happy you must be to be back in New York. And how I envy you. I am jealous as hell that you are going to get to see all those new shows. Merde on this war!

. . . I feel horribly lonely and out of the way here in Corpus. So do come and see me *soon* SOON SOON. Have a good time, but hurry. You can get Eastern Airlines right from N.Y.C. and they come through here. . . . do make it soon, my darling. . . .

When Tyrone learned of her illness, he insisted that she come to Corpus Christi, where he kept a suite at the Driscoll Hotel for his own use whenever he could get away. He told her she could stay in bed every day until four o'clock and get rested up, and then each evening he would come. In early October, when her doctor gave her permission to leave New York, she flew to Texas and recuperated there.

Annabella does not recall meeting Tyrone's recent companion, Lieutenant Tabelling, but he introduced her to an older officer, Lt. Comdr. Thomas White, of the Navy, who often had dinner with them, along with his wife, Midge. Midge White was staying in Corpus Christi, and they became a foursome for a while, when Annabella was stronger. Later in California, Midge would be introduced to sister Anne Hardenbergh.

Annabella remained in Corpus Christi until the end of October. They did all that there was to do in Corpus, which is not comparable to New Orleans or other Gulf cities, but still is a sailor's town and lively enough. Tyrone believed that any city or town is redeemed by being on the water. They had reached a point in their marriage, which is not at all uncommon, where much had happened between them so that each understood the other better. There was far more acceptance and tolerance than passion now.

Annabella was now committed to do *Jacobowsky and the Colonel* for the Theatre Guild, with rehearsals beginning in New York just before Christmas. Tyrone had resigned himself to spending the holidays alone in Texas. He told Watson his only desire "is to get this God damned training over, and get out of this place. It can certainly get on one's nerves after a time. And I think that I have had just about enough of Texas. For my dough they can give it back to the Indians, or Mexicans, or whoever the hell it is that wants it."

But he *was* as comfortable as any other lieutenant at the base. He had a "cozy" little room in the officers quarters, where he kept his books, records (many of them sent by Watson) and Victrola. On weekends, he would go to his room at the Driscoll Hotel to live "in the lap of luxury" for a couple of days. He said that the people there were terribly nice to him, but complained that they were a bit dull. Some of his Hollywood cronies, among them Keenan Wynn and Laird Cregar, already had been sent to the South Pacific, and he wanted "desperately," he believed, to be going to "someplace like that. I should talk. . . . I probably will." But he did not, or if he did, none in a higher authority listened to him.

Watson had been made chief editor of a semidocumentary war film by Henry Hathaway. It was originally called *Torpedo Squadron Eight*, and told of life aboard an aircraft carrier and of an attack on a Pacific island. It was a difficult and challenging assignment, since much of the responsibility for blending fact and fiction rested with Watson as cutter. But it resulted in a brilliant and memorable film, finally called *A Wing and a Prayer*. It starred Dana Andrews, one of those "new people" Tyrone had complained about in his letter to Annabella and, in Goetz's master plan, the one most likely to succeed Tyrone in the affections of the public.

Tyrone managed, in his spare time, to help Watson's mother, Ma Webb, obtain the Roxy Theatre in New York for a benefit. He had gotten close to the Roxy management through several personal appearances there. It gave him considerable satisfaction to be doing something even remotely connected with his Hollywood career. In his airplane recognition class at the base, he helped handle some editing of the film through Watson's help (via the mails).

That New Year's Eve, the Langs again had their party, and Watson went along. Tyrone wrote him, ". . . probably just as well that I wasn't there . . . would have gotten into some mischief, no doubt." He started the New Year by getting permission to live off the base and moved into the Driscoll on a permanent basis.

Annabella opened in the Theatre Guild production, *Jacobowsky and the Colonel*, with Louis Calhern, Oscar Karlweis, and J. Edward Bromberg on January 26, beginning a break-in tour in New Haven. The company then moved on to Boston, where she spent much of her free time with Midge White, wife of Tyrone's friend at Corpus Christi, Captain Tom White. Midge was an amusing companion; dynamic, wry, and as refreshing as a breeze off Boston Harbor.

The play's reviews on the road were excellent, and when Tyrone read them, it revived his own stage ambitions. He had made a game effort to reshape his future when the war was over, including the stage, but that was going to be almost as difficult now as it had been before. He had re-signed with the studio, forced to compromise on nearly everything. He would do two pictures a year for them, not one. He had story approval, but he could not make independent deals with other studios, although a "loan-out" would be permitted. Tyrone's feelings about the whole matter were bitter. His financial obligations had compelled him to sign. He told those closest to him that he was glad to be away from Zanuck during those war years, away from the studio, which he now looked upon as a kind of bondage.

In early February, he saw the movie thriller, *The Lodger*, starring his old pal from the Fox lot, Laird Cregar, as Jack the Ripper. Watson had edited it, and Tyrone wrote him that he was "thrilled to see your name on the credit sheet. . . ." Then he went on to criticize Cregar's performance as being very "naughty" in some scenes and he wished the director had "tamed Laird down a bit." He was referring to Cregar's obvious projection of the killer as a homosexual, an interpretation Cregar knew well how to play since he was quite open in his sexual preference around the studio.

On March 13, Annabella opened in New York to rave notices. Even though most of a continent separated them, Tyrone's thoughts were very much with her that night. Yet she knew that their future together was cloudy. Over the years of their marriage, she had developed a kind of sixth sense about Tyrone and she no longer had any illusions about holding him after the war. She was prescient about such matters, and while she was touring with her play on the way to New York, Tyrone had sent Judy a valentine (again not acknowledged) and had bought every one of her records then available. Then in the squadron projection room, they showed film of a Command Performance and Judy sang "Over the Rainbow." The executive officer of the squadron was a young man named Dick Davis, who remembered the Gumm family, especially Judy and her sister Virginia, back in Lancaster, California.

Annabella's success had revived all of her old spirit, and off-stage, she was having a grand time feuding with a New York critic, who had said some very unkind things about her. Nearly every working member of Actors' Equity got into the scrap and signed petitions in her behalf. The publicity ensuing from this brou-ha-ha did the play no harm, and it was sold out for weeks in advance.

In mid-April, Tyrone got his orders transferring him to the Naval Air Station at Atlanta on May 1. There, he would be given advanced flight training, including instrument landings. Since he now had been in the Marine Corps sixteen months and was still undergoing training, one might well ask *why*? There were many pilots in combat who had been rushed there after only a fraction of the hours of flying time and ground school Tyrone already had received. When he enlisted, he was still number one at the box office. Could it be that Zanuck had little or nothing to do with all of this drawnout process, but that men on the highest level of government deemed Tyrone Power a national icon too precious to be risked in battle? There were some stars, like Jimmy Stewart and Henry Fonda, who had gone on to battle action at their insistence. Tyrone had begun his tour in the Marines with that in mind, but somewhere along the line, those heroic ambitions had been dissipated. Even Clark Gable, who had risked his life for months in aerial battles, was out of the service by the spring of 1944.

Tyrone and Annabella spent four days together in New York as he was "en route" to Atlanta from Corpus Christi. They were not truly able to rid themselves of the specters of the past year, but they were very much in love.

He was two months in Atlanta, which he vastly preferred to Corpus Christi, and then he was sent, finally, to the Marine Corps Air Station at Cherry Point, North Carolina. During his first free moment, he wrote Watson:

Just a line, to let you know that I am thinking of you. I

just arrived here yesterday, and I must say that this is
really the last place. It is horrible. There are about a
million people here, and none of them seem to know
what the hell they're doing. They haven't the slightest
idea what to do with me, so I guess that I will just sit,
until someone makes up their [sic] mind. The base is
huge, and terribly impersonal and I just think it stinks.
Especially after Atlanta, which was like a dream. God,
but I had a divine time there, and how I hated to leave.
. . . Have been hearing some rather lurid tales of our
friend [Judy] lately . . . but I can't say that I blame her a
hell of a lot. I just hope she doesn't get hurt . . . she's
much too nice and sweet a person, to have anything happen to her.

I wish that you would ask Clark [Gable] to please send
me a written document that I can hand out to the people
that ask me why he's out of the service. Christ! I'll bet if
one has asked me, there have been a thousand . . . and all
I can say is that I don't know, but that I envy him like hell.

At last, the Marine Corps seemed to be preparing Tyrone
for battle action. He was assigned to a Transport Squadron,
learning to fly DC-3's. The training program called for 340
hours in the air, so it would go on for several months. He also
flew a B-25 bomber and said that it was "one wonderful airplane."

The good life still held him, however, and he and a new-
found friend, Major Little, took a place at Atlantic Beach
about twenty miles from the air station. He planned to com-
mute to the base, so he could have a dip after classes in the
evening and lie on the sand on weekends. Still, he complained
about actor George Montgomery getting a deferment because
of his family (wife Dinah Shore) and said he would like to see
him in the Marine Corps for half an hour. "It makes it very
handy," he railed on, "not to have one's home life disrupted
by any nasty old war." The truth was that he felt sorry for
those men not in the war. "They really don't know what the
hell they're missing. And they will come out of this whole
thing, without having gotten one damn thing. Why, I
wouldn't take anything for what this all has taught
me."—This to Watson, forgetting that Watson was not in the
war either.

In late July, he got up to New York for a two-day visit withAnnabella, where he heard about a Marine outfit being sent overseas. By the time he rushed over to place his application, they were all filled up.

While they were dining in the Champagne Room at El Morocco, Tyrone and Annabella saw Judy Garland at another table with five or six people. She was laughing loudly and talking almost without interruption, perhaps made edgy by noticing Tyrone, although she made a great show of not seeing him. At their corner table, Tyrone took Annabella's hand and pressed it under the table.

On August 22, Paris was liberated by the Allies. Annabella was in mid-performance as "Marianne" in *Jacobowsky and the Colonel* when the curtain was lowered and the lights were raised. Someone whispered the news to her from the wings and said, "Go on! Tell them!" The curtain came up again and Annabella went alone to center stage, where with tears streaming down her cheeks, she told the audience that her native city had been freed. Everyone stood up and began singing "La Marseillaise" spontaneously, with Annabella sobbing for joy in accompaniment.

From that moment on, Annabella was desperate to get to her family. As soon as Paris was liberated, the Charpentiers had moved to Paris, where they were staying with a cousin. Earlier that year, brother Pierre had been called up by the Nazi-controlled Vichy army for conscription. Everyone knew that Frenchmen taken for duty in Vichy, France, were transported into Germany as slave laborers. Pierre's delicate health would have doomed him there, not to mention his hatred for the Germans, so he ran away and hid for days in the forest. When he was caught, he was suffering from pneumonia and very soon thereafter died in a sanitorium. His parents joined him there just before his death, and father Paul Charpentier was devastated.

In October, the Theatre Guild realized how much Annabella wanted to get to liberated Paris and released her from her run-of-the-play contract in *Jacobowsky*. She immediately offered her services to the USO with the stipulation that she would be touring in Europe. She thought that wherever they sent her, she somehow would manage to fly to Paris for a brief reunion with her parents.

She was again asked to do Elvira in Noël Coward's *Blithe Spirit*, and the USO Camp Shows production opened in Long Island the first week of November, where the soldiers were most enthusiastic. Within two weeks, they were on their way to Italy by way of Newfoundland and the Azores, where they opened at Mediterranean headquarters in Caserta, before touring with the Fifth Army throughout the boot of Italy. There was fierce fighting going on at Cassino and around the Po Valley. Annabella had got into the thick of it before Tyrone did, and it upset him. "The whole thing seems more unbelievable every day—the life we all used to live before—and now *this*." Her arrival in the battle areas of Italy while he was still safely in the States was clearly an emasculating thing with him. It would never leave him, even when he had arrived in the war zone of the Pacific, because he would be seeing the war from the air, a kind of abstraction veiled by mountains of clouds, while Annabella was slogging through mud, sleeping in rude tents and in the cold, and seeing the bloodied wounded everywhere.

Coincidentally, while she was moving among the "dog-faces" ("doughboys" had been outmoded by the length of the various Italian battles, preventing most of the infantrymen from shaving regularly), a programmer film she had made on loan-out to Republic Pictures, *Tonight We Raid Calais*, was playing the Fifth Army circuit. She was supposed to have played the Parisian girl in Fox's *Paris After Dark*. Studio head Goetz had promised her the part, but when she went into his office to see him once production was scheduled, he told her that Brenda Marshall, an American girl who was married to actor William Holden, was going to play the Parisienne.

There, in Naples, Caserta, Rome, and finally Bologna, Annabella was totally caught up in the war, and while her heart broke at the sight of the wounded and the misery, she felt fulfilled. She adored the young soldiers and even allowed them to come back to her dressing room tent and watch her remove the gray, phosphorescent makeup she wore as the dead Elvira. "See the Annabella underneath?" she would ask, and they grinned as her own high color emerged when the Kleenex and cold cream had removed the last vestiges of her "spirit" pallor.

Tyrone had completed his 340 hours of flying time at Cherry Point and was waiting for his final assignment or transfer. On December 14, he got his orders and he flew to Los Angeles en route to the staging encampment at El Centro. He had two days' leave and he went to Watson's, since his own home was still rented.

When he was inside the Crescenda Street house, he headed for the den, where the fireplace was blazing. It was his favorite room in the house, small enough to encourage intimate conversation but clearly a man's retreat and study with its natural wood paneling, built-in bookcases, and gun case (Watson no longer hunted; like Tyrone, he had begun to hate killing animals for the sport of it, although his father was noted for his foxhounds and the hunts on his huge estate in northern Vermont and even his mother had killed a huge Kodiak bear, among other game, now mounted and on display in the Webb mansion at Shelburne). Watson's New England colonial house had a natural warmth built into it. The cherry paneling of the living room had come from a room his mother "had left over" from her vast collection of rooms and had lain in storage for years. There was a raised brick hearth on which guests could sit close to the fire.

Then Tyrone went back to the Marine Corps Air Station at El Centro, the departure point for Marine pilots and crew leaving for the Pacific war. From there, he wrote Watson:

> . . . You will never know how much it meant to me to be able to just sit in that beautiful garden, and then to have a wonderful dinner, such as we had. It was all so new and strange after the life that I had been living, that I supposed I had difficulty in expressing my gratitude, but believe me it was really deeply felt.
>
> Enclosed is the card, and I'm sure the gift is just what I want. Please see that it is delivered to the proper party [Judy, still, more than two years after their first meeting], and in time.

Over the next ten days, Tyrone methodically packed everything he had collected during his two years in the Marines—books, records, photos and letters, and shipped them in large boxes to Watson to hold until he returned to "redeem it all." Then he drew his overseas gear for himself, his plane, and all his four crew members. He retained a few of his favorite records, including *Daphnis and Chloë*, a handful of books, and a leather twin photo frame with portraits of Annabella and daughter Annie.

While waiting for the weather to clear for their final journey to an as-yet-unknown destination in the Pacific, Tyrone managed to fly up to Palm Springs for a half-day visit with the new president of Fox, Spyros Skouras, who had succeeded Annabella's friend Sidney Kent, and Joe Schenck, who was chairman of the board. Later that morning, he chatted with Zanuck, who was just back from the war, and he felt considerable relief over their reassurances about his future, saying afterward, "they are pretty obliging old bastards at that."

The waiting depressed him. It made him "lower than hell." These bouts of melancholia had come with the realities of war, the sudden awakening to the facts of life about film stardom following his struggle over his contract, and the foredoomed romance with Judy Garland and the damage that had caused his relationship with Annabella. As partial redress, Tyrone adopted Annie before going overseas to protect her in case anything happened to him during the battle action. He wanted them to have the same name.

Life for this young man was no longer something to be lived and enjoyed a day at a time; whatever was done had to be paid for somehow, sometime. The maturing Tyrone often hated the cost.

VI

TYRONE CATCHES UP
WITH THE WAR

TYRONE spent his last night in the United States sitting in his small, sparsely furnished room in the officers quarters at the edge of the Air Station in El Centro. He could catch a glimpse of distant lights scattered here and there in the Imperial Valley beyond the base, and it was a night of sharp contrasts. There was every galaxy visible in the black sky above the valley; there were stars that moved and then blinked out as planes took off for remote Pacific points. The sound of their motors revving for takeoff and then the hum overhead never stopped the whole night.

It was a wry departure. Not what he had planned at all. Annabella was in Europe, doing what she could for the soldiers. But despite her good intentions, he resented her absence at such a critical time. He had hurt her deeply and he must have realized that she needed to do something meaningful to fill her life as the wound healed.

During their last reunion, he had given her a ruby-encrusted gold heart on a chain. "Here is my heart," he had told her. "Take good care of it." And he had meant it, every word. Of course, she wept and everything was fine and wonderful. Yet she was gone in the war and there was no hearth being kept warm for Tyrone. Home, to Tyrone, during the months he would spend in the Pacific, became an abstraction, fondly remembered, but no longer a solid reality awaiting his return.

But if Annabella had asked the one question that needed to be asked when she first knew how serious it was between him and Judy, then he was convinced that she would not be in the USO, wading in the mud of northern Italy. If she had asked, "What is it that she gives you that I do not?" everything might have been simplified. He needed a relationship that was

181

free, sensually. Judy had caught on to that immediately. He was not a conventional lover. He wanted to do everything, try everything, and, if it was good, do it again and again.

Tyrone was not bitter toward Annabella, nor Judy, nor even the Fates. He knew that what he wanted from his bedroom encounters could not last forever. The trouble was, he had endowed these episodes with romance, drenched them with it. That was his nature. And what he felt for Annabella was far more profound than any transitory shacking-up. So why did he insist on combining the two?

In his pursuit of perfection in all things in life, Tyrone knew he had to take chances. Here he had taken a gamble and lost. Now, in the months ahead, he would have to recoup. The Marine Corps had given him that opportunity. His situation with Annabella had been put on "hold" for the rest of the war. He had been given a second chance.

23 Feb. 1945

My dear Watty:

We have finally arrived at our destination, and have a few days at our disposal, while some work is being done on the airplanes. It has been a job getting settled in the squadron, and in our new living quarters. They are not half bad, by the way. A sort of tent affair, which they call Fales (it is pronounced as though it were spelled f-o-l-l-y) . . . 'nuf sed! The days are brilliant with sunshine. . . . and warm enough, and the nights are really beautiful under the new moon which is coming up. Last night for example, I had quite an experience. . . . I went to the movies!! Yes . . . we had to take our own chairs. I managed to scrape up something that after the first three reels began to lead to the belief that I was being ridden out of camp on a rail. However, it was a beautiful night, and we saw 'Meet Me in St. L.[ouis]' It was quite an odd sensation, as you may imagine, sitting here on this place and seeing the picture. I thought it was wonderful, and my God, but she [Judy] never looked more beautiful. Minellee (?) is really a very clever fellow. I don't know, but the whole thing seemed to make a very deep impression, and promoted quite a mood. . . . sitting there in the moonlight (of course the theatre is outdoors), with all the other fellows, with that breeze blowing in off the sea.

. . . oh, you know what I mean. Please present my compliments to our friend and tell her how much I enjoyed it. . . . We live in shorts all day, and drink quantities of fruit juice . . . and then, all the sleep. . . . there's nothing else to do. . . .

You will never have any idea what all the records mean to us. We have our machine in the tent, and a concert every evening. . . .

Before Tyrone and his squadron could get into the action, they were moved again, this time to Saipan, a volcanic island in the Marianas in the western Pacific. It had been wrested from the Japanese in 1944 and now served as an air base for American attacks on the mainland of Japan. Tyrone's transport squadron was now in the thick of it. Because it was wooded and mountainous, Tyrone thought it was far lovelier than their first island headquarters. There were exotic birds singing much of the time and Tyrone wrote that "it suddenly occurred to me, that it was the first one I had heard since I left Calif. It's amazing how those things come to one all of a sudden, and you realize, not that you are actually hearing the song, but that you haven't heard anything like it, for so long."

At about this time, through the generous intervention of then Congresswoman Clare Boothe Luce, Annabella was given permission to fly from Naples to Paris in an air force plane. She was in Lucca just out of Bologna, and the ragged front line was in the mountains just above her. The sound of artillery exchanges was constant. She had been told that if you could hear the whistle of the shell above your head, you were safe. *Blithe Spirit* was playing at a station hospital in Lucca when permission finally came through for the flight to Paris. She had dinner that evening with a young surgeon who had spent all day in the operating room. She had met him as she and some of the others of the cast performed for those patients in the surgical ward who could not get to the improvised theatre. He had been weeping because he had just performed an amputation of the leg of his best friend who had been maimed by a mine that very morning, but when she and some of the others did some foolish songs, dances, and jokes, he began laughing. Annabella thought, "Migod! This USO means something!" The two of them talked after dinner, and she told him that she was flying to see her parents. He told her that he had received some cakes from his mother and insisted that she take them to her family. The corporal in charge of the *Blithe Spirit* company managed to find her a huge bag full of K-rations (tinned meat, chocolate, canned soup, cigarettes). She was so loaded down with goodies that the soldier-chauffeur in Paris had to help her into the apartment building and up the stairs. The apartment door had been locked for the night, but when she knocked, somehow they knew. She heard cries inside: "Here she is! Here she is! She's back! Here she is!"

Then there was a grand reunion and everyone wept. Annabella took the bag of K-rations and the cake from the surgeon and piled everything on the floor in a grand display of plenty. Her family could only stare at it in wonder. She saw then how thin and undernourished her parents were, and she was nearly mad with joy at being part of the American liberation of Europe and being able to help them. She was inordinately proud of her uniform and of what the Americans had done for France.

When she left them after several weeks, during which she managed to perform for her own people, she attempted to catch up with General Patton's Third Army in Germany, but his forces were moving so fast, the *Blithe Spirit* company could not catch up with them.

Tyrone and his squadron ferried supplies to the advancing forces as the ring around Japan tightened. He described one hop as lasting ten and a half hours.

You find yourself devising all manner of ways to make the time pass more quickly. . . . It was a beautiful day, with only a few lovely puffs of clouds, here and there. . . . and that interminable blue sea. We played a game . . . imagining that we were flying into New York, and that in a little while we would land at Floyd Bennett, or LaGuardia. Then we planned a whole evening . . . from the first drink, and then the hot shower . . . to dinner, the theatre, and a club, or two afterwards. It was a lot of fun, but a train of thought that is destined to drive one mad, if followed too far. . . .

•   •   •

His closest friend in the squadron was Lieutenant Chubb Church. Chubb had visited Watson's home with Tyrone during that last hurried leave before departing the States. Tyrone was living with the commander of the squadron, a Captain Webb, with whom he was comfortable but not terribly close. They shared a fale (tropical tent) as well as an army of mosquitoes. Frequently, they had to wear netting over the bare parts of their bodies and a grease repellent.

There was one near mishap when they were attempting to lift off in the *Blithe Spirit* (Tyrone had chosen the name of their plane) and the ailurons failed to work. Finally, after circling the runway several times, they got them unlocked at the last moment. Japanese artillery, or ack-ack, was frequent as they passed over Japanese-held areas on their way to the bases close to the ever-changing front, but they were never hit.

Between missions, he began work on a "novel," told in the first person, which was completely autobiographical. Inexperienced as he was with the form, he was an old hand at letter-writing and a gifted one, too, and the surviving pages are fascinating for their intimate glimpse of the man, even though the autobiographical material keeps shifting back and forth between Tyrone and "Fred," who was probably Chubb Church. To further distance himself, it was "Fred" who was going to write the book, and Tyrone's piece of fiction is about "Fred's" talking of the book he is planning to write.

In one excerpt, "Fred" is lying back "plucking at his right eyebrow" (a tic that Tyrone had), and says

> It is going to be about me . . . but not so much about me as a person, as a whole, as about the people, and places and things that are me. All the way along the line, little things have rubbed off, you might say. A word here, a color there, a gesture someplace else . . . a taste, an aversion, a habit. They're all here, little bits and pieces that I've picked up. Some of them are speaking to you now, and some of them listen to you, when you talk. Others are saying what a wonderful day this is, and how beautifully the sea dances. . . . I wouldn't be here today if it weren't for every one of them, and I think it only right that they know about it. And how I feel about them.

When "Fred" is asked if he would like to live it all again, he says, "Not even one little part of it. I wouldn't have missed any of it, for anything . . . but I couldn't stand it again. . . ." Then the narrator observes that the tide is out and has littered the sand-bar with "little dead things" . . . "the broken shells of anger, hurt pride, spite. The rotting shapes of envy, covetousness, greed, and jealousy . . . gleaming white and naked, under the brilliant, calcine light of criticism, censure, gossip and fault-finding. And then presently the floodtide of hope, ambition, reason, or its substitute, love, will return to obliterate all those nasty shapes. . . ." It is noteworthy, perhaps, that Tyrone sees "reason" on a higher plane than "its substitute, love." Here is Tyrone, setting down for the record his inability ever to be reasonable in affairs of the heart.

He tries to recall those figures who were most memorable in his life . . . "Those vague shapes that stalk the paths of memory. This gesture that I use . . . where did I get it? This manner of speech, this slight inflection, this way of walking, of sitting down, this getting up . . . where did I get them? Who gave them to me? Where is their counterpart? For just as surely as god gave me arms and legs, a head, eyes and certain masculine paraphernalia . . . someone taught me how to use them."

And then he comes as close as ever he would to an acknowledgment of all that Annabella had given him. " . . . don't for a minute make the mistake of asking what the 'little lady' has given him. What is it that she has contributed toward molding him into this model of manhood that he is today. No . . . for God's sake don't ask questions like that, because, for him, they are unanswerable. And for that reason, embarrassing. And if there is anything in this work that Brer Rabbitt hates . . . it's to be embarrassed. . . . Why don't they come right out and say that *we* did this thing, or *we* made this or that decision. Either, my mother and I, or my wife and I, or my sweetheart and I. No, after the age of ten, or thereabouts, they deny the necessity of reliance on anyone, or anything." Here, he is referring to a "Babbitt of commerce," but it seems clearly some reprehensible part of himself that he is excoriating.

Tyrone has shifted the setting from his present situation back to the Atlantic, probably Atlantic Beach, North Carolina, for he next describes two young women, curvaceous and striking, "swinging along with that easy, empty grace . . . Take the one on the inside, for instance . . . the blonde one. Now, I don't know her, never have seen her before in my life. But if I were to meet her, spend the evening with her, and then if I were never to see her again, why, just from talking with her, and so on, she might leave with me something that would become a part of me for the rest of my life. It might even be some little something of which I am not even conscious. But it would be a part of herself, which she has left with me. . . ."

Tyrone rarely spoke about his father's abandonment of the Power family, but here he speaks openly of what that has done to him. "Fred" asks what it was like to be part of a regular family. "I have often wondered what it would have been like, to have been raised in a family with a father. A family where all the pieces are in their proper places, just as everyone says they should be. Would it have been better . . . who knows? Different, yes . . . but better. . . ." "Fred's" shoulders ever so slightly raise themselves, and fall again. "Too often," he continues, "I have observed that inviolable halo, known as the 'family circle,' and never, except in certain very rare instances, can I regard them without experiencing the sensation of escape. I can't really put it into words. And escape from what, I don't know. But, too often have I seen that circle become a noose, a pair of mental and emotional hand-cuffs, a garrote, and a shroud; and invariably, I whisper a prayer of thanks. . . . You've seen them too, I'm sure. At dinner particularly . . . in some restaurant. Four monuments to repression. Why don't they sometimes jump up and scream, I don't know. They sit there, with nothing to say to each other, wishing to hell they were someplace else, and masking this quite natural revulsion to the whole thing, by keeping up a stream of banalities. They must not allow a silence to ensue, for in those voids, they become even more conscious of their trap." The friend who has enjoyed the warmth and support of a whole family, the "I" character, tells his cynical friend, "I don't remember the time that we weren't more than glad to share the company of any of the others . . . I think (what you are saying) is a lot of bunk. . . . In a family relationship, just as in any other, business or marital, one must work at it, to make it a success. . . . And as for having grown up with a father, it is a wonderful experience. It would be difficult to tell you what it is like, if you have never had one. It must be rather like trying to fly with one of your most important instruments missing." To which "Fred" counters: "If . . . you try to learn to fly, lacking certain means of recognizing attitudes, or reactions, you . . . develop other methods of appreciating them. And I believe that those other resources, in cases like this, come from within a person. And I'm not at all sure that it wasn't better this way . . . I learned self-reliance, dependence, and laid a foundation for a feeling of confidence in myself, and my own ability to do things, far earlier than I would have, had I possessed a paternal buffer. I had to figure a great many things out for myself . . . had to find the answer to a lot of questions through my own processes of trial and error. Things that my mother just would not have known. Then, if I were burned, I would stay away the next time. If it was good, and I liked it, I would come back again. And if it burned me, and yet I liked it . . . I would still be back again. . . . Oh, later on, I did go and see my father. Saw quite a bit of him, in fact. But that's another story. However, all the time that he was gone, and I was growing up, his influence was felt. He was a man I admired, in so many ways, and I used to urge people to tell me stories about him. And there were many. When he had passed, there were none who could deny that he had gone that way. My mother never forgot him, that I know, and she wore the years of their life together, as a beautiful cloak against the bitterness of later days."

Tyrone broke off his "novel" when "Fred's" mother remarried. Here, doubtless he had struck something too painful to explore, even on a fictional level. But he had made intelligible on paper something that had been inchoate in his mind for years. He was very pleased with it; it was reassuring as well. He saw that he had emerged from both the deprivations and the intimate bond of surviving Powers passably well. There was no bitterness in him, even though there was a sense of loss.

Tyrone had been given the additional chore (happily accepted) of supervising the primitive amphitheatre with its graded hillside where the Marines could sit on the ground. When the squadron was not on a run, or cargo mission, he would go up to the film exchange every morning and get a new feature, check it out, and then test the projectors. In March, they showed *A Tree Grows in Brooklyn* with Peggy Ann Garner, James Dunn, and Joan Blondell, as the blowzy, sensual, rough-talking aunt. Its direction by Elia Kazan and the Blondell performance excited Tyrone, and he thought that lady, the veteran of a dozen Warner backstage musicals, was about as fine and sexy as any character actress to come along since Gladys George, who had been "wasted" along with himself in *Marie Antoinette*. He made a mental note to keep Miss Blondell in mind. The cinematographer on *Tree* was his old friend Leon Shamroy, and he sat down and wrote "Shammy" a note of congratulations. Such thoughtfulness did Tyrone no harm when he returned from the war.

During Tyrone's movie season, he obtained a print of Vincente Minnelli's *The Clock*, which was Judy Garland's first non-singing role. Tyrone was becoming a bit more objective about her films at last. He found it "studied," and the love scene in the park "sheer affectation." He thought Keenan Wynn, who was now back from the war, "marvelous. . . . That whole scene was a gem. I thought I would die at that damned old hag at the counter . . . and when she got her fork caught in her pearls I fell off the bench." *The Clock* was followed by *A Royal Scandal*, starring Tallulah Bankhead and Bill Eythe, who was a young leading man the studio was advancing quickly to replace "the old guard," represented by Tyrone, Henry Fonda, et al., in their absence. Eythe was close to both Tyrone and Watson, and Tyrone did not knock him, although he thought his part in the Bankhead film was "jerky." What distressed Tyrone was that there was a cadre of these young men—Eythe, John Dall, Dana Andrews, captained by Van Johnson, who had "seniority" and was another close friend—moving ahead solely because the majority of their peers were in uniform. A punctured eardrum, a heart murmur, a discreet admission of homosexual encounters; these were the distinctions that kept them before the cameras while the others were fighting.

As a moviehouse "manager," Tyrone projected the same qualities which he had around the Fox lot, especially an almost obsessive perfectionism. He was outraged when someone, not in his group, broke the title from one of the features and instead of splicing it back on, simply threw it away. Another fool used adhesive tape as a splicing agent, and Tyrone nearly threw a fit.

In mid-May, an ENSA company arrived on Saipan. This was the British equivalent of the USO. The star of the show was Gertrude Lawrence, whom Tyrone had met in New York through Noël Coward. He wrote Annabella, ". . . I would have loved to have seen another Coward play instead (meaning her *Blithe Spirit*)." To Watson, he confided how much he really had enjoyed it: "We have had more laughs, and while it all hasn't added up to a damn thing, at least it allows you to forget for a few moments, that this is a pretty stinking life. In the evenings when the show is over, we have been going up to the radio station; it is the one place where lights all night are not looked upon with suspicion, and play the piano and sing, and have a wonderful time long after the normal hour for retiring in these parts. . . . And while we are on the subject of the radio. I don't know whether or not you know it, but I am doing a show for the Marine Corps every Sunday afternoon." Tyrone was afraid that Zanuck would hear of it and reinvoke his radio ban on Tyrone. He thought Watson might be able to pick it up on his short wave radio.

The Gertrude Lawrence appearance pointed up the fact to Tyrone that there really was no adequate stage for artists of that caliber. He very soon stopped apologizing to Miss Lawrence as they began a party that was only interrupted by her performances, but after the ENSA company's departure several days later, he decided to rectify the situation. In late May, there was a long, rather ominous lull before the mighty invasion armies would move ashore in Japan. Tyrone made a rough sketch of an outdoor stage and improved amphitheatre, and he, along with Chubb Church and the rest of the crew began constructing what was soon dubbed "The Roosevelt Theatre," in honor of the late President, who had died in April. They toiled over a period of about ten days with the help of a few carpenters who volunteered from the men stationed there. Tyrone was the expert who guided the building crew in shaping the proscenium, the stage apron, and the wings with minuscule dressing rooms. Even so, he did not stand back while the work was going on, but hammered away along with the others.

By the end of the first week of June, the theatre was ready. Opening night gave Tyrone's spirits an enormous lift. He had exhausted himself over the preceding three or four days working on the finishing touches—hauling coral for the

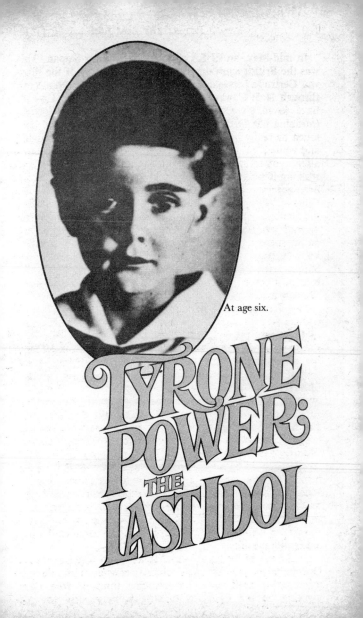

At age six.

TYRONE POWER: THE LAST IDOL

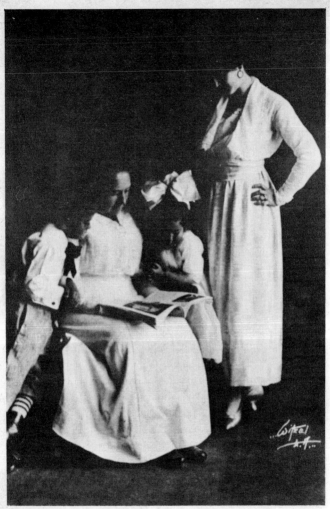

Tyrone and Anne Power with Frieda "Pet" Tracy
while mother Patia looks on. Circa 1917–1918.

Tyrone's father Frederick Tyrone Power, a star in his own right, at the peak of his success in 1917.

TYRONE E. POWER
"Ty"

Dramatics, '30, '31; Senior "B" Treasurer, '31; German Club, '31; Class Basketball, '29, '30.

"Ty" came to Purcell from Dayton Prep, and in a short time became a favorite with students and teachers alike. "Ty" is a good student, but his acting makes him the logical successor of John Barrymore.

At the time of his graduation from a Catholic high school in Cincinnati, Tyrone was already known for his acting abilities.

Father and son at the depot in Montreal, 1930.

Father and son in *The Merchant of Venice,*
Chicago, 1931.

Tyrone with Madeleine Carroll in *Lloyds of London*
(1936), the film that launched him as a leading man.

With Irving Berlin on the set of *Alexander's Ragtime Band* (1938).

Tyrone as Count Axel de Fersen with Norma Shearer
as *Marie Antoinette* (1938).

With Alice Faye, a torrid scene from *In Old Chicago* (1938).

Rare group shot of "Fox family" on promotional tour, 1939.
From left: Darryl F. Zanuck, Virginia Zanuck, Sonja Henie,
Mayor Rossi, Anita Louise, Annabella, Tyrone, Loretta Young,
Don Ameche; Sidney Toler and Cesar Romero behind Miss Louise.

Lunch break on set of *Suez* (1939). Tyrone and Annabella
with Director Allan Dwan (left) and cameraman Peverell Marley.

Annabella brings her new husband to her native city, Paris, 1939.

Tyrone mobbed by London fans on his honeymoon, 1939.

Henry Fonda, Annabella, Frances Brokaw Fonda and Tyrone inspect the Powers' new Brentwood property, 1939.

Tyrone with another Fonda, Jane, 1939.

Tyrone as *Liliom* with Betty Garde, 1941.

Relaxing on *The Black Swan* location with co-star Laird Cregar, 1942.

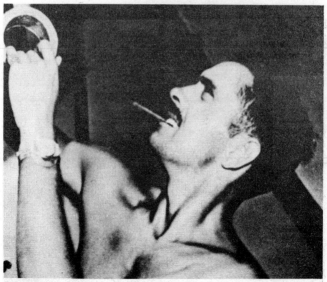
Construction work in the Pacific, Saipan, 1945.

Linda Christian with Tyrone on location for *The Black Rose,* Africa, 1950.

Tyrone and Watson Webb, 1942.

Tyrone with Judith Anderson and Raymond Massey
recording *John Brown's Body*, New York, 1953.

A new romance: Tyrone with writer Mary Roblee
on location for *The Eddy Duchin Story*, New York, 1955.

Tyrone and Debbie on the patio of Watson's
Lake Arrowhead home, 1958.

The skipper of *The Black Swan*, 1958.

On location in Spain, 1958.

Tyrone Power, actor, 1914–1958.

decor, hanging the curtains. Dick Jergens, a popular recording artist for years with his dance band, now was in the
Marines, where he had gathered a group of musicians from
among the Corps to form a new sweet and swing band.
Jergens opened the Roosevelt Theatre with an evening concert
of old and new favorites, receiving an enthusiastic reception
and having the occasion graced by the appearance of
"manager" Tyrone Power, thanking everyone involved in
creating the facility.

Meanwhile, Annabella was in Paris on May 8, which was
V-E Day (Victory in Europe) and celebrated with her family
and friends. It was a day, for her, of nearly incredible events.
And yet there was in Annabella a remarkable prescience about
key occurrences in life. She had a sometimes frightening
ability to be in the right place at just the right moment. In the
tumultuous aftermath. she performed again, playing two
weeks in English at the Théâtre de la Madeleine for the troops
lucky enough to be in Paris. Annabella was fiercely patriotic
toward all things American, and the mere sight of the Stars
and Stripes made her weep and filled her heart with gratitude.
Once again, Annabella conveyed to Tyrone in a flimsy
V-mail-type letter sent from Paris to Saipan that she had
never felt so needed in her life as during those months with the
USO. She loved performing for the troops, and they
responded in kind. Few performers during the war won the affection from the soldiers in the field that Annabella had. She
found roughing it in peculiar and often perilous places to be
exhilarating rather than an ordeal. Ironically, Annabella was
apparently happiest away from home, "soldiering" in a good
cause; Tyrone couldn't wait for it all to be over. Everywhere
he was sent was uncomfortable to him, although he attempted
to upgrade his living conditions the moment he arrived in a
new place. On Saipan, he and his tentmates installed a ceiling
of nylon material made from a red cargo chute, making "the
whole drab establishment look like something out of the
Arabian Nights."
The tempo of cargo flights was stepped up as they moved
into midsummer. In one week, Tyrone was in the air forty-
seven hours. The invasion of the island empire was set for late
August or early September, or so rumor had it, and the
heightened activity seemed to make that probable. In his

exhaustion, he had occasional nightmares, and in one of them he approached Judy, who was with Watson, and they gave him "the freeze-out." This nightmare coincided with Judy's marriage in late July to director Vincente Minnelli, and may have been sired by Tyrone's custom of following her activities in detail through reports from Watson, from other friends in Hollywood, and the gossip columns of newspapers and magazines sent him.

Consciously, all of Tyrone's thoughts of home always centered around Annabella. He felt that their being apart had brought them closer together. He was attempting to purge himself of the flaws he knew had shaken their marriage to its foundations. He was reading Freud in his spare moments. This absorption in self-analysis came soon after his attempt at fiction. But he thought the Viennese father of psychoanalysis should be taken in small doses.

Not unexpectedly, Twentieth Century–Fox saw the end of the war looming just ahead, and they began repairing relations between themselves and their top star of two and a half years ago. Lew Schreiber, business aide to Zanuck, wrote Tyrone a long, warm letter, telling him how wonderful it would be when all of this horror was past and they were making pictures together again. Edie Goetz, wife of the head of the studio through much of the war, finally decided to write Tyrone (after a silence of more than two years), giving him all the latest gossip, and informing him that everyone is giving "tent parties."

Annabella put her mother, Mama Lily, on a liner bound for New York on July 16. Father Paul Charpentier had died earlier that summer of heart failure, induced by the loss of his adored son, Pierre, the strain of months of malnutrition, and of the monumental damage inflicted on his country, not to mention his own property. Annabella was to follow by plane that same week. Mother and daughter would meet in New York, and Annabella planned to return to the Saltair house, which had been reopened, after word of their imminent arrival, by Anne Power Hardenbergh, who had come up from Point Loma.

On August 6, the U. S. Air Force dropped the world's second atomic bomb on the city of Hiroshima, wiping out the heart of that city and killing over 100,000 Japanese; on the ninth, even before the damage to Hiroshima could be assessed, the Americans annihilated Nagasaki. The word on Saipan and aboard the invasion convoys already steaming across the Pacific toward Japan was that the Japanese would surrender before their great cities were reduced to smoldering craters. On August 10, Tyrone wrote Watson:

. . . the thought in everyone's mind, and the subject of all conversation these days is a new bomb. And it is not just the immediate effect that it is going to have on the Japs, and the war in general . . . but the effect it is going to have on us all for the rest of our lives. For as surely as I sit here writing to you this morning . . . our whole lives have changed. They are no more the same than they were the day the first horseless carriage appeared. . . . They are well on the road to destroying it all, of course you know that. The only question everyone asks is, "How much more time do we have . . . how many years?"

Yesterday I was fortunate enough to be able to see some of the pictures that were taken just after the first one was dropped. Even if I were allowed to tell you what it was like, I doubt whether I could. It actually defies description. There are no words in our poor vocabulary, at present to draw an adequate picture of it. The human mind cannot grasp it, at present. Watty, it is simply staggering. One can only look at it, and say, "My God!" . . . this has changed the picture entirely. It just cannot be humanly possible for anyone, or anything to hold out very long. . . . With us too, it's particularly in mind, for we know that they [the bombs] must be around here someplace. . . . Just let them be careful . . . that's all I have to say.

Annabella was settled in the Saltair house again by Labor Day. Daughter Annie returned from Minnie Astor's estate in Rhinebeck, Dutchess County, New York, where she had remained while her mother was overseas. Birdlike Mama Lily was given the small guest room and seemed very happy to be secure and with close family again. Her English was poor, even though she had studied intensively just before coming over and on the boat. Something of a household staff was pulled together. Ysidro, the gardener, had remained throughout the leasing of the house, and Addy Branch, the cook, returned. With Anne Hardenbergh and daughter Pixie already there, Annabella felt that everything was just as it was when Tyrone last was in the house.

Zanuck was back at Fox and making preparations to film W. Somerset Maugham's latest and best-selling novel, *The Razor's Edge*, the story of a young American's quest for spiritual serenity in a materialistic world. The studio head was telling everyone, including Tyrone by cable, that he had bought it as the vehicle for Tyrone's return to films, following his war service. His intention was to make it the most distinguished film in the history of his studio. In typical Zanuck fashion, a production schedule already had been set up, based upon the assumption that Tyrone would be out of the service by November, a date which Zanuck considered conservative.

But Tyrone never had been more wretched. He had come down with dengue fever, also known as "break-bone fever." All he could say was "Fuck the whole damned business . . . everything." He was about as far from the serenity of *Razor's Edge* hero, Larry Darrell, as a man could get—aching, constipated, burning up with fever and the tropical heat, and with a case of athlete's foot blistering his toes. Life itself seemed futile and pointless, and he was fearful that he would be so late in being separated from the Marines, they would give his part to Dana Andrews and hand him something like *Son of Zorro* "or other trash" for his "triumphant" return to the screen. In the midst of these *douleurs*, some reporters found him stretched out on his bed and began to interview him. He gave them one to remember, much of it unprintable.

Then the fever left him as suddenly as it had come. He was his eager, curious, and enthusiastic self again, and his superiors gave him permission to make two cargo flights to "The Empire" of Japan. He wrote Annabella:

. . . We had a most wonderful see around the country, and got a little more the feeling of the people. If there is one thing of which I am sure in this world it is that they hate us! You can feel it in the air. You can see it on their faces, when they pass you on the street. They don't do anything outwardly . . . but you can sense that it is deep down inside. If you meet their gaze, they turn their eyes away . . . just little things like that, but if you see enough of them it all adds up to the big fact that, they hate us.

Yesterday we got a jeep and took a drive up toward Tokyo. The roads are horrible, and we couldn't get all the way there in the time allotted to us. But we did get to Yokohama, and spent about an hour driving around that graveyard of what was once a great and beautiful city. It staggers the imagination and beggars description. I'm sure that if you had seen Rotterdam, or some of the places in Europe you might have been prepared for what we saw, but for us, it was just unbelievable. Mile after mile of nothingness . . . rubble . . . nothing to even indicate where streets and homes or shops had been. The downtown section fared a little better. . . .

We drove up on the heights to the south of town, where the beautiful homes had been. There things were a little better. It seems that the fires did most of their damage in the valleys, and the hills escaped the worst of the damage. At least one can get an idea of what it was once like. . . . A beautiful church . . . the Sacred Heart, still dominates one of the heights, and is completely untouched. . . . There is so much I want to tell you . . . so much I have seen to be able to put it all down on paper. But I have it all locked in the "book and volume" of my brain, and I will describe it all to you one day. . . .

I miss you, my darling . . . more than you can imagine. I hope you are not still too mad at me for getting you to cancel your tour out this way. I know now that we would never have met, and it would have just been too maddening to know you were out here some place, and that I might be going home at any moment. I'm sure I did the right thing in asking you to forget it. . . .

Give Annie my love, and explain to her why I haven't had a chance to write lately. There has just been too much to do. A kiss to Maman, and Anne, and tell them I think of them, and miss them very much.

Each morning brings us a day closer to the garden, and days by the pool, and at night my dreams are full of you . . . and moments we will have.

> All my love,
> Tyrone.

• • •

To his mother, he wrote of his exhaustion:

> . . . Physically, I am well, although I get very tired from
> time to time. I notice it first in my right eye. Strange, but
> that's where it seems to get me. Everything goes kind of
> soft, and I have a time getting it into focus.

By the first of November, Tyrone was on Guam, waiting
for papers and a ship that would take him the rest of the way
home. He had secured passage on a ship leaving on the sixth
for Portland, which would bring him home by Thanksgiving.
He was apprehensive, perhaps even a little fearful, about his
first meeting with Annabella. Her letters had not suggested
that there would be recriminations; it was just a feeling he
had.

VII

RETURN TO
ANNABELLA

THE U.S.S. *Marvin McIntyre* eased into its berth in Portland. It was November 21, 1945, and there was a huge crowd of civilians waving and craning to see on the dock below. Then Tyrone's spirits soared as he spotted Annabella, dressed in a white raincoat. In a second he knew that all of his forebodings had been baseless; she had come all the way up the coast to meet him.

The moment the ship was secure to the pier, Tyrone vaulted over the ship rail and jumped to the dock in a real-life scene every bit as acrobatic as anything in his Douglas Fairbanks cycle. Several hundred other homeward-bound Marines and soldiers screamed their encouragement as Tyrone embraced and kissed her. One soldier yelled, "Take it easy, Jesse." Annabella, weeping with emotion, had her eyes squeezed tightly shut. Someone with a Graflex press camera managed to take a picture as he released his hold a moment to take a good look at her. "How'd you get so smart, Blondie?" he asked, wondering how she knew when his transport would be docking.

"I have friends," Annabella said cryptically. He said later that when the brief conversation stopped and their eyes met finally, "It was the top moment I've ever lived . . . It was as though you'd died and gone to hell and then you'd come back and there was an angel holding open the door of a heaven you'd ceased to believe existed at all. . . . When I looked around at the other guys—I knew they were thinking the same thing about the women that were waiting for them."

The idyll lasted several months. Annabella had got the Saltair house back to the beautiful, slightly formal and stately home it had been before Tyrone had gone away. There were no recriminations, no apologies, on either side. Life moved on.

In January, Spyros Skouras and other Fox high executives threw a huge "Welcome Home" party in New York's Hotel Pierre Ballroom to honor Tyrone and, just so no feelings would be ruffled, they elected to co-honor Dana Andrews, who had taken his place so willingly and competently. Unfortunately, some of the guests were clearly not as familiar with Mr. Andrews as the Fox officials were, for he was frequently addressed as "Mr. Dana." Annabella and Tyrone found this quite amusing, although they were most gracious to the usurper.

Patia was very much involved with her work for the woman electrotherapist, Dr. Drown. Since Annabella seemed a little run-down, Patia urged her daughter-in-law to come in for at least one treatment, which Annabella agreed to. In Dr. Drown's office, she was hitched up to a buzzing machine and told to stand on the "magnetic mat" so the electrons could work their magic. During the session, Annabella surreptitiously stepped off the mat, but Dr. Drown was not aware and subsequently told her that the treatment had done this and that for her system. Tyrone was amused to hear of the exposure of Dr. Drown, but let his mother's enthusiasm (often, so like his own) run its course rather than disillusion her. He was more philosophical than shrewd about such matters. He believed that a little deception did no one much harm.

W. Somerset Maugham was seventy years old when what he called "my last major work," *The Razor's Edge*, was published. Darryl Zanuck had paid him a quarter of a million dollars for it, and when shooting began more than a year and a half later in May 1946, the budget on the film had gone to three million dollars. It would involve the skills of nearly all of the four thousand employees at Fox, its various offices scattered around the world, and, almost for the first time, bring out in Zanuck a quest for perfection that he had not shown previously, even in such films as *In Old Chicago* and *A Tree Grows in Brooklyn*.

That special care had begun early. Originally, Zanuck had wanted George Cukor to direct the picture. He had made arrangements to borrow the brilliant director of *Dinner at*

Eight (1933), *David Copperfield* (1935), *Camille* (1936), *The Philadelphia Story* (1940), and *Gaslight* (1944), to name a few of his greatest successes, from his home studio, Metro-Goldwyn-Mayer. This was in the winter of 1944-45, long before the end of the war. Cukor had read the book in typescript before publication and had admired it very much.

Lamar Trotti's adaptation was sent to Cukor from Zanuck's office, but his reaction was negative. He thought it was "entertainment, which means dancing and country clubs and all that crap. Nothing to indicate you were supposed to sit down and listen to what was being said. Whatever important things this script retained [of the novel] were sandwiched between all kinds of nonsense." So Cukor told him he would direct if Zanuck would get Maugham to write a new script. Zanuck protested, saying that Maugham would want too much money, but when Cukor phoned his old friend, Maugham, in New York, the novelist said, "I'll do it for nothing."

Maugham came to California and stayed in Cukor's lovely Mediterranean-style villa for several weeks, turning out a screenplay which Cukor thought "wonderful." Maugham wrote a little prologue for the players and director: "Please note that this is, on the whole, a comedy and should be played lightly by everyone except in the definitely serious passages. The actors should pick-up one another's cues as smartly as possible, and there's no harm if they cut in on one another as people do in ordinary life. I'm all against pauses and silences. If the actors cannot give significance to their lines without these, they're not worth their salaries. The lines are written to be spoken; they have all the significance needed if they are spoken with intelligence and feeling. The director is respectfully reminded that the action should accompany and illustrate the dialogue. Speed, speed, speed."

Maugham wrote the script mornings in longhand. He was very pleased with it. It was obviously a labor of love. Zanuck liked the Maugham screenplay, or so he said, but he added there were a few problems. He said that he had written his top leading man, Tyrone Power, about the project and Tyrone begged Zanuck to hold up production until the war was over and he was free. By November 1945, when Tyrone was discharged from the Marines, Cukor was deeply committed to another project for Metro, *Desire Me*, with Greer Garson and

Robert Mitchum, a film far more plagued by problems than any *The Razor's Edge* might endure and eventually disowned by Cukor.

Zanuck then assigned *The Razor's Edge* to Edmund Goulding and, feeling no obligation to Cukor any longer, returned to Trotti's original script. He sent Maugham an original Matisse as compensation for his weeks of unfilmed work and one can but wonder how the film would have turned out had the Maugham screenplay been produced. Probably the old adage held firm; great novelists make poor screenwriters.

Goulding was an Englishman who had been in Hollywood since the mid-Twenties. Although he had been married, he was considered a bachelor through many of his Hollywood years and, as such, palled around with Tyrone, Errol Flynn, David Niven, and other "playboys" whenever they were free of domestic entanglements.

Despite some mild criticism he would receive upon the film's release, Zanuck was more than justified in holding out for Tyrone as the central character, Larry Darrell. He seemed born for the part. There were so many facets of Larry within him. Larry was sensitive, introspective, curious about God and why we are here. What Larry was not, of course, was sensual, but he was so damnably attractive, women pursued him everlastingly. In Lamar Trotti's rather careful, journeyman version of the book and in Tyrone's interpretation, Larry moves beyond sensuality to celibacy.

In order to achieve this saintly mien, director Goulding took Tyrone aside and asked him to abstain from having relations with Annabella until the crucial meeting with the holy man in India, Shri Ganesha, has taken place in that guru's mountain retreat. Later, Larry was to say (in the book), "I am in the fortunate position that sexual indulgence with me has been a pleasure rather than a need. I know by personal experience that in nothing are the wise men of India more dead right than in their contention that chastity intensely enhances the power of the spirit."

For several nights that week, Annabella brooded about Tyrone's perfunctory kiss and then his abrupt posture of sleep, "so unlike Tyrone." She had heard the usual stories that accompanied the production of his films—Gene Tierney was madly in love with him and a torrid romance was under way in their dressing rooms—but she saw or felt no disinterest on his part. This seemed to be an elective thing, as though he had read that it was bad for his health.

Tyrone, very much like the Tyrone who had wondered about walking out on their publicity man, told her that Goulding had forbidden them to have sex. Annabella then remembered something Pat Boyer, her matron of honor, had told her a long time ago. When Goulding was directing her husband, Charles, in *The Constant Nymph* (1943), he had told him the same thing. When Tyrone heard that this was his director's way of purging his leading men's faces of any carnal hint, he doubled up with laughter, then reached out and they fell into bed together. When he arrived on the set the next day, his face was blanched and his eyes glassy. Goulding took one look, nodded, and said, "That is what I was looking for," and shot the scene.

Maugham himself appears in the film, played with his usual suave nonchalance by Herbert Marshall. A much stronger character with a number of Maugham's own prejudices is Elliott Templeton, a snobbish Chicagoan who much prefers the salons of Paris, and played in the movie by waspish and stylishly cantankerous Clifton Webb. Templeton's character and details of his life were taken almost directly from Sir Henry "Chips" Channon, an American who lived most of his life in England and took British citizenship. The parallels here are endless. Channon was flattered by the borrowings for literary reasons, calling the book a masterpiece.

Because of the clear derivation from real life, Clifton Webb's Elliott is much the most memorable performance in the picture, but one other character deserves mention, since she, too, was drawn from life. And that is Sophie Mac-Donald, whose young husband has been killed in a motor accident and thereafter cannot cope with life, drifting into a world of demimondaines in France and eventually being murdered in Toulon and dumped into the bay.

According to Anne Baxter, who played Sophie and won an Academy Award for it, there were thirteen other actresses tested for the part before Gregory Ratoff, one of Zanuck's favorite toadies, proposed her. Like Tyrone in his role, Miss Baxter understood Sophie right down to the Illinois ground they both had walked on. "I was born fifty miles from Chicago and went to the same kind of dances. Who could forget a country club named The Pottawattomi?''

A more idealized girl in the book is Isabel Bradley, who really only comes to life when she behaves rottenly. Isabel, played by the gorgeous exotic beauty Gene Tierney, who had proved she was an actress in *Leave Her to Heaven* (1945), is desperately in love with Larry, and does her best to trap him, even at one point trying to seduce him and failing. Eventually, Isabel does something that leads by an indirect path to Sophie's murder, so she grows in interest as the book progresses.

Tyrone had to fight to sustain a magnetism that would believably attract not only the various women to him but the audience as well. Larry is a man in search of perfection in character and as he becomes progressively more saintly, the burden on Tyrone becomes greater. In the end, when he renounces every last worldly thing in his life, both Larry and Tyrone lose their audience. Bosley Crowther in the New York *Times* was to write: ''His [Tyrone's] face glows like Mr. Sunshine's and he affects a sublime serenity. But the quality of 'goodness' that is in him must depend for demonstration on no more.'' *Life* magazine was far more generous. They named the picture their ''Movie of the Week,'' called the film ''superb'', and said, ''Tyrone Power and Gene Tierney, who have reached success more on good looks than on ability, have put themselves in the company of the movies' most accomplished actors.'' The production had been touted twice by *Life*; first in a photo essay by Ralph Crane published in its August 12, 1946, issue, and then again in its review, which followed by a number of weeks. Photographer Crane covered everything and everyone connected with the film, including a shot of ''Cutter Watson Webb, whose job is one of Hollywood's trickiest.'' Watson, after his magnificent job of editing *A Wing and a Prayer* for Hathaway (1944), was now one of Zanuck's favorite technicians. There was also another friend of Tyrone's pictured in *Life*—his stand-in Tommy Noonan, who had been brought out of Cincinnati by his school chum's success.

The movie, despite the inherent weakness of Tyrone's part, had everything going for it. During the filming, Anne Baxter had to leave the production for three or four weeks for major surgery, and during her absence, everyone, especially Tyrone and Gene Tierney, got terribly close, the way people do when

they are together in a movie or a play, but she was the outsider
upon her return. Since the character of Sophie MacDonald
becomes an outsider once she takes to alcohol, drugs, and
men following her husband's death, in her words, "I used
that like mad. It was very good for me." There was another
accidental plus for the movie in its music. The two main
themes—Isabel's Waltz and Sophie's Theme—had been composed by their director, Edmund Goulding. Miss Baxter did
not know that he was a composer until one day when "he took
us to his bungalow with his interesting, fascinating mother,
who was a psychic. He played the music [Sophie's Theme] for
us, a hairdresser, Ione, and myself. Then he went to sleep at
his desk [it was said that Goulding was an occasional drug-
user]." The song he played for them was "Mam'selle," the
alternate title for Sophie's Theme. Before the movie opened at
the Roxy in New York in November, Goulding's song, a
haunting, nostalgic ballad with a Gallic flavor, had become
the most popular song in the nation, as reported by the weekly
radio show, "Your Hit Parade," which it remained for a
number of weeks.

Tyrone grew to admire Goulding as a director more every
day. The man knew what Tyrone was fighting both within
himself and within the character and he tried to balance the
two and draw out the best in each for dramatic impact. Miss
Baxter remembers Goulding's "language." "It was a peculiar
shorthand. An emotional shorthand. I remember the day of
the test, he said, 'Oh, oh, the violins. Steady. The violins. The
violins.' A lot of people didn't understand a word he said. I
think he was especially good with women. He had an inner
sense . . . totally different [from Mankiewicz]. Eddie was
much less precise. And he didn't have the sense of humor that
Joe had. You had to be very careful with Eddie. He was both
man and woman, and sometimes when you'd expect him to
react like a man, he'd react like a woman. There was one
disastrous scene, which was never in the final picture and
never should have been shot. It wouldn't work. It wouldn't
play and it wouldn't move. And, I don't know, we were still
working at eight o'clock at night and I'd been weeping for
hours. And we were behind two Whitney steamer trunks and
there was this picture of two heads above the steamer trunks,
and I said, 'God, Eddie, doesn't that look like two crows on a
fence.' Well, never in his life had he directed a scene that

looked like crows on a fence. I felt terrible and sorry about it, but I also knew it would never be in the picture. It wasn't his fault or our fault (Tyrone's or mine) or anybody's fault. An overbalance.'' Fussing over every inch of footage, Zanuck did all of the final cutting on the picture, and he was brilliant in that. He was an autocrat there, and only one director, Joe Mankiewicz, could really assert himself in the cutting room.

Zanuck hovered around and over the production in a state of agitation, worry, and total possessiveness. It was to be the picture he wanted to be remembered by. His "yes-men" and even more disinterested parties who had seen parts of it in the cutting room (from the studio, of course; no outsiders were permitted to see so much as a frame) were tossing the word "masterpiece" around.

When the final cut had been scored by Alfred Newman and it was ready for release, Watson was personally ordered to carry it by private compartment on the Twentieth Century to New York, guarding it with his life until it was handed over to the projectionist at the Roxy. Unfortunately, that print was not checked out for flaws, and when it was screened opening night for the press and invited guests, there were some imperfections in the sound that would have to be cleared up.

The reviews were mixed; they were certainly not the unanimous raves which Zanuck had been hoping for. But everyone conceded that something important had been attempted and that it was worthwhile. In its persistent effort to show the folly of most everyday pursuits, it was far ahead of its time. If it had been released in the nineteen-sixties, when Zen Buddhism was beginning to attract many followers in the Western world, it would have been even considered topical. As it was, nearly everyone considered it an offbeat love story with a most peculiar hero—the antithesis of Clark Gable—a man who renounced women, material goods, and earthbound adventure for a long pilgrimage in quest of perfect goodness. While *The Razor's Edge* was nominated for an Academy Award that year, it did not have a ghost of a chance of winning against *The Best Years of Our Lives*, which was about a different sort of pilgrimage—that of life as it was before war had disrupted everything. Clifton Webb was nominated for his splendid Elliott Templeton and should have won, but he was denied it by an emotional reaction (understandably so) to Harold Russell's first acting effort as the paraplegic (which

Russell himself was) in *Best Years*. Annie Baxter won hers, much to her surprise, over Ethel Barrymore's chilling performance in *The Spiral Staircase*. Tyrone was not even nominated, nor would he ever be, although he should have been the following year for his next film, the controversial *Nightmare Alley*.

Life with Annabella was once again strained. It was not simply that Tyrone had changed much during the war, but Annabella, too, had gone off to war and new worlds had opened up for her. She had hoped that something of their old love would be rekindled by proximity and a resumption of their old life in the Saltair house. But that had not happened.

Everything seemed against them, even the house itself. In late May 1946, when *The Razor's Edge* was in its earliest stages of production, Tyrone and Annabella hosted another of their Sunday play parties, with all of the old crowd—Rex Harrison and wife Lilli Palmer, Cesar Romero, John McClain (of the New York *Sun* and the handsomest of New York's drama critics), and the David Nivens. Primula Niven had just arrived from England with their five-month-old son, and this would be her first Hollywood party. After a cookout by the poolside, they all came indoors where the crowd decided that they were bored with charades and Cesar suggested a new game called "Sardines," which he remembered playing as a child, in which the lights are turned out and everyone hides until there is just one person left with no available closet or table to conceal himself in or under. The Saltair house did not especially lend itself to such nonsense. It was a mansion of spacious rooms; the furniture was uncrowded; there were steps down into the living room; *and*, unfortunately, there was an unlocked door leading onto a flight of steps into the basement.

Lilli Palmer heard a tumbling sound and then a cry. Cesar knew immediately what had happened and, knowing the house, headed for a light switch and the cellar door. It was open, and lying at the foot, unconscious, was "Primmie" Niven. Annabella and Lilli were more used to seeing injured people than any of the other women present, having both undergone air raids during the war. Lilli laid Primmie's head in her lap and made her comfortable while an ambulance was called. Annabella fetched a bowl of ice water and put cold compresses on her forehead. Then the ambulance arrived, Primmie was put inside with Niven following, and everyone waited in a state of shock for Niven to phone from the hospital.

Instead, Niven himself returned to the party with "good news." "She's very concussed," he said, repeating the doctor's words, but he assured them that there was nothing to worry about. The doctor told him, "She'll have to stay absolutely quiet and in the dark for a few days. She'll be fine."

On the following day, Primmie's condition remained unchanged, which her doctors considered hopeful, and Niven worked throughout the day at his studio, where he was making a dreadful picture with Ginger Rogers (*The Magnificent Doll*). He dropped by the hospital on his way home and sat with his wife for a while, but the matron urged him to go home and get some sleep. Primmie's eyes were open and she recognized him, so he was encouraged enough to leave. But then around eleven that evening, a call came to the Nivens' "Little Pink House," of which he was so proud, that a blood clot had developed and they would have to operate. Primmie Niven died during the operation at the age of twenty-five.

Of course, the Sunday parties stopped after that. A Yale lock was affixed to the cellar door . . . too late. It seemed too late for both Annabella and Tyrone as well. Something wonderful between them had died during the war. It seemed impossible to recall it to life.

Annabella took the first long step away from the situation. She was asked to play the lesbian in Jean-Paul Sartre's *Huis Clos* (*No Exit*), which had been translated for a New York production. She would be co-starring with Claude Dauphin and Ruth Ford for Jed Harris, and the opening was set for early September. Tyrone had completed retakes on *The Razor's Edge*, and he followed her East, attending the first reading of the play (and satisfying himself that Annabella's lesbian role was "a classic"). He even was asked to stand in as the porter who opens the door to hell, ushering in the doomed characters "who find that hell is other people."

John Huston directed *No Exit*, and his only great error was to break the longish one-acter into two parts with an intermission. The mood was broken while the audience went out for a smoke, but most of the critics praised both the play and the performers, most of them singling out Annabella for special commendation. It was still running when *The Razor's Edge* had its premiere in New York on November 19. The Powers were reunited, but breathing life into that romance was impossible. Yet the bond between them remained strong. They were rarely out of touch until he died.

VIII

---

*NIGHTMARE
ALLEY*

THE RAZOR'S EDGE, despite its artistic pretensions, turned out to be a smash, eventually bringing in more than five million dollars. Any doubts Zanuck may have had about Tyrone's status as a superstar vanished in a torrent of box-office receipts. The two men became close again, and Tyrone's domestic crisis was discussed briefly. Zanuck's solution was to get Tyrone away for a while.

In mid-August, 1946, Tyrone was off on a good-will tour of South America sponsored by the Fox Studios. His hand-picked companions were actor Cesar Romero, secretary Bill Gallagher, publicist Jim Denton, and co-pilot and navigator John Jeffries. They were flying in a twin-engine Beechcraft christened *Saludos Amigos* and they flew down the west coast of South America, crossed over to Argentina, where they were given a state dinner by Juan and Evita Perón; then came back by way of Cuba, where there was a gala party for them at the club in the Hotel Nacional. In the several days of their stay in Argentina, the Peróns looked after them and even wept at their departure. Even though both Tyrone and Cesar had recently returned from war duty, Cesar had been in the Pacific in the Coast Guard, they both felt honored by the Peróns' attention and were doubtless ignorant of the close ties between the Peróns government and the Nazis and of the presence in Argentina at that time of many Nazi fugitives. Tyrone remained a political naïf to the end.

Yet another best-selling novel was on Zanuck's shelf awaiting Tyrone's return to films. *Captain from Castile* would mark his return to the swashbuckling hero, a genre he had made his own. There were several distinct differences, however, from your run-of-the-Main derring-do. It was the work of one of the two most popular and literate authors of historical romance then writing, Samuel Shellabarger (the other being Thomas Costain); it was more epic in scope than anything of the sort attempted before; and it was to be shot on location where most of the historical action had taken place, Mexico.

While Lamar Trotti was preparing the screenplay and director Henry King scouting out locations, Tyrone, who was now formally separated from Annabella, had become involved, inevitably perhaps, with his female counterpart, Lana Turner.

Lana had had as many affairs as Tyrone, but she had married many of her lovers. Evie Wynn had brought them together, even though they had been acquaintances for years. To Evie, and to a great many others, they seemed perfectly matched. When King's assistant, Bob Webb, saw them chasing each other down a stretch of beach, both in white swimwear, tanned and glowing with health and with what everyone took to be delight in one another's company, it struck Webb as one of the most beautiful sights he had ever seen.

Lana, too, had come from a broken home, and there was a dominant mother-figure in her background, but Mildred Turner was not on the same social level as Patia Power. Mildred had been a beautician, and worked in a beauty parlor while daughter Julia Jean (her name was changed to "Lana" by her first director, Mervyn Leroy) attended Hollywood High School. Her father had been murdered after winning a large amount of money at cards. Much of this background was unknown to Tyrone before their affair began.

Nevertheless, the couple had much in common. They both needed to be surrounded by supportive, close friends much of the time, *and* left alone the rest of the time. Lana was bright and witty and she loved a ribald joke—she had quite a few of her own in her repertoire. Sometimes she would get nearly hysterical with laughter. Yet Lana and Tyrone were very private people, loners in a very real sense.

They were both sensualists. Touch and proximity were as important to them as sex. When their affair first began, Lana was living in a large home on Crown Drive in the heart of Brentwood. Tyrone began spending a great deal of time there, but he felt it was awkward because her three-year-old daughter, Cheryl, also was in the house. On the other hand, he was very good with the child, as he was with most children. He seemed far more relaxed with Lana in her dressing room at Metro, where she was making *Cass Timberlane* from a Sinclair Lewis potboiler. Since the film was a drama, Tyrone contributed a little something by keeping Lana in a bubbly mood off-camera, saving herself for the emotion-charged exchanges with co-star Spencer Tracy.

Tyrone, for a change, was completely faithful to Lana. When, by some chance, a rival might threaten their relationship, at a party or on a soundstage, Lana had no compunction about going up to the girl and telling her "hands off."

Tyrone's alliance with Lana Turner might well have led to marriage, following a divorce from Annabella, but for one distressing element. Lana was in the hands of one of Hollywood's "Dr. Feel goods." Given to bouts of melancholia far deeper than anything Tyrone ever had to endure, she was given amphetamines in a mild dosage that kept her gay most of the time and ready to party all night. But there were times when she was clearly out of control, her laughter too shrill and her moods irrational. These occasions frightened Tyrone and he suggested that she change doctors, but, apparently, she would not.

When production began on *Captain from Castile* near Patzcuaro, Mexico, Tyrone was considerably relieved to be far from Hollywood and its complications. As Pedro de Vargas, he was playing a youth about fourteen years younger than he was. But that was all right, because they cast old-time movie star Antonio Moreno as his father, Don Francisco. Pedro's adventures in Spain and Mexico were epic in scope and spectacular in execution. He took on the Spanish Inquisition at home and, in Mexico, many of Montezuma's bravest warriors, as well as Spanish turncoats, maturing by the sword, you might say. Not least of the film's pictorial treasures was Cesar Romero, a giant monument in the helmet and armor of the Conquistador Hernando Cortez. As the camera tracked in for a close shot of Cortez, his magnificence fairly took one's breath away.

Jean Peters, who already had attracted Howard Hughes and whose screen career would be brief, plays the whore who

follows Pedro through all of the battles in the New World and
Lee J. Cobb the embittered warrior who is forced to kill his
own mother so that the Inquisition will not burn her at the
stake.

One of Lana's irrational whims struck her over New Year's.
She was starring in *Green Dolphin Street*, a period piece also
derived from a best-seller and intended for the women fans,
when she decided that she and Tyrone should not be separated
on New Year's Eve. When she arrived in Mexico City, her im-
pulsive mood had worn off. In something of a panic, she
phoned Tyrone in Patzcuaro, nearly a hundred miles away in
the mountains.

Tyrone did not sound elated to learn that she was just over
the mountains. "Jesus Christ!" he said, and asked what she
was doing in Mexico City.

"I'm here to have a belated Christmas dinner with you.
Now how do I get to where you are?"

"Jesus Christ!" he repeated.

But Tyrone had a small plane sent over to pick her up, and
the situation eased a bit when they were together. The cast and
crew brightened, too, when they heard her gutsy laughter.
They remember her as "a good-natured dame." They, too,
had knocked off work until after New Year's, and the
partying didn't stop while Lana was there.

When reporters heard that Lana had flown to Tyrone's
side, Annabella was awakened at her hotel in New York by a
gossip columnist, who wanted to know what she thought
about Tyrone's Mexican meeting. "Why don't you ask
heem?" she wanted to know.

Then bad weather set in. Lana said, "It rained. It roared.
. . . I wept for two days." There was no way even a small
plane could take her away from Patzcuaro back to Mexico
City and a scheduled airline. She was more than twenty-four
hours late arriving on the set of *Green Dolphin Street*. Instead
of being reprimanded, she writes that "Suddenly all the
blazing lights went up and there they were, Saville [the
director] and the whole cast—in serapes and sombreros just
like mine! Someone hit a big note on the piano and they began
to sing 'South of the Border.' "

The ensuing publicity did not enhance Lana's reputation.
For perhaps the first time, instead of the pursued beauty, she

was the pursuer. This sort of aggressiveness was nothing new in Tyrone's life; he was now used to it. But it added a blemish to her image.

Still, Lana was too much in love to care. When she learned later that month that the little Beechcraft that had picked her up had crashed in those same mountains, even though the two members of the *Castile* company suffered only minor injuries, she must have shuddered just a little at her impetuosity. She told Tyrone that she would be coming down again when she finished her picture, but that she was planning the trip with greater care than before.

Tyrone wrote Watson from Patzcuaro:

> . . . I am out on the set, and the sun is beating down like mad [the set was a reproduction of Tenochtitlan or the precursor of Mexico City, terraced with shimmering canals, soon to be destroyed by the Spanish and all of its inhabitants slaughtered, the climax of the film], but it is quite beautiful . . . that is, if you haven't been here three weeks. Oh, brother, will I be glad to get the hell out of here. It is not only the dirtiest place you can imagine, but they have killed four people here in the last two days, and that is just four too many for this character. Two of them were knifings and two of them were pistol. Cute little place. . . . do you suppose it would be possible for me to come and bunk with you for awhile when I return. I promise not to make it too long, and I will keep out of the way as much as possible. I don't think I will have a place by that time, and as the house will be rented . . . yours truly will be buying a tent. . . .

The letter is significant because nowhere does Tyrone suggest that his friendship with Lana will affect his future in any way. The Saltair house is to be rented, and he obviously is planning to find his own bachelor quarters as quickly as possible.

Studio work began on the picture in February and word circulated among his friends on the lot that he was in the market for a house. Henry Hathaway and wife, Skip, were about to move into a hilltop contemporary from their huge Cape Cod on North Rockingham. Tyrone went to look at it and decided that it would suit him fine. There was a large master suite upstairs with lots of storage space and a study for his growing library. He bought the house.

Tyrone had hoped that his moving into North Rockingham would help clarify the situation with Lana. He thought that he loved her, but there was not only the drug problem; she was also far more possessive than Annabella ever had been.

Lana seemed unconcerned about their each having a house. Houses are disposable, but men like Tyrone were not, despite her reputation for treating men like Kleenex. She would prove her critics wrong through the passing of the days and months. She would stick with Tyrone as long as he would have her, and she declared to her friends that she hoped it would be forever. Tyrone became panicky whenever he felt the tug of Lana's possessiveness, and implored Annabella not to divorce him.

On May 19, 1947, Tyrone began work on the film that would remain his personal favorite—*Nightmare Alley*. It had taken some doing. Although the screenplay was ready to shoot while he was completing *Captain from Castile*, the lead had been difficult to cast. The central character, Stan Carlisle, is a con-artist who climbs to success through the women who are drawn to his striking good looks.

George Jessel, the former song-and-dance man, had become a Zanuck intimate. Zanuck loved his old yarns about the early vaudeville and blackface days and in 1946 had made him a producer. He had done two musicals, including *I Wonder Who's Kissing Her Now* (1947), when Zanuck urged him to take on *Nightmare Alley*. Its sleazy, carnival background was something Jessel knew at firsthand.

By chance, Tyrone had read William Lindsay Gresham's novel, which was favorably reviewed at the time of its publication in 1946 because of its Chandler-like toughness and the accuracy of its setting. "Intelligent trash," someone called it. Tyrone went to Jessel, while *Captain from Castile* was in its final phase, and asked to be cast as Stan. Jessel was surprised or even shocked that the studio's top leading man would want to play a "Geek." A Geek is a carny attraction on the lowest level, an alcoholic who rips up live chickens and swallows their quivering flesh in front of sideshow audiences in order to get another bottle of cheap booze. Stan Carlisle gets his comeuppance from the last of the women he exploits, and in the last ten minutes of the film is an unshaven, disheveled, trembling Geek.

Zanuck was appalled. *Nightmare Alley* was not a major film; it was offbeat, with a modest budget and a cast of no great star power. Only Joan Blondell, who had scored as the Aunt in *A Tree Grows in Brooklyn*, had any marquee value. But Tyrone said that he loved Miss Blondell in *A Tree*; had in fact very nearly written her a fan letter when he had seen it on Saipan. Here was a chance, he told his boss, for him to prove to everyone that he was an actor of depth and conviction and not just a movie hero in the grand tradition.

Zanuck urged Henry King to talk some sense into him. King told him that his fans would be shaken to see him as the Geek. Tyrone pointed out, justifiably, that he would be playing a handsome young con-man for nearly an hour and a half before that shocker. Then King told him that there were other serious dramatic roles he could play. "Name one!" Tyrone dared him, but King could not think of any. It was unlikely that Zanuck was about to authorize any film versions of Shakespeare, Shaw, Ibsen, or even Arthur Miller.

Lana had done a role equally reprehensible at Metro, *The Postman Always Rings Twice* (1946), and, rather than hurting her, it had finally endeared her to the critics and won her a whole new audience. She was behind Tyrone throughout these preliminaries, and it was not a small gesture.

Very briefly, the story revolves about Stan, a barker for Madame Zeena (Joan Blondell), a telepathic act or mentalist. When her husband, Pete, is too drunk to perform, Stan fills in. He is ill-educated but bright and attractive. He takes to it immediately. "This gets me," he tells Zeena. "I like it, all of it. The crowds, the noise, always keeping on the move. When you look at all the yokels out there, it gives you a sort of superior feeling . . . as if you were 'in the know' and everybody else was on the outside, looking in. . . ."

Zeena is taken in by Stan's glib banter until a card from her Tarot deck, the Hanged Man, which she believes must represent Pete, frightens her. Stan can't believe she is serious, telling her, "Honest, Zeena, to see a smart girl like you fall for one of your own boob-catchers."

Stan manages to smuggle some forbidden whiskey to Pete before a performance so that he can take his place and, before finishing the bottle and starting on some lamp-oil, which Stan has placed in Pete's locker and which will kill him, he goes into his spiel, which Stan memorizes:

> Since the dawn of history, mankind has sought to see behind the veil which hides him from tomorrow. And through the ages certain men have gazed into the polished crystal and seen. Is it some property of the crystal itself? Or does the gazer use it to turn his gaze inward. . . .

Pete dies, but no one suspects Stan, and he and Zeena form a team. Meanwhile, Stan is also working over Molly, a beautiful but dimwitted girl who is "Miss Electra" and whose hair stands on end every performance. He runs off with Molly, taking Zeena's mentalist act with him, although he does so at the risk of his life since strong man Bruno has been Molly's boyfriend and catches up with Stan before they leave, making Stan promise to marry Molly.

The Production Code Office was much concerned about *Nightmare Alley*. There were heavy restrictions on Stan's bedroom encounters, and in one note in the shooting script, that Office has requested that they shoot "the latter part of bedroom scene in a manner which will exclude the bed."

Stan is now the Great Stanton. They are playing in a smart hotel clubroom in Chicago with Stan in white tie and tails and blindfolded. Molly moves among the tables in a spotlight. An attractive woman slightly older than Stan, Lilith, who turns out to be a psychoanalyst, is in the audience with a client or patient, a tycoon by the name of Ezra Grindle. They are amused and skeptical. But Lilith is intrigued and asks him something about her mother. Stan astonishes her by telling her that her mother is dead. Then she invites him to her office, where she asks how he happened to know about her mother being dead. "I just had a feeling your mother wasn't on the level. So I figured you were trying to make a chump out of me . . . just common sense." When an emergency call comes in and she dismisses him, he exits, but leaves the door a little ajar so that he can sneak back in and observe her at work. He notices that she makes a recording of each session with a patient. He knows now that she is a con-artist, too. "It takes one to catch one," he says.

By using data on her clients from Lilith's confidential files,

Stan is able to con some real estate, a spiritualist church, out of a wealthy old lady and persuade the skeptical Grindle that he can resurrect from the dead his first love, Dorrie, whom he had wronged. He forces Molly to appear in Grindle's garden in the moonlight costumed as Dorrie, circa 1900, following an old photo of the girl, and Grindle is staggered by the "apparition." He is ready to back Stan in every conceivable way, but Molly is sickened by the ruse, and screams in protest, "I can't do this, Stan!" The con is off and Stan flees, hurrying to Lilith's to pick up the swag of about $150,000 he has taken from suckers so far, including Grindle and the old lady. She does a "gypsy switch" on him and hands him a bag of 150 dollar bills. He hurries off to meet Molly at the railway station, but in the taxi sees what Lilith has done and orders the driver to turn around. He enters Lilith's place through a window and is confronted by the housekeeper brandishing a revolver. Surprisingly, Lilith tells her everything is all right, that this is "a patient," and she leaves them alone. Then she tells Stan: "When you first came to me, you were in bad shape. I had hoped that by getting at the roots of your anxiety, I could avert a serious upset. Well . . . I seem to have failed." Stan is puzzled and does not get her drift. It is clear that she is too smart for him. "Please, Mr. Carlisle," she continues,"try to understand that these delusions of yours in regard to me are a part of your mental condition. When I first examined you, you were being tortured by guilt reactions connected with the death of that drunken mentalist during your carnival days. . . . " Stan is now startled and frightened. "I'm a psychologist, not a judge. What I want to explain to you is, all of these things you think you have done—or that have been done to you lately—are merely the fancied guilt of your past life projected on the present. . . . You must regard it all as a nightmare. . . . Police records show that a carnival employee by the name of Peter Krumbein actually died of wood-alcohol poisoning in Burleigh, Mississippi, self-administered. You told me that you gave him the bottle, but I suppose that was just another one of your homicidal hallucinations. . . . Or was the homicide a reality, too. . . . " She tells him that she has a recording of his "confession" to her about Pete, but she really thinks he needs a long rest in a mental hospital. A police siren can be heard coming closer, but she pretends not to hear—this is just another of his "hallucinations." He backs to the window and flees into the night.

Stan sends Molly back to the carnival and retreats to a series of cheap hotels, where he holes up, sending out for gin as long as his meager bankroll holds out. A year later, all funds gone, he is in a hobo jungle enthralling the bums with his spiel: "Since the dawn of history" beside their campfire next to the railway tracks.

Finally, he reappears at the carnival, unrecognized by the owner, stubble covering his haggard boozer face. He tries to convince the man that he is a capable mentalist, but the owner tells him that he knows he is an "alky" and unreliable. Then he says, "You know what a geek is. . . . Think you can do it?" Stan tells him with a queer smile: "Mister, I was made for it."

His total comedown, however, is more than Stan's mind can handle, and he runs amuck. A posse of carny hands, including the owner, pursue him. They are afraid of him, since he has armed himself with a tent stake. Molly sees the commotion and watches, then it dawns on her who the new Geek really is. When she approaches, he makes menacing gestures, but then there is a feeble ray of recognition. "It's me, Stan," she says, and she leads him away from the disbelieving knot of carny people.

Edmund Goulding was asked personally by Tyrone to direct the film. What Goulding and Tyrone did was bring a wry detachment to the whole proceedings so that it did not become a grim melodrama, but had a zingy vaudeville spirit about it. In their gifted hands, it became a fable of a lost soul rather than a chapter from the "Inferno."

As one can see from this brief reprise of Jules Furthman's screenplay, there were elements in Stan's character and life that came very close to Tyrone himself. There was the same easy flirtatiousness, the charm, *and* the self-destructiveness. That was a side to Tyrone that seemed to have begun during the war years and would continue to grow. He knew it, but could do nothing to root it out. In *Nightmare Alley*, he was able to use it.

Every discerning critic in America saw the long step Tyrone had taken as an actor. James Agee pointed out that "Joan Blondell, as the fading carnival queen, is excellent and Tyrone Power—who asked to be cast in the picture—steps into a new class as an actor."

If Tyrone's liaison with Lana produced nothing beyond this

film and its superior quality, then the relationship must be considered as one of the most valuable in Tyrone's life. With her encouragement every step of the way, he had gone far beyond the Fairbanks-Haines-Valentino cardboard characters and contributed a portrayal of enduring satisfaction. The film lost money not because his fans rejected him in such an off-beat casting but because Zanuck had no faith in the project as a Tyrone Power vehicle. His fans were not given much of a chance to catch it, it made the rounds of the moviehouses so fast.

Partially because of Zanuck's lack of faith in *Nightmare Alley*, it was rushed into the moviehouses as soon as it was completed, being released two months ahead of *Captain from Castile*, made months earlier. Zanuck felt that the public's faith had to be restored in Tyrone Power as a romantic hero after this folly, and he justified the booking by calling *Captain* the studio's "Christmas release."

Toward the end of summer, Lana began planning a party. Tyrone's studio was about to send him off on another long vacation *cum* press junket in a DC-3 which he renamed *The Geek*. Tyrone never had seen Africa and they planned to do the whole continent with a skilled pilot, Bob Buck, later with TWA, at the controls. Jim Denton and Bill Gallagher were invited, too. Perhaps Lana wanted her relationship with Tyrone made clear to everyone before his departure.

In any case, the party was catered and the guests were all properly astonished to see the motif was Cupid, and all of the specially created frosted glassware had two entwined hearts initialed "T" and "L" pierced by Cupid's arrow. Tyrone hand't been informed of this detail, and when friends came over to congratulate him, he gave them a cold stare. He couldn't wait for the departure of *The Geek*, although he was not the only party up in the air on takeoff.

The trip was beautifully timed. Tyrone could sort matters out much better while airborne. He said later that he was thinking much of the time about how he could make a graceful exit from his entanglement with Lana. He was not very good about such matters; in fact, he was surprisingly abrupt and, occasionally to others, cruel. But he clearly wanted out.

In Johannesburg, there were receptions. He was, it seems,

about as popular with the Afrikaaners as he was with the Americans, Europeans, and South Americans. It was strange being cheered by people in such an alien country, but that was part of the miracle of the movies. Then they flew over the Sudan and the Sahara, which, of course, reminded Tyrone again of Annabella. Still another matter up in the air.

They made a long side trip to Australia, where Tyrone judged a beauty contest. There, again, were throngs and wild adulation. The public receptions seemed curative in some special way for Tyrone. These strangers knew nothing of his private turmoil over Annabella, over Lana. Despite his being a man who cherished privacy, very public excursions such as these lifted him up from the depths.

Tyrone came back by way of Rome, which was perhaps his favorite city in all the world. He checked into the Excelsior Hotel to spend a few days of just plain rest, with some good Roman cuisine and a bit of visiting with friends. Rather late in the evening of his second day, his phone rang. "This is Linda Christian," the slightly accented voice announced. "My little sister was carried away when she heard you were here in the same hotel. She picked up the phone and asked for you, and I'm terribly sorry."

Tyrone was not annoyed by the intrusion. He had spent more than six weeks in the company of male friends and endless mobs of adoring, matronly ladies. He invited her over for a nightcap, and suggested she bring her "inquisitive sister," Ariadne.

It was not really by chance that Linda Christian turned up that evening with her sister in tow. Linda was then under contract to Metro-Goldwyn-Mayer (and had played a small role in Lana's *Green Dolphin Street*), and Metro's Rome representative, Signor Minghelli, had cued her about Tyrone's presence in her hotel and made the suggestion that she call.

Neither was it her first meeting with Tyrone. She was in Acapulco with Turhan Bey on holiday when Tyrone was completing *Captain from Castile* and they had a chance encounter there when Lana was visiting him, pointedly clinging to his arm, in fact. As with the con-artists in *Nightmare Alley*, it took one temptress to know another.

Their conversation was interrupted by a phone call. Linda could hear a woman's strident voice shouting: "I've been trying to get you all day. Where the hell have you been?'' Linda describes him as being uncomfortable, ''almost in apology, for he knew that I could hear the voice and would recognize it.''

''Tell me you love me,'' the voice shouted. ''Right now!''

Without taking his eyes from Linda's, he spoke into the phone: ''I love you.'' Somehow Linda knew that the message was intended for her, and it put her in a state of confused emotions.

During the next few days, Tyrone resolved his romantic problems in his usual fashion by falling in love with somebody new. Within two days he declared his love and insisted that he was going to marry Linda. ''I have a wife I used to love,'' he told her, ''and a girl I used to love. . . . The big problem still left to settle with Annabella is the how-much of a divorce. . . .''

In November 1947, his romance with Lana Turner was offically over when a news release was sent out by his studio saying that ''Ty Gives Up Lana for Fight on Reds.'' The political activism came from Lana, not Tyrone. She told the press: ''He saw so much suffering in Europe. He came back determined to spend his time fighting Communism, which he believes, as we all do, is the scourge of the world.'' With one stroke, she had endeared both of them to the House UnAmerican Activities Committee, which was already investigating charges of red propaganda in films. Such an obsession, however, was far from his mind. They met briefly upon his return to California, discussed their problems, ''like grownups,'' according to Lana, and decided to go their separate ways. ''From now on,'' she said, ''I will carry my chin a little higher and work harder.''

In truth, friends say that Lana was devastated by the breakup. For her, it was by far the most important relationship of her life. In Tyrone, she had a bright companion, lover, family man, and protector. But all of that was lost now to someone else. Tyrone had told Lana about Linda Christian.

Annabella had flown into Los Angeles quietly a couple of weeks earlier to file for divorce. Most of Tyrone's time following her arrival was spent with her lawyers. It was costing him dearly to win his freedom so that he and Linda could marry. Annabella would get the house (which she had paid half the cost of anyway), and a settlement of no less than $50,000 a year that could go to $87,500, if his earnings warranted it.

Bob and Eadie Allen, old friends whom Tyrone had met when he was training at Quantico, accompanied him to the courthouse for the settlement. He needed someone to hold his hand because he knew he would be broke when he left the place. Judge Thurmond Clarke approved the settlement, although he advised Tyrone that he was being terribly generous. Tyrone simply said that he wanted it over with regardless, and the deed was done.

In the brief divorce action, Annabella was compelled to admit that Tyrone was "moody and unpredictable. . . . If there were friends in our home, he would suddenly go to his room and remain there the rest of the evening. . . . Sometimes when we were at a party, he would leave without warning, and I would have to be driven home by friends. . . . I became so nervous I couldn't eat. I had to go under the care of a doctor."

But the slate was wiped as clean as Tyrone's assets, and Annabella was granted a divorce on January 26, 1948.

IX

FAREWELL, CALIFORNIA

IN SEPTEMBER 1948, Laurence Olivier's *Hamlet* opened in moviehouses around the world. That same month, Tyrone's *The Luck of the Irish* also went into the major circuits. This was a harmless comedy-romance having a great deal to do with a leprechaun, and the leads (Anne Baxter was Tyrone's leading lady) and leprechaun Cecil Kellaway had far more fun making it than any audience did seeing it.

Shooting on the film had followed Tyrone's return from Europe to the old Henry Hathaway house on North Rockingham Drive. From there, he wrote an impassioned, yet oddly clinical letter to Linda, clinical in its detachment about Lana:

My dearest Puss—

It is so strange to sit here and look out over the hills, the old familiar view. The hills, the trees, the houses are all in their accustomed places—they haven't changed at all, I know—and yet they are so, so very different. The whole thing looks like something I never saw before in my life. The first thing I did—even before I unpacked my bags—was to unwrap my records and I have been lost in a dream of "Passione," "Monasteria Santa Chiara," and "Core 'Ngrato." They make all the difference in the place—and make live again all those fantastically beautiful moments of my life when we were together—but that was in another world, I think—on another planet at least. Oh, my most dear Puss, what have you done?

Last evening I drove to the airport to meet the plane

229

from New York. We came back here to talk. There was
no doubt that things were different and she [*Lana*] sensed
it immediately. I was surprised how frighteningly easy it
was to say the things I said. The "Iron Curtain," I call it,
came down—and there was no mistaking it. I'm afraid
that I'm a fantastically bad actor at moments like that.
But now it's finished and done with. Today has been
strange and quiet. I have been here alone straightening
things up. . . .

Anne Baxter recalls that Linda came once to the set, and
while the three of them were gathered in Tyrone's dressing-
room trailer, Miss Baxter noticed "a very feline, animal
quality about her. In other words, a panther as opposed to a
poodle. She seemed extraordinarily possessive. She took her
hand and ran it down his thigh in a way that made me shudder
because it was predatory and possessive, and that's a bad
combination."

Criticism of Linda Christian ran high among Tyrone's
friends. Although she kept an apartment for legal reasons
until Tyrone's final decree came through from Annabella, she
was thought to be living in the Rockingham Drive house. It
was Tyrone's wish that she do so, not simply Linda's
aggressiveness. All of his friends, except for the Hathaways,
the Bob Allens, and one or two others, urged him to have his
fling, but "don't marry her." At twenty-five, her aristocratic,
even arrogant, beauty had won her the admiration and protec-
tion of world figures such as President Miguel Alemán of
Mexico and movie star Errol Flynn. Although Linda always
kept in touch with Alemán, she had fled the Flynn mansion.
Tyrone had heard several versions of the reason behind that,
most of them sordid.

The Hathaways knew a different Linda, a girl who loved
some action around her most of the time, but a decent person
under all the layers of sexuality and intellectual pretensions.
This was the Linda Christian with whom Tyrone fell in love.
And there is small doubt about Linda's feelings. She had
never felt so strongly about anyone before and she wanted to
marry him as quickly as possible.

But Blanca Welter, her dear "Mommie" now living in
Mexico, insisted that she wait. Blanca wanted only the best
for her children, and Tyrone, for all of his success and fine

looks, had a bad reputation with the ladies. Blanca made inquiries; she was as protective of her offspring as any tigress. Tyrone went to visit her Mexican home and buttered her up, but while she laughed at his foolish romanticism and she came to like him, she still said no, not now.

With yet another puzzling piece of trash in release (*That Wonderful Urge*, 1948, a remake of Tyrone's second starring production, *Love Is News*), Tyrone got his final divorce decree and the path was clear for their wedding. They were at the time in Italy, where Tyrone had begun work on a second Samuel Shellabarger historical melodrama, *Prince of Foxes*, set in Renaissance Italy at the time of the Borgias.

The popular and indefatigable Hollywood hostess Dorothy di Frasso had a large villa at the edge of Rome, the Villa Madama, and Tyrone and Linda were invited to stay there. Tyrone had written his sister, Anne, who had a rich appreciation of fine, historic places such as the film company was discovering on location, and asked her to come over and share this experience with him. She came for a few weeks and stayed in the converted stable of the villa, which was no second-rate annex to the villa itself, but an elegant restoration with marble floors and Old Masters hanging on the paneled walls. Linda's sister Ariadne was there in the stable, too, at the time.

Linda had style and looked simply smashing as she strode down the Via Veneto; all heads turned. Anne Hardenbergh noticed it throughout her stay; Linda's beauty was something that could not be easily dismissed. Linda, too, wanted Anne to look her best, and took her to the Fontana Sisters, who did her clothes, so that Anne was able to move about in the Roman society Tyrone had come to know well in some finery.

Because Annabella and Tyrone had had a civil ceremony, the Catholic Church declared that they had never been legally married. There were no children, so the papal pronouncement was relatively simple to procure. Tyrone and Linda looked about Rome for a small chapel, where the ceremony could take place.

Near the Forum and its ruins, they found their church. As Linda writes in her memoirs:

. . . And there, amid the glory that was Rome, we

suddenly came upon a lovely little church with steps
mounting to a colonnade. Its weathered stone walls were
certainly aged, but it stood there whole and entire, and
attached to one side was a building that was apparently
occupied, and had a medieval tower rising from it. . . .

But a monk in a white robe told them that no one had ever
been married there. Their disappointment was so keen, he told
them that he would seek permission. The church, called Santa
Francesca Romana, is today busy with the traffic of one
wedding after another, because the Tyrone Power–Linda
Christian ceremony was the biggest thing of its kind in the
history of modern Rome.

Anne had gone home by the time of the wedding rites, and
Patia could not come over, although she liked Linda and, in
fact, kept a picture of Linda and her son in an informal
pose in a frame on her night stand. Tyrone insisted that an in-
vitation had gone to Watson, but it was never received. It was
only natural that Linda would not care for Watson, since he
had advised Tyrone not to marry her. Linda's dearest friend
in Los Angeles, a sort of second mother to her, Maya Van
Horn or "Popsi," thought Linda was jealous of Watson. But
perhaps feelings there went deeper than mere jealousy. Linda
was free, uninhibited, totally sensual, while Watson was shy,
cautious, and rarely allowed anyone to read his feelings. They
could not help but clash.

Some of Tyrone's Italian friends, like a number of his
American friends, were not above using his celebrity for their
own ends. He had thought that one of his best friends was
Count Rudi Crespi, and he even had spent his last "bachelor"
night in Crespi's house. But Crespi also owned a news
magazine, and Tyrone awoke on his wedding morning to find
himself surrounded by a battery of cameras. The crew from a
newsreel owned by the same Crespi firm formed a second ring
around him, as he got out of his pajamas, shaved, had his
breakfast, and then dressed for the ceremony.

His old friend publicist Jim Denton, was trying to handle or
at least placate the hordes of journalists from all over the
world who had converged on Rome. This was the largest
gathering of the media for any event in the Holy City aside
from the convocation of cardinals for the naming of a Pope.

No one remembered to have a wedding cake ordered for the

reception, but the American embassy obliged them by having one baked in their kitchen. Streets surrounding the little church began to fill with a sea of people, all chanting the names, "Tee-ronee!" and "Leenda!" over and over again.

Linda's own account of what followed is worth recording here:

Tyrone's arrival at the church created a near-hysteria, and as my car arrived I heard the insistent roar of: "Ty-ro-ne—Magnifico!" Even the motorcycle-police escort made no impression on the wall of humanity. The car could only inch its way forward. When at last we drew up, my two bridesmaids, Ariadne and my school friend Luisa Costero from the days in Haifa and Florence, glanced apprehensively at the frenzy that surrounded us. "Linda, Linda!" the crowds were screaming as they threw themselves in a solid block against the phalanx of policemen struggling to lead us to the steps of Santa Francesca Romana. People seemed to be everywhere, even hanging from the walls outside.

Our church had been transformed from quiet stone and marble to a blaze of candles. Garlands of flowers hung everywhere, with white lilies and carnations marking every pew. . . . Standing ready to lead me down the aisle was an old friend of my family, Leone Miglievich, tall and erect though in his seventies, with a distinguished white beard. Luisa and I had stayed in his house on the Tevere for our Christmas holidays before the war, when snow had blanketed Rome for the first time in seventeen years. Slowly we moved forward, and among the hundreds standing there I saw few faces that were familiar. The invitations had been duplicated, we learned afterward, and sold in great numbers on the black market. How I missed Mother and Father! Mother was in Mexico, having a baby son—and Father [Gerard Welter, a Dutch petroleum engineer] was in Cyprus on his honeymoon, unable to arrange a visa for his new bride. . . . And there stood Tyrone, quiet and beautiful at this great moment in our lives. Monsignor William Hemmick, our dear friend, who was canon of St. Peter's, came forward from the altar, and as Tyrone and I knelt side by side on small cushions he began to read the vows that pledged us to each other for the rest of our lives.

Behind the wall of flowers surrounding our altar were dozens of photographers and newsreel cameras, their presence by happy chance made less conspicuous, their lights adding to the brilliance. . . .

The ceremony was followed by a nuptial mass, during which the couple took Holy Communion, and then they proceeded with a motorcycle escort through the sea of people to the Vatican for a private audience with Pope Pius XII, who doubtless could hear their approach. The Pope told them, "I am happy that you have chosen my country for your wedding. The people love you here . . . The eyes of the world are upon you. Your industry can do a lot of good in the world, but it can also give bad examples. You must show everyone the meaning of a Catholic marriage." After receiving the papal blessing, they left hand-in-hand, Linda calling herself "the happiest woman in the world." A decade ago, that same Pope had blessed Tyrone and Annabella during their wedding trip, but papal memories are doubtless and short as secular ones.

They honeymooned in the Alps, spending three weeks in Kitzbühel, Austria, where they attempted to ski. Linda was more skillful at it than Tyrone; he fell frequently but laughed about it. Unlike fencing, for example, it was not a sport he needed for his work or to maintain his physique, and he was by nature indolent. In at least one skiing snapshot, his downhill course is abruptly ended by his skis crossing in an "x."

After stops in Salzburg and Vienna, an American Army colonel took them on a guided tour of Hitler's mountain retreat, Berchtesgaden. Tyrone was impressed by it; especially by the magnificent view of the mountain valley from the picture window where Hitler had sat to catch his breath between savageries. A few weeks later, the place was bulldozed to rubble because of the many surviving and new Nazis coming there on pilgrimages.

Ahead of them was the very uncertain future. They both had been extra careful to put themselves in the best possible light through the sixteen months of their friendship and now marriage. They both had pasts and reputations to live down or beyond. But what man could say that they were not happy?

It was the best time of their years together. Tyrone was still courting Linda. His studio had yet another massive production of a best-selling adventure yarn ready to roll, also on location—this time in Africa—Thomas Costain's *The Black Rose*, the story of Walter of Gurnie, at the time of the Saxon and Norman skirmishes in England. Walter's mother is out of favor with her lord, the boy's nobleman father, who has taken a Norman wife. The mother languishes because of it, taking a secluded apartment within the Gurnie castle.

Although Walter must go all the way to Cathay, apparently following roughly the route of Marco Polo, whose own adventures somewhat resemble Walter's, he comes back with a great fortune, a beautiful damsel in distress saved from bondage, and support to repulse the Normans, even including his wicked stepmother. En route to Cathay, Walter meets an awesome warlord, not unlike Genghis Khan, named Bayan of the Thousand Eyes, played by Orson Welles. This was Welles's second film in a row with Tyrone, since he had played Cesare Borgia in *Prince of Foxes*. Welles was now principally based in Europe, where he was much in demand as an actor, although he would shoot his own version of *Macbeth* the following year in California for, of all studios, Republic, known for its Westerns.

The second male lead in the picture, the part of companion Tristram, was played by Jack Hawkins, a British actor who, with his wife Noreen, would remain close to Tyrone until his death.

Hathaway recalls that Tyrone was the "perfect star. Never caused a moment's trouble. Always up in his lines. Affable. Didn't mind the sirocco that blew up every day on the dot of 12:27 for two hours, but climbed under a tent or inside a truck and seemed to love it." Orson was another matter. He liked to play against the character as drawn. On one occasion, Hathaway had him doing retakes all day. Finally, Orson told his director: "Henry, I've done this loud; I've done it soft. I've done it slow; I've done it fast. I've done it backwards and forwards. Now how would you like it done?" And Hathaway said, "Orson, you've done it every way except the way I told you to do it." Nevertheless, Hathaway called him "brilliant."

The location shooting started off on a grand note when the company convened at the Mamounian Hotel in Marrakech, sometimes described as the most beautiful hotel in the world. They worked out of Marrakech briefly, then they were off for a remote Foreign Legion outpost, where they lived in the barracks. There were three couples who ordinarily would have commanded the best suites in the place, had such existed—the Henry Hathaways (Skip had come along), the Tyrone Powers, and the Jack Hawkinses, plus one single male lead, Orson Welles. Orson kept chasing the native woman used as interpreter by Hathaway, but never got anywhere, since she only had eyes for Tyrone. Linda kept her worries at bay by keeping him in view most of the time, and by realizing that there were few women around as beautiful as she. Artists and sculptors already had discovered that.

Once, when Tyrone made the mistake of going to the next location—in the Atlas Mountains—by car instead of plane, they found a bridge washed out, and the Powers, Jack Hawkinses, and Bill Gallagher had to spend the night in a cockroach-infested Berber inn.

In Quarzazate, in an abandoned Foreign Legion outpost, the company doctor discovered that Linda was pregnant. Linda was quite sure that she was carrying Tyrone Power IV.

The Black Rose wound up production in London, after which Tyrone rented a little Cessna and flew with Linda for a month's rest at St. Tropez. While there, they befriended French actor Jean Murat, who once had been Annabella's husband. Murat's daughter by his present marriage liked Linda very much and followed her everywhere. Murat turned to Tyrone and said: "You know who is in love with your wife? My daughter. Further complications in our lives, no?"

After the location shooting was completed, the couple flew around Europe in a light plane, following their whims. They even managed to spend some time in Paris, and it did not seem haunted by Annabella's presence. But it was there that tragedy struck.

It was bumpy coming into Paris and they were bounced around in the light plane a great deal. Linda seemed all right and they made plans to have dinner with Charles Boyer and Annabella's dear friend, Pat Patterson Boyer. But Linda went into premature labor; she was rushed to the hospital, and an infant son was born dead after six months of pregnancy.

On the first anniversary of their marriage, Tyrone was at

the Shepperton Studios in London completing interiors on *The Black Rose* and wrote Linda:

My dearest one—

Well, here it is. One year has gone by and that famous morning is here again.

There is not much I can add to what already has been said except to say again how happy you have made me this past year. And to tell you again how much I love you.

I know that in many ways this has been a very difficult year for you—physically and mentally, and that also there are many ways in which I have been lacking. I'm sure there were so many times that I could have helped, with a word or an action, and I let you down. Then I get angry with myself because I realize the need—and the whole thing ends in a shambles. I have always been so much better at expressing myself on paper. That is why I am writing this.

I just wanted you to know how wonderful this year has been, and what a wonderful future I see, as I look into the years ahead. I wish I could have made this first year of adjustment a little easier for you, as I appreciate only too well the problems connected with sharing my life, and just how unrewarding it must seem at times.

For you, I could wish that I were so many things—particularly that I could more easily express myself. But I wouldn't trade these last twelve months for any others I could dream up.

Your understanding and patience can help more than anything else to give me the confidence I need. And I assure you I will try to be more considerate and less demanding.

I do so wish that we were together at this moment, but know that you are in my thoughts as you are deep in my heart.

I hold you close and tell you again—I love you.

Always,
Tyrone

They seemed to be building a life together. There were some carry-overs from Tyrone's days before Linda to help stabilize the Powers—his own family (Patia and sister Anne, both of whom seemed to have developed a real affection for Linda), Cesar Romero, who never challenged Tyrone's judgment, the Hathaways, the Zanucks when they were together, Bill Walsh, and Wil Wright. Then there were Linda's closest friends, especially Madelyn FioRito and Maya "Popsi" Van Horn, also known as "the Countess," whose Dutch accent and general manner suggested a Breughel painting come to life. Madelyn apparently had a permanent crush on Tyrone, never requited except on the most formal level. Popsi had just married a young man thirty-eight years younger than herself simply because she had seen him pumping gas near her house and thought he was beautiful. She even waited a year until his eighteenth birthday for the wedding because someone told her that she might be breaking the law if she married him before. Tyrone thought all of this was richly human and sufficiently ribald to capture his imagination. Here was one aspect of himself run riot in another person.

In the spring of 1950, Tyrone had to go to the Philippines to make a dreadful picture, *An American Guerilla in the Philippines*, directed by Fritz Lang, who hated the assignment nearly as much as Tyrone did. Although it was based upon an Ira Wolfert novel, and Wolfert had provided the story for the Abe Polonsky classic *Force of Evil* (1948), it was one of Lamar Trotti's weakest scripts. What sustained Tyrone throughout that production was the consolation that upon its completion, he was to go to London to appear on the stage for the first time in many years.

At a cocktail party in New York attended by the Powers, director Josh Logan's wife, Nedda, had approached Tyrone and asked him point-blank, "How would you like to star in *Mister Roberts* in London for six months?" Tyrone's face lit up and he said, "I'd be absolutely delighted!" And so it was done.

Joshs Logan was then one of the most successful directors in the New York theatre, having collaborated on and brought in the biggest hit of the decade in *South Pacific* a year earlier. A year before that (1948), he had collaborated with novelist Tom Heggen on *Mister Roberts*, which was still running; and with *The Wisteria Trees*, his own adaptation of Chekhov's *The Cherry Orchard*, he had three of his productions running at the same time. He was the only American director ever to have actually studied under Stanislavsky in Russia.

Taking *Mister Roberts* to England was no small enterprise. Despite its American success and the general enthusiasm for it on the American continent (Leland Hayward had said, "It's probably the greatest play that's ever been written in the history of the world . . . Aristophanes could never have written as good a play as that"), its humor was decidedly American and no one really knew whether the British would take to it. But the Tennant organization, represented by producer Hugh "Binkie" Beaumont, decided to risk it in a large theatre where the Navy cargo ship, which was the single set, could be constructed and where a sufficient number of Britishers could be attracted to pay the enormous overhead of the show. Beaumont insisted that Logan find an American film star to play "Mister Roberts," otherwise, the customers would not come out in the thousands required.

Tyrone was quite suitable to Beaumont and contracts were signed, Tyrone flying to New York for intensive rehearsals there throughout June prior to sailing. Others in the cast were Jackie Cooper, Russell Collins, Hildy Parks, and George Matthews. The theatre selected by Beaumont was the Coliseum, about the size of a football field, and the cargo ship designed by Jo Mielziner took on the dimensions of a battleship in that setting.

The play opened in mid-July to mixed notices. It seemed clear that much of American humor is not exportable, but Tyrone was astonishingly good as Mister Roberts. Throughout the rehearsal period, he had urged Logan to keep "digging. The first thing I do may be facile. That's because I did all my films on that level. That was all that was required. But I'm better than that."

Patia had gone over for the opening, and had sat with Cesar Romero, who was then shooting a film in London, and Linda. The opening-night audience clearly had come to see Tyrone and the curtain ovation was the high point of Patia's life. Here was her son succeeding in one of the greatest theatrical centers in the world at the profession she had helped train him for—acting on the stage.

There was a great deal of entertaining throughout the six months of their stay in England. One weekend, the Powers were invited to Notley Abbey, the country estate of Laurence Olivier and wife Vivien Leigh. Olivier was quite the opposite of Tyrone in manner; he was shy and unsure of himself. What they shared was a robust sense of humor and a passion for the theatre. Olivier was a little astonished by Tyrone's dedication.

Linda spent some of her leisure by posing for sculptor Jacob Epstein. She earlier had been asked to pose by painter Diego de Rivera, who had worked her long-necked beauty into two separate murals. When the bust was finished, after many sittings, Tyrone admired it so excessively that he asked Epstein if he would consider selling it and finally persuaded him to part with it for three hundred pounds. Then another sculptor named Peter Lambda, having seen the Epstein head in the newspaper, asked to do a nude statue of Linda. He wanted Tyrone standing behind her, "the ideal couple," also presumably nude, a sort of latter-day Adam and Eve.

The work, _sans_ Tyrone, later became a notable addition to the entrance patio of their new home on Copa de Oro in Bel Air, to which they moved early in 1951. A _Look_ magazine reporter conned them both into posing beside it for a layout, telling them it would be handled "in the best possible taste."

Mister Roberts began to slip at the box office before the first six-month period was over. The British were not responding to the locker-room and sailor humor at all; it was just too American for them. After the rush of fans had passed, everything was downhill.

It was during the winter following their return that Linda discovered that she was again pregnant. With rest and strict medical supervision, there were no complications and even though Tyrone lost his way trying to find Cedars Hospital, they made it in time and on October 2, 1951, the Powers had a baby daughter, whom they named Romina Francesca after the city where they fell in love and the church where they were married. She had dark hair like her parents and eyes of a blue so deep that Linda thought they looked black.

Tyrone worshiped his daughter and did not seem in the least distressed that he had not had Tyrone Power IV. At almost the same moment, the studio seemed bent upon tearing down his reputation with undistinguished films and came up with two in the same year, 1951, first _Rawhide_, on which he met Mike Steckler, who came to the location as Tyrone's stand-in to replace Tommy Noonan, who had fallen ill and later died; and then a remake of _Berkeley Square_, which would seem to be the last thing movie audiences needed in the early fifties, retitled *I'll Never Forget You*. But Tyrone would rush home every night to be with Romina. If love and affection were all that fatherhood demanded, Tyrone would have been the greatest father in the world.

His contract with Fox would expire in 1952 and he had no intention of renewing. It became common knowledge among his friends that he was disgusted by the way his studio had treated him ever since *The Black Rose* had turned out to be something less than a smash at the box office, even though it had done respectable business. Word filtered back to the studio, and Zanuck must have felt some contrition and a flicker of his old loyalty to Tyrone because his last films under his contract sharply improved in quality—in story particularly, and *Diplomatic Courier*, which was an entertaining spy yarn in which he co-starred with Annabella's good friend, Pat Neal, did surprisingly well, while *Pony Soldier* did even better. But gone were the days of the great vehicles—*In Old Chicago, The Razor's Edge*. These last contractual films were just not in the same league with them, and Tyrone was determined to make his exit. He turned down one certain success, *Lydia Bailey* from a Kenneth Roberts best seller, because he was sick to death of costume dramas and by the summer of 1952 he was a free agent.

Linda was a little free herself. She was not the best of mothers, although she loved Romina dearly and gave her affection and sometimes even made a stronger effort. But Romina was to be raised largely by her nanny and her grandmother Blanca.

Around 1952, Linda and Tyrone were drawn into a morally liberated group of film people who had swimming-pool parties *cum* drinking parties, and the gatherings became very sexual by midnight. These groups exist in France, in Italy, and possibly in every country where there is a large film industry and a great many amoral people. Tyrone, who always had kept his side affairs very much apart from his marriages, now crossed over the line, apparently quite willingly. The marriage was coming apart.

As his first picture following his release from bondage, Tyrone chose *The Mississippi Gambler*, which producer Ted H. Richmond was doing at Universal. His new agent, George Chasin, had arranged for him to be paid $250,000 plus half of

50 per cent of the studio's net profits, and Tyrone's take from this film eventually was to swell to over a million dollars. At almost the same time, he signed to play the lead in *The Robe*, which would follow *The Mississippi Gambler*. For this he would be paid $250,000 plus 10 per cent of the net profits. He had not shaken off the shackles soon enough.

There was some acrimony over the first film, however, between Tyrone and Linda. Apparently, Tyrone originally had told Richmond that he wanted Linda to play opposite him. He had seen her restlessness and thought that the work would help lessen the tension between them. She even had made a test for the part. But then suddenly the studio phoned to inform Linda that they had decided to cast Piper Laurie in the role. Linda asked to speak to her husband, but was told that he was at an important meeting and could not be disturbed.

There was a scene when Tyrone finally returned the call. "Why did that man have to call," Linda wanted to know. "What does he have to do with our life?" She was weeping bitterly. "Oh," she moaned, "why didn't you call me!"

The picture then proceeded, Linda noticing that Tyrone was becoming more and more exhausted each day. While Popsi, who was a gifted and distinguished character actress, was given the role of a madame, she was hardly an ideal chaperone. During the course of *The Mississippi Gambler*, Tyrone met Anita Ekberg, a Swedish actress then in bit roles in Hollywood.

Tyrone also became close to his producer, Ted Richmond, and before shooting was completed, they discussed forming their own independent company, which within three years would be an active reality.

In August 1952, following completion of *The Mississippi Gambler*, the Powers took Romina to Mexico for a brief holiday. Naturally enough, there was a great deal of traveling back and forth between their new home on Copa de Oro in Bel Air and Mexico City, where Linda's mother was living with her present husband and infant son. While there, Tyrone received a phone call from stage producer Paul Gregory, who had become celebrated for reviving interest in staged readings or "concert performances" of plays. His tour of Charles Laughton's production of Shaw's *Don Juan in Hell* had been a sellout nearly everywhere. Now he asked Tyrone if he would be interested in joining a tour of *John Brown's Body* by Stephen Vincent Benét.

Laughton had been an actor Tyrone had admired ever since *The Devil and the Deep* (1932) when Tyrone was making his film debut in *Tom Brown of Culver*. Tyrone agreed to the offer at once, and returned for rehearsals in Los Angeles for an opening in the fall. He got out of his commitment to do *The Robe*, the financial sacrifice amounting, with percentages, to over half a million dollars.

His fellow players would be Raymond Massey and Judith Anderson. They were also actors who had Tyrone's most profound respect and admiration. He was elated.

In his biography of Laughton, film historian Charles Higham writes:

> The stage presentation of *John Brown's Body* was beautifully worked out by Charles. As in *Don Juan in Hell*, the actors were dressed in contemporary evening clothes. But this time the eye was relieved: there was a brown balustrade with a red bench top that the actors rested on, and red velvet chairs spread out in the darkness for the chorus. On this occasion, the actors did not sit still, but moved about freely, sometimes actually leaving the stage while one or other of them gave a long speech, sometimes sitting while another stood. As the poem moved on throught the history of the Civil War, the mood of the actors became more intense, Judith Anderson in particular rising to a great force of feeling.

Linda was afraid that their marriage might not survive such a long separation, but she couched her fears in other terms. She told him that it sounded exhausting. *"Exhilarating,"* he corrected her. She was not reassured when he told her firmly that he didn't want her at the opening.

In her memoirs, Linda describes a hastily arranged flight to Chicago, where the *John Brown* company was headquartering while doing one night stands in the Midwest:

> . . . He was in his room preparing to leave for that night's performance when I knocked, and I wondered whether or not he would be glad to see me. It was a sweet reunion, if not an ecstatic one; he was warm and friendly,

yet there was unmistakable restraint between us—
touching physically but not in spirit. But we were
together, and that was vital.

The show had become his life. . . . "Don't you think
you husband is wonderful?" Charles Laughton asked.

I agreed—he was wonderful.

John Brown's Body opened at the Century Theatre in New
York on February 14, 1953. The critics hailed it as one of the
most exciting productions to come into town that season and
singled out Tyrone for praise, especially as the soldier Jack
Ellyat. Ellyat, a Yankee, recalls the simple things that seem
lost to him now, everyday things at home that have taken the
shape of miracles in his memory.

Tyrone's voice, with that deep, resonant timbre, evoked the
humanness in Ellyat that gave his performance a permanent
distinction:

Jack Ellyat, in prison deep in the South,
Lay on his back and stared at the flies on the wall
And tried to remember through an indifferent mist
A green place lost in the wood and a herd of black swine.
They came and went.
The two Michigan men had died last night.
The Ohio brothers were going to die this week,
You got pretty soon so you knew when people would die.
It was only the mist and counting the flies that bothered
    him. . . .

Then Judith Anderson, crisp and incisive, would cut in:

John Brown lies dead in his grave and does not stir,
The South goes ever forward, the slave is not free.

The male chorus behind them would then chant mournfully:

John Brown's Body lies A-*moulder*ing in the grave.

When Tyrone reached Jack Ellyat's death, his voice raised in
pitch to a near shout:

A yellow-fanged face

Was aiming a pistol over a chunk of rock.
He fired and the face went down like a broken pipe
While something hit him sharply and took his breath.
"Get back there, you suckers," he croaked, "Get back
   there, you suckers!"
(Rebel yells are heard.)
He wouldn't have time to load now—they were too near.
He was up and *screaming*. He swung his gun like a club
Through a twilight full of bright stabbings, and felt it
   crash
On a thing that broke. He had no breath any more.
He was down in the grass. . . .

Tyrone had discarded the persona of Tyrone Power, star, for this production, with the help of Laughton. He told Harry Gilroy, a reporter on the New York *Times*: "When Charles Laughton talked with me about the way in which we should begin each performance, he said that we had to do something at the outset to get rid of the monster. 'When you come out on the stage,' he said, 'you will be the fellow who is going to recite some stirring lines and portray some interesting characters in Benét's very much admired literary work. But you will also be the monster, made up of all the characters you have played on the screen. Many people will come to see that monster. You must go out there and dispose of him with a little speech which demonstrates that you can talk and breathe and move, and then you must draw the people along to an interest in the story we are going to tell.'" He added to Gilroy that he felt some antagonism against himself because he had played so many glamour boys on the screen. "If I ever get psychoanalyzed it will be found that half the things I do are to try to compensate for reactions like that in people I meet. For instance, I drive my wife crazy insisting that we have to be absolutely punctual about things—I hate to have anyone put out in any way by us."

Linda had been allowed to attend the New York opening, and had come East with Romina and the nanny, moving into Tyrone's suite at the Hampshire House. On March 12, he wrote his old friend from the Annabella years, producer Lothar Wolff, who was then filming in Germany, that doing *John Brown* "seems to be the answer to a lot of questions we have been asking ourselves for many years . . . and it has presented me with a lot of opportunities that heretofore we have only dreamed of. I am sure you know what I mean." Tyrone now equated "opportunities" with his talent altogether and not with how much he was to be paid. In the wake of the huge success of *The Mississippi Gambler*, his agent, George Chasin, was forced to turn down numerous offers in the neighborhood of a quarter of a million dollars and more for pictures while Tyrone spent all of 1953 touring.

During that opening week in New York, Tyrone acknowledged a wire and a letter from Watson, who had seen little of him since his marriage to Linda. He wrote Watson:

> . . . Your letter arrived this A.M. and I was deeply touched. Yes—we've been through a lot one way or another, and it's heartwarming to realize that basically things don't *really* change.
>
> I was so glad that you could come that evening to Occidental [college, a one-night stand on the tour] and your reactions have given me great heart. I am so happy you like it.
>
> There are many things we will talk about one day—but in the meantime, my very best, & thanks again for your understanding & thoughtfulness.
>
> Always,
> Tyrone

It was a warm letter and the first step taken to bridge the gap that had widened between them.

During the summer of 1953, Judith Anderson left the cast and Anne Baxter, Tyrone's former co-star in at least three pictures for Fox, joined them in San Francisco. She saw at once how excited he was by his involvement with live theatre and how well he had risen to the challenge. She recalls that he was "very good indeed . . . his peak point in John Brown he handled very well.... He trusted Charles Laughton. Charlie was his mentor. No question. And he soaked up Charlie's attitudes and talents, and wanted very much to learn from him. And I think at that time he wanted to direct. He asked me to dinner when we played San Francisco. . . . I'd played it maybe three weeks and he broached the subject of him directing the rest of the tour. And I knew there were changes he wanted to make because he'd played it a lot longer, he and Ray

(Massey), than I had. And I was still shaky on my pins, but I was still finding all kinds of things. And *this* suddenly. I'd opened cold in ten days. That's a tall order. He wanted to take over the direction, and I very gently deflected this, demurred. I mean I wanted it perfectly harmonious on the tour because there were really only three of us and the chorus. And I really felt that I had to lean on Charles. I knew Ty wanted to change the ending of the first act. I knew he wanted to do this and that. I wasn't able at that point to fiddle around with it. . . . He wanted to have fun with it, you know . . . but right at that point I wasn't able to do it. I think he was upset by that . . . he really wanted to take charge. And I had a talk with Charles, and Charles understood my point of view very much and frankly agreed with it. Changing it would have distressed Charles. It was his baby, his *second* baby. He'd had the first with *Don Juan in Hell* and done extremely well. The other two were champing at the bit because they liked to pull the taffy when they've pulled it as long as they had and make new shapes. It's like the old saw, you know. The director comes back in five months and takes out the 'improvement.' ''

Miss Baxter remembers, too, that Tyrone was under a lot of strain throughout the tour because of Linda. He never knew when she would show up, and when she did, he withdrew, tightened up, and remained so until she left. Secretary Bill Gallagher, as always, tried to be the buffer and run back and forth between the two and try to explain to Linda that he badly needed this time to himself. Bill always got on well with Linda and felt for her, too. It is a wonder that the man survived relatively intact during this war of nerves. Of course, Bill didn't emerge from his many years of deflecting trouble from Tyrone without some inroads on his well-being. Those years with Tyrone sapped his vitality; he was simply too dedicated to his employer.

On December 1, the tour was in Vermont and they made an overnight stop at Watson's family mansion, The Brick House, at Shelburne, next to Lake Champlain. There was a turnout of the Webbs for the company—Ma, Watson's brother Harry, and other family members. They were given a tour of the Shelburne Museum of Americana, founded by Ma Webb, filled with patchwork quilts, weathervanes, cigar-store Indians, and crockery.

•   •   •

Following the run of *John Brown's Body*, which had closed in Los Angeles where all of Tyrone's peers were overwhelmed by his stage presence and power, he decided that he could not take the strains of his marriage to Linda any longer and their relationship had to be terminated. She may have sensed what was coming and used words to ward off the blow. Before Tyrone could speak, she told him, "I'm going to have another child."

But a new Tyrone seemed to have taken over, a cooler species. "What a shame, Linda," he said. "I was going to have a long talk with you. I had made up my mind . . . about a divorce. I want my freedom. . . . "

He was not being as callous as he sounded. During a summer haitus of *John Brown's Body* in 1953, Tyrone had gone home to California and back to his old studio to star in *King of the Khyber Rifles* (1954), a remake of the successful British colonial adventure set in India, *The Black Watch*. Director Henry King had asked for him, and they had resumed their old professional camaraderie as though there had been no lapse. The studio seemed quite agreeable to Tyrone again.

But life at Copa de Oro had become nearly intolerable. While he was touring in *John Brown's Body*, Metro had brought over from England a young actor as strikingly handsome as Tyrone had been, Edmund Purdom. After a loan-out to Fox for a disaster film, *Titanic* (1953), Purdom was rushed into a remake of *The Student Prince* to replace Mario Lanza, who had walked out, his nerves frayed by too many years of crash diets and bouts of high living. Linda was invited by Angela Lansbury to dinner, where she met Purdom and his wife, Tita. Linda says she was first drawn to Purdom because of his love of music. She also thought that his wife was not "sweet enough" toward him.

Whether it was a common interest in serious music or Linda's concern for his happiness, an affair began that summer. When Tyrone returned, it was disguised as a close friendship with both Purdoms, and Tyrone helped the Purdoms find a more comfortable home in Beverly Hills. Linda also suggested and supervised a junket of the two couples to Acapulco.

Linda now wanted to resume her acting career in earnest and she began studying with a coach nearby. The Purdoms had separated, and eventually in the divorce action, Linda was named as correspondent. Her classes seemed to drag out into the night and she would not come home. She began lying to Tyrone about it and throughout the shooting of *Khyber Rifles*, he would get home before Linda, then listen to her excuses and quietly go to his room. He told Popsi that he couldn't take her lying; he could take everything else, but not that.

Madelyn FioRito was in the room when the conversation about divorce took place. Linda wanted her there, possibly because it might prevent Tyrone from saying something that would be irrevocable. But it didn't stop him for a moment; he ignored Madelyn's presence.

Then Linda fell to her knees and grabbed him about the legs. She seemed quite beside herself. "You can't go!" she was crying. "You can't!" And she began, with closed eyes, saying her rosary and imploring the Blessed Mother to stop this. Tyrone seemed startled by the unexpected religiosity of the moment, then left the room and, within minutes, left the house.

The Powers were reconciled briefly during the remainder of the *John Brown* tour. Their second child, a daughter whom they named Taryn, was born at Cedars Hospital on September 13, 1953. Not long out of infancy, Taryn had her mother's look of mischievous wonder and her father's profile and long eyelashes. She was a little beauty.

Meanwhile, Edmund Purdom had been selected by Twentieth Century–Fox as their second choice for the plum role of *The Egyptian* from the Mika Waltari best-selling novel. Marlon Brando had turned it down. A loan-out was again arranged, and a tremendous buildup began for Purdom. Tyrone told his friends that Linda seemed to have become convinced that he was on the way down and Purdom was the bright new film idol.

It was a deceptively quiet time in America. The Korean War had officially ended, but American troops were still there in large numbers. Dropouts from society were closer to middle age than youth and called themselves "beatniks," gathering in cheap apartments in North Beach, San Francisco, and Venice, in California; and the East Village in Manhattan. There was a beatnik literature emerging with Jack Kerouac,

Allen Ginsberg, and Gregory Corso; beards were becoming a sign of individualism in an increasingly conformist age.

Films had gone wide-screen, and Judy Garland, long considered unbankable because of her emotional problems, had waged a miraculous comeback via the concert circuit and was filming an independent remake of Janet Gaynor's old hit, *A Star Is Born*. Tyrone must have observed the irony of that. Marlon Brando was the hottest male star of the day with *On the Waterfront* and *The Wild One*. Marilyn Monroe was the tabloids' favorite and it was difficult to avoid some mention of her in the daily gossip columns. Emotions on the screen were no longer muted; they were close to the bone. If true maturity in films could not yet be accepted in those Eisenhower years, open sensuality was considered a satisfactory alternative.

It was against this background that Tyrone joined forces with director John Ford to make a picture that was really an ode to the noble traditions and ideals of the nineteenth and early twentieth century in America. It was like Tyrone to go against the grain of contemporary moods; it was John Ford's credo.

Despite Ford's vision being toward the past, he was a director who ranked with Wyler, Griffith, von Stroheim, and Wilder. *The Long Gray Line* was basically a character study, but Ford knew that Tyrone was now mature enough as an actor to handle it. Harry Cohn at Columbia, who would be releasing it, was still very much a fan of Tyrone's, and contracts were signed.

Much of the film was to be shot at West Point, since it was the story of Marty Mahar, an Irishman who becomes the head physical instructor at the military academy. The script called for a dark Irishman just off the boat, "a Paddy," and within days, Tyrone had mastered an authentic Irish brogue as thick as Mulligan stew.

On Tyrone's first night at West Point, John Ford threw a buffet reception at the only decent restaurant in town. During the preliminary cocktails, he was introduced to a blond, rather aristocratic-looking young lady named Mary Roblee, who was a friend of the Ford family. The director had phoned her in Manhattan, where she was attempting to get a foothold in writing and publishing as a junior editor on *Vogue* magazine, and she was asked to come to the Point to be leading lady Maureen O'Hara's stand-in.

The room was candlelit and Tyrone maneuvered Mary into the seat across from him. Mary recalled: "Sitting across from him, his eyes were incredibly beautiful, almost hypnotic. . . . It was a thunderbolt for me. We collided like shooting stars, glancing off each other into rare and reluctant areas of the heart and mind." For Tyrone, Mary represented the elegance and graciousness that had been denied him for too long. Besides, she spoke four languages and informed him that she was basically a pagan, in love with Italy and France, and the Latin side of Europe. She had come at a moment of fierce emotional stress in his life and she, innocent of all that, was sublimely serene. It was the beginning of an affair that would last well beyond a year and a half and a friendship that would survive until his death.

Although Tyrone was now forty years old, he was a convincing young Marty with his immigrant tag still pinned to his jacket, looking about in growing wonder at the young cadets drilling, exercising and doing everything in cadence. "Is it a prison or a looney house?" he asks.

Marty's first job as a helper in the mess hall ends in disaster as he breaks nearly every piece of crockery that comes into his hands, but someone wises him up to the fact that he can enlist in the Army, which he does. After some initial bewilderment (he finds that the cannonballs stacked on the parapet of West Point since the Civil or an earlier war don't fit the cannons), he finds himself assigned to the chief physical instructor. Marty Mahar was born for the job and begins training his first corps of cadets before the beginning of World War I. The young men become very fond of him, and when he marries another "Paddy" just off the boat, Mary O'Donnell, they become the sons the O'Donnells are denied (she loses their only child, a son, shortly after giving birth). The film takes on much of the complexion, but on a more virile level, of *Goodbye, Mr. Chips*. It spans an entire generation and goes beyond World War II, with Tyrone aging convincingly in appearance and speech as the film proceeds.

Under Ford's strong direction, Tyrone's Marty Mahar is a film tour-de-force, much the strongest piece of acting he had done since *Nightmare Alley*. While he was just beginning to pick up the pieces of his private life, his career finally was on the course he had charted for himself many years ago.

When location shooting was completed, Mary Roblee returned to her *Vogue* job and Tyrone went with the company back to Hollywood to finish the picture. She was rather surprised, then pleased to find that he remained in constant contact with her. There were letters nearly every day, and he had a habit of phoning her at three every morning. There was much discussion of a future sojourn in Italy together, a romp of seduction in a sunny land they both loved.

After the film was completed, Tyrone flew East immediately and phoned Mary from the airport. She was his constant companion throughout most of the winter and well into the following year. He learned that she looked with both fascination and dismay on Hollywood people, startled by their casual four-letter words, "gutter talk" then considered vulgar by her own set at *Vogue*. She was thought to be too proper and priggish by Tyrone's Broadway and Hollywood friends, although she formed close and lasting friendships with many of his theatrical colleagues in New York and London. They attended opera and ballet together, listened to classical records, and he recited poetry endlessly to her. She was flattered to realize that she had become *la femme inspiratrice*.

Mary introduced Tyrone to the founders and managers of Caedmon Records, Barbara Cohen and Marianne Roney, whose mission it was to record the greatest English poetry and prose. Already among their "best-sellers" were selections from Dylan Thomas, Sean O'Casey, and both Dame Edith and Sir Osbert Sitwell. The women all agreed that few noted actors possessed Tyrone's pitch and resonance.

He was then leasing the Garson Kanins' townhouse at Turtle Bay on East Forty-ninth Street and, in the living room there, with Mary seated by the hearth, leaning against Tyrone's legs and staring into the fire, he read aloud Canto I of Byron's *Don Juan*. He was now calling her "Cara," and they had eased into an intimacy that led Mary to the verge of accepting his proposals for a life together. But this was all *too* perfect, *too* much the ideal of a relationship, she thought. Alarms sounded somewhere within her.

Sister Anne Hardenbergh seemed to agree that her brother had found someone who could rid him finally of the unsavory, recent past. With her painter's eye, Anne saw them as "all light, even glittering, light and uncomplicated, everything being light and all nice, nothing ever mean or drab."

The recording of *Don Juan*, along with *She Walks in Beauty* and selections from *Childe Harold's Pilgrimage* was made in the Caedmon loft in Greenwich Village, where he delighted the Misses Cohen and Roney with his quick smile, easy manner, and spontaneous intimacy. Mary recalled that "his voice, touched with irony and wit, seemed to sing with the cadence of the poetry. . . . "

He decided to put some roots down in New York. With Mary's help, he found a small two-bedroom penthouse at 760 Park Avenue, and began furnishing it. He was finding a full panoply of life in Manhattan—theatre, art, friendships, things happening, and, with Mary, romance. The only small difficulty was her fierce independence. She wanted nothing of his fame or his fortune; she only wanted his company. Here was *a lady*, and she loved him. Tyrone threw off the melancholy that had pursued him during his last months with Linda.

He came home briefly to California, carrying with him a photo of Mary. Linda used this discovery, not without justification, to give Tyrone the "news" that she and Purdom had become lovers. Tyrone was scarcely surprised, and told her, "All right, then—if it keeps you happy that way."

Taryn grew up seeing her father only at random meetings. She and Romina spent most of their childhood years with Blanca in Mexico City. Taryn recalls: "We didn't really have parents. Mother and Father had their own lives and interests. We didn't miss them. We didn't know any better, and we loved Blanca. I know my father had his weaknesses; that's only human. And Mother, too. But she's very bright and sensitive. She did things and suffered for it. I remember after Romina married, I was visiting them in Italy and Albano's mother said something nasty about Mother and I got so angry, I threw a pan of pasta at her. I don't think I hit her, but after that they never said another word against Mother."

But Mary Roblee remembers meeting both little girls. And she was introduced to sister Anne Hardenbergh. "He was a very inclusive kind of man," she recalled. "That was one of the dear things about him, and he took you into his world; he never screened you out. He wanted me to know his sister; he wanted me to know his children. He never excluded me. There were times when a screen would come down with certain people and you could tell he was acting. He was a wonderful actor.''

Within weeks, Tyrone was proposing marriage, but Mary simply said, ''We'll talk about it later. We can't think about that now.'' He was not free, and as the months went on and she saw other women pursuing Tyrone and sometimes managing to wind up in his bed, she was relieved that she had had the courage to resist. Still, she often would have moments of regret in the years ahead. They were so much alike. They both loved to read, and Tyrone never packed for a trip without including a book. ''Always take something to read,'' he would say. He gave her a copy of Eleanor Clark's very personal travel book *Rome and a Villa*, and inside wrote, '' . . . and you, Tyrone.''

Two weeks later, hand in hand, they explored that Roman villa, which was Hadrian's. As they stumbled through the dusty ruins, Tyrone spoke of yet another of his favorite books, *Hadrian's Memoirs*, and said that he would try to find a copy for her. The thought struck her that in some fashion Tyrone used literature as a cohesive agent in his life, making everything fit together. It no longer seemed a coincidence that the heroine of the novel *Sparkenbroke*, which he insisted everyone dear to him read *at once*, was named Mary, and her affair with Lord Sparkenbroke doomed. She made no foolish plans for an improbable future.

But something of his old zest for life returned in the city. He rented a Lancia, and he and Mary raced around Rome, occasionally leaving the car to stroll through piazzas, to eat pasta along with cool white Frascati wine at the trattorias, sometimes in the golden sunlight but often at night under the stars. Tyrone was recognized everywhere, but Mary was so obviously his girl, his lady love, they respectfully kept their distance. Mary was not sure that he even noticed all those Roman eyes upon them. He was too caught up in living out their dream of having some time together in this city that was so much his spirit's home.

In the fall of 1954, Tyrone was approached by Guthrie Mc-Clintic, husband of Katharine Cornell, to play opposite her in a new Christopher Fry play, *The Dark Is Light Enough*. As the McClintics' production manager, Gertrude Macy, recalls:

"Mr. McClintic thought htis play needed a movie name with the theatre in the condition it is today. You've got to have a star for the male lead. And Ty had worked for them in those early plays and was very fond of them and said, 'Yes.'"

He more than said yes; he couldn't get over the miracle of it. He would be co-billed *with Katharine Cornell*. The first lady of the stage. The name that came first to his mind when anyone mentioned the American theatre. Life was indeed brightening again.

The play was pretentious and elaborately written by Fry, who had turned out the marvelous *The Lady's Not for Burning* and *A Phoenix Too Frequent* earlier. Set in the middle of the nineteenth century during an abortive uprising of the Hungarians against Austrian rule, it took place in an Austrian country house, the home of the Countess Rosmarin Ostenburg, played by Miss Cornell. Tyrone was playing a heavy co-star, the sort of bounder Trevor Howard made such a specialty of in the British cinema. As Richard Gettner, he represented the evil forces that brought the rebellion to a quick end (and the Countess's death at the curtain). But his success with Marty Mahar had given him the confidence to pull it off.

Evenings, Mary Roblee would leave her *Vogue* job and rush to the theatre to attend rehearsals of the play. Often, in his dressing room and elsewhere, she would go over Tyrone's lines with him. As always, he was letter perfect in them, and never fluffed a line in rehearsal or performance. But he got little help from McClintic. The play was murky, the motivations of the central characters unclear, and McClintic was often drinking heavily. Tyrone said nothing about it and his relationship with both director and star, Miss Cornell, remained warm and affectionate. When he found McClintic unresponsive on something, he would quietly ask Miss Cornell's opinion. She sustained him, understanding only too well what the situation was.

Tyrone had hired a male secretary to handle his correspondence and keep track of his appointments, an attractive Irish-American from Kentucky, Henry Edward Lea. Back in California, Bill Gallagher was helping to set up Tyrone's own production firm, Copa Productions, with Ted Richmond, producer of *The Mississippi Gambler*.

Noël Coward was in town, promoting the latest volume of

his memoirs, *Future Indefinite*. Tyrone slipped back into the casual duality he had pursued when he was last with Cornell twenty years earlier. Their friendship was one of friendly rivalry and good-natured ribbing. He was seeing Mary almost nightly in a different setting and with different friends. On weekends, they would drive up to Connecticut to visit with the Raymond Masseys, who had the kind of humor and grace Mary appreciated.

Miss Macy describes the tour: " . . . he worked hard, religiously. He looked marvelous. And he did four weeks on the road, a try-out tour before New York, in Washington. That was our last road week and he wasn't feeling well and we opened in Washington to a sold-out audience. He was terribly sick, with diarrhea, etc. He had hepatitis. During the tour, he had roomed or boarded with actor Christopher Plummer, a good actor who had a small part in the play. And Christopher Plummer came down with hepatitis in Baltimore, and we had to leave him there to open in Washington. And then we suspected what Ty's illness might be, since it was more than ptomaine or a momentary upset. And the doctor in Washington said, 'This fellow has hepatitis.' We put him in a Washington hospital and canceled our New York opening, *for Tyrone Power*."

Secretary Henry Lea was phoned personally by Miss Cornell and informed that he must get a blood test immediately. Apparently, she feared an epidemic among the men surrounding her production. Mr. Lea went to the doctor and had blood taken, and the report was dispatched to Miss Cornell at her request. It was negative, much to his relief.

Miss Macy continues: "Well, you know hepatitis isn't a quickie. It's really terrible. Ty had a marvelous recuperation from it. So did Christopher Plummer. They were both young [Plummer was thirteen years younger than Tyrone]. They both were immobilized and in bed for five weeks. To postpone a New York opening of a Katharine Cornell play by Christopher Fry was really serious. The house manager of the theatre in New York where we were to open came down with hepatitis. Oh, it was terribly costly, but we had to keep the cast together. We did have a little insurance of the 'act of God' sort, but it wasn't half enough to pay what it cost us. We had to change all the newspaper ads and magazine ads, everything that had been publicized. Here's where I come in badly—at least for Tyrone Power's sake—I said to Cornell, 'Don't wait for Ty Power. He's not as good as his understudy [Christopher Plummer]. And I'd been to the understudy rehearsal, and Plummer is a really very talented man. But Miss Cornell and McClintic said, 'But Plummer has no name. Who's ever heard of him?' "

They waited another week for Tyrone to get on his feet. His New York internist, Dr. John T. Parente, was treating him at the Leroy Clinic in Manhattan. He was put on a high-protein diet and all liquor was banned for a long time. And despite Miss Macy's reservations about his talent, he received far better notices than the play. When it opened at the ANTA Theatre on February 23, Brooks Atkinson writing in the New York *Times* said: "Katharine Cornell has found a good part in a heavy play . . . At least, it seems like a good part. For Miss Cornell plays it with the regality, kindness and nobility of her best art . . . Tyrone Power, who is co-starred with Miss Cornell, gives a forthright, vigorous performance in a negative part. . . . It is a graceless role, unredeemed by wit, brilliance or cleverness. It is greatly to Mr. Power's credit that he can give it such a solid performance. . . . 'The Dark Is Light Enough' is a literary exercise—somber in tone and labyrinthine in thought, despite its high-minded attitude toward life. In his early plays Mr. Fry wrote for the theatre. He is writing for posterity now, and not with much passion or enthusiasm."

The play closed on April 23, 1955, after sixty-nine performances, and then toured for another month. The final curtain rang down in Boston after two weeks there—joyous weeks spent mostly with sister Anne, who now was living in Winthrop with Midge White and her daughter Sheila. Midge had been widowed a year earlier by the death of Tom White. The Whites had helped Anne and her husband Peter find an apartment near Harvard when he was teaching there just before their separation and divorce.

Mary Roblee came up to meet Anne, and Tyrone was hopeful that seeing him in a loving, supportive, and intelligent family environment might help his cause. He was keen on marrying Mary just as soon as he and Linda were divorced. But Mary's own innate wisdom now warned her that Tyrone was constitutionally unable to be true forever the way she wanted a husband to be. She was beginning to give herself the advice others had given Judy Garland. She had heard that

Anita Ekberg had turned up on the road while they were touring. Miss Ekberg even had to be invited by Miss Cornell to the *en famille* Christmas dinner she had for select members of the company while they were in Cincinnati. Although Tyrone and some of his friends pointed out to Mary that Miss Ekberg would just turn up uninvited and unannounced, Mary remained unconvinced.

Eddy Duchin was an attractive, dark-haired bandleader who played the Central Park Casino and other posh spots around the country throughout the late thirties and the forties. He was about as close as a bandleader can get to the status of matinee idol. He had a great smile and was never photographed except while flashing those very white teeth. He married Marjorie Oelrichs, a Manhattan socialite and ex-debutante, who died soon after giving birth to a son.

Averell Harriman and his wife had been close to Eddy and Marjorie, and had a great deal to do with raising the boy. Eddy himself died young of a mysterious illness, and the son, Peter, went on to become a society bandleader of some celebrity himself. All of this biographical matter was worked into a story by a writer named Leo Katcher, and it was sold to Metro for a movie with a musical background.

Metro's leading director of musicals in the forties and fifties was George Sidney, who had done *Anchors Aweigh* (1945), *Annie Get Your Gun* (1950), and *Kiss Me, Kate* (1953). He liked the Duchin project, had known Eddy, and worked closely with screenwriter Samuel Taylor in developing a screenplay.

Then Sidney was enticed over to Columbia Pictures by Harry Cohn in the mid-fifties, and he somehow managed to take the "Eddy Duchin" project with him. At about this time, Sidney was on a plane en route from New York to Los Angeles and his seatmate was Tyrone. They were old acquaintances in Hollywood and Sidney had followed his career, especially its latest phase of more important screen and stage work, with much interest. He told Tyrone that he was working on a movie called *The Eddy Duchin Story*.

Tyrone brightened and told Sidney that Duchin was a frequent guest at his Saltair house when he was married to Annabella and often had performed in their living room for guests. "Who's going to play him?"

"You are," Sidney told him.

Before leaving Boston, after *The Dark Is Light Enough* went into mothballs, Tyrone wrote:

My dear Watty:

The wonderfully thoughtful gifty [a gold charm consisting solely of the number five, meaning 5-5-55, Tyrone's last birthday] arrived last evening, & I hasten to thank you for your kindness. It is a wonderful thought, & makes a welcome addition to the 'Life Begins' and the air-raid wardens' hat etc. Seems I have everything on my key chain *but* keys to a house—but then I have no house [Linda had it]—and who the hell cares. I somehow would rather have my mementos & memories.

These last few weeks have been a bitch—but it's all behind us now, & I must say the future looks rosy indeed. We closed last Saturday after a rousing two weeks in Boston, & it was nice to go out on that note—packed, enthusiastic houses & excellent notices. Then too I had the two weeks with Anne, & they were so pleasant. She is a darling, & I do enjoy being with her.

The children are with me now, & we fly to England on the 3rd of June. Only three weeks—but quiet ones & then back here. The picture begins July 18th—but whether here or in Calif. I don't know as yet. Imagine doing the 'Duchin Story'—what memories that brings back!! So, I am up to my you-know-what in piano lessons, conferences with George Sidney & God knows what else. . . . But I love it—and I am so happy here. *Merde to Calif!*

Annabella flew to Paris yesterday *with* her passport, so she is happy. . . .

Anne, who was a trained pianist and even something of a composer, was helping Tyrone daily during his Boston stay with piano fingering. Nat Brandwynne, who had played with Duchin, would be taking over this chore in New York, and soon Tyrone's fingering would be foolproof. No one could possibly know that Carmen Cavallaro was doing the actual playing in the film.

Kim Novak joined the company in New York for location

shooting, and a young lady by the name of Victoria Shaw came in as the ingenue.

Once again, as in the Marty Mahar role, Tyrone was required to open the picture as a youth full of beans and ambition as he dashes into the Central Park Casino. He may just have been the most convincing forty-year-old juvenile ever. The movie slowly unfolded an elegiac tale of foredoomed lovers, first one pair and then another as Eddy loses his first wife and goes on to the younger woman who is governess to his boy. George Sidney kept the sentiment under control at all times, and there is even an air of sophistication about the movie.

In the latter half of the picture, Tyrone is allowed to look his age. When the fatal illness strikes, we care very much, not least because he is so likable and talented. And Manhattan never looked more inviting. This was about the last time it would appear so attractive in films for *Blackboard Jungle* had set the tone for movies about the city a year earlier. The mood of the film was captured beautifully by Harry Stradling's camera.

The Eddy Duchin Story opened at the Radio City Music Hall on June 22, 1956, and Tyrone's film career was back where it had been a full decade earlier. He had made the transition into middle age gracefully and profitably. Two months after that, Linda obtained her final divorce decree in London.

Merde to California!

X

ALONE

A QUIET PLACE was the study of a deteriorating marriage and producer Roger Stevens must have thought that it was a theme Tyrone knew well. The protagonist, Oliver Lucas, is a concert pianist, who takes his wife to Italy, where they first fell in love, to try to salvage their relationship. Unfortunately, an attractive Italian girl, played by Susan Kohner, catches his eye and everything goes to pieces, including the play. Leora Dana brought her usual intelligent grace and sensibility to the part of the wife and Tyrone contributed his nicely aging handsomeness and Irish charm, but the audience was clearly unable to identify with any of it. Delbert Mann had directed a long series of successful one-hour dramas on television. This was nearly the end of the golden era of live TV theatre, but he was a comparative novice in the legitimate theatre bigtime. Nothing he suggested worked.

The opening at the Shubert in New Haven on November 23, 1955, was a fiasco. Leora Dana had been in turkeys before—she was an actress who was in almost constant demand—and she could sense that the evening was an intensive exercise in futility. Leora was the wife of actor Kurt Kasznar, and had met Tyrone when he came up to the Stratford Festival to see *Julius Caesar* with Raymond Massey, when she was playing Portia. The Kasznars were Tyrone's kind of people, and it was a case of love at first sight. They had become a very important part of his small New York theatrical social circle.

Despite the uniformly bad notices the play received, the New Haven engagement was pretty much of a sellout. The same was true in Cincinnati, where several of Tyrone's cousins came backstage and there was a Power reunion at his

263

hotel. Audiences seemed to regard *A Quiet Place* as a star turn, and business was brisk everywhere.

Playwright Julian Claman was so demoralized by the reviews, he quietly went home. Director Del Mann slipped away. Roger Stevens decided to recoup part of his and his angels' investment by allowing the tour to proceed all the way to Washington, but canceled the New York opening.

Tyrone and Leora dedicated the next several weeks to saving the show. They swapped lines. They even exchanged reactions so that he got angry instead of the wife. It reached a point where Tyrone told Leora that they really must stop short of exchanging clothes.

By the time they reached Washington, somehow they nearly managed to breathe new life into the play. Leora's husband, Kurt Kasznar, was then about to do *Six Characters in Search of an Author*. Tyrone suggested that they had a play in search of an author because, despite all their labors, neither he nor Leora were playwrights and the battle was lost. They closed in Washington, and ever afterward Tyrone would often muse, "I wonder what became of Julian Claman?"

Christmas of 1955 was spent at the Kasznars' beautiful garden apartment on East Forty-eighth Street in Manhattan. Other intimate New York friends shared the holiday with them. Talent agent Gloria Safier got on especially well with Tyrone; they each had a wicked sense of humor. The only Hollywood personality among them was Eva Gabor, then a girlfriend who was showing up with increasing frequency as the affair with Mary began to founder on the shoals of infidelity. Eva helped make the occasion gay. She was the most subdued of the Gabor sisters and thought Tyrone was an exceptionally sweet and dear person. She had hosted a party for him at her California home following the run of *The Dark Is Light Enough* when, as she recalled, "all Hollywood was at his feet." Their affair was not very serious on either side.

Tyrone had given up on finding something of real value to do in films, although he was ever on the lookout for a book or a play which Copa Productions might take on. He felt that he now belonged to the theatre, and there he hoped to remain with only an occasional film to clear up bills or alimony payments. The latter were a serious matter to him. According to his friend Leora Dana, they were walking down a New

York street when he asked, "Want to see something awful?" and he showed her a check to be forwarded to Annabella's lawyer for an amount she considered outrageous; then he mailed it at the next corner. Actually, his feelings for Annabella were warm and somewhat rueful. At about this time (Tyrone rarely dated letters), he wrote her from New York, thanking her for the offer to use her Paris apartment as a retreat while he was involved with an upcoming theatrical engagement in England.

> . . . I accept with great pleasure. Will let you know from London when, & if, I can be coming over. However, will see you for lunch on the 4th at Orly. . . .
> The children are well, & having a divine time. Every day to Central Park, & all the children are getting together for tea, etc. . . .
> A kiss to Mama Lili, & thank you again *so* much. . . .
> Until the 4th, take care
>
> > Love,
> >
> > > Tyrone

Then in mid-January, Tyrone was off to London. Hugh "Binkie" Beaumont had signed him to play the role of Dick Dudgeon, the irreligious son, in *The Devil's Disciple*, in a revival of the Shaw play. The last London production had starred Robert Donat in 1940. A long break-in tour was planned under the direction of Noel Willman, who also was playing General Burgoyne.

A whole new life loomed ahead. He had been acclaimed in London before in *Mister Roberts*. Now was the chance to solidify that stage-star status and perhaps even stay indefinitely. He was determined to play Dublin, too, where the first Tyrone Power had begun his successful stage career. He even thought of living in Ireland. The tax break was highly favorable and it was the land of his ancestors.

On January 26, 1956, rehearsals began on *The Devil's Disciple*. The company was first-rate. David Langton was playing Anthony, the pastor whose place Dick Dudgeon takes on the gallows. They rehearsed at the Lyric Theatre, and after one "read through," they were on their feet beginning the work of staging it. An opening was scheduled in Manchester on February 20.

Tyrone's social life diminished, although he was expecting
Eva (Gabor) to join him at any moment. Evenings, he dined
quietly with friends such as Lilli Palmer, who was now hap-
pily married to actor Carlos Thompson, and the Jack
Hawkinses or attended the theatre. He saw one new play on
its way to the West End because they were lacking a "Mrs.
Anderson" in the Shaw play and he endured two hours of *The
Long Echo* by Lesley Storm, going down to Worthing to catch
it; but the play put him off so entirely, he didn't find his last
needed player there. He called it "Worthing's answer to *A
Quiet Place*. Wow!" But he hugely enjoyed *La Plume de Ma
Tante* at the Garrick.

Snowstorms raged. Quite often, he remained in his suite at
the Connaught Hotel and read. His long-term and intimate
friend, Dr. Johnny Parente, passed through London and they
had a quiet evening together. He worried over a small dispute
with New York Actors Equity about his status as a member,
since he had indicated all of his future theatrical plans were in
England, but through the intercession of the Kaszners, he got
a new membership card.

Clipping from a medical advice column in a London
tabloid:

CHOOSE YOUR FRUIT

Q—Is there something specially wrong with me, because
I just seem to shrivel up in winter? My feet and hands go
completely numb no matter how many pairs of gloves or
socks I wear under my boots. I feel cold all over, get
covered with goose pimples, and my make-up goes blue.
Can you suggest a remedy?

The headline was clearly spliced onto the question by Tyrone
from the home economics page, and the whole thing Scotch-
taped to a letter to the Kasznars with the handwritten
question: "Never mind about the other things. What *do* I do
about the make-up???"

He had seen a production of Samuel Beckett's *Waiting for
Godot* and he thought Peter Bull was especially good as
"Pozzo," but he kept seeing his friend Kasznar in the part
(and Kasznar did it in New York later that year). His schedule

was becoming more hectic. He was asked to open a new TV network in Birmingham on his way to Manchester for the play's opening. He wrote the Kasznars, "Do you think there is any chance your coming over at all—anytime? Please try—it's all so sad & empty." He was trying to get Kurt Kasznar's production of *Six Characters* done in England. To Leora, he added,

> . . . My darling Lelee, what a joy to work with Willman—*here is a director*. Can't really tell you what he does nor how he does it—but HE KNOWS, and he's articulate, & he's sure, & he's talented, & *right*. He had me doing things I would never have dreamed of doing—nor even thought I could do. Most stimulating. . . . I'm dead—so good night my darlings—will try to write this week. No promises, but love—and loads of it.
>
> Sempre,
> Tyrone

Upon receiving this last warm letter and word of Tyrone's sense of desolation at opening to strangers in Manchester, Kurt turned to his wife and said, "I think we should go."

"Go where?" Leora asked.

"To Manchester! Why not? We're both free right now." And the next moment, Kasznar was on the phone to BOAC, inquiring about flights to London. The opening was set for the next night. The airline said that it was sorry, but they had nothing except a flight to Manchester. Kasznar couldn't believe his ears.

Within hours, the Kasznars were packed and aboard the British airliner en route to Manchester. When they arrived, they had about half an hour to get to their hotel and change for the theatre. There was no time for dinner, but that could wait.

The theatre was packed, and it had taken some finagling for the Kasznars to get seats at all. Tyrone's first appearance stirred the audience to a high pitch and his spirited performance carried the evening. There were cheers and bravos at the curtain, even though Leora privately felt that his overall projection of the role was on the weak side. Perhaps it had something to do with his voice, which was beautifully resonant and reminded her of a great many past movies.

But no matter. The audience loved him, even though he holed himself up in his dressing room and refused to see anyone after the curtain. The Kasznars sent two little notes back that "a couple of American friends" would like to say "hello." He politely instructed the doorman to give his regrets. The Kasznars were aghast. It wasn't every day that they flew across an ocean on an impulse. Then the doorman informed Tyrone that "the American friends" refused to leave. He sighed and said he would see them. When they appeared at the doorway, his eyes popped and the makeup seemed to rise right off his face. Later, when he had his fatal heart attack, they regretted all the times they surprised him like that. It was a running joke between them—who could top whom?

After Manchester came Liverpool, which he described as "fairly grim, the houses like Manchester—but away from the theatre, death. Plus *very* active 'pointed-heads.' Beastly." But then the company reached Edinburgh, Tyrone calling it

> heaven. The hotel [George] is most comfortable, the people warm, reserved, but friendly, and the audiences—well! The theatre is a dream, and as soon as I can I want to explore the town a bit—it looks fascinating.
>
> The trip up here by car was wonderful. Beautiful sunshine—so clear & sparkling, and the colours almost hurt the eye they were so vivid. That mauve haze on the hills, & the damp slate roofs—green trees, & the road a ribbon of blue after the rain. All this washed in golden sunshine—bliss.

Although Tyrone was fighting a cold, the Edinburgh premiere (the first production ever of the play in Scotland) won an enthusiastic press. The *Evening Dispatch* said that he is "a likeable . . . robust and thoroughly convincing Dick," although they had one small reservation which was that he lacked sufficient insolence, weakening the scene with Judith before the court-martial. The Glasgow *Herald* sent their man, who wrote that Tyrone's performance "lacks something of the necessary fire—for Dick is, after all, a saint turned inside out—but it has considerable panache instead."

And so it went throughout the tour. Great reviews with unstinting praise for Tyrone in all the provincial places and some back-handed compliments in the large cities. These more knowledgeable critics seemed to sense that Tyrone had all of the equipment for greatness save passion. He was one step removed from the very heart of the matter in whatever he did, which would make his last, magnificent performance on film for Billy Wilder in *Witness for the Prosecution* so very right. Leonard Vole, despite his probable guilt, is a man outside the action, a man in search of a goal he can't articulate. Tyrone accepted the plaudits and only took umbrage when a man on the *Lancashire Evening Post* in Blackpool called his work "a brilliant new interpretation of Dudgeon in the Hollywood manner." Was there no escape?

The theatres were another matter. They were either exquisite or underheated "football fields." He called the theatre in Bournemouth "just horrible: rather like the South Duchsbury High School Auditorium—and the audiences have all been embalmed, or should be." But in Bournemouth, too, were Jack and Doreen Hawkins, so there was a grand reunion, although his cold, in that bitter, snowy season hung on. Then agent Maynard Morris sent him copies of all of Rex Harrison's rave notices in *My Fair Lady*, which had just opened in New York. Tyrone read them, "put them on the board for the company, and then we all cut our throats!! My God! How far can one go?" Bill Gallagher arrived the first week of May, while Tyrone was in Leeds, and that boosted his morale.

Finally, during their week's run at the Hippodrome in Bristol, word came from the Tennant office, for which Binkie Beaumont was the principal producer, that the play would be closing with its Dublin engagement "because of a lack of a suitable theatre." He began making more definite plans for the future and relaxed a bit with the company. He even stayed at a theatrical boardinghouse in Bristol, Mrs. Brierly's, along with the rest of the cast.

Tyrone scheduled the start of his first British-based film for his Copa Productions, *Seven Waves Away*, which was written and was to be directed by Richard Sale, for July 2 at Shepperton Studios. He signed Mai Zetterling, who had done Strindberg's *Miss Julie* with him on British television before the tour began, as his leading lady. He even leased a furnished house in London for June, July, and August at 30 Chester

Street, and arranged with Linda to have the children for part
of the summer, although he cursed when he heard that Linda
was bringing them over herself. The bitterness there was
lasting. There was no cure for it.

On May 29, he wrote the Kasznars:

> Shelbourne Hotel, Dublin, Monday
> My darlings—
>   Well, here we are—into the last week. It seems almost
> yesterday that you were in Manchester, and now it's
> over. Well, it's been a glorious time and I've loved every
> minute of it. We are certainly going out in a blaze of
> glory. This is *really* the place. They pack the theatre, they
> love the show, & the reception is staggering. It's nice to
> leave it this way.
>   I'll not say anything about the opening here. . . . It was
> the full stomping bit though and really choked me up. In
> my curtain speech I made reference to the fact that this
> was the 1st time in 130 years that there had been a Tyrone
> Power on the stage of an Irish theatre. I blush to tell you
> the response that got. You *must* play here one day. It's
> better than cocaine.

What Tyrone failed to tell the Kasznars was that Mary
Roblee had come to the Dublin opening and they had spent
the night roistering in a local pub, where Tyrone was
congratulated the night through. Mary was not popular with
the Kasznars, and she thought they were Hollywood types,
despite both Leora and Kurt's substantial and distinguished
theatrical reputations. Mary was delighted to be with him that
night, however, since they were headed for a breakup and this
was one of the last wonderful times together.

The Dublin reviews were ecstatic. This engagement rated
very high with Tyrone, nearly on a level with the delayed
London one. The *Sunday Press* said: "Tyrone Power's first
stage appearance in Dublin was an undoubted success. He
proved even greater on the stage than on the screen, and as a
magnificent Dick Dudgeon, he added to his own prestige,
while raising the reputation of G.B.S. in Dublin, so far as it
lay on this melodrama." The *Sunday Independent* wrote that
Tyrone Power was giving "a spectacularly successful performance as Dick Dudgeon," while the *Evening Press* called

the production "the finest . . . yet seen in this country. And, thanks to Noel Willman's production (direction) and Tyrone Power's acting, it is pure Shaw."

The glow from those Irish reviews lasted a long, long time for Tyrone. He had proved himself to his own kind, and despite his mixed Irish-French ancestry, he was most loyal to the Irish side. Yet he temporarily put aside his intention of settling in Ireland. It seemed much too damp, and Irish though he was, he had to confess that he preferred London to Dublin. Perhaps if he had gone there years earlier and had enjoyed a similar success, he would look for an Irish estate in deadly earnest. Now he was forty-two years old (he celebrated his birthday in Leeds on the eve of their opening there), and he wanted only comfort and loving friends. Still, it remained a dream of his, which he would take up again.

London was crowded at the time with American film stars. Marilyn Monroe was shooting *The Prince and the Showgirl* with Laurence Olivier at Pinewood, and getting into trouble with the press for seeming surprisingly cool to them. She was, of course, terrified by the prospect of working with Olivier. Charlie Chaplin was still editing his *A King in New York*, shot at the Shepperton Studios, a film about the McCarthy Era in America just ended although not quite buried. The furor over the U.S. Immigration Agency's vicious denial of his re-entry into the United States had long since died down, and he had settled with Oona, his childlike wife with the beatific smile, in Switzerland; but both he and his film were considered too controversial for an Eisenhower America and the film was banned there for several years. Tyrone and his Copa crew would take over the same sound stages at Shepperton used by Chaplin, a matter of no great significance. The two stars had not been friends, Tyrone being about as active politically as he was religiously, which put him slightly right of center.

In a way, it was as if he had never left California. There were familiar faces at all the best dining rooms—Ava Gardner, David Niven, Robert Mitchum, Esther Williams, Stewart Granger, Ingrid Bergman, Merle Oberon, Jennifer Jones, and even his old friend Jack Benny with wife Mary Livingstone.

A surprise birthday party was planned by Jack, and Merle and Tyrone were pressed into service to see that Mary arrived "to meet the Queen" on time. Instead of the Queen, there were several dozen of her closest friends, most of them from California, to greet her.

The girls, Romina and Taryn, arrived with their mother, who tactfully moved on to the Continent. Tyrone was already deeply involved with his leading lady, Mai Zetterling, who had left a lover, a young American writer and publisher, stranded with an apartment in Paris and imploring her to come back to him when the picture was finished. But Tyrone was very discreet around the girls and told a friend that he preferred to curtail some of his social or love life while they were with him because it meant far more to him to have one of them shaking him at eight-fifteen in the morning, telling him "Wake up, Daddy!"

Production on the first Copa film production, *Seven Waves Away* with script and direction by Richard Sale, began early that summer. He and Dick Sale bought almost identical 1935 vintage Rolls-Royce Silver Clouds and got them fitted out with initialed license plates. Sale's wife, the writer Mary Loos, threw together a California-style dinner for the film company, since she felt that Tyrone, despite all of his protests to the contrary, really missed the movie colony. The only one who seemed to be moved by the gesture was Lloyd Nolan, who began to weep, and when asked why, told her, "It's your goddamned hot chili!"

Tyrone told a London reporter, Thomas Wiseman, that the fun had gone out of Hollywood.

I've made 42 films, and I am dissatisfied with 90 per cent of them. If you ask me what films of mine I liked, I can name you about three—and then I have to start thinking. . . . You can't go on always being a knight in shining armour. I'm 42 and there are too many young fellows better equipped for that sort of role coming along. You can kid everybody but the fellow you shave every morning. The day might come when your phone isn't ringing any more and nobody knocks at your door. . . . There [in Hollywood], your social activities are restricted to the people you work with. You meet the same people at party after party. The cast is always the same—and the dialogue doesn't change much either. Always shop talk . . .

When asked about his two wives, he said, "I wouldn't say I had made a mistake in my choice of wives. I would not have missed the experience of knowing the two ladies in question for anything. I think I have emerged from the experience a better, more understanding, human being." But he added that he had no intention of marrying again, because he lacked the enthusiasm for it.

Still, Mary Roblee had arrived in London from her brief stay in Ireland. Earlier, she had subleased his penthouse on Park Avenue while he was away. But now she was in town, and their relationship was very amicable. Perhaps the interview with Mr. Wiseman had clarified things a bit. That was often the way around Tyrone. There was no tension over Miss Zetterling; she had been forewarned. And Miss Zetterling, a bright lady herself, understood how he felt about Mary and did not monopolize his time.

And so the summer passed. The title of the movie, on which photography was now complete, was changed to *Abandon Ship!* (1957). It concerned a luxury liner on a world cruise which explodes when it strikes a derelict mine from World War II in the South Atlantic. Much of the action takes place in a lifeboat, and is involved with the decision (by executive officer Tyrone) as to who shall survive, since it is not only overloaded, but has many desperate passengers clinging to its sides. He is forced to order a dozen of them off the boat at gunpoint in order to save those "who won't fall faint when the food gives out and the water runs dry." The survivors have complete faith in him until rescue is near and they realize that husbands, mothers, and fathers have been lost to them through the iron will of Tyrone. Mai Zetterling, as a nurse, has fallen in love with him and remains true, as does an unhappily married member of Café Society, who is infatuated. Richard Sale's story was gripping, his direction taut, and Tyrone's performance flawless.

Because so much of the film had been made in the "tank" at Shepperton, the actors were more concerned about not drowning, pneumonia, and facing howling winds than dialogue. Much of it had to be dubbed, which took Tyrone and the cast into the fall. Before that task was begun he flew to Sicily with Mai for two weeks, leaving his new London house, a charming old place at 51 Abingdon Road, in the hands of Mrs. Lilian Ruddy, who had been recommended as housekeeper by Esther Williams. Although not on a mews, it had the feeling of being on one. It was very small, with one or two fair-sized rooms on each of three floors, and you entered through a dining area adjacent to the kitchen. There was no garden to speak of and it was right on the street, but it was delightfully cozy and seemed exactly right for Tyrone.

Mrs. Ruddy's husband had been paralyzed for five years and had had both legs amputated after gangrene set in. She was devoted to him, and Tyrone always allowed her to leave early each day to visit her husband in the hospital and eventually helped get him into a nursing home. There would be a long stream of close friends staying as guests of Tyrone's at the Abingdon Road house, in the Kensington section of London, including Charles and Elsa Laughton, Louis Jourdan and his wife, and the Kurt Kasznars.

Professionally, Mai and Tyrone were moving in different directions. She was wild about films, even spoke of an ambition to direct. He was convinced that the theatre meant far more to him and was looking forward to the London premiere of *The Devil's Disciple* in November. The Berliner Ensemble had come to London late that summer with Bertolt Brecht directing his own work and featuring, among many others, the gifted Helene Weigel. Tyrone saw *The Caucasian Chalk Circle* and *Mother Courage*. He found the performances "tremendous. *Most* interesting and wonderfully stimulating."

Following its West End opening at the Winter Garden in mid-November, *The Times* called *The Devil's Disciple* "a notable salute" to Shaw in his centenary year (1956), and went on to say that Tyrone's performance could not have disappointed the huge audience attracted to the theatre by his celebrity.

Darryl F. Zanuck finally had resigned as head of production at Twentieth Century–Fox to become an independent producer. He left his wife and family and went to France to set up temporary headquarters in Paris. His mistress, Bella Darvi, whose professional last name was composed of the first letters of his given name and that of his wife, Virginia, was now a gambling addict and heavily in debt to the Monte Carlo casinos. One of his first acts in Paris was to bail her out and then send her packing. In a few years, she would die a suicide.

His first production for DFZ films was Alec Waugh's *Island in the Sun*, a potboiler best-seller about miscegenation. In it, Harry Belafonte was required to kiss Joan Fontaine, resulting in the picture's being banned throughout the South in the United States. Zanuck made "significant pronouncements" in the press about the controversy in which he brought up the furor over *Pinky* and *The Grapes of Wrath*. But there was nothing memorable about usually brilliant Robert Rossen's work on *Island in the Sun*. The reviews were mixed, while the box-office receipts were piling up. Zanuck was launched with a controversial and melodramatic *succès de banque*.

Zanuck then turned all of his attention to a second project, Ernest Hemingway's *The Sun Also Rises*. This was something Zanuck could get excited about. He knew Hemingway from encounters at Sun Valley, Idaho, a ski resort financed by Averell Harriman. Zanuck told his biographer, Mel Gussow, "He was a great companion—eating, drinking, storytelling companion. He had great attraction for women, even during the period when he was overweight. He had style with women and his conversation was so good." Unfortunately, the two men were no longer close. There had been a falling out over the filming of *The Snows of Kilimanjaro* (1952), Hemingway feeling that his work had been made into melodramatic trash, even though it had earned a great deal of money.

Although Tyrone was more than a dozen years older than the protagonist, Jake Barnes, of *Sun*, Zanuck considered no one else at any time. To him, Tyrone was "the truest, the handsomest, the best of the lot." Zanuck considered his age unimportant. Ava Gardner was his other first and only choice, as Lady Brett. Finally, he invited Henry King to direct. Since the Zanuck films were being released by Fox, there was no contractual problem.

Upon receipt of her copy of the script, co-star Ava Gardner, then living in Spain, allowed her next-door neighbor, who just happened to be Hemingway, to read it. Hemingway was appalled. He immediately wired Zanuck to stop everything or he would sue. Peter Viertel then rewrote the script, but it never did suit Hemingway, who finally shrugged and fell out of touch with the project, simply taking the money.

Errol Flynn, near the end of his film career because of his many dissipations, was playing a man very like himself at that point, Mike Campbell, doing so well in the part he would follow it with an expanded version, playing John Barrymore in *Too Much, Too Soon* (1958). All of the male beauty was now gone and in its place was a wry, pasty lost grandeur. Tyrone, who was only five years younger, was saddened by his presence, although delighted that Zanuck had cast him. It had been a depressing year for Tyrone, far too full of reminders of lost opportunities and impregnable mountains walling him off finally from his personal Shangri-La.

Mel Ferrer was brought in as Jake's rival for Lady Brett, Robert Cohn, and here was another once brilliant leading man in the twilight of his career, although he never had shone with the magnitude of Flynn. Added to this gallery of leading men no longer at the zenith was a curious young man, Robert Evans, who had come to Hollywood at the instigation of Norma Shearer because, so she said, he resembled her late husband, Irving Thalberg, and Evans had been hired to play the studio head in a film biography of Lon Chaney, *The Man with a Thousand Faces* (1957). Evans was a darkly handsome New York garment manufacturer with limited acting experience. He was a sort of beautiful, male Sonja Henie, only he couldn't skate. Evans was to play "Pedro Romero," the matador. Naturally, he made a magnificent figure of a bullfighter alone in the arena with his suit of lights and the bull, but the bull won all of the acting honors. While Tyrone had made a genuine effort to become an *aficionado* during his time with Linda, it seemed evident that his approach to the art of bullfighting was entirely intellectual; his emotions were nearly always ripped by such excursions.

Tyrone's reaction to Evans' first appearance in the rushes was so negative, he was afraid that this bad actor would sink the entire project. Shooting on the film was nearly all done on location. It was in Pamplona, Spain, that Tyrone and director Henry King prevailed upon Zanuck to replace Evans. Tyrone thought that the matador instructing Evans in the movements of the *corrida* would be a better choice. Still, Zanuck refused to yield, telling them that Evans had sex appeal. He would make one final effort to launch Evans as a leading man in *The*

Fiend Who Walked the West (1958) and then turn Evans free to rise in the industry as production head of Paramount Pictures within less than a decade.

In Paris, Tyrone stayed in an apartment of Annabella's. She was then living part of the time at a thirty-acre farm she bought in the south of France near Biarritz, which she called "Contra-mundo." Zanuck was so totally involved in the production that he even took over its direction for ten days while Henry King scouted out locations at Biarritz.

The Sun Also Rises is probably Hemingway's finest novel. Jake Barnes has been wounded in the groin during World War I and has been rendered impotent. There are women who would love him (Lady Brett et al.), but his condition leaves them something less than fulfilled. Lady Brett is Circe, and feels compelled to castrate her lovers, except for bullfighter Romero, who is allowed to escape with his balls intact. Hemingway told a professor with a major interest in his work, Fraser Drew, that *The Sun Also Rises* was the most moral book he had ever written, a "tract against promiscuity," and added that critics had a tendency to overidentify him with Jake Barnes.

> It is true [he told Drew], that I got the idea when I was in the hospital in Italy after I had been wounded. I too had been wounded in the groin and there had been wool infection there. I was swollen up like footballs . . . but I was not made impotent like Jake Barnes, obviously. I was put into a so-called genito-urinary ward where there were many guys with groin wounds, and it was pretty bad. That is where I got the idea for Jake, not from myself. But of course people thought that he was a self-portrait.

Since the novel's main concern is with Jake's mourning his loss of manhood, it may be assumed that it was close to Hemingway's own confusions about himself. Hemingway felt compelled to prove his own identity as a man again and again, often brushing with death in the attempt. He honestly believed that he had convinced everyone, and told Professor Drew: "They've said everything about me except that I'm homosexual, and that will be the end. . . . "

Tyrone, as we already know, shared some of these con-

fusions about himself, but he was more honest than
Hemingway personally in dealing with them. There were no
trophied heads of big game in his living room; he was never
heard to brag about an amorous exploit or conquest; and
there was no bluff heartiness about him. Tyrone could have
made a compelling Jake Barnes, but in Zanuck and Henry
King's hands, he was not. The production cried out for
creative innovation and liberation from the printed page,
which is never sacred in moviemaking. There was the air of a
dead classic beginning to permeate the studios and locations
where it was being shot.

But the production moved ponderously on, for months,
and soon was in Biarritz, where Tyrone visited Annabella's
farm and was relieved that his beloved Saltair house, sold by
Annabella in 1954, had helped buy the place. Annabella was
astonished by the change in him. He seemed like a man who
had outlived his time and felt alien in the new one. It was a
rueful meeting.

Final shooting on *Sun* was done in Mexico. It was a noble
gamble that already seemed to be lost (and curiously, that
feeling of being a lost cause seeped into the film and became
the truest thing about it as an adaptation of the original).
When it was released in 1957, co-stars Eddie Albert and Errol
Flynn got the best notices.

Life as a bachelor at Copa de Oro was not much fun. The
truth seemed to be that he had come to dislike much of
Hollywood. Those who had survived the two decades with
him were often comforting, but not terribly exciting. Watson
had left Zanuck over a personal falling out, but had remained
in touch somehow, although on a very stiff and formal basis.
Now, when he gossiped or chatted about Hollywood
parochial matters, Tyrone had to strain to sustain an interest
in the subjects under discussion. Tyrone had matured; he had
grown beyond the town.

Even before the winter snows had melted, Tyrone was back
in New York, snug in his penthouse at 760 Park Avenue. Here
he could breathe; here he could talk, and listen with interest.
Mai Zetterling was in town, having settled her rather tangled
affairs in Europe; and there were the Garson Kanins, the Kurt
Kasznars, and an actor who was Machiavellian in appearance
but full of charm and talent, Arnold Moss. Moss was involved

in a great many theatrical projects and managed to attract Tyrone's interest in some of them.

On an impulse, Tyrone took off for Europe. Before committing himself to anything in the American theatre, he wanted to know if there were anything doing in London. He also had some business to transact for Copa Productions. Gina Lollobrigida, who was then riding a great wave of popularity, had read a rough draft of a huge costume drama revolving around the Queen of Sheba and King Solomon. It was the sort of swashbuckler he had hoped he was done with, but his producer Ted Richmond thought it would make a lot of money and so did producer Eddie Small, who had been an admirer of Tyrone's for a long time.

In March, Tyrone was back in Paris. He had wired Annabella from London, saying "Keep Thursday evening open." She went to his suite at the Hotel Loti, where Louis Jourdan and his wife, Quique, joined them for drinks. Then Tyrone and Annabella left the Jourdans and went to the Berkley Restaurant for an early dinner. The maître d' knew them and led them to a private booth.

Tyrone began talking almost at once. He said, "I've made many mistakes in my life, but the biggest one was when I let you go." Annabella was silent much of the time. This was obviously something Tyrone had had on his mind for a long time. Finally, he suggested that they go up to her apartment on the rue Marceau "for a last drink."

There, Tyrone told her that his life was empty, almost purposeless. Annabella was moved and torn apart by her emotions. Before leaving Hollywood, he said that he had spoken with Billy Wilder about doing the role of the defendant, Leonard Vole, in *Witness for the Prosecution*. Billy had assured him that the part would make him hotter than ever in Hollywood, but, Tyrone explained, he couldn't stand the place any more. Not alone.

The conversation was taking Annabella into a deep melancholy, and she wanted to stop, to talk of less dangerous things. "Why don't we try again?" she heard Tyrone asking. "I know it won't be the same. Couldn't be. But isn't it worth trying?"

With that, he kissed her, and Annabella confessed much later that she had wanted to say "yes," but she had heard too many things and didn't want to be hurt again. This was no

longer the vivacious girl just off the boat from the French
cinema. Annabella was now a woman who had learned to live
with her past sorrows, and practical enough to go on living
her own life, often with some measure of happiness and
gaiety. She had not been without men. There were many
things to be considered, other people. It was not a thing to be
decided on the moment.

Then Tyrone got to his feet and said he was going to walk
down the stairs. He understood her hesitancy, he said. Who
could blame her? He told her that he wouldn't take the
elevator because he wanted one last chance. She could call
down to him at any time. And so he left, and she listened to
his footsteps as they descended. She wanted to cry out to him
to come back, but something prevented her. Perhaps her
present involvement; perhaps a sudden bitter memory of the
past. A thousand times since, she regretted that she did not.
But a year later, three years later, a dozen years, in California; in Deerfield, Massachusetts; in Mexico; in Paris, when
she saw young Tyrone growing up—the son Tyrone did not
live to see or know—and so well brought up by his mother,
Annabella thought that fate had been kind after all, and she
thanked Providence that she had said "No."

On that brief trip, Tyrone also visited his adopted daughter
Annie. She was now married to German actor Oskar Werner
and living in Liechtenstein. The two had met when he was
making *Decision Before Dawn* (1951), and Annie Power was
handling the horses. When Tyrone gave her her first horse, he
couldn't have known that they would become a passion with
her. She loved grooming them, riding them, and looking after
them. Werner, a most sensitive actor, noticed immediately
how tenderly she handled the mounts, and became interested
in her. Within a few months, they were married. Life for
Annie Werner since then had been full of more ups and downs
than her mother's. The temperament of an actor is a far more
volatile thing than that of the most intractable stallion.
Tyrone, however, found Werner rather sweet-tempered and
contemplative on all the occasions when they met.

XI

A BAREFOOT LORELEI

IN MAY 1957, Tyrone flew back to California to begin interiors (nearly all consisting of scenes to be shot in a splendid reproduction of London's Old Bailey Courtroom) at the old Sam Goldwyn Studios in Hollywood for Billy Wilder's production of Agatha Christie's *Witness for the Prosecution*. Some location work already had been done in London.

Professionally, his life had never been more fulfilling. *Witness* was already a smash stage success throughout the world. Wilder believed in him, in that serious part of him which Zanuck had rarely touched. Max Youngstein at United Artists had okayed a multi-million dollar budget on the biblical spectacle, which would follow next year for his own company. There were several stage prospects awaiting his return to New York.

But he needed a woman so badly, he ached. Not an easily-available roll in the hay, but a woman's company, feel, spirit, *presence*. He had not really held out any hope of a reconciliation with Annabella. That was a gambler's plunge.

Then one evening, there she was. He had allowed some close friends, the Charles Skipseys, to honeymoon in the guest house at Copa de Oro. The bride was a Mexican girl named Lourdes Nieto, and one evening just as *Witness* was well under way, Tyrone entertained the Skipseys for dinner and a friend of Lourdes Skipsey, Deborah Ann Minardos, then divorced from Nico Minardos, an actor better known for circulating about Hollywood than for working in films.

Deborah Montgomery Minardos was a brunette beauty with a directness about her that Tyrone found enchanting. There was in her a hint of what Linda might have been like if she had forgotten appearances and the hair stylist and her eleven languages and decided to be just plain Blanca Welter.

A bit earlier, she had set her cap for Elvis Presley, and they had gone around Hollywood for several months. But Presley, while liking Debbie's effulgent spirit, wanted nothing to do with matrimony at that time. For her part, Debbie was not about to become one of the singer's available girls, and they broke up.

So it would seem that Tyrone had come a long distance away from the likes of Annabella, despite their recent meeting. Perhaps, as he approached his mid-forties, he was turning his back on the glamorous life, on the world of aristocratic and monied "piss-elegance," as he termed it. On the surface, at least, it seemed a healthy tack to pursue.

Debbie impressed Tyrone's friends as being a simple, wide-eyed, ingenuous young woman (she was about to be twenty-six) with a slightly nasal whine in her voice, marking her as a native of the Deep South. Her mother and stepfather still lived in her home town of Tunica, Mississippi. Where Linda's free spirit seemed something that was the end product of rebellion against conformity, Debbie's seemed innate. Nineteen fifty-seven was the last gasp of the beatnik era and the onset of the hippies' time. At twenty-five, Debbie Minardos still liked to go barefoot, let her hair down, eschew makeup except for a little lipstick, and generally enjoy life. But a true beatnik she was not. A poetry reading doubtless would have bored the bejeezus out of her. She was often blunt-spoken. Tyrone had considerable accommodation to undertake while with Debbie. Yet it all seemed worthwhile.

Debbie was around Copa de Oro much of that summer. She seemed to adore Tyrone, and took some pains to dress up for more formal occasions, which were becoming fewer and fewer as he began moving in her direction, if not in her world.

Witness would make Tyrone financially comfortable again. His agent, George Chasin, had been able to get him a large salary plus 10 per cent of the gross. That percentage would mean more than any other asset to Tyrone and his estate in the years ahead.

Billy Wilder was relentless in seeking just the right reaction, but he was no martinet. He was one of the few authentic geniuses left in Hollywood since the collapse of the great studios in the 1950s. Pixielike, always smiling quizzically, myopic, forever wearing a battered fedora, he *cajoled* brilliance out of his players. Naturally, he had to begin with a good script, and he always assured this by writing it himself, often with a collaborator, I. A. L. Diamond. *Witness*, however, had been written with Harry Kurnitz, an old poker crony of Wilder's who had an ear for sardonic wit.

This was Wilder's first (and last) time directing either Tyrone or Charles Laughton, who played Tyrone's lawyer (barrister), Sir Wilfrid Roberts. Wilder made two decisions—play down Tyrone or have him underplay or underreact to everything, and play up Laughton, allowing him full latitude in chewing down the very walls of the courtroom in Old Bailey, if he so desired.

Tyrone was delighted to be working with Laughton again. They both indulged in the same impish humor, and Tyrone admired him professionally almost as much as he did Olivier, and cheered him on in his mugging and flamboyant scenery-shredding. He got close to Charles and Elsa again. Elsa was very outspoken and Tyrone was often surprised by her.

Wilder, in turn, got quite close to Tyrone, whom he had rescued from too many years of trashy films. He met Debbie, but it is unlikely that he encouraged a match. Tyrone's friends were urging him to caution; yet Tyrone himself had once written that if a man gets burned once but likes what he is doing, he will do it again regardless.

After the shooting was over on *Witness*, Tyrone and Wilder went together to Wilder's native Austria to unwind. It was September, and he wrote Debbie that "flaming autumn has me by the throat. I have felt a few times almost on the point of strangulation from the sheer beauty of the time and place. The crystal lakes, towering white-crowned mountains, deep blue-green armies of pine trees marching up their slopes—or the sweeping farm and cattle-decked meadows." Always, these flights of lyric at-oneness with the beautiful were induced by a new romance. Incredibly, at forty-three, they were just as ardent as those he had penned to sweethearts in his twenties.

> I have a growing suspicion [he confirms], it is really not these glories of nature that has produced this feeling. I really believe it's because of you. . . . how I wished for you knowing how you too would have loved that gentle sweeping drive (albeit in the rain) from Paris to Dijon. The next day in rich, golden sunshine through Burgundy, over the Jura into Switzerland & the dazzling brilliance of

the lake at Neuchatel, on to the quiet solid beauty of
Lucerne. . . . Then yesterday over the Arlberg pass—with
snow even now—gliding down that long valley to
Innsbruck. . . . like something out of a Tyrolean dream.
It was the most heavenly 4 days, blessed by unbelievable
sunshine. . . .

It has taught me a great lesson, my darling. A lesson
that I will whisper to you some bleak, rain-bound New
York night when we are together. . . .

The lesson, apparently, was that nature and the forces of
nature were the most significant things in life. His relationship with Debbie had been marked by his tossing aside all ar-
tifice and what he now looked upon as "phony" gentility.

By October, the two men were in Bad-Gastein taking the
baths, where they were joined by Charles Laughton. Tyrone
wrote Debbie that he was getting sunburned "in October. The
weather has just been crazy—*way* far out. A real swinging sun
every day in a cloudless sky, and we lap it up." He was beginning to use her argot, which was hippie talk. But he did still
cling to certain proprieties. The children, Romina and Taryn,
were coming to New York, and he wrote Bill Gallagher to find
Debbie a suite at the Hotel Carlisle, politely hinting that she
should leave his penthouse during their visit. "I think it's
better that way," he wrote Debbie. "There just wouldn't be
room for us all, plus a nurse."

Tyrone's vitality returned at Bad-Gastein. He and Wilder
even took a train two stops away from the resort town and
walked back through the mountain trails.

Wilder's wife Audrey went East to stay at Tyrone's penthouse for a while, and seemed to get on well with Debbie.
Tyrone was frequently an international host, and, of course,
loved doing it. As for Wilder, he hugely enjoyed Tyrone's
company. Unlike so many actors, he really listened to a man
and he had the kind of agile mind Wilder liked to parry with.
There would have been other Wilder-Power successes in the
years ahead, had Tyrone lived, of that there is absolutely no
doubt. Perhaps the next one would have been Wilder's version
of *Sherlock Holmes*, which Tyrone could have redeemed with
his wry humor.

Tyrone returned from Europe to his penthouse, now living
openly with Debbie there. He seemed in no rush to marry her,
but he later wrote her of that month together:

. . . The last four weeks have been a dream, & I really believe that being with you for that time is the closest I have come to real & complete happiness. I never really believed it existed, you see. We're never too old to learn. . . . It's going to be a wonderful winter—and let's enjoy every moment of it. But then, we have so many things to look forward to, don't we? And in case any of the local inhabitants want to know what you are doing with "that old man," you'll tell them, won't you?

Debbie saw in him the same vital spirit, the same enjoyment and savoring of each moment of life, which she had in abundance. It was something Tyrone shared, too, with Laughton, and he wrote of walking for two hours through the gardens at Versailles with him—"pure bliss."

The three men came in the afternoon to Annie Werner's house in Trisen, Liechtenstein. Tyrone stayed the night at Annie's, where Annabella was visiting, while his two companions returned for breakfast the following morning. The men were happy together, still euphoric from having made such a great film. A few days later, the travelers had a farewell dinner for Laughton, who was flying back to Los Angeles on the northern route, by way of Copenhagen.

Tyrone had plans to do a lot of reading to Debbie when he got back home; he was afraid of "getting on the merry-go-round" again. Then there was a flurry of personal appearances with *Witness* in Vienna, Berlin, and Stockholm. His "grand tour" wound up in the Swedish capital, where he ran into his old friends from England, the Charles Hughesdons, and had drinks with them. They were charming, gay, and amusing people, very much the sort Tyrone had cultivated everywhere. He urged Charles Hughesdon to look Debbie up on his way through New York.

Upon Tyrone's return from Europe, there were almost daily meetings with actor Arnold Moss. Moss had persuaded Armina Marshall (Mrs. Lawrence Langner) to provide Theatre Guild backing for a tour of Shaw's *Back to Methuselah*, followed by a limited run on Broadway. A leading lady, Faye Emerson, had been secured, and they would spend a long enough time on the road to get it polished for Broadway. Miss Emerson was a bosomy, flirtatious lady then much in demand on television, where she had had her own show. Even though she was married to Elliott Roosevelt, one of the sons of the late President, Debbie observed the lady's endowments and was relieved that Tyrone had made elaborate plans for her to accompany him on the tour. This was not an easy matter for Debbie, since this would be a bus tour and they would bounce around half of the eastern seaboard before coming into the Ambassador Theatre in New York on March 26, 1958.

It was the iron determination of Arnold Moss that brought the almost insurmountable project of getting Shaw's *Back to Methuselah* revived in America. This broadside attack on the Book of Genesis, on immortality as promised by the Bible, and on all those "fools" who chose not to believe Darwin's theory of evolution, was considered too controversial in its own day (1921). Shaw wrote in a lengthy preface to a reprint: "I threw over all economic considerations and faced the apparent impossibility of a performance during my lifetime." It received its world premiere in America in 1922, when the then youthful and brash Theatre Guild presented it in three installments and three nights, all 90,000 words of it, and lost $20,000 in the process.

In an article for the New York *Times* just before the play's Broadway opening, Moss wrote of his drastic cutting of the play and said that he had the blessing of the Shaw estate, but in his own lifetime, Shaw, who died in 1950, would not allow his works to be edited or tampered with in any way. In the case of this version of *Methuselah*, it is a wonder that he did not return from across the Styx to stir up a ghostly clamor. After this episode, surely the conclusive test of whether the departed can communicate with this world, we may safely assume that Shaw truly has moved on to another plane, or, as he insisted, gone into nothingness.

Tyrone's participation was chiefly as star in the multiple role of an Adam rebelling against everlasting life ("I am not strong enough to bear eternity"); an intellectual and prolix pastor, Franklyn Barnabas, who says of Adam's son Cain, "he slew his beefsteak-eating brother, and thus invented murder. That was a steep step. It was so exciting that all the others began to kill one another for sport, and thus invented war, the steepest step of all. They even took to killing animals as a means of killing time, and then, of course, ate them to save the long and difficult labor of agriculture." Pure, iconoclastic Shaw, the very essence of his beliefs (he was a pacifist and vegetarian); and in the last act, he is an old man in the year 31,920 A.D., whose "head is finely domed and utterly bald. Except for his eyelashes he is quite hairless," but "in the prime of life." Moss needed Tyrone's marquee value, and knew that he could handle the parts with distinction.

Armina Marshall Langner, of the Theatre Guild, was co-sponsoring the production. With the names of Tyrone Power and Faye Emerson as lures, audiences came to fill houses from Florida to Canada over a period of eleven weeks. According to Moss's article, audiences were larger for *Back to Methuselah* than for any other Shaw play except *My Fair Lady*, which was adapted from *Pygmalion*. Curiously, Moss omits Tyrone's and Miss Emerson's names in the *Times* piece, when their popularity was the central reason for the tour's success. Perhaps unconsciously, Moss refused to accept the fact that box-office idols have more audience appeal than a neglected Shavian classic. Following polite reviews, the play expired in New York after twenty-nine performances. Glamour is a coin of little value to the tougher New York theatregoers.

Tyrone good-naturedly accepted the failure. Unfortunately, it left him with an unexpected void of several weeks. Personal matters, which can be kept at bay when a star is on a frantic schedule, pressed in on him, chief among them Debbie Minardos. She may have had bohemian tendencies, but she was a firm believer in marriage. She had no interest in being Tyrone's live-in companion, but she was not ready to rush into another marriage.

In February 1958, he wrote "Freddie" Hungerford, Debbie's mother, in Tunica, Mississippi: "You have doubtless wondered at my actions & probably questioned my intentions as far as Debbie is concerned. Well, it looks as though everything is going to straighten itself out. I must be quite frank in admitting that until I met her, I had no intention at all of embarking on another matrimonial venture, but the more I am with her, the more I see of her & get to know her, the more I believe it would be more than a possibility. I am trying to talk her into it—and if she will agree eventually, I think June sometime will be the date. This is a long way around to tell you that I am very much in love with your daughter.''

The couple flew to Tunica, Mississippi, and there they were married on May 7, 1958. Rice Hungerford, Debbie's step-father, was best man and her mother the matron of honor. The Hollywood gossips were quick to spread the rumor that Debbie must have been pregnant, since Tyrone had said repeatedly to reporters and others that he would never marry again. But the fact was that Debbie was examined on May 13, a week after their marriage, by Dr. Leon Krohn, a Beverly Hills gynecologist, and found not to be. Her pregnancy would not be confirmed by Dr. Krohn until June 23, 1958.

Tyrone, eighteen years older than his bride, must have felt a little like his father when he married Patia—also a third marriage for him and a last chance for a family. For Tyrone, it would be his last chance to have a son.

They honeymooned at Newport Beach, where they became so enthusiastic about boating after spending some time aboard the boat belonging to assistant director Bob Webb and his wife, cutter Bobby McLean, that Tyrone bought a powered sloop with a spacious cabin and fine rigging. It cost $35,000, but some of the profits from *Witness for the Prosecution* had come in and he could afford it. It had been a season of improvisation for Tyrone; he was vamping, and the sloop, which he immediately christened *The Black Swan*, was a new theme on which he might embroider a future. Everyone thought the name referred to his popular movie, but he told a friend that it really referred to him. He was now getting his toes in the mud; his new bride disdained makeup and designer elegance—she even drove an old Volkswagen—and he was doing his best to please her. Debbie was a close friend of actor (and author) Sterling Hayden, who spent much of his time on the water. Hayden wore old clothes, spoke in a tough sailor argot, and generally rejected all pretensions to refinement. He was Debbie's kind of man.

The Powers stayed about ten days at Lido Island in Newport, seeing a great deal of the Webbs, Rock Hudson, and the Milton Brens (she was actress Claire Trevor), who also had a boat. Claire was a gifted painter and began a por-trait of Tyrone in the beard he was growing for his role as Solomon.

XII

SOLOMON AND SHEBA

MIKE STECKLER had become Tyrone's stand-in at the time of *Rawhide*, when Tommy Noonan fell ill. They had become good friends, and became even closer after Mike saved little Taryn from drowning in the Power pool. One Sunday at Copa de Oro, they were all sunning by the pool—this was in the time of Linda—when Mike happened to see two-year-old Taryn floating by, face down. She was not even unconscious, just terrified by their frantic efforts to get about a tablespoon of water out of her. Ever since then, Mike had been a special sort of pal to Tyrone. There was also a daredeviltry in both of them and sailing *The Black Swan* was even more thrilling than flying. Mike became the first mate and caretaker of the boat.

Tyrone told Mike that he thought they might sail her across the Atlantic to Spain by way of the Panama Canal. Everyone connected with the management at Copa Productions and United Artists thought this a harebrained idea, and it had to be abandoned.

The Black Swan was hoisted aboard an Italian freighter, the *Volta*, for shipment to Barcelona also by way of the Panama Canal, but firmly lashed to the deck of the big ship. Mike bunked down in the sloop, and it was an eerie feeling, sailing the Atlantic about thirty feet above the water. Once, the captain asked to check *The Black Swan*'s automatic pilot, which the *Volta* lacked, to get his bearings, and corrected the ship's course by five degrees. Tyrone had supervised the business of hoisting the sloop aboard; he had an obsessional interest in the craft. Then he gracefully thanked the whole crew and posed for a group photo with captain and crew on the deck.

In August, the Powers were off from New York to England

293

aboard the *Liberté* of the French Line. His old friends Lothar Wolff and his wife, Vee, from his days with Anna-bella, had come to the pier to see them off, bringing flowers and a thick volume on Spain and its people. Wolff and Tyrone had discussed several projects while the Powers were in New York awaiting the ship's departure. One was a film version of James Thurber's adult fable, *The Thirteen Clocks*. While crossing the Atlantic, Tyrone wrote Wolff:

> . . . Debbie was so excited [about sailing on the *Liberté*], and really hasn't come out of it yet. It was a glorious day to glide down the Hudson, and we made good use of the movie camera on the top deck. The weather has not been too kind to us the last two days however, and the fog-horn serves as a mournful obligato to the days activities. It's been a magnificent rest, and the food and service . . . well, I don't need to tell you. . . . I have read three books and as many scripts these last days. The first item on the list was the Thurber book, and then the script. I think it is absolutely fascinating, and can cer-tainly understand your enthusiasm for the subject. Without even consulting Ted [Richmond] I would like to say that we should get started. . . . It is the sort of story that fires the imagination, and gives one immeasurable scope for improvisation. . . . My last word to you at this time is: "Let's get going"! . . . Also, if you have time would you get a copy of 'The Lost Steps' by Alejo Car-pentier, and after you have read it let me have your com-ments on same? . . .

Tyrone already had purchased *The Lost Steps* for his Copa Productions, paying $100,000 for it. It was to be his next film project, and Irwin Shaw, another close friend, had written a script, which would arrive while Tyrone was in Madrid. To Wolff, he wrote from Madrid:

> . . . You will be happy to know that we received the first draft screenplay of "Lost Steps" from Irwin Shaw, and it's one of the best I've read in a hell of a long time. He has done, what I consider to be a masterful job with a most difficult subject. It's long, of course, but he has managed to retain the flavor of the book, say everything

that Carpentier wanted to say, and his dialogue is both penetrating & brilliant. I believe we can really have something here. Irwin is now in N.Y. for the opening of his play. If you would care to I will ask him to get you a copy of the script. . . .

In London, they stayed at Tyrone's favorite hotel, the Connaught, Tyrone using the suite as an office, pulling together the final arrangements for the biblical spectacle about to be filmed. He checked in, too, at the London office of the U.S. Marine Reserve and underwent a physical, following which he was promoted to major in the Reserve. That pleased him very much, especially since he had some apprehension about the physical. In March, when he was having a physical requested by the insurers for *Solomon and Sheba*, the cardiologist said that he found nothing specifically wrong but asked to take a second cardiogram. Tyrone refused, since if they had found something wrong, his future as a film star would have been imperiled. He told Linda about it in one of their infrequent conversations, but added, "If there *is* something wrong, I don't want to know."

While they were in London, he phoned Mrs. Lilian Ruddy, his former housekeeper, to see how she and her ailing husband were faring. He had shut down the Abingdon Road house earlier that year. As he had shaken hands with her on that occasion, Mrs. Ruddy said, "I'm sorry this is ending, Mr. Power," and Tyrone had told her, "Well, Mrs. Ruddy, when a thing ends, there is always a new beginning."

His beard for Solomon now gave his face a severe expression, making him look all of his forty-four years. He was chain-smoking Camels, and drinking more. There were so many pressures on him, responsibilities. Debbie's pregnancy was now quite obvious, and she confidently expected a son. She was such a tomboy, he half believed her. While still in London, he leased a furnished villa in Lausanne for the winter. They would go there after the movie was wrapped up and wait for the arrival of the baby, which was due in February. He also had a London real estate agent on the lookout for an Irish estate.

The impending production had Tyrone all keyed up. It was much the biggest thing that his company ever had attempted.

There were fifty horses required, a huge cast of players and extras. Besides Miss Lollobrigida, there was George Sanders, who was playing Solomon's brother Adonijah. Copa producer Ted Richmond already was in Spain with his wife, along with their director, veteran King Vidor, who would be winding up nearly forty years as a leading filmmaker (*The Big Parade*, 1925; *Show People*, 1928; *Our Daily Bread*, 1934; *Duel in the Sun*, 1947). Vidor was a man equally at home with epics and small domestic comedies and dramas. Tyrone wrote Mike in Spain:

> . . . we have a lot of work to do in Europe & it's all exciting & we will talk all about it when we meet. . . . Debbie is beaming. . . .

Secretary Bill Gallagher joined the Powers in London before they took off for the flight to Madrid on the third of September. The Power professional family was complete.

The Black Swan had not remained in Barcelona Harbor very long. Tyrone urged Mike to move her to the Costa Brava, calling the situation at Barcelona "ghastly."

The move of the boat to the Club Nautico at Arenys de Mar had climaxed a week of chaos for Mike Steckler. When the Italian crewmen lowered the boat into Barcelona Harbor, they forgot to tie a towline to it, and it began floating away. Mike had to find a rowboat to take out in pursuit of the $35,000 derelict vessel. Then when the mainmast was lowered in place by some Spanish stevedores, it was found to be backward. Even when the mainmast was righted, trouble plagued *The Black Swan*. When Mike finally anchored her in the harbor, he found that he was in a direct path of oceangoing liners and freighters and was constantly afraid of being crushed. The news from his beloved boat was just part of the over-all confusions and alarms that moved in on Tyrone that September. But he tried to remain upbeat. He wrote Wolff:

> . . . The Liberté is an idyllic mirage & we are now plunging furiously over the Aragon countryside. It seems to be going well and if 2500 Spanish soldiers dressed as Egyptians & Israelites can add anything to the cinema —we have it made. Another 10 days here [in Valdespar-

tera at the military reservation], then we return to
Madrid. We have an apartment there at the Castellana
Hilton—so that will be our address until further notice.
. . . No, we didn't find a place yet in Ireland, although we
have a few more leads we will investigate when this is
over. The west is just too rugged & isolated. We are off
on another tack now.

This is a fascinating old city, and though the countryside is pretty barren & bleak, there are interesting
spots in town to explore when one has time off. We spent
a divine Sunday in Toledo getting giddy on roomfuls of
El Greco, & an afternoon at the Prado in Madrid
prostrate at the shrine of Goya. What magnificence! We
are pretty small potatoes, after all. . . .

By the end of September, they had been shooting fourteen
days on the dusty plains of the military reservation. That day,
in addition to the twenty-five hundred extras, there were forty
horses required, twelve Egyptian chariots, five Sheban
chariots, horsemen, and ten stuntment to engage in a sword
fight. According to yet another diary-like letter to Wolff,
Tyrone found the weather

    . . . on our side. Day after day of clear sunshine. A
little on the chilly side, but sunny nevertheless. This week
will see us finished with our exteriors, and then it can do
whatever it likes. Have not done very much work with La
Lollo as yet, but I must say she looks "smashing." As for
me? Well, I may not do as great a dis-service to the Jews
as would appear at first blush. . . .

Debbie goes to Lausanne next Friday to make
arrangements for the Clinic, in February. As nearly as I
can tell you now, we will be here until sometime the
middle of December. Then we go to Klosters to spend the
Holidays with Irwin Shaw. After that to Rome to do the
dubbing and scoreing, and then to Lausanne to
"wait". . . .

If you have the time, and your stomach is in a not too
delicate condition, I submit for your interest Alexander
King's autobiography *Mine Enemy Grows Older*. All I
can say is . . . WOW!"

                    •   •   •

When the company moved inside the Madrid studios to shoot the interiors on *Solomon*, Tyrone seemed to visibly age. His right eye, which he had described to his mother in a wartime letter, as tiring first, ahead of the rest of his body, began to trouble him. Numerous photographs and closeups attest to the weakness of that eye. He began to get short-tempered, especially around Bill Gallagher and, occasionally, with Debbie. Bill would take it and skulk away; it seemed that he had made a career lately of being the whipped cur. Debbie sometimes engaged in shouting matches with Tyrone.

In mid-October, producer Ted Richmond saw how tired Tyrone had begun to look and he worked out a schedule with director Vidor so that they could shoot around him. Tyrone was sent off on a brief vacation.

Tyrone and Debbie went straight to the Costa Brava to board *The Black Swan*. Mike was delighted to help take the boat to sea, but warned Tyrone that the weather was not good. *Mal tiempo*, according to the Spanish, with gusts and rains. The wind was too erratic to use the sails, so they turned on the motor and headed for Majorca to the south.

Tyrone thought he saw a whale and got very excited. Debbie was terrified, surprisingly, and when an entire school of whales appeared, Tyrone distracted her by pointing out peculiar conformations of the storm clouds all the while directing his home movie camera at the whales. She didn't learn about the actual existence of the whale school until the films came back from the developer two weeks later.

After a full day of gray skies and drizzle, the clouds opened up and a shaft of sunlight struck the water on the horizon. A steady breeze came up. Mike couldn't believe it. Without saying a word, Tyrone raised the mainsail, the mizzen, and the jib, and they began sailing the waters off Majorca. "What are you telling me?" Tyrone asked Mike. "That the weather's lousy down here! I know! You've been having a ball sailing down here while I'm up in Madrid working my balls off."

When they got back to the Club Nautico Marina on the Costa Brava and prepared to tie up, Tyrone tried to help with the ropes, but he couldn't use one hand. "What do you make of this?" he asked Mike. It appeared that the tendons were too tight and he couldn't open his left hand.

By early November, they were nearly halfway through

production, but Tyrone was still not himself. Some in the company wondered if the marriage would survive the shooting of the picture. Tyrone proposed that Debbie accompany him on the weekend up into the Basque country over the border to visit Annabella.

They inspected Contramundo; it was Tyrone's second visit. There had been extensive renovation done to the interior of the great estate house, bathrooms installed, new appliances, and a general look of expensive but unpretentious comfort: Debbie seemed very subdued to Annabella, not at all what she had expected. The three of them collaborated on a postcard to Watson back in California. As they left, Annabella promised that she would come to visit them in Madrid, which was not a great distance from her farm.

On Thursday, November 6, Tyrone was in the steam room with Bill Gallagher after a rigorous day's shooting. The tendons in his hand were still bothering him, but it was not his sword hand and they were into a dueling scene. Even more bothersome than the tendons was his growing exhaustion, and he hoped that the therapeutic effects of a Turkish bath might help. Suddenly, he gripped his upper torso and told Bill that he had a terrific pain in his chest. "Where in your chest?" Bill asked him. "All over. A bad case of heartburn, I guess. I've got to lay off this Spanish food."

On November 10, Annabella came to the set. The sound stage did not seem to be heated, and she kept her coat on. But it was the emotional climate that disturbed her now. Annabella was a barometer of Tyrone's moods, and she felt immediately that something had died inside him. This was far worse than their meeting in Paris. "What is it?" she asked. "What's wrong?"

"Life isn't worth the living right now," he told her.

Annabella went home, praying that his marriage could be salvaged somehow. Perhaps the child would do it. If it were a son . . . She prayed a lot these days. In 1948, nearly ten years earlier, her Hollywood friends Pat Boyer and Veronica "Rocky" Cooper had spent an entire luncheon date with her talking about an exciting American Catholic writer, Thomas Merton, and his book, *The Seven Storey Mountain*. Annabella read it and, in a sense, her life was changed by it. She identified with former sinner Merton. Here was a young man caught up in the same empty idiocies and materialism most everyone else was, but he had rebelled, thrown it all over and gone into one of the most austere orders of the Church, the Trappists at Gethsemani, Kentucky, where the priests took vows of not only chastity, purity of thought and spirit, but of *silence* as well. The enormity of such a vow as that quite overwhelmed Annabella, who adored good conversation. She sought out Merton's poems, published as *Tears of the Blind Lions*. In *The Seven Storey Mountain*, Merton had written:

> If my nature had been more stubborn in clinging to the pleasures that disgusted me: if I had refused to admit that I was beaten by this futile search for satisfaction where it could not be found, and if my moral and nervous constitution had not caved in under the weight of my own emptiness, who can tell what would eventually have happened to me? Who could tell where I would have ended?
>
> I had come very far, to find myself in this blind-alley: but the very anguish and helplessness of my position was something to which I rapidly succumbed. And it was my defeat that was to be the occasion of my rescue.

Annabella had asked Tyrone to read Merton then, in 1948, when he was so involved with Lana and then Linda, but she was sure that he had not. Now, the saddest thing to Annabella was that she felt it was too late for Father Merton's eloquent book or anything else to do any good.

On the morning of November 15, Gina Lollobrigida reached the sound stage at the Madrid studios in a state of despair. The producers had agreed to some accommodation or other, perhaps such a nicety as space heaters, but they had not come through. She did not look upon Tyrone as anything but a fellow actor (and not her employer, as in part he was). "Don't upset yourself," he told her. "Life goes on."

It was so cold on the set that puddles of water called for in the screenplay description froze. The dueling scene between Solomon and his hostile brother, played by George Sanders, kept going wrong at one point or another. Once, Tyrone slipped ungracefully on the icy floor and landed on his bottom.

Tyrone did all of his own fencing. Sanders used a double for the rear or reverse shots and appeared with the sword only when the cameras were on his face. This meant double work for Tyrone, who moved quickly between the two camera setups. This was not a situation imposed upon the production by Sanders; he was very unskilled with a sword. At one point, however, the camera had to show both men's faces, and that was where most of the retakes happened, despite extensive rehearsal with Sanders.

Between retakes, Tyrone asked the wardrobe man for a coat, but when it was brought to him, he said, "Give it to Steckler. He's turning blue."

Then it happened. During a retake, Tyrone suddenly clutched his shoulder and stopped the action. He staggered back, and several crewmen reached out to keep him from falling. With trembling hands, he lit up a Camel. "I've got to stop," he said. "I don't feel well." He complained of a terrible pain in his chest and abdomen. There was a trace of fear in his eyes.

He was helped back to his dressing-room trailer, where he lay down on the cot, face up. His breathing was shallow, and someone went to the portable bar and poured out a tot of brandy, which Tyrone drank. Medically, the liquor was possibly the worst thing that could have been given him. Then he said, as he saw Mike Steckler's anxious face, "Don't worry. The same thing happened about a week ago." With that, he lifted his head, gasped, and fell unconscious.

Ted Richmond was now in the trailer, nearly beside himself. Several people were milling around, but one of them was cool enough to phone for a doctor. Why there was not a physician attached to such a large company as *Solomon and Sheba* remains a mystery.

Bill Gallagher, paler than usual and shaking, phoned the Castellano Hilton switchboard and told them, "Absolutely no phone calls must be put through to Mrs. Power." He wanted no reporters to upset her needlessly until they knew just how bad the situation was.

Makeup man Ray Sebastian alerted a newspaperman he knew who had come to cover the day's shooting that he might have a scoop. Ray was not being insensitive, just typically "Hollywood" in his reaction to catastrophe.

Several minutes after Tyrone's collapse, it was decided that they couldn't wait for a doctor, and he was carried to Miss Lollobrigida's Mercedes, which was nearest the dressing-room trailer. The trip at top speed through Madrid's streets to the Ruber Sanitorium and Clinic, the nearest medical facility, took twelve minutes. Three minutes into the trip, Tyrone died.

Before the set was shut down, Spanish extras milled around for an hour or more, some of them frightened for their jobs, others grief-stricken, since Tyrone was still enormously popular in Spain. The general feeling was "Such a tragic waste!" But, of course, it was far from being a waste. Tyrone had lived the equivalent of several lives, all of them lived to the fullest possible measure. He was the last of the great male idols, and it was inevitable that he fade out sometime. Better to go quickly as he did, "like a skyrocket," as Anne Baxter described his passing. But for those who loved him, and rarely, as this book in your hands suggests, has any man been loved by so many, it was cruel soon.

EPILOGUE

Anne Power Hardenbergh was still living with Midge White and respective daughters Nieltje and Sheila. Their restored colonial house was on the edge of Marblehead, Massachusetts, and Tyrone had helped with the down payment. He and Debbie had stayed overnight en route to Europe. Now Bill Gallagher phoned her from Madrid with the incredible news. She was stunned, of course. Although the Powers tended to steer clear of one another's private affairs, they were a tight little family and with mother Patia invalided with a variety of serious ailments in Hollywood, Anne felt terribly alone for the first time in her life.

Patia was really too ill to be informed. She lived with a nurse in a small bungalow just off Sunset, all paid for by Tyrone. She would survive for nearly another year, but die a hard death, the kind of death Tyrone was spared, and she never knew that her son had gone ahead of her.

Annabella was reached at Contramundo and told newsmen: "The most wonderful man in the world is gone." But in the privacy of her farmhouse, she took out an unmailed letter, written to Tyrone years ago soon after their divorce.

Whatever you did afterward [she had written him], had no importance really. You made me so completely happy at the beginning. You gave me the adolescence and the youth I never had time to have.

You were so sweet and romantic, so happy, maybe even prouder to have me than I was to have you. You knew how to make each hour a little more exciting than the hour before.

Your letters brought each moment of your day to life for me . . . the flowers, the poems, the musicians under the village windows, the jewels, the voices, the trips, our house, your glorious youth and your beauty.

It was during our marriage that I came to believe in God.

Why didn't he come . . . our little baby? So much wishing, so much waiting.

Spain, 1949

Zanuck was gravely shocked by the news. From his Paris headquarters, he said, "Tyrone was a great star and equally a great actor. It was my good fortune to have launched his screen career. As the then head of Twentieth Century-Fox, I cast Tyrone in a small bit in his first picture. But so striking was his personality and so perfected was his talent that we had no hesitancy in starring him in his very next picture, *Lloyds of London*. The rest is history."

Copa producer Ted Richmond recovered from his shock sufficiently to begin searching for a replacement in the role of *Solomon*. Within a week, Yul Brynner was signed and would be on his way to Spain following the final work on William Faulkner's *The Sound and the Fury*. All of Tyrone's footage would have to be reshot.

Meanwhile, another drama was beginning for Linda Christian, who was in La Haye, France. She had had a strong premonition that something might happen to Tyrone that day while she was en route to Paris by train. She had told her friend, Sonja Hoogeweegen, "Maybe he's dying." The reporters waiting for her train at the Gare du Nord confirmed what she had feared. "They're coming to tell me," she thought.

It was the second calamity in a year for Linda; she had lost her lover, Fon Portago, in a racing accident during the summer.

On orders from Major General Stanley "Moose" Donovan, in charge of that sector of Spain for the U. S. Army, Tyrone's body was moved by ambulance from the Ruber Clinic to the American Air Base, Torrejon de Ardoz, where it was embalmed while complicated paperwork attendant to getting a body removed from Spain went on. General Donovan and his wife, Peggy, were expecting Tyrone and Debbie for dinner that very evening. They had entertained the Powers frequently during their Madrid stay, Peggy being the twin sister of Tyrone's old New York girlfriend Mary Roblee. Impersonality was impossible around Tyrone, even in death. He knew and was admired by too many people.

There was a military honor guard at the door to the improvised viewing room, and there was a steady flow of friends in and out: Gina Lollobrigida, who said that she had never met a more generous man, a finer professional companion and a more thorough actor; Mike Steckler; co-star Marisa Pavan and her husband, Jean-Pierre Aumont; and Richmond.

A memorial service was hastily arranged there at the Air Base, George Sanders delivering an eloquent eulogy:

> I shall always remember Tyrone Power as a bountiful man. A man who gave freely of himself. It mattered not to whom he gave. His concern was in the giving.
>
> I shall always remember his wonderful smile. A smile that would light up the darkest hour of the day like a sunburst.
>
> I shall always remember Tyrone Power as a man who gave more of himself than it was wise for him to give. Until in the end he gave his life.

Debbie was so moved by this tribute, she had it printed up and distributed to all members of the cast and crew, as well as Tyrone's many friends at home.

Spanish officials did what they could to cut the red tape and two days after Tyrone's death, a special TWA plane appeared at the Madrid airport, sent from America to pick up the body of Tyrone and those closest to him. Debbie was too shocked to realize that the flight was unusual in any way until she was nearly home. Then she decided that his old studio, Twentieth Century–Fox, must have sent it as a last gesture of courtesy. When she was able to do so, Debbie wrote them a thank-you note. But their reply puzzled her. They had not sent the plane. Finally, after asking everyone she knew at TWA, including Tyrone's old friend, pilot Bob Buck, the truth emerged. The plane had been dispatched at the express wish of Howard Hughes, who controlled the airline. Hughes and Tyrone had been friends for more than a dozen years and had flown together, but then during Tyrone's last years with Linda, there had been a falling out.

• • •

Anne Hardenbergh flew west with Midge to make funeral plans in Los Angeles with Watson, who met them at the airport. Anne moved into Watson's guest house, and Midge stayed with the Powers' old friends, the Franzen sisters, in Hollywood.

Madelyn FioRito met Linda at the airport. The girls would arrive the next day with Jerry Welter, Linda's brother. Linda checked into the Bel Air Hotel and was barely settled when the phone rang. It was Watson, who said, "Linda, I'm sorry to be the bearer of bad news, but Deborah has instructed me to tell you that you will not be welcome at the funeral chapel and if you do appear, I'm to turn you away." Linda was silent for a moment and then said quietly, "Thank you, Watson."

That shock was somehow crueler than word of Tyrone's death, about which she had had such a strong premonition. When she had spoken to Bill Gallagher in Madrid before leaving Paris, nothing was said to indicate that it would be out of order for her and the girls to be at the funeral. Linda knew social protocol as well as anyone around Tyrone and it was customary for ex-wives and ex-husbands to attend funerals discreetly, away from the widow and family.

Her friend Madelyn was outraged, but then took command and made arrangements for a funeral mass to be said just for Linda and the girls at a Catholic church on Sunset Boulevard.

The chapel at Hollywood Memorial Park only held 150 people and Watson had excluded many friends with regret.

Tyrone was denied Catholic funeral rites because of his divorces, and Commander Thomas M. Gibson, a Presbyterian Navy chaplain, conducted the service. His friend for more than twenty years, Cesar Romero, delivered the eulogy, quoting from something by Thomas Wolfe, which was a favorite of Tyrone's, especially when he read it aloud to friends—"The Promise of America" from the novel *You Can't Go Home Again*:

Go, seeker, if you will, throughout the land and you will find us burning in the night.
    There where the hackles of the Rocky Mountains blaze in the blank and naked radiance of the moon, go make your resting stool upon the highest peak. Can you not see

us now? The continental wall juts sheer and flat, its huge black shadow on the plain, and the plain sweeps out against the East, two thousand miles away. The great snake that you see there is the Mississippi River.

Behold the gem-strung towns and cities of the good, green East, flung like star-dust through the field of night. That spreading constellation to the north is called Chicago, and that giant wink that blazes in the moon is the pendant lake that it is built upon. . . . There's Boston, ringed with the bracelet of its shining little towns, and all the lights that sparkle on the rocky indentations of New England. Here, southward and a little to the west, and yet still coasted to the sea, is our intensest ray, the splintered firmament of the towered island of Manhattan. Round about her, sown thick as grain, is the glitter of a hundred towns and cities. . . . look another thousand miles or so across moon-blazing fiend-worlds of the Painted Desert and beyond Sierras' ridge. That magic congeries of lights there to the west, ringed like a studded belt around the magic setting of its lovely harbor, is the fabled town of San Francisco. Below it, Los Angeles and all the cities of the California shore. . . .

Observe the whole of it, survey it as you might survey a field. Make it your garden, seeker, or your backyard patch. Be at ease in it. It's your oyster—yours to open if you will. . . . Reach out and dip a hatful of cold water from Lake Michigan. . . . Take your shoes off and work your toes down in the river oozes of the Mississippi bottom—it's very refreshing on a hot night in the summertime. . . .

So, then, to every man his chance—to every man, regardless of his birth, his shining, golden opportunity—to every man the right to live, to work, to be himself, and to become whatever thing his manhood and his vision can combine to make him—this, seeker, is the promise of America.

And Tyrone had known these towns and they had been his oyster. He had done it all, seen it all, experienced it all, drinking it in like that hatful of Lake Michigan water. His sights had been high, and he had come so close to achieving everything he had set out to do, the failures were minimal and scarcely worth mentioning, except for that most elusive thing—contentment. Had anyone ever been so restless, so agitated to move on? This man who was still seeking to put down his roots in the very last year of his life?

Cesar concluded by paraphrasing George Sanders' tribute: "He constantly gave of himself until one day he gave a little too much." There was a din outside, a babble of voices and Cesar strained to be heard, nearly shouting, "He was a beautiful man . . . beautiful outside and . . . beautiful inside. Rest well, my friend."

Especially near the back, the noise outside drowned out his words for many of the mourners, including Henry Fonda, Yul Brynner, Gregory Peck, James Stewart, and Loretta Young, who came in an oriental costume which she was wearing that day while shooting an episode for her "Loretta Young Show" on television.

Outside, a carnival atmosphere prevailed. Curious throngs, excluding hundreds of Tyrone's fans, were eating hot dogs and box lunches, and trampling over the graves; parents had brought infants. The fans themselves were silent, reverent, a little angry at being denied the service at least over loud-speakers. Earlier, Debbie had barred microphones and speakers. She was a lady who would fight for her privacy now and in the years ahead for her son as yet unborn.

The widow sat next to the open coffin, holding Tyrone's dead hand as someone sang, "I'll Be Loving You Always." Following the service, there was a delay before interment when Debbie asked that she be allowed to sit alone with Tyrone for a while. She remained in the chapel for twenty minutes; then funeral attendants closed the coffin lid and transported the body to the burial site, which was just eight yards from the mausoleum of Marion Davies and her family (the Dourases) and about forty yards from the large com-munal mausoleum where Rudolph Valentino and dozens of other stars were interred. A Marine honor guard of pall-bearers carried the coffin to its grave.

A bit later that month, in New York, there was a memorial service held at the Music Box Theatre by his circle of friends there, including Josh Logan, the Kasznars, Lothar Wolff, Johnny Parente, Katharine Cornell, and Mary Roblee. Several of his most intimate friends rose and spoke movingly of the way he had touched and warmed their lives.

Watson's loyalty, of course, did not stop at any point. He arranged to have a memorial bench erected with the familiar "Good night, sweet prince" quotation from *Hamlet* inscribed on one end. It already had been appropriated by Gene Fowler for his book on John Barrymore, but no matter; it evoked Tyrone's origins, a boy steeped in Shakespearean theatre.

Tyrone William Power was born on January 22, 1959, at Cedars of Lebanon Hospital in Los Angeles, weighing nearly six pounds. Debbie said, "I hope he has the gentleness of his father and the toughness of his mother." The boy would grow up to look strikingly like his father, "almost too good-looking," his friend Hank Fonda said. Then in November 1978, Tyrone Power IV stepped upon a stage for the first time on the campus of a college in Southern California, where he played Malcolm in *Macbeth*. Another chapter in the 150-year career of actor Tyrone Power had begun.

FILMOGRAPHY

TOM BROWN OF CULVER (Released July 29, 1932)

A Universal Picture, directed by William Wyler.
Screenplay by Tom Buckingham; story by Dale Van Every and George
   Green.
Cinematography by Charles Stumar, A.S.C.

Tom Brown	Tom Brown
Dr. Brown	H. B. Warner
Bob Randolph	Richard Cromwell
Ralph	Ben Alexander
Slim	Slim Summerville
Major Wharton	Sidney Toler
Captain White	Willard Robertson
Carruthers	Norman Phillips, Jr.
John	Tyrone Power, Jr.
Call Boy	Andy Devine
Doctor	Russell Hopton

The story traces Tom Brown's conversion from a moody, rebellious
youngster into a misty-eyed young stalwart contemplating the
traditions of Culver Academy and the United States Army. The plebes
are depicted in a convincing fashion by Wyler and the atmosphere is
right. Tyrone is not mentioned in any of the reviews, all of which were
favorable.

FLIRTATION WALK (Released November 28, 1934)

A First National Picture, directed by Frank Borzage.
Produced by Robert Lord.
Screenplay by Delmar Daves.
Songs by Mort Dixon and Allie Wrubel; musical director—Leo
   Forbstein; choreography by Bobby Connolly.
Art direction by Jack Okey; costumes by Orry-Kelly.

Cinematography by George Barnes, A.S.C., and Sol Polito, A.S.C.;
edited by William Holmes.

Dick Dorcy	Dick Powell
Kit Fitts	Ruby Keeler
Sergeant Scrapper Thornhill	Pat O'Brien
Oskie	Ross Alexander
General Jack Fitts	Henry O'Neill
Lieutenant Robert Biddle	John Eldredge
Sleepy	Guinn "Big Boy" Williams
Spike	John Arledge
Eight Ball	Glen Boles
General Paul Landacre	Frederick Burton
Cadets	Carlyle Blackwell, Jr.,

Lieutenant Joe Cummins, Tyrone Power, Jr., and Dick Winslow
and Sol Bright, Paul Fix, Maude Turner Gordon, Avis Johnson,
Gertrude Keeler, Frances Lee, Colonel Tim Lonergan, Mary
Russell, and Cliff Saum; with Army and University of Southern
California polo teams played by professional polo players.

This is a pleasant musical comedy set in West Point. It tells about the
joys, difficulties and collegiate fun of life among the cadets at the
Military Academy; hand-crafted by First National for the Powell-
Keeler team.

* * *

GIRLS' DORMITORY (Released August 28, 1936)

A Twentieth Century-Fox Picture, directed by Irving Cummings.
Screenplay by Gene Markey, from a play by Ladislaus Fodor.
Cinematography by Merritt Gerstad, A.S.C.; edited by Jack Murray.
Art direction by Hans Peters.

Dr. Stephen Dominik	Herbert Marshall
Professor Anne Mathe	Ruth Chatterton
Marie Claudel	Simone Simon
Professor Augusta Wimmer	Constance Collier
Dr. Spindler	J. Edward Bromberg
Luisa	Dixie Dunbar
Toni	John Qualen
Fritzi	Shirley Deane
Count Vallais	Tyrone Power, Jr.

and Lynne Berkley, Symona Boniface, Rita Gould, George Hassell,
Frank Reicher, Christian Rub, June Storey, and Lillian West.

● ● ●

Prepared as the American screen debut of French actress Simone Simon (pronounced See-MOAN See-MOAN). She is a schoolgirl who falls in love with her headmaster (*Marshall*) in Switzerland. One of the faculty, Professor Anne Mathe (*Miss Chatterton*), is also secretly in love with him. He is totally absorbed in writing history textbooks and is blind to all of this adoration.

An immature letter, filled with recollections of rapturous moments in the arms of a lover, falls into the hands of the school authorities, and the writing is traced to Marie Claudel (*Simone Simon*). She confesses that she wrote it as a piece of fiction, but they insist that she name the man who inspired this. Marie learns of Professor Mathe's love for the headmaster and courageously renounces her own love so that the older couple can pursue their newly discovered romance into a happy future.

The critical consensus was that Simone Simon was the greatest gift from France since the Statue of Liberty.

LADIES IN LOVE (Released October 28, 1936)

A Twentieth Century–Fox picture, directed by Edward H. Griffith. Screenplay by Melville Baker, from the play by Ladislaus Bus-Fekete. Cinematography by Hal Mohr, A.S.C.; edited by Ralph Dietrich.

Martha Kerenye	Janet Gaynor
Susie Schmidt	Loretta Young
Yoli Haydn	Constance Bennett
Marie Armand	Simone Simon
Dr. Rudi Imre	Don Ameche
John Barta	Paul Lukas
Karl Lanyi	Tyrone Power, Jr.
Paul Sandor	Alan Mowbray
Ben Horvath	Wilfrid Lawson
Brenner	J. Edward Bromberg
Countess Helena	Virginia Field
Johann	Frank Dawson

and Lynn Bari, John Bleifer, Egon Brecher, William Brisbane, Helen Dickson, Maxine Hicks, Paul McVey, Tony Merlo, Vesey O'Davoren, Edward Peil, Jr., Jayne Regan, Hector Sarno, Paul Weigel, Eleanor Wesselhoeft, and Monty Woolley.

A typical "woman's" picture of the day. A love story in four parts, each concentrating on, in turn, Janet Gaynor, Loretta Young, Constance Bennett, and Simone Simon. Paul Lukas, Tyrone Power, Jr., and Don Ameche play the lovers.

The New York *Times*: "(The leading men) play the passive lovers with complete resignation, gratefully accepting the few dramatic crumbs the ladies brushed from their make-up tables."

LLOYDS OF LONDON (Released November 25, 1936)

A Twentieth Century–Fox Production, Darryl F. Zanuck in charge, directed by Henry King.
Screenplay by Ernest Pascal and Walter Freeis.
Cinematography by Bert Glennon, A.S.C.; edited by Barbara McLean.
Musical director: Louis Silvers.

Young Jonathan	Freddie Bartholomew
Lady Elizabeth Stacy	Madeleine Carroll
Jonathan Blake	Tyrone Power
John Julius Angerstein	Sir Guy Standing
Old "Q"	C. Aubrey Smith
Polly	Virginia Field
Hawkins	Montague Love
Sir Gavin Gore	Gavin Muir
Lord Everett Stacy	George Sanders
Young Horatio Nelson	Douglas Scott
Brook Watson	J. M. Kerrigan
Captain Suckling	Lumsden Hare
Lord Nelson	John Burton
Ann	Yvonne Severn
Jukes	Miles Mander
Rev. Nelson	Murray Kinnell
Widow Blake	Una O'Connor
Smutt	Will Stanton
Forrester Harvey	Percival Potts
Lord Drayton	Robert Greig
Lady Markham	May Beatty
Prince of Wales	Hugh Huntley
Willoughby	Charles Croker-King
Captain Hardy	Lester Mathews
Dr. Sam Johnson	Yorke Sherwood
Boswell	William Wagner

and Reginald Barlow, Thomas A. Braiden, Rita Carlyle, E. E. Clive, Charles Coleman, D'Arcy Corrigan, Jean de Briac, Arthur Hohl, Olaf Hytten, Charles McNaughton, Leonard Mudie, Georges Renavent, Ivan F. Simpson, Leonard Walker, and Cecil Weston.

● ● ●

An impressive, largely fictional account of the famous British underwriting syndicate during the years immediately before the Battle of Trafalgar. Tyrone plays "Jonathan Blake," who is supposed to have (in this movie chronicle) insured everything from an actress's leg to a King's coronation. A friend of Lord Nelson, Blake becomes a hero through his struggle to keep Nelson's fleet intact. For love interest, there is his involvement with the wife (*Madeleine Carroll*) of a mean-spirited Lord (*George Sanders*).

The New York *Times*: "Power plays a much more vital role than any he has had previously for the screen. He is excellent where sheer action and character delineation are concerned."

LOVE IS NEWS (Released March 6, 1937)

A Twentieth Century–Fox Picture, directed by Tay Garnett.
Screenplay by Harry Tugend and Jack Yellen; story by William Lipman and Frederick Stephani.
Cinematography by Ernest Palmer, A.S.C.

Steve Layton	Tyrone Power
Tony Gateson	Loretta Young
Marty Canavan	Don Ameche
Mrs. Flaherty	Jane Darwell
Cyrus Jeffrey	Dudley Digges
Johnson	Walter Catlett
Judge	Slim Summerville
Penrod	Stepin Fetchit
Count André de Guyon	George Sanders
Lois Westcott	Pauline Moore
Findlay	Frank Conroy
Eggleston	Elisha Cook, Jr.
Bevins	Charles Coleman
Alvord	Paul McVey

and Sam Ash, Frederick Burton, Jack Byron, Sterling Campbell, Ed Dearing, Art Dupuis, Sidney Fields, Paul Frawley, Dick French, Al Jenson, Ray Johnson, Jack Mulhall, George Offerman, Jr., Richard Powell, Charles Tannen, and Julius Tannen.

Loretta Young plays a madcap heiress, Tony Gateson, whose antics are reported and often exaggerated or fictionalized by newspaperman Steve Layton (*Tyrone*). She is so furious at the lurid and scandalous stories that she announces her engagement to him, and, as a consequence, his boss (*Don Ameche*) fires him. Through a bizarre chain of events, both Steve and Tony wind up in jail. After their extended and unnecessary ordeal, they find they are really in love, much to their mutual amazement.

Even though the character of the heiress was drawn from the same blueprint as that of Claudette Colbert in *It Happened One Night*, most reviewers were charmed by this trifle, and Tyrone found himself quite at home in screwball comedy. While the New York *Times* called it "a furiously unimportant farce," the New York *Herald Tribune* noted Tyrone's "engaging performance," and added that he fully justified the promise he showed in *Lloyds of London*.

CAFÉ METROPOLE (Released April 28, 1937)

A Twentieth Century–Fox Picture, directed by Edward H. Griffith. Screenplay by Jacques Duval; story by Gregory Ratoff. Cinematography by Lucien Andriot, A.S.C.; edited by Irene Morra.

Monsieur Victor	Adolphe Menjou
Laura Ridgeway	Loretta Young
Alexis Penayev, a.k.a.	
Alexander Brown	Tyrone Power
Mr. Ridgeway	Charles Winninger
Paul	Gregory Ratoff
Margaret Ridgeway	Helen Westley
Maxey Schinner	Christian Rub
Thorndyke	Hal K. Dawson

and George Andre Beranger, Eugene Borden, Fred Cavens, Gino Corrado, Charles deRavenne, Leonid Kinsky, Louis Mercier, Alberto Morin, Jean Perry, Albert Pollet, Paul Porcasi, Jules Raucourt, Georges Renanvent, Rolfe Sedan, and Leonid Snegoff. Specialty dance by Bill Robinson.

A diverting comedy with Paris and the baccarat tables of the Café Metropole as background. Tyrone, as a penniless opportunist from Princeton, is converted into phony Prince Alexis of Russia; his object, to win the affections of wealthy Laura Ridgeway (*Miss Young*), whose family is title-mad. Remorse overtakes ambition and he realizes that he loves her for her sake alone.

Graham Greene wrote: "Here is a very amusing script, admirable acting by Mr. Menjou, Miss Loretta Young and Mr. Tyrone Power, all thrown away by inferior direction: the wrong angle, the ugly shot, the cluttered set . . . and the camera is planked down four-square before the characters like a plain, honest, inexpressibly dull guest at a light and loony party."

THIN ICE (Released September 3, 1937)

A Twentieth Century-Fox Picture, directed by Sidney Lanfield.
Screenplay by Boris Ingster and Milton Sperling.
Songs by Sidney Mitchell and Lew Pollack; Mack Gordon and Harry
  Revel; musical direction by Louis Silvers; choreography by Harry
  Losee.
Cinematography by Robert Planck, A.S.C., and Edward Cronjager,
  A.S.C.; edited by Robert Simpson.

Lili Heiser	Sonja Henie
Prince Rudolph	Tyrone Power
Nottingham	Arthur Treacher
Uncle Dornick	Raymond Walburn
Prime Minister	Sig Rumann
Orchestra Leader	Joan Davis
Baron	Alan Hale
Krantz	Melville Cooper
Alex	George Givot
Count	Maurice Cass
Singer	Leah Ray

and Rudolph Anders, Monica Bannister, Bonnie Bannon, Walter
  Bonn, Egon Brecher, Lon Chaney, Jr., Diane Cook, Pauline Craig,
  Doris Davenport, George Davis, June Gale, Ruth Hart, Dorothy
  Jones, Margaret Lyman, Alphonse Martell, Greta Meyer, Torben
  Meyer, Alberto Morin, Wanda Perry, Christian Rub, Clarice
  Sherry, Iva Stewart, June Storey, and June Wilkins.

A romance set in a winter resort. Sonja is a skating instructor in a
Swiss hotel, and Tyrone is an engaging stranger who turns out to be a
prince. Through his backstage manipulations, she becomes a famous
skating star, while she remains ignorant of how it all came about. Of
course, they are falling in love.

The New York *Times* called the film one of the brightest comedies
of the year. The *Herald Tribune* wrote that "Power does his best to
make it palatable, and his best is something to enliven virtually any
nonsense."

SECOND HONEYMOON (Released November 12, 1937)

A Twentieth Century-Fox Picture, directed by Walter Lang.
Screenplay by Kathryn Scola and Darrell Ware; story by Philip Wylie.

Cinematography by Ernest Palmer, A.S.C.; edited by Walter Thompson.
Art direction by Bernard Herzbrun and David Hall.
Music direction by David Buttolph.

Raoul	Tyrone Power
Vicky	Loretta Young
Marcia	Claire Trevor
McTavish	Stuart Erwin
Joy	Marjorie Weaver
Rob	Lyle Talbot
Herbie	J. Edward Bromberg
Huggins	Paul Hurst
Paula	Jayne Regan
Elsie	Mary Treen
Andy	Hal K. Dawson
Dr. Sneed	William Wagner

and Stanley Blystone, Wade Boteler, Troy Brown, Harry Burkhardt, Lon Chaney, Jr., Sarah Edwards, Herbert Fortier, Phillipa Hilbere, Arthur Stuart Hull, Fred Kelsey, Joseph King, Robert Lowery, Don Marion, Major McBride, Alex Novinsky, Thomas Pogue, Lillian Porter, Arthur Rankin, Henry Roquemore, and Charles Tannen.

Tyrone plays a wealthy idler married to Miss Young, but she leaves him, insisting that he do something worthwhile, and marries Rob, who is a fussbudget. Miss Young stamps her foot at Rob's dullness and runs back to her first mate.

The New York *Herald Tribune* called Tyrone "again expert and handsome in the chief role, although none too plausible in the bibulous scene."

•

IN OLD CHICAGO (Released January 6, 1938)

A Twentieth Century-Fox Picture, Darryl F. Zanuck in charge of production; directed by Henry King.
Screenplay by Lamar Trotti and Sonya Levien; story by Niven Busch.
Cinematography by Peverell Marley, A.S.C.; special effects photographed by Daniel B. Clarke, A.S.C.; edited by Barbara McLean.
Special effects directed by H. Bruce Humberstone.
Art direction by William Darling and Rudolph Sternad; costumes by Royer.
Songs by Mack Gordon and Harry Revel; Sidney Mitchell and Lew Pollack; and James Bland. Music direction by Louis Silvers.

Dion O'Leary	Tyrone Power
Belle Fawcett	Alice Faye
Jack O'Leary	Don Ameche
Molly O'Leary	Alice Brady
Gil Warren	Brian Donlevy
Pickle Bixby	Andy Devine
Ann Colby	Phyllis Brooks
Bob O'Leary	Tom Brown
Hattie	Madame Sul-Te-Wan
General Phil Sheridan	Sidney Blackmer
Senator Colby	Berton Churchill
Gretchen	June Storey

and Wade Boteler, Spencer Charters, Eddie Collins, Frank Dae, Francis Ford, Rondo Hatton, Russell Hicks, J. Anthony Hughes, Paul Hurst, Joe King, Charles Lane, Scotty Mattraw, Thelma Manning, Robert Murphy, Gene Reynolds, Gustav von Seyffertitz, Billy Watson, Bobs Watson, and Clarence Hummel Wilson.

When Molly O'Leary (*Alice Brady*) loses her husband in a terrible accident on the trail west, she takes her brood of three boys to Chicago, where she survives by taking in washing.

The most solid of her sons (*Don Ameche*) becomes a lawyer, while scapegrace Dion (*Tyrone*) hangs around with the wrong crowd, mostly in gambling and rough-and-tumble politics.

"The Patch" is a seamy section where the red-light and gambling district is located. There, in a saloon run by tough and racketeering Gil Warren (*Donlevy*), Dion hears Belle Fawcett (*Miss Faye*) sing, and is so taken with her, he charms her into an affair with her, against her better judgment. He even convinces her to become a partner in his own saloon, the Senate.

Brushing off a bribe from Warren, who is trying to become mayor, Dion persuades his brother Jack to run, and then is horrified to learn that Jack is going to clean up the Patch, if elected. He wins and launches an investigation, which incriminates Dion. Dion thereupon marries Belle, so that she cannot testify against him. He laughs at her when she becomes Mrs. O'Leary; she is sick at heart and prepares to leave both him and Chicago. The brothers engage in a slugfest.

Mother O'Leary is so disturbed by the fight, she forgets to put a bar between the legs of her milk cow; the cow kicks over a lantern and the barn begins to burn, thus starting the great Chicago fire.

Mayor Jack O'Leary with General Sheridan begin dynamiting sections of the city as a fire-break. Dion learns that his brother is in one of the most dangerous areas of the city and rushes to save him when the building behind Jack comes crashing to the ground, burying him.

Dion and Tom search for Molly, and Tom's wife Gretchen and find them in knee-deep water at the lake shore. Belle is found, and she now sees Dion as a hero.

At a cost of nearly two million dollars, this disaster film went on to earn back enormous returns for the studio. Most of the critics found it historically inaccurate but hugely entertaining. Alice Brady was singled out by nearly all reviewers for special praise and went on to win an Academy Award for her role.

ALEXANDER'S RAGTIME BAND (Released August 5, 1938)

A Twentieth Century-Fox Picture, Darryl F. Zanuck in charge; directed by Henry King.

Screenplay by Kathryn Scola and Lamar Trotti; adaptation by Richard Sherman from a story idea by Darryl F. Zanuck and Irving Berlin.

Cinematography by Peverell Marley, A.S.C.; edited by Barbara McLean.

Art direction by Bernard Herzbrun and Boris Leven.

Music by Irving Berlin; musical direction by Alfred Newman.

A Darryl F. Zanuck Production; Harry Joe Brown, Associate Producer.

Alexander (Roger Grant)	Tyrone Power
Stella Kirby	Alice Faye
Charlie Dwyer	Don Ameche
Jerry Allen	Ethel Merman
Davey Lane	Jack Haley
Professor Heinrich	Jean Hersholt
Aunt Sophie	Helen Westley
Taxi Driver	John Carradine
Bill	Paul Hurst
Wally Vernon	Himself
Ruby	Ruth Terry
Snapper	Douglas Fowley
Louie	Chick Chandler
Specialty	Dixie Dunbar

and Stanley Andrews, Tyler Brooke, Charles Coleman, Eddie Collins, Joseph Crehan, Donald Douglas, Otto Fries, Robert Gleckler, Selmar Jackson, Jane Jones, Mel Kalish, Joe King, Grady Sutton, and Charles Williams.

Roger Grant (*Tyrone*), of an old San Francisco family, chooses to lead a small jazz band rather than follow serious violin studies as his family wishes. Unfortunately, his band can get only cheap Barbary Coast gigs until they meet up with a befeathered and cheap-looking singer named Stella Kirby (*Alice Faye*), who has acquired a rag tune which suits the band fine, "Alexander's Ragtime Band."

Roger grooms Stella for classier dates as his band singer; piano player Charlie (*Don Ameche*) falls in love with her, but she already has fallen for Roger. The bandleader is much too ambitious and busy to notice.

The First World War intervenes and Roger, in uniform, is asked to form an army band to entertain the troops. He and his army band march off to a snappy beat to a waiting boat to take them to France. Meanwhile, Charlie marries Stella, even though he knows she still loves Roger. The marriage does not work out, and they part friends.

Roger returns from the war to form a new band, hiring a brass-voiced singer, Jerry Allen (*Ethel Merman*), who helps their popularity during the jazz craze of the twenties. They are playing Carnegie Hall when Stella comes to see them, and she is in the wings where Roger sees her and pulls her onstage to do a reprise of "Alexander's Ragtime Band," the song that brought them together and broke them apart.

Written as an Irving Berlin showcase of tunes, the film includes nearly all the great ones ("Alexander," "Blue Skies," "All Alone," "Oh, How I Hate to Get Up in the Morning," "What'll I Do?" "Remember," and a new one, "Now It Can Be Told").

Hailed by all of the critics as one of the most entertaining films of the year, the film remains the most enduringly popular of all of Tyrone's forty-seven pictures. It is director Henry King's personal favorite among his own work.

MARIE ANTOINETTE (Released August 16, 1938)

A Metro-Goldwyn-Mayer Picture, directed by W. S. Van Dyke II.
Screenplay by Donald Ogden Stewart, Claudine West, and Ernest Vajda; based in part on the book by Stefan Zweig.
Produced by Hunt Stromberg.
Cinematography by William Daniels, A.S.C.; edited by Robert J. Kern; montage effects by Slavko Vorkapich.
Art direction by Cedric Gibbons with William A. Horning and Edwin B. Willis; costumes by Adrian and Gile Steele.
Musical score by Herbert Stothart; choreography by Albertina Rasch.
Technical Adviser—George Richelavie.

Marie Antoinette	Norma Shearer
Count Axel de Fersen	Tyrone Power
King Louis XV	John Barrymore

King Louis XVI	Robert Morley
Princess de Lamballe	Anita Louise
Duke d'Orléans	Joseph Schildkraut
Mme. du Barry	Gladys George
Count de Mercey	Henry Stephenson
Comtesse de Noailles	Cora Witherspoon
Prince de Rohan	Barnett Parker
Comte d'Artois	Reginald Gardiner
La Motte	Henry Daniell
Toulan	Leonard Penn
Comte de Provence	Albert Van Dekker
Empress Marie Thérèse	Alma Kruger
Drouet	Joseph Calleia
Robespierre	George Meeker
The Dauphin	Scotty Beckett
Princess Thérèse	Marilyn Knowlden

Young Marie (*Miss Shearer*) is given over by her mother, Empress Marie Thérèse of Austria (*Alma Kruger*), in a bargain with France to keep the peace. She is betrothed to the foolish heir to the throne (*Robert Morley*). She enters a corrupt Paris, where the world-weary Sun King, Louis XV (*John Barrymore*), reigns by the side of his mistress, Mme. du Barry (*Gladys George*), with Marie carefully guided into decadence by a master of intrigue, the Duke d'Orléans (*Joseph Schildkraut*).

Louis XV dies, and his grandson ascends the throne. It is tottering as the embittered peasants are carefully organized for revolution. Meanwhile, Marie parties and embarks on a series of escapades that make her notorious. One evening, bored by losing at the gaming tables, she wanders to a balcony where she sees a handsome young man passing by. It is Count Axel de Fersen (*Tyrone*). In his innocence and integrity, she sees herself as she was when she arrived in Paris.

Eventually, Marie has a son. The Duke d'Orléans then feels thwarted by her new-found strength and prestige—she has given France a future king—and he goes over to the side of the revolution. There, he persuades the people that Marie is the symbol of their suffering. She is condemned to death with d'Orléans casting the decisive ballot.

Fersen tries to help her and her small family to escape, but they are discovered at Varennes and returned to Paris and the guillotine, where she dies at thirty-seven.

Most reviewers were overwhelmed by the spectacular production values. The New York *Times* said: "The splendors of the French monarchy in its dying days have not simply been equaled, they have been surpassed by Metro-Goldwyn-Mayer's film biography." In the program Metro prepared for its premiere engagements, they boasted that the film production "involved more people directly and indirectly than participated in the Paris riots which led to the French Revolution and a new era in world history.''

SUEZ (Released October 14, 1938)

A Twentieth Century-Fox Picture, Darryl F. Zanuck in charge of production; Gene Markey—Associate Producer; directed by Allan Dwan.

Screenplay by Philip Dunne and Julien Josephson, from a story by Sam Duncan.

Cinematography by Peverell Marley, A.S.C.; edited by Barbara McLean.

Special effects by Fred Sersen.

Art direction by Bernard Herzbrun and Rudolph Sternad; costumes by Royer.

Ferdinand de Lesseps	Tyrone Power
Empress Eugénie	Loretta Young
Toni	Annabella
La Tour	Joseph Schildkraut
Said	J. Edward Bromberg
Count de Lesseps	Henry Stephenson
Du Brey	Sidney Blackmer
Sir Malcolm Cameron	Nigel Bruce
Louis Napoleon	Leon Ames
Sergeant Pellerin	Sig Rumann
Prime Minister	George Zucco

and Egon Breecher, Albert Conti, Marcelle Corday, Denis D'Auburn, Jean De Briac, Jerome De Nuccio, Robert Graves, Brandon Hurst, Louis LaBey, Frank Lackteen, Jacques Lory, Fred Malatesta, Miles Mander, Christina Mantt, Alphone Martel, Alberto Morin, Maurice Moscovich, Leonard Mudie, Odette Myrtil, Rafaela Ottiano, Jean Perry, Anita Pike, Frank Reicher, C. Montague Shaw, George Sorel, Tony Urchal, Carlos Valdez, Jacques Vanaire, Victor Varconi, Louis Vincenot, and Michael Visaroff.

Ferdinand de Lesseps (*Tyrone*) is a young French engineer who masterminds construction of the Suez Canal. In attempting to sell his dream, he moves on the highest level of government and society and meets a countess (*Miss Young*), who is already betrothed to Louis Napoleon, who will make her the Empress Eugénie.

In Egypt, where he is supervising the construction against the incalculable hazards of the desert, he meets a gamine, Toni (*Annabella*), the daughter of a Foreign Legion regimental sergeant. She is illiterate and prankish, and instantly falls in love with him. It is Toni who encourages him to proceed against all the odds and finish his canal.

When construction is far advanced, a huge sandstorm blows up, during which Ferdinand and Toni flee for their lives. He is knocked unconscious, but she ties him to a post and then is herself blown away to death.

The New York *Times* wrote: "Power is playing de Lesseps with fully the seriousness he accorded the bandleader role in 'Alexander's Ragtime Band.' . . . Annabella represents a veritable Cigarette (*the heroine of another desert romance*)." Most reviewers across the country liked the film and it went on to long runs everywhere. It is the most frequently revived of all of Tyrone's non-musical films on television and elsewhere.

JESSE JAMES (Released January 13, 1939)

A Twentieth Century-Fox Picture, Darryl F. Zanuck in charge of production; directed by Henry King.
Associate Producer—Nunnally Johnson.
Screenplay by Nunnally Johnson, based upon historical material from Jo Frances James and Rosaline Shaeffer.
Cinematography by George Barnes, A.S.C.; edited by Barbara McLean.
Art direction by William Darling and George Dudley.
Music by Louis Silvers.

Jesse James	Tyrone Power
Frank James	Henry Fonda
Zee	Nancy Kelly
Barshee	Brian Donlevy
Will Wright	Randolph Scott
Major Rufus Cobb	Henry Hull
Mrs. Samuels	Jane Darwell
Bob Ford	John Carradine
McCoy	Donald Meek
George Runyon, a.k.a. Remington	J. Edward Bromberg
Jailer	Slim Summerville
Mrs. Ford	Claire Du Brey

and Erville Alderon, Arthur Aylesworth, George Breakston, Virginia Brissac, Paul Burns, George Chandler, Lon Chaney, Jr., Spencer Charters, Don Douglas, Wylie Grant, Charles Halton, Harry Holman, Leonard Kilbrick, Edward J. Le Saint, Tom London, Charles Middleton, Willard Robertson, John Russell, Paul Sutton, Charles Tannen, Harry Tyler, and Eddy Waller.

Young Jesse (*Tyrone*) and his brother Frank (*Henry Fonda*) are peaceable farmers when the railway trust attempts to take over their farmland and that of their neighbors for a right of way. They are offered next to nothing for it, and Jesse organizes the farmers to fight the railway. The company hires thugs, led by a man named Barshee, to harass Jesse, and Barshee finally firebombs Jesse's mother's house, killing her.

From then on, Jesse vows to destroy the railway, turns outlaw and with a band of men, including his brother and neighboring farmers, begins holding up trains.

Despite his status as a wanted man by the law, Jesse survives until one of his own men, Bob Ford, shoots him in the back in his own house, for the reward money.

The New York *Herald Tribune* called the picture "first-class entertainment," but thought Tyrone was miscast. The New York *Times* tended to agree, saying "it isn't Jesse James."

ROSE OF WASHINGTON SQUARE (Released May 5, 1939)

A Twentieth Century–Fox Picture, Darryl F. Zanuck in charge of production; directed by Gregory Ratoff.

Associate Producer—Nunnally Johnson.

Screenplay by Nunnally Johnson, based on a story by John Larkin and Jerry Horwin.

Cinematography by Karl Freund, A.S.C.; edited by Louis Loeffler.

Art direction by Richard Day and Rudolph Sternad; costumes by Royer.

Songs by Mack Gordon and Harry Revel, James F. Hanley and others.

Musical direction by Louis Silvers; choreography by Seymour Felix.

Bart Clinton	Tyrone Power
Rose Sargent	Alice Faye
Ted Cotter	Al Jolson
Peggy	Joyce Compton
Harry Long	William Frawley
Whitey Boone	Hobart Cavanaugh
Buck Russell	Moroni Olsen
Mike Cavanaugh	Charles Wilson
Band Leader	Louis Prima

and Paul Burns, E. E. Clive, Hal K. Dawson, John Hamilton, Harry Hayden, Horace MacMahon, Paul Stanton, and Bed Welden.

This was obviously based on the Fanny Brice story (the Fox Studio settled with her out of court). Rose Sargent (*Alice Faye*) rises as a singer from amateur nights. At a resort, she meets Bart Clinton (*Tyrone*), a small-time con-artist. She is interested, but before any romance can ripen, he is in flight over a missing necklace, a detective on his trail.

From then on, Bart is in and out of her life, as she rises to the top, finally landing in the Ziegfeld Follies. Bart is constantly in trouble with the law. Rose's close friend, Ted Cotter (*Al Jolson*), who knew her when they both were still small-time, tries to be helpful. It is no use, as Bart cannot avoid jail. Meanwhile, Rose, remembering Bart, is a sensation singing "My Man," the torch song to end all torch songs, and at the end, she is at the railway station bidding Bart farewell on his way to Sing Sing.

The New York *Times* wrote: "Twentieth Century-Fox's latest tour down Melody Lane has come to the Roxy under the blushing title *Rose of Washington Square*, the Rose being neither Al Jolson nor Tyrone Power (as we had feared), but Alice Faye, who flowers lushly in the cabarets and flounces of the post-war years."

SECOND FIDDLE (Released June 30, 1939)

A Twentieth Century–Fox Picture, directed by Sidney Lanfield.
Produced by Gene Markey.
Screenplay by Harry Tugend; story by George Bradshaw.
Songs by Irving Berlin; music director—Louis Silvers.
Cinematography by Leon Shamroy, A.S.C.; edited by Robert Simpson.

Trudi Hovland	Sonja Henie
Jimmy Sutton	Tyrone Power
Roger Maxwell	Rudy Vallee
Jean Varick	Mary Healy
Aunt Phoebe	Edna May Oliver
Willie Hogger	Lyle Talbot
George Whitney	Alan Dinehart
Jenny	Minna Gombell
Joe Clayton	Spencer Charters

and Irving Bacon, Ralph Brooks, A. S. Byron, Maurice Cass, George Chandler, Frank Coghlan, Jr., Don Douglas, Fern Emmett, Harold Goodwin, John Hiestand, Leyland Hodgson, Charles Lane, Robert Lowery, Lillian Porter, Purnell Pratt, Dick Redman, Cyril Ring, Gertrude Sutton, Minerva Urecal, Dale Van Sickel, the Brian Sisters, and the King Sisters.

Jimmy Sutton (*Tyrone*) is a movie studio press agent, who trumps up a romance (fake) between the company's new skating star (*Sonja Henie*) and one of their leading men (*Vallee*). But to no one's surprise, the lady falls for the press agent. In the end, the feeling is mutual.

The New York *Herald Tribune* wrote that Tyrone and Edna May Oliver carried the picture.

THE RAINS CAME (Released September 8, 1939)

A Twentieth Century-Fox Picture, Darryl F. Zanuck in charge of production; directed by Clarence Brown.

Associate Producer—Harry Joe Brown.

Screenplay by Philip Dunne and Julien Josephson, from the novel by Louis Bromfield.

Musical score by Alfred Newman.

Art direction by Thomas Little; costumes by Gwen Wakeling.

Cinematography by Arthur Miller, A.S.C.; edited by Barbara McLean; special effects by Fred Sersen.

Major Rama Safti	Tyrone Power
Lady Edwina Esketh	Myrna Loy
Tom Ransome	George Brent
Fern Simon	Brenda Joyce
Maharani	Maria Ouspenskaya
Lord Albert Esketh	Nigel Bruce
Mr. Bannerjee	Joseph Schildkraut
Aunt Phoebe Smiley	Jane Darwell
Rev. Homer Smiley	Henry Travers
Mrs. Simon	Marjorie Rambeau
Rev. Elmer Simon	Harry Hayden
Miss MacDaid	Mary Nash
Maharajah	H. B. Warner
Lily Hoggett-Egbury	Laura Hope Crews

and Mara Alexander, Abner Biberman, Sonia Charsky, Guy d'Ennery, William Edmunds, Herbert Evans, Major Sam Harris, Harry Hayden, Adele Labansent, Rita Page, Pedro Regas, William Royle, and Montague Shaw.

Major Rama Safti (*Tyrone*), a surgeon trained in America, returns to his native village of Ranchipur, India, to devote his life to helping his people. The British Colonial government is represented by Lord and Lady Esketh (*Nigel Bruce* and *Myrna Loy*). He is bumbling; she is bored and being courted by a drunken Tom Ransome (*George Brent*).

Lady Esketh falls for Major Safti. When the rains come, they never stop and floods soon begin washing everything away.

The New York *Herald Tribune* wrote that Tyrone "plays with skill and restraint." The New York *Times* was less charitable and said that it was "badly assembled" with Tyrone "young, impetuous and charming with all the depth of a coat of skin dye."

DAYTIME WIFE (Released November 23, 1939)

A Twentieth Century-Fox Picture, directed by Gregory Ratoff.
Associate Producer—Raymond Griffith.
Screenplay by Art Arthur and Robert Harari, from a story by Rex Taylor.
Art direction by Richard Day and Joseph C. Wright.
Musical director—Cyril J. Mockridge.
Cinematography by Peverell Marley; edited by Francis Lyons.

Ken Norton	Tyrone Power
Jane	Linda Darnell
Dexter	Warren William
Kitty	Wendy Barrie
Blanche	Binnie Barnes
Miss Applegate	Joan Davis
Mrs. Dexter	Joan Valerie
Coco	Leonid Kinsky

and Marie Blake, Frank Coghlan, Jr., Mary Gordon, Mildred Glover, Otto Han, Robert Lowery, David Newell, Alex Pollard, and Renie Riano.

In his roofing company office, Ken Norton (*Tyrone*), engages in a mild flirtation with his secretary (*Wendy Barrie*). His wife flares when he forgets their wedding anniversary and takes a job as secretary to a business friend (*Warren William*). It is all resolved happily.

Most of the critics thought Tyrone did well in this attempt at screwball comedy.

JOHNNY APOLLO (Released April 12, 1940)

A Twentieth Century-Fox Picture, Darryl F. Zanuck in charge of production; directed by Henry Hathaway.
Associate Producer—Harry Joe Brown.

Screenplay by Philip Dunne, Rowland Brown; story by Samuel G. Engel and Hal Long.

Song: "This Is the Beginning of the End" by Mack Gordon.

Cinematography by Arthur Miller, A.S.C.; edited by Robert Bischoff.

Bob Cain	Tyrone Power
"Lucky" Dubarry	Dorothy Lamour
Robert Cain, Sr.	Edward Arnold
Mickey Dwyer	Lloyd Nolan
Judge Emmett F. Brennan	Charles Grapewin
Jim McLaughlin	Lionel Atwill
John Bates	Marc Lawrence
Dr. Brown	Jonathan Hale
District Attorney	Russell Hicks

and Wally Albright, Stanley Andrews, James Blain, Stanley Blystone, Anthony Caruso, Tom Dugan, James Flavin, Bess Flowers, Ed Gargan, William Haado, Louis Jean Heydt, George Irving, Selmar Jackson, Fuzzy Knight, Charles Lane, Eddie Marr, Walter Miller, Jim Pierce, Don Rowan, Harry Rosenthal, Milburn Stone, Charles Tannen, Phil Tead, Charles Trowbridge, Eric Wilton, and Charles Williams.

Young Bob Cain (*Tyrone*) is the son of a Wall Street broker (*Arnold*) who is in the process of being convicted of fraudulent manipulations of funds. When his father's friends turn their backs on him, Bob Cain falls in with a group of gangsters, becoming the right-hand man of Mickey Dwyer (*Nolan*). He brushes death when he becomes enamored of Lucky (*Dorothy Lamour*), Nicky's moll.

Bob is eventually sent to prison, where he is reunited with his father. The latter risks his life to save his son when Bob tries to break out.

Eileen Creelman in the New York *Sun* wrote: "It's been quite a while since Twentieth Century-Fox ventured into the Warner's fields and took a crack at a gangster story. These underworld thrillers take a certain knack—a knack that sometimes seems to consist mainly of speed and still more speed. 'Johnny Apollo' does not maintain a particularly racing pace."

BRIGHAM YOUNG—FRONTIERSMAN (Released September 20, 1940)

A Twentieth Century-Fox Picture, Darryl F. Zanuck in charge of production; directed by Henry Hathaway.

Associate Producer—Kenneth MacGowan.

Screenplay by Lamar Trotti, from a story by Louis Bromfield.

Cinematography by Arthur Miller, A.S.C.; edited by Robert Bischoff.

Musical score by Alfred Newman.

Art direction by William Darling and Maurice Ransford.

Brigham Young	Dean Jagger
Jonathan Kent	Tyrone Power
Zina Webb	Linda Darnell
Angus Duncan	Brian Donlevy
Porter Rockwell	John Carradine
Mary Ann Young	Mary Astor
Eliza Kent	Jane Darwell
Joseph Smith	Vincent Price
Clara Young	Jean Rogers
Mary Kent	Ann Todd
Doc Richards	Moroni Olsen
Heber Kimball	Willard Robertson

and Stanley Andrews, Arthur Aylesworth, Chief Big Tree, Frederick Burton, Claire Du Brey, Ralph Dunn, Selmar Jackson, Dickie Jones, Frank LaRue, Fuzzy Knight, Tully Marshall, George Melford, Charles Middleton, Lee Shumway, Russell Simpson, Frank Thomas, Harry Tyler, Eddy Waller, Cecil Weston, and Blackie Whiteford.

Designed primarily as a vehicle to make a character leading man of Dean Jagger, the film succeeded in part to that end. It tells of the great Mormon trek to Utah and is a retread of the familiar "Covered Wagon" story. Jonathan Kent (*Tyrone*) is merely one of Young's followers and sometime scout as they make their way across the plains.

The *Times*'s man said: "You'll hardly believe it, but his (*Tyrone's*) role is utterly incidental."

THE MARK OF ZORRO (Released November 3, 1940)

A Twentieth Century-Fox Picture, Darryl F. Zanuck in charge of production; directed by Rouben Mamoulian.

Associate Producer—Raymond Griffith.

Screenplay by John Tainton Foote, based on the story, "The Curse of Capistrano" by Johnston McCulley, adapted by Garrett Fort and Bess Meredyth.

Cinematography by Arthur Miller, A.S.C.; edited by Robert Bischoff.

Musical score by Alfred Newman.

Art direction by Richard Day and Joseph C. Wright; costumes by Travis Banton.

Don Diego Vega, a.k.a. Zorro	Tyrone Power
Lolita Quintero	Linda Darnell
Captain Esteban Pasquale	Basil Rathbone
Inez Quintero	Gale Sondergaard
Father Filippe	Eugene Pallette
Don Luis Quintero	J. Edward Bromberg
Senora Isabella Vega	Janet Beecher
Don Alejandro Vega	Montagu Love
Rodrigo	Robert Lowery

and John Bleifer, Eugene Borden, Ralph Byrd, Gino Corrado, Pedro de Cordoba, Jean Del Val, Guy d'Ennery, Victor Kilian, Chris-Pin Martin, Belle Mitchell, Frank Puglia, George Regas, Hector Sarno, and Frank Yaconelli.

Filmed as a satire by director Mamoulian, Don Diego Vega (*Tyrone*) is a dandyish colonial scion by day and a reckless, masked terror, named Zorro, by night, whose sole aim is to destroy the corrupt Spanish rulers in California.

This was a film Tyrone enjoyed making enormously. His flair for this sort of parody was noted by nearly all perceptive film critics, although the New York *Times* missed the whole point, saying, "rather overdoes the swashing and the swash is more beautiful than bold." A great success everywhere.

BLOOD AND SAND (Released May 22, 1941)

A Twentieth Century-Fox Picture, directed by Rouben Mamoulian.

Produced by Darryl F. Zanuck; Associate Producer—Robert T. Kane.

Screenplay by Jo Swerling, based on the novel by Vicente Blasco Ibáñez.

Cinematography by Ernest Palmer, A.S.C., and Ray Rennahan, A.S.C.; edited by Robert Bischoff; Technicolor director—Natalie Kalmus.

Art direction by Richard Day and Joseph C. Wright.

Costumes by Travis Banton.

Musical score by Alfred Newman; choreography by Hermes Pan.

Juan Gallardo	Tyrone Power
Dona Sol	Rita Hayworth

Carmen Espinosa	Linda Darnell
Senora Augustias	Alla Nazimova
Manolo de Palma	Anthony Quinn
Natalio Curro	Laird Cregar
Garabato	J. Carrol Naish
Nacional	John Carradine
Antonio Lopez	William Montague
Don Jose Alvarez	Pedro de Cordoba
Guitarist	Vicente Gomez
Encarnacion	Lynn Bari
Captain Pierre Lauren	George Reeves
Pedro Espinosa	Fortuntio Bonanova
Priest	Victor Kilian
La Pulga	Michael Morris
Pablo Gomez	Charles Stevens

and Armillita, Maurice Cass, Cora Sue Collins, Jacqueline Dalya, Rex Downing, Ted Frye, Larry Harris, Russell Hicks, Cullen Johnson, Schuyler Standish, Ann Todd, and John Wallace.

After launching Tyrone successfully as the heir to the Douglas Fairbanks athletic swashbucklers, his studio now made a bold effort to place him in the scented ranks of Valentino.

The story tells of a Spanish poor boy (*Tyrone*) who wants to follow in the footsteps of his father before him, killed in the bullring, and against the wishes of his scrubwoman mother (*Nazimova*). He proceeds through the steps necessary to become a matador, marrying his village sweetheart (*Linda Darnell*) along the way, and finally making it big as a bullfighter. Then, success begins to spoil him; he is nearly seduced by Dona Sol (*Rita Hayworth*), and in the end, dies in the ring like his father before him.

The New York *Morning Telegraph* wrote: " . . . there is the general effect, the impact on the eye, rather than on the intellect, that 'Blood and Sand' tries to manage. For instance, there's that first view of Mr. Power himself, the dark and tousled head lying against a rich, crimson drape, there are the bull fighting costumes in which he appears in the ring, more than enough to make all the ladies in the audience swoon with desire, and there is, once again, Miss Hayworth, and her wham, more than enough to make the men in the audience do precisely the same thing." The *Herald Tribune* echoed this feeling, saying, " . . . his fans will become delirious with pleasure at the figure he cuts with his host of costumes."

A YANK IN THE R.A.F. (Released September 26, 1941)

A Twentieth Century-Fox Picture, Darryl F. Zanuck in charge of production, directed by Henry King.

Screenplay by Karl Tunberg and Darrell Ware; story by Melville Crossman.

Cinematography by Leon Shamroy, A.S.C.; edited by Barbara McLean.

Songs by Leo Robin and Ralph Rainger.

Art direction by Richard Day and James Basevi.

Tim Baker	Tyrone Power
Carol Brown	Betty Grable
Wing Commander Morley	John Sutton
Roger Phillby	Reginald Gardiner
Corporal Harry Baker	Donald Stuart
Squadron Leader	Morton Lowery
Al	Ralph Byrd
Thorndyke	Richard Fraser
Redmond	Denis Green
Richardson	Bruce Lester
Mrs. Fitzhugh	Ethel Griffies

and Claude Allister, Fortunio Bonanova, Gladys Cooper, James Craven, Bobbie Hale, Dennis Hoey, G.P. Huntley, Jr., Crauford Kent, Kurt Kreuger, Lester Mathews, Gavin Muir, Gil Perkins, Lillian Porter, Otto Reichow, Lynne Roberts, Stuart Robertson, Maureen Roden-Ryan, Hans von Morhart, and Frederick Worlock.

This is set during the defeat of the British landing party at Dunkirk and the aerial cover given the rescue. Tim Baker (*Tyrone*) is a cocky American, who joins up with the R.A.F. because he craves excitement. While on a brief leave, he meets an old American girlfriend (*Grable*) and their romance begins anew. During the ensuing aerial action, he is nearly killed, but the lovers are reunited.

The New York *Times* said that Tyrone and Betty Grable play the lovers "with becoming gusto . . . both are as good as they have ever been."

SON OF FURY (Released January 29, 1942)

A Twentieth Century-Fox Picture, Darryl F. Zanuck in charge of production; directed by John Cromwell.

Associate Producer—William Perlberg.

Screenplay by Philip Dunne, based on the novel, "Benjamin Blake"
   by Edison Marshall.
Cinematography by Arthur Miller, A.S.C.; edited by Walter
   Thompson.
Musical direction by Alfred Newman.

Benjamin Blake	Tyrone Power
Eve	Gene Tierney
Isabel Blake	Frances Farmer
Sir Arthur Blake	George Sanders
Ben as a boy	Roddy McDowall
Bristol Isabel	Elsa Lanchester
Caleb Greene	John Carradine
Amos Kidder	Harry Davenport
Helen Blake	Kay Johnson
Bartholomew Pratt	Dudley Digges
Purdy	Halliwell Hobbes
Captain Greenough	Arthur Hohl
Kenneth Hobart	Martin Lamont
Fennou	Pedro de Cordoba
Judge	Robert Greig

and Leonard Carey, Harry Cording, Ethel Griffies, Olaf Hytten,
   Charles Irwin, Marilyn Knowlden, Ray Mala, Mae Marsh, Lester
   Mathews, Clive Morgan, Ignacio Sanchez, Clifford Severn, and
   Heather Thatcher.

Benjamin Blake is the base-born son (*Tyrone*) of an English gentleman, his rightful inheritance taken over by his bounder uncle
(*George Sanders*). He is so mistreated by Sanders that he runs off to
the South Seas, where he meets the half-caste Eve (*Gene Tierney*). He
becomes a pearl merchant and returns to London wealthy enough to
clear his name.
   At the end, he goes back to Eve in the South Seas.
   The New York *Herald Tribune* wrote: " . . . Power bears the brunt
of the acting. He is the proud handsome lover of two women but also
convincing as the 'Son of Fury.' "

THIS ABOVE ALL (Released May 12, 1942)

A Twentieth Century–Fox Picture, Darryl F. Zanuck in charge of
   production; directed by Anetole Litvak.
Screenplay by R. G. Sheriff, based on the novel by Eric Knight.
Cinematography by Arthur Miller, A.S.C.; edited by Walter Thompson.

Clive Briggs	Tyrone Power
Prudence	Joan Fontaine
Monty	Thomas Mitchell
Ramsbottom	Nigel Bruce
General Cathaway	Henry Stephenson
Iris Cathaway	Gladys Cooper
Roger	Philip Merivale
Rector	Alexander Knox
Waitress	Sara Allgood
Violet	Queenie Leonard
Wilbur	Melville Cooper
Nurse Emily	Jill Esmond

and John Abbott, Billy Bevan, Colin Campbell, Herbert Clifton, Carol Curtis-Brown, Harold de Becker, Mary Field, Brenda Forbes, Denis Green, Lumsden Hare, Forrester Harvey, Holmes Herbert, Dennis Hoey, Olaf Hytten, Doris Lloyd, Thomas Louden, Miles Mander, Aubrey Mather, Virginia McDowall, Rita Page, Jean Prescott, Arthur Shields, Will Stanton, Heather Thatcher, Cyril Thornton, Clare Verdera, Cecil Weston, and Rhys Williams.

Clive Briggs (*Tyrone*) is from the lower classes in England and, once conscripted and caught in the war, broods over his situation and feels that he is really fighting to preserve upper- and middle-class values. He deserts and during his time hiding from the authorities, he meets a WAAF, Prudence (*Joan Fontaine*), with whom he falls in love; they have a rag-tag affair in haystacks, abandoned places, and cheap rooms. Finally, she convinces him that England is worth fighting for and he returns to his unit, but not before showing his true colors in saving lives during an aerial bombardment of a town.

The New York *Herald Tribune* said that Tyrone was "extremely clever" in the role of Clive Briggs. The reviews were fine all across the country.

THE BLACK SWAN (Released December 23, 1942)

A Twentieth Century–Fox Picture, directed by Henry King.
Produced by Robert Bassler.
Screenplay by Ben Hecht and Seton I. Miller, based on the novel by Rafael Sabatini.
Cinematography by Leon Shamroy, A.S.C.; edited by Barbara McLean.
Musical score by Alfred Newman.
Art direction by Richard Day and James Basevi.

Jamie Waring	Tyrone Power
Margaret Denby	Maureen O'Hara
Henry Morgan	Laird Cregar
Leech	George Sanders
Blue	Thomas Mitchell
Wogan	Anthony Quinn
Lord Denby	George Zucco
Don Miguel	Fortunio Bonanova
Ingraham	Edward Ashley
Captain Graham	Stuart Robertson
Fenner	Charles McNaughton
Speaker	Frederick Worlock
Captain Higgs	Charles Francis
Chinese Cook	Willie Fong

and John Burton, Rita Christiani, Bryn Davis, William Edmunds, Jody Gilbert, Arthur Gould-Porter, Rondo Hatton, Keith Hitchcock, Olaf Hytten, Boyd Irwin, Charles Irwin, George Kirby, Frank Leigh, Cyril McLaglen, Clarence Muse, C. Montague Shaw, Arthur Shields, and David Thursby.

Jamie Waring (*Tyrone*) is a pirate in the days of the Spanish Main, vying for booty with such types as red-bearded Leech (*Sanders*), seizing an attractive girl (*O'Hara*), whom he has to knock almost cold, as she is a rebellious wench, and outwitting nearly everyone who attempts to capture him.

The critics in the large cities enjoyed the tinge of parody in Tyrone's performance, while everyone else found the action exciting and worth seeing.

CRASH DIVE (Released April 28, 1943)

A Twentieth Century–Fox Picture, directed by Archie Mayo.
Produced by Milton Sperling.
Screenplay by Jo Swerling from an original story by W. R. Burnett.
Cinematography by Leon Shamroy, A.S.C.; edited by Walter Thompson and Ray Curtiss.

Lieutenant Ward Stewart	Tyrone Power
Jean Hewlitt	Anne Baxter
Lieutenant Comdr.	
Dewey Connors	Dana Andrews
McDonnell	James Gleason
Pop	Charley Grapewin
Grandmother	Dame May Whitty

Brownie	Henry Morgan
Oliver Cromwell Jones	Ben Carter
Hammond	Charles Tannen
Captain Byrson	Frank Conroy
Doris	Florence Lake

and Stanley Andrews, John Archer, David Bacon, Frank Dawson, Kathleen Howard, George Holmes, Edward McWade, and Minor Watson.

A "pig-boat" officer (*Tyrone*) pursues a young woman (*Anne Baxter*), who is engaged to his lieutenant commander (*Dana Andrews*) and seems unattainable. There is intense rivalry between the two men, each trying to prove that his form of craft is superior. Then they are both involved in a commando-type raid on a Nazi base. When all the shooting is over, the girl winds up with the young officer.

The New York *Times* found this "Hollywood at its wildest . . . Mr. Power is his usual snappy self, and Dana Andrews plays the submarine commander with commendable second-lead charm."

THE RAZOR'S EDGE (Released November 19, 1946)

A Twentieth Century–Fox Picture, Darryl F. Zanuck in charge of production; directed by Edmund Goulding.

Screenplay by Lamar Trotti, based on the novel by W. Somerset Maugham.

Musical themes by Edmund Goulding; the song, "Mam'Selle" by Goulding and Mack Gordon; musical score by Alfred Newman.

Cinematography by Arthur Miller, A.S.C.; edited by J. Watson Webb, Jr.

Art direction by Richard Day and Nathan Juran.

Larry Darrell	Tyrone Power
Isabel Bradley	Gene Tierney
Elliott Templeton	Clifton Webb
Sophie MacDonald	Anne Baxter
Gray Maturin	John Payne
Somerset Maugham	Herbert Marshall
Mrs. Louise Bradley	Lucille Watson
Bob McDonald	Frank Latimore
Miss Keith	Elsa Lanchester
Kosti	Fritz Kortner
Joseph	John Wengraf
Holy Man	Cecil Humphreys

and Dorothy Abbott, Stanislas Bielski, Walter Bonn, Mary Brewer,

Jean de Briac, Renee Carson, Andre Charlot, Noel Cravat, Eddie Das, Marcel De La Brosse, Jean Del Val, Dr. Gerald Echeverria, Helen Fasquelle, Bess Flowers, Greta Granstedt, Hassan Khayyam, Edward Kover, Isabelle Lamore, Robert Laurent, Ruth Miles, Mayo Newhall, Barry Norton, Peggy O'Neill, Marge Pemberton, Albert Petit, Marie Rabasse, Richard Sisson, George Sorel, Lillian Stanford, Blanche Taylor, Betty Lou Volder, and Cobina Wright, Sr.

A young man in Chicago, Larry Darrell (*Tyrone*), gives up a successful career to search for the true meaning of life, a search which takes him to India. He gives up his fiancée, Isabel (*Gene Tierney*), who can't understand his motives. She tries to seduce him in an effort to hold him, but fails.

Another Chicagoan, Sophie MacDonald (*Anne Baxter*), has lost her husband in a car accident, and begins to go to pieces. Larry finds her in Paris, where she has become an entertainer in a low dive and sleeping with the low life surrounding her. She is eventually murdered and Larry has to identify the body.

Isabel's uncle, Elliott Templeton (*Clifton Webb*), is an American who is more at home in Paris. She goes to visit him and runs into Larry there, on his way to India. Isabel realizes that all is lost with Larry and marries ambitious Gray Maturin (*John Payne*).

In India, Larry goes up a mountain and confronts a Holy Man who tells him to reconcile himself to the world as it is, seek serenity, and try to live a life free of materialism. He returns to Chicago to do just that, living simply and finding the peace of mind that eludes all the others around him.

Life magazine picked this film as their "Movie of the Week," calling it one of the very best movies made in years. Commenting on the leads, *Life* said: "Playing them, Tyrone Power and Gene Tierney, who have reached success more on good looks than on ability, have put themselves in the company of the movies' most accomplished actors."

The New York *Times*, parodying an old Gable ad, wrote: "Goodness is back and Power has it." However, the *Herald Tribune* was once again partial to Tyrone, writing, "The Larry of Tyrone Power, engaged in a quest for spiritual sustenance, is as remarkable as he is good, as Maugham thought him."

NIGHTMARE ALLEY (Released October 9, 1947)

A Twentieth Century–Fox Picture, directed by Edmund Goulding. Produced by George Jessel.

Screenplay by Jules Furthman, based on the novel by William Lindsay
Gresham.
Cinematography by Lee Garmes, A.S.C.; edited by Barbara McLean.
Musical score by Cyril Mockridge, conducted by Lionel Newman.
Art direction by Lyle Wheeler and J. Russell Spencer.

Stan Carlisle	Tyrone Power
Zeena	Joan Blondell
Lilith Ritter	Helen Walker
Molly	Coleen Gray
Bruno	Mike Mazurki
Ezra Grindle	Taylor Holmes
Pete	Ian Keith
Mrs. Peabody	Julia Dean
Hoatley	James Flavin
McGraw	Roy Roberts
Town Marshal	James Burke

and Florence Aver, George Berenger, Oliver Blake, June Bolyn,
George Chandler, Harry Cheshire, Leo Gray, Al Herman, Robert
Karnes, Emmet Lynn, George Lloyd, George Mathews, Maurice
Navarre, Jack Raymond, John Wald, Eddy Waller, and Marjorie
Wood.

Stan Carlisle (*Tyrone*) is an ambitious young man who joins a carnival
with no background in the business, but with a great deal of surface
charm and an attractiveness that endears him to the ladies. Zeena, the
mentalist (*Joan Blondell*), engages in a serious flirtation with him
because her partner, Pete, is drunk most of the time. Pete is supposed
to work the crowd and, using a code, give Zeena the clues she needs to
"read" the minds of the members of the audience.

Stan, wittingly or otherwise, slips Pete some wood alcohol, and
Pete dies, paving the way for Stan to become Zeena's partner. When
he has mastered the Code, he runs off with Molly (*Coleen Gray*), the
girl in the electrical sideshow whose hair stands on end. Molly is pretty
and dumb.

With his good looks and the Code, Stan and Molly rise to the top
among mentalist acts. He finally meets Lilith (*Helen Walker*), a
psychologist who is interested in him physically as well as
professionally. She is a con-artist herself. Through her help, he
manages to promote a Spiritualist Church and attempts to summon
back the dead sweetheart of tycoon Ezra Grindle. He has Molly
dressed to look like the dead woman, copying an old photo Lilith has
given him. The "apparition" is at night in Grindle's garden. But
Molly can't go through with it and breaks out of character, exposing
the scheme. Stan is then a fugitive and eventually becomes a hobo,
finally returning to the carnival begging to become "a geek," a freak

who bites off the heads of live chickens in exchange for a bottle of booze. This comedown is so shattering, Stan goes berserk and only when Molly recognizes him and gets through to his alcohol-saturated brain, does he finally call out her name, and there is some hope that he can become a human being again.

James Agee, writing in *The Nation*, said: " . . . two or three sharply comic and cynical scenes make it worth seeing—Power's wrangle over 'God' with his wonderfully stupid but not-that-stupid wife (*Coleen Gray*), a scene which has some of the hard, gay audacity of *Monsieur Verdoux*; and every scene in which Taylor Holmes impersonates a skeptical but vulnerable industrialist. Later, in *Time* magazine, Agee added: "From top to bottom of the cast, the playing is good. Joan Blondell, as the fading carnival queen, is excellent and Tyrone Power—who asked to be cast in the picture—steps into a new class as an actor."

CAPTAIN FROM CASTILE (Released December 25, 1947)

A Twentieth Century–Fox Picture; produced by Lamar Trotti; directed by Henry King.

Screenplay by Lamar Trotti, based on the novel by Samuel Shellabarger.

Cinematography by Charles Clarke, A.S.C., and Arthur E. Arling; edited by Barbara McLean.

Musical score by Alfred Newman.

Art direction by Richard Day and James Basevi.

Pedro de Vargas	Tyrone Power
Catana Perez	Jean Peters
Hernand Cortez	Cesar Romero
Juan Garcia	Lee J. Cobb
Don Francisco de Vargas	Antonio Moreno
Diego de Silva	John Sutton
Father Bartolome Romero	Thomas Gomez
Luiza de Caravajal	Barbara Lawrence
Marquis de Caravajal	George Zucco
Professor Botello	Alan Mowbray
Corio	Marc Lawrence
Hernand Soler	Fred Libby
Manuel Perez	Robert Karnes
Dona Maria de Vargas	Virginia Brissac
Coatl	Jay Silverheels
Captain Alvarado	Roy Roberts

Cermeno	John Laurenz
Mercedes	Dolly Arriaga

and Robert Adler, Mimi Aguglia, Willie Calles, Harry Carter, David Cato, Gilberto Gonzales, Reed Hadley, Stella Inda, Chris-Pin Martin, Edward Mundy, Julian Rivero, Ramon Sanchez, Bud Wolfe, and Vincente Gomez (guitarist).

Pedro de Vargas (*Tyrone*) is the young, vigorous son of an aristocratic and pious family in Spain. It is the time of the Inquisition and crimes by the Church against neighbors are frequent. Diego de Silva (*John Sutton*) owns an adjoining estate to that of de Vargas and wants it. Old Don Francisco de Vargas (*Antonio Moreno*) refuses to sell, so de Silva plots to get it anyway. He learns that Pedro has helped Juan Garcia (*Lee J. Cobb*) in his efforts to get his mother out of the clutches of the torturers of the Inquisition. He has the entire de Vargas family jailed as suspected heretics, and during the subsequent tortures, frail daughter Mercedes dies.

With the help of a barmaid whom he has loved (*Jean Peters*), Pedro escapes and goes to the New World as part of Cortez's (*Cesar Romero*) army of conquistadors. They conquer parts of Mexico and capture Montezuma, pillage the capital and come back rich heroes. Catana, the barmaid, has joined him in the New World as a soldier by his side, but thinks once home he will marry Luiza de Caravajal, a wealthy snob who married de Silva when she thought the tide was against the de Vargas family. She has had that marriage annulled. Pedro sees how foolish she is and instead takes Catana as his bride.

The New York *Herald Tribune* wrote that Tyrone was excellent in the passages describing his flight from the Inquisition. The *Times*, always chipping away at Tyrone's pedestal, said that he had "little temper in his mettle." Nothing like a lousy pun to put a man down.

THE LUCK OF THE IRISH (Released September 15, 1948)

A Twentieth Century-Fox Picture, directed by Henry Koster.
Produced by Fred Kohlmar.
Screenplay by Philip Dunne, based on the novel by Guy and Constance Jones.
Cinematography by Joseph La Shelle, A.S.C.; edited by J. Watson Webb, Jr.
Music by Lionel Newman.
Art direction by Lyle Wheeler and J. Russell Spencer.

Stephen Fitzgerald	Tyrone Power

Nora	Anne Baxter
Horace	Cecil Kellaway
D. C. Augur	Lee J. Cobb
Frances	Jayne Meadows
Bill Clark	James Todd
Taedy	J. M. Kerrigan
Higginbotham	Phil Brown
Clancy	Tim Ryan
Augur's Secretary	Louise Lorimer
Senator Ransom	Harry Antrim
Cornelius	Charles Irwin
Mrs. Augur	Margaret Wells

and Robert Adler, Don Brodie, John Davidson, Gene Garrick, Douglas Gerrard, John Goldsworthy, Hollis Jewell, Robert Karnes, Norman Leavitt, J. Farrel MacDonald, Marion Marshall, Frank Mitchell, George Melford, Eddie Parks, John Roy, Tom Stevenson, Bill Swingley, Tito Vuolo, and Wilson Wood.

Cecil Kellaway as an Irish leprechaun named Horace attempts to keep a romance between a New York newspaper reporter (*Tyrone*) and Nora (*Anne Baxter*), a pretty young colleen, from foundering. He nearly fails, but all turns out well in the end. The leprechaun was the most convincing thing in the story, and Kellaway was charming in the role.

The *Herald Tribune*, usually kind, couldn't find words to praise Tyrone and said instead, "As the fellow who gives up fame and fortune at the behest of the leprechaun, Tyrone Power looks and acts like a person who isn't quite certain he isn't a fool."

THAT WONDERFUL URGE (Released December 21, 1948)

A Twentieth Century-Fox Picture, directed by Robert B. Sinclair.
Produced by Fred Kohlmar.
Screenplay by Jay Dratler, based on the movie, *Love Is News*, by William R. Lipman and Frederick Stephani.
Cinematography by Charles Clarke, A.S.C.; edited by Louis Loeffler.

Thomas Jefferson Tyler	Tyrone Power
Sara Farley	Gene Tierney
Count André de Guyon	Reginald Gardiner
Jessica Woods	Arlene Whelan
Judge Parker	Gene Lockhart
Aunt Cornelia	Lucille Watson

Duffy	Lloyd Gough
Mr. Whitson	Richard Gaines
Justice Homer Beggs	Chill Wills
Attorney Ketchell	Porter Hall
Mrs. Riley	Hope Emerson

and Charles Arnt, John Butler, Hal K. Dawson, Frank Ferguson, Robert Foulk, Bess Flowers, Eula Guy, Charles Hamilton, Joe Haworth, Gertrude Michael, Forbes Murray, David Newell, Eddie Parks, Norman Phillips, Francis Pierlot, Edwin Randolph, Isabel Randolph, Mickey Simpson, David Thursby, Robert Williams, Marjorie Wood, and Wilson Wood.

Resembling an old Robert Montgomery–Myrna Loy comedy of the mid-thirties, *Petticoat Fever*, more than a little, this comedy has a supposedly mismatched couple isolated in the north country, where they thaw out enough to see that they were meant for each other.

The New York *Times* had a new reviewer who said that "Mr. Power and Miss Tierney are a congenial team." While the *Herald Tribune* man still was peevish about Tyrone and wrote that "the stars march through their parts with the technical accomplishments and goods so often used as a substitute for lively, imaginative acting."

PRINCE OF FOXES (Released December 23, 1949)

A Twentieth Century–Fox Picture; produced by Sol C. Siegel; directed by Henry King.
Screenplay by Milton Krims; based on the novel by Samuel Shellabarger.
Cinematography by Leon Shamroy, A.S.C.; edited by Barbara McLean.
Music by Alfred Newman.
Art direction by Lyle Wheeler and Mark-Lee Kirk.

Andrea Orsini	Tyrone Power
Cesare Borgia	Orson Welles
Camilla Verano	Wanda Hendrix
Belli	Everett Sloane
Mono Zoppo	Katina Paxinou
Angela	Marina Berti
Count Verano	Felix Aylmer
Esteban	Leslie Bradley
D'Este	Joop van Hulzen
Alphonso D'Este	James Carney
Art Dealer	Eduardo Ciannelli

and Adriano Ambrogi, Eva Breuer, Franco Corsaro, Ludmilla
  Durarowa, Guiseppe Faeti, Albert Latasha, Rena Lennart,
  Njntsky, and Ves Vanghielova.

An elaborate and macabre account of the life of the wicked Borgias,
whose behind the scenes power governed much of Renaissance Italy.
Orsini (*Tyrone*) is a charming aide to Cesare Borgia, although not
above working for the other side from time to time, and eventually he
defies Cesare and proves to be the foxiest of his enemies.

The *Herald Tribune* wrote: "Power achieves his vengeance on the
house of Borgia with meticulous skill."

The film was mounted elaborately and filmed almost entirely in
northern Italy in actual locations. If nothing else, it is a beautiful
panoramic re-creation of life in the high Renaissance.

THE BLACK ROSE (Released September 1, 1950)

A Twentieth Century–Fox Picture, directed by Henry Hathaway.
Produced by Louis D. Lighton.
Screenplay by Talbot Jennings, from the novel by Thomas B. Costain.
Cinematography by Jack Cardiff; special effects by W. Percy Day,
  O.B.E.; edited by Manuel Del Campo.
Art direction by Paul Sherriff and W. Andrews; costumes by Michael
  Whittaker.
Music composed by Richard Addinsell; directed by Muir Mathieson.

Walter of Gurnie	Tyrone Power
Bayan	Orson Welles
Miriam	Cecile Aubry
Tristram	Jack Hawkins
King Edward	Michael Rennie
Alfgar	Finlay Currie
Anthemus	Herbert Lom
Countess of Lessford	Mary Clare
Mahmoud	Bobby Blake
Edmond	Laurence Harvey

and Alfonso Bedoya, James Robertson Justice, Gibb McLaughlin,
  Henry Oscar, and Hilary Pritchard.

Walter of Gurnie (*Tyrone*), whose mother is in disfavor with his father
and the master of Belaire Castle, is summoned there upon the death of
his father. His father has married a Norman, an embittered, mean-
tempered woman, and Walter knows that he cannot stay. Instead, he

goes far out into the world to seek his fortune and vows to return to clear his name and that of his mother.

Before leaving England, he joins up with Tristram, also an outsider, and together they follow the route of Marco Polo toward Cathay, where they expect to find riches. As they near their goal, they encounter a fierce warlord, Bayan of the Thousand Eyes (*Welles*), but the men prove themselves worthy and he helps them. In a captured caravan, Walter sees Miriam, who is from England. He rescues her and together they reach Cathay.

There, they are separated, and Walter returns to England, but, through Tristram, Miriam is returned to him. With his wealth, he comes back to Belaire in triumph, deposes the Normans, and clears his name.

The *Herald Tribune* said: "Whatever slight suspense there is in the picture is supplied by Power's defiance of the ruthless Mongol warlord, played to the hilt by Orson Welles."

AMERICAN GUERILLA IN THE PHILIPPINES
(Released November 7, 1950)

A Twentieth Century-Fox Picture, directed by Fritz Lang.
Produced by Lamar Trotti from his screenplay; based on the novel by Ira Wolfert.
Cinematography by Harry Jackson, A.S.C.; edited by Robert Simpson.
Art direction by Lyle Wheeler and J. Russell Spencer; costumes by Travilla.

Ensign Chuck Palmer	Tyrone Power
Jeanne Martinez	Micheline Presle
Jim Mitchell	Tom Ewell
Lovejoy	Bob Patten
The Speaker	Jack Elam
Miguel	Tommy Cook
Juan Torena	Juan Martinez
General Douglas MacArthur	Robert Barrat
Señora Martinez	Maria Del Val
Colonel Phillips	Carleton Young
Colonel Dimalanta	Eddie Infante

and Miguel Anzures, Erlingda Cortez, Rosa del Rosario, Chris De Varga, Arling Gonzales, Captain Slim Martin, Eduardo Rivera, and Kathy Ruby.

Ensign Chuck Palmer (*Tyrone*) is stranded in the Philippines following the war, and attempts to help the natives fight off the Huks (Communists) in their raids on villages. Filmed on location, it is nevertheless contrived material, done at a time when McCarthyism was riding high in the land.

The *Herald Tribune* was quite fair in saying "Power, as the chief protagonist, plays the various episodes with a solemn, lackluster attitude that suggests that he was painfully conscious of their basic emptiness."

Tyrone disliked Lang intensely and wrote of "putting a firecracker under his behind" to keep the production moving because of his slowness.

RAWHIDE (Released March 25, 1951)

A Twentieth Century-Fox Picture, directed by Henry Hathaway.
Produced by Samuel G. Engel.
Screenplay and story by Dudley Nichols.
Cinematography by Milton Krasner, A.S.C.; edited by Robert Simpson.
Music composed by Sol Kaplan, directed by Lionel Newman.
Art direction by Lyle Wheeler and George W. Davis.

Tom Owens	Tyrone Power
Vinnie Holt	Susan Hayward
Zimmerman	Hugh Marlowe
Yancy	Dean Jagger
Sam Todd	Edgar Buchanan
Tevis	Jack Elam
Gratz	George Tobias
Luke Davis	Jeff Corey

and Robert Adler, Milton Corey, Sr., Dick Curtis, Judy Ann Dunn, Edith Evanson, William Haade, Louis Jean Heydt, Si Jenks, Howard Negley, Vincent Neptune, Walter Sande, Max Terhune, Ken Tobey, and Dan White.

Tom Owens (*Tyrone*) and Vinnie Holt (*Miss Hayward*) are victims held hostage by four desperadoes who have broken jail.

The reviewers complained that Tyrone had little to do in this.

I'LL NEVER FORGET YOU (Released December 7, 1951)

A Twentieth Century–Fox Picture, directed by Roy Baker.
Produced by Sol C. Siegel.
Screenplay by Ranald MacDougall, based on the play *Berkeley Square* by John Balderston.
Cinematography by George Perinal; edited by Alan Obiston.
Music composed by William Alwyn, directed by Muir Mathieson.
Art direction by C.P. Norman.

Peter Standish	Tyrone Power
Helen Pettigrew/Martha Forsyth	Ann Blyth
Roger Forsyth	Michael Rennie
Tom Pettigrew	Dennis Price
Kate Pettigrew	Beatrice Campbell
Duchess of Devonshire	Kathleen Byron
Mr. Throstle	Raymond Huntley
Lady Anne Pettigrew	Irene Browne
Dr. Samuel Johnston	Robert Atkins
Jacob	Gibb McLaughlin

and Ronald Adam, Felix Aylmer, Hamlyn Benson, Catherine Carlton, Richard Carrickford, Jill Clifford, Arthur Denton, Peter Drury, Alec Finter, Tom Gill, Diane Hart, Rose Howlett, Victor Maddern, Alexander McCrindle, Anthony Pelly, and Ronald Simpson.

A nuclear physicist, Peter Standish (*Tyrone*), finds himself transported back to the London of 1784. He falls in love with his cousin, Helen (*Ann Blyth*). Still retaining his twentieth-century knowledge, he sets up a lab with a camera, a steamboat and other latter-day inventions. He is considered quite mad and returns to the present, where he meets Martha (also *Ann Blyth*) and feels he has the best of both times.

Both the *Times* and the *Herald Tribune* were unkind to this film and to Tyrone, the *Times* saying that they thought Tyrone acted as though he had been tapped on the head. It was not a success.

DIPLOMATIC COURIER (Released June 13, 1952)

A Twentieth Century–Fox Picture, directed by Henry Hathaway.
Produced by Casey Robinson.
Screenplay by Casey Robinson and Liam O'Brien, based on the novel, *Sinister Errand* by Peter Cheyney.

Cinematography by Lucien Ballard, A.S.C.; edited by James B.
    Clark.
Musical director—Lionel Newman; music by Sol Kaplan.
Art direction by Lyle Wheeler and John de Cuir.

Mike Kells	Tyrone Power
Joan Ross	Patricia Neal
Colonel Cargle	Stephen McNally
Janine	Hildegarde Neff
Ernie	Karl Malden
Sam Carew	James Millican
Platov	Stefan Schnabel
Arnov	Herbert Berghof

and Michael Ansara, Sig Arno, Arthur Blake, Monique Chantal, Russ
    Conway, Peter Coe, Dabbs Greer, Lumsden Hare, Charles La
    Torre, Alfred Linder, E. G. Marshall, Lee Marvin, Tyler McVey,
    Tom Powers, and Carleton Young.

Mike Kells (*Tyrone*) is an American courier for the State Department
who scours Trieste for a secret plan by the Russians for an invasion of
Yugoslavia. He meets an apparent American sightseer (*Miss Neal*),
who turns out to be working for the Reds. Janine (*Miss Neff*), a
European, is cryptic and puzzling to him, but on our side.

The critics were nearly unanimous in finding this one too complicated to follow and Tyrone too naïve to be believed. The story,
however, was better than his other recent films and his fans were
reassured.

PONY SOLDIER (Released December 19, 1952)

A Twentieth Century–Fox Picture, directed by Joseph M. Newman.
Produced by Samuel G. Engel.
Screenplay by John C. Higgins based on a story by Garnett Weston.
Cinematography by Harry Jackson, A.S.C.; edited by John
    McCafferty.
Music composed by Alex North and directed by Lionel Newman.
Art direction by Lyle Wheeler and Chester Gore.

Duncan MacDonald	Tyrone Power
Konah	Cameron Mitchell
Natayo	Thomas Gomez
Emerald	Penny Edwards
Jess Calhoun	Robert Horton
Comes Running	Anthony Earl Numkena

Inspector Frazier	Howard Petrie
Standing Bear	Stuart Randall
White Moon	Adeline DeWalt Reynolds

and Frank De Kova, John War Eagle, Chief Bright Fire, Grady Galloway, Carlow Loya, James Hayward, Muriel Landers, Anthony Numkena, Richard Shackleton, Nipo T. Strongheart, and Richard Thunder-Sky.

It is the job of Canadian Mountie Duncan MacDonald (*Tyrone*) to return the migrating Cree Indians to their old reservation. Konah, their chief, has other plans and nearly thwarts the Mountie's plan.

The New York *Times* wrote that Tyrone gallantly represents "the Queen and sets a fair example of White Supremacy."

THE MISSISSIPPI GAMBLER (Released January 29, 1953)

A Universal-International Picture, directed by Rudolph Maté.
Produced by Ted Richmond.
Screenplay and story by Seton I. Miller.
Music by Frank Skinner; choreography by Gwen Verdon.
Cinematography by Irving Glassberg; edited by Edward Curtiss.

Mark Fallon	Tyrone Power
Angélique Duroux	Piper Laurie
Ann Conant	Julia Adams
Edmund Duroux	Paul Cavanagh
Kansas John Polly	John McIntire
Laurent Duroux	John Baer
Andre	Guy Williams
Pierre	William Reynolds
Paul O. Monet	Robert Warwick
Kennerly	Hugh Beaumont
Spud	King Donovan
Voodoo Dancer	Gwen Verdon
Caldwell	Ralph Dumke

and Paul Bradley, Dorothy Bruce, Eduardo Cansino, Jr., Michael Dale, Alan Dexter, Marcel de la Brosse, Edward Earle, Anita Ekberg, George Hamilton, Renate Hoy, Tony Hughes, Jackie Loughery, Bert LeBaron, Saul Martell, David Newell, Buddy Roosevelt, Rolfe Sedan, Jon Shepold, Angela Stevens, Jeanne Thompson, Maya Van Horn, Dale Van Sickel, Bill Walker, and LeRoi Antienne (Singer), and Gwen Verdon (Dancer).

Here, Mark Fallon (*Tyrone*) goes through some rather conventional situations as a gambling man; good at cards, ready with his fists, and handy with the ladies. But much to everyone's surprise, it was one of the top-grossing films of the year. The critics mostly nixed it, but the public came in droves.

KING OF THE KHYBER RIFLES (Released December 23, 1953)

A Twentieth Century-Fox Picture, directed by Henry King.
Screenplay by Ivan Goff and Ben Roberts, based on the novel by Talbot Mundy.
Cinematography by Leon Shamroy, A.S.C.; edited by Barbara McLean.
Music composed by Bernard Herrmann.
Art direction by Lyle Wheeler and Maurice Ransford.

Captain Alan King	Tyrone Power
Susan Maitland	Terry Moore
Brigadier General Maitland	Michael Rennie
Karram Kahn	Guy Rolfe
Lieutenant Heath	John Justin
Major MacAllister	Murray Matheson
Lieutenant Baird	Richard Stapley
Ali Nur	Frank de Kova
Native Dancer	Sujata
Lali	Argentina Brunetti
Ahmed	Frank Lackteen

and Mohinder Bedi, Naji Cabbay, David Cota, Karam Dhaliwal, John Farrow, Aram Katcher, Alberto Morin, Gavin Muir, Richard Peel, Gilchrist Stuart, Aly Wassil, and Patrick Whyte.

This Cinemascope production shot on location in India has Tyrone as Captain King, the son of a British officer and a native woman. He is dispatched to the northwestern frontier where most uprisings occur, and he is led against the hill people by an old friend, Indian Karram Kahn, whom he has known for many years.

The New York *Times* described Tyrone as "solemn and efficient as befits a man of courage and pride."

THE LONG GRAY LINE (Released February 11, 1955)

A Columbia Picture, directed by John Ford.
Screenplay by Edward Hope, from the book, *Bringing Up the Brass*, by Marty Mahar and Nardi Reeder Campion.
Produced by Robert Arthur.
Cinematography by Charles Lawton, A.S.C.; edited by William Lyon.
Music composed by Morris Stoloff.
Art direction by Robert Peterson; gowns by Jean-Louis.

Marty Mahar	Tyrone Power
Mary O'Donnell	Maureen O'Hara
"Da"	Donald Crisp
Kitty Carter	Betsy Palmer
James Sundstrom, Jr.	Robert Francis
Captain Herman J. Koehler	Ward Bond
Charles Dotson	Phil Carey
Red Sundstrom	William Leslie
Dinny Mahar	Sean McClory
Corporal Rudy Heinz	Peter Graves

and Don Barclay, Willis Bouchey, Chuck Courtney, Dona Cole, Ken Curtis, Lisa Davis, Diane Delaire, Mimi Doyle, Robert Ellis, Walter D. Ehlers, Major Philip Kieffer, Martin Milner, Erin O'Brien Moore, Donald Murphy, Jack Pennick, Robert Roark, Mickey Roth, James Sears, Elbert Steele, Milburn Stone, Norman Van Brocklin, and Patrick Wayne.

Twenty-year-old Marty Mahar (*Tyrone*) is a "paddy" just off the boat, hired as a cook's helper at West Point. Feeling a slave, he enlists as a rookie but stays on at the Point, finally winning the interest of the chief of physical training, Captain Koehler, "Master of the Sword." He becomes his first assistant. The cadets find him enormously likable and through the years he sees an entire generation pass through, first on their way to the World War.

His father and brother come over from Ireland, after he is married to Mary O'Donnell (*Miss O'Hara*). They have no children; she loses her only son right after birth, so the cadets become their boys.

As an old man, he asks President Eisenhower, whom Marty had seen graduate (in 1915, a class "the stars fell on") to intercede to allow him to stay on at the Point. The President agrees and Marty returns to find the Dress Parade that day is in his honor.

The New York *Times* wrote: "Duty, pride and honor are the virtues that glow warmly in this film, which might better be called 'The Long Green Line'—especially when the customers start flocking in. . . . " It is a beautiful, elegiac tribute to the Academy, strong on sentiment, but never mawkish. Tyrone came as close as he ever would to the power and dramatic excitement of Olivier as Marty Mahar, closer even than his Stan Carlisle in *Nightmare Alley*.

UNTAMED (Released March 11, 1955)

A Twentieth Century-Fox Picture, directed by Henry King.
Screenplay by Talbot Jennings, Frank Fenton and Michael Blankfort, from a book by Helga Moray.
Produced by Bert E. Friedlob and William Bacher.
Music composed by Franz Waxman.
Cinematography by Leo Tover, A.S.C.; edited by Barbara McLean.
Art direction by Lyle Wheeler and Addison Hehr.

Paul Van Riebeck	Tyrone Power
Katie O'Neill	Susan Hayward
Aggie	Agnes Moorehead
Kurt	Richard Egan
Shawn Kildare	John Justin
Julia	Rita Moreno
Maria de Groot	Hope Emerson
Squire O'Neill	Henry O'Neill
Christian	Brad Dexter
Jan	Alexander D. Havemann
Jantsie	Emmett Smith
Joubert	Louis Mercier

and Eleanor Audley, Louis Polliman Brown, Forest Burns, Leonard Carey, Brian Corcoran, Kevin Corcoran, Bobby Diamond, Gary Diamond, Jean Dodsworth, Robin Hughes, Linda Lowell, Jack Macy, Edward Mundy, Paul Thompson, Tina Thompson, Maya Van Horn, Philip Van Zandt, and Cecil Weston.

Tyrone as Paul Van Riebeck is a Dutchman who comes upon a wagon train of settlers and saves them from the Zulus. Aboard the wagon is Katie (*Miss Hayward*), who has lost her husband in the attack. They fall in love, but do not marry, although she waits for his child while married to a farmer (*Richard Egan*) and for him.

Susan Hayward won most of the reviewer attention. She was moving into a spot once occupied by Bette Davis, and Academy Awards were coming her way, although not for this one.

THE EDDY DUCHIN STORY (Released June 22, 1956)

A Columbia Picture, directed by George Sidney; produced by Jerry Wald.

Screenplay by Samuel Taylor from a story by Leo Katcher.

Cinematography by Harry Stradling, A.S.C.; edited by Viola Lawrence and Jack Ogilvie.

Music score composed and directed by Morris Stoloff; piano by Carmen Cavallaro.

Eddy Duchin	Tyrone Power
Marjorie Oelrichs	Kim Novak
Chiquita	Victoria Shaw
Lou Sherwood	James Whitmore
Peter Duchin	Rex Thompson
Peter at Five Years	Mickey Maga
Mr. Wadsworth	Shepperd Strudwick
Mrs. Wadsworth	Frieda Inescort
Mrs. Duchin	Gloria Holden
Leo Reisman	Larry Keating
Mr. Duchin	John Mylong

and Jack Albertson, Kirk Alyn, Arline Anderson, Jacqueline Blanchard, Oliver Cliff, Richard Crane, Richard Cutting, Ralph Gamble, Butler Hixson, Lois Kimbrell, Peter Norman, Howard Price, Gloria Ann Simpson, Richard Walsh, and Gregory Gay.

The film has a sprightly opening to the offscreen tune of "We'll Take Manhattan, the Bronx and Staten Island, too," as Eddy, son of a Jewish druggist, just down from his New England home town, prepares to storm the Central Park Casino and get a job as pianist with Leo Reisman's band. He fails, and his comedown is witnessed by a high-society deb, Marjorie (*Kim Novak*), who is having a big bash at the Casino and urges Reisman to allow Eddy to play. He does, and is something of a sensation. Then Miss Oelrichs' aunt hires him to play at a private party given in their home (her aunt and uncle have raised her). He doesn't know whether he is a hired hand or a guest and becomes a little of both.

He and Marjorie marry and soon he has his own band at the Casino, a record contract and a swank terrace apartment overlooking the Park. Marjorie is soon pregnant, but she is also very ill with a rare disease. The baby, a son, lives, but Marjorie dies. For a long time, he will have nothing to do with the boy, blaming him for his wife's death. Then finally through the boy's governess (*Victoria Shaw*), he relents, and soon he and Chiquita are in love and it all begins again until it is learned that Eddy, too, is stricken with an incurable malady.

He tells his son that he will soon leave him as they walk in the Park, and the boy understands.

Critics from coast-to-coast loved this film and found Tyrone far more mature and compelling as an actor than ever before. It played long runs everywhere, and is the most frequently revived of all of Tyrone's musical films.

ABANDON SHIP (Released April 17, 1957)

A Columbia Picture, directed by Richard Sale.
Produced by Ted Richmond.
Screenplay by Richard Sale from his story, *Seven Waves Away*.
Music by Sir Arthur Bliss.
Cinematography by Wilkie Cooper; edited by Ray Poulton.
Art direction by Ray Simm.

Alec Holmes	Tyrone Power
Julie	Mai Zetterling
Frank Kelly	Lloyd Nolan
Will McKinley	Stephen Boyd
Edith Middleton	Moire Lister
"Cookie" Morrow	James Hayter
Mrs. Knudsen	Marie Lohr
Daniel Cane	Moultrie Kelsall
Aubrey Clark	Noel Willman

and Clare Austin, Colin Broadley, Finlay Currie, John Gray, Danny Green, Gordon Jackson, David Langton, Victor Maddern, Orlando Martins, Ralph Michael, Clive Morton, Laurence Naismith, Derek Sidney, John Stratton, and Meurig Wyn-Jones.

As the executive officer of a liner on a world cruise, Tyrone is forced to take charge when the ship hits a floating mine from World War II and blows up. There is only room in the lifeboat for fourteen people, but there are numerous others, many injured and clinging to the sides. It is up to Tyrone to get rid of the extra ones if any will survive. He orders half a dozen off the boat at gunpoint, and it seems that he was right. But when days and weeks later, they sight land, those survivors who lost family and loved ones resent him and a grumbling is felt that threatens him for a time.

The nurse (*Mai Z.*) who helped him through the ordeal has fallen in love with him in the process, but the ending is not sentimental.

Since it was made for Tyrone's own Copa Productions, he was especially interested in critical reaction. It got uniformly fine reviews but was not properly promoted by Columbia, which released it, and it died.

THE SUN ALSO RISES (Released August 23, 1957)

A Twentieth Century–Fox Picture, produced by Darryl F. Zanuck, and directed by Henry King.
Screenplay by Peter Viertel, based on the novel by Ernest Hemingway.
Cinematography by Leo Tover, A.S.C.; edited by William Mace.
Music composed by Hugo Friedhofer, conducted by Lionel Newman.
Art direction by Lyle R. Wheeler and Mark-Lee Kirk.

Jake Barnes	Tyrone Power
Lady Brett Ashley	Ava Gardner
Mike Campbell	Errol Flynn
Robert Cohn	Mel Ferrer
Bill Gorton	Eddie Albert
Georgette	Juliette Greco
Count Mippipopolous	Gregory Ratoff
Zizi	Marcel Dalio
Doctor	Henry Daniell
Harris	Bob Cunningham
Pedro Romero	Robert Evans

and Jacqueline Evans, Lilia Guizar, Rebecca Iturbi, Lee Morgan, Carlos Muzuiz, Eduardo Noriega, Carlos David Ortigos, and Danik Patisson.

This screen treatment of Hemingway's most successful novel is set in Paris, Pamplona, Biarritz, and other resorts of the rich. The atmosphere is heavy and right. Jack Barnes (*Tyrone*) has been wounded in the groin by the war and cannot have a satisfactory love affair, but women pursue him, most notably Lady Brett (*Miss Gardner*), who is herself pursued by Robert Cohn (*Ferrer*).

Unfortunately, the bullfighter, as played by Robert Evans, is wooden and stops everything dead; the direction is heavy and pedestrian rather than wry and profound. Henry King, usually so fine, was out of his depth here. Still, the New York *Herald Tribune* called it a good film version of the book. "Power is a handsome and dignified Jake Barnes, not quite as insistently masculine as Hemingway's character suggests but manful enough in his struggles with himself."

WITNESS FOR THE PROSECUTION (Released February 6, 1958)

A Theme Pictures Production presented by Edward Small and distributed by United Artists; directed by Billy Wilder.
Produced by Arthur Hornblow, Jr.
Screenplay by Billy Wilder and Harry Kurnitz from the novel and play by Agatha Christie, from an adaptation by Larry Marcus.
Cinematography by Russell Harlan; edited by Daniel Manhell.
Art direction by Alexander Trauner.

Leonard Vole	Tyrone Power
Christine Vole	Marlene Dietrich
Sir Wilfrid Robarts	Charles Laughton
Miss Plimsoll	Elsa Lanchester
Mayhew	Henry Daniell
Brogan-Moore	John Williams
Carter	Ian Wolfe
Janet McKenzie	Una O'Connor
Mr. Meyers	Torin Thatcher
Judge	Francis Compton
Mrs. French	Norma Varden

and Marjorie Eaton, Ruta Lee, Ottola Nesmith, Molly Roden, and Philip Tonge.

Leonard Vole (*Tyrone*) is accused of murdering his wealthy lady admirer, whom he has visited often and, he tells the court, has regarded as his friend. His wife, Christine (*Dietrich*) knows of this friendship and has not criticized it. She also is his chief alibi, since she has accounted for his presence with her at the time of the lady's death. Vole's lawyer (barrister) is a semi-invalid, Sir Wilfrid Robarts (*Laughton*), who is invariably accompanied by his nurse, Miss Plimsoll (*Elsa Lanchester*). Mid-trial, the prosecution, however, presents a surprise witness, a woman who has strong evidence to indicate that Vole has been lying. We will not give away anything of the shocking surprise here by telling who that woman is.

A smash success with long runs everywhere; most critics were impressed by the skillful shading and nuances given the role of Leonard Vole by Tyrone, once again playing a character of much duplicity.

BIBLIOGRAPHY

Agee, James. *Agee on Film*, Volume I. New York: Grosset & Dunlap, 1967.

Baxter, Anne. *Intermission*: A True Tale. New York: Putnam, 1976.

Baxter, John. *Hollywood in the Thirties*. New York: A. S. Barnes, 1968.

Benêt, Stephen Vincent. *John Brown's Body*. Garden City: Doubleday, 1928.

Benny, Mary Livingstone, and Hilliard Marks with Marcia Borie. *Jack Benny*, a Biography. Garden City: Doubleday, 1978.

Bradley, Larry. *Jesse James as Filmed in Pineville, Missouri*. Noel, Missouri: McDonald County Press, 1970.

Calder, Robert Lorin. *W. Somerset Maugham and the Quest for Freedom*. Garden City: Doubleday, 1973.

Christian, Linda. *Linda*. New York: Crown, 1962.

Costain, Thomas. *The Black Rose*. Garden City: Doubleday, Doran, 1945.

Drew, Fraser. *April 8, 1955 with Hemingway*: Unedited Notes on a Visit to Finca Vigia. From the Fitzgerald/Hemingway *Annual*, 1970, edited by Matthew J. Bruccoli and C. E. Fraser Clark, Jr., Washington: Microcard Editions, 1970.

Ewen, David. *The Story of Irving Berlin*. New York: Henry Holt, 1950.

Flynn, Errol. *My Wicked, Wicked Ways*. New York: Putnam, 1959.

Frank, Gerold. *Judy*. New York: Dell, 1976.

Frank, Gerold and Diana Barrymore. *Too Much, Too Soon*. New York: Henry Holt, 1957.

Fredrik, Nathalie. *Hollywood and the Academy Awards*. Beverly Hills: Hollywood Awards Publications, 1970.

Fry, Christopher. *The Dark Is Light Enough*. London: Oxford University Press, 1954.

Gow, Gordon. *Hollywood in the Fifties*. New York: A. S. Barnes, 1971.

Gresham, William Lindsay. *Nightmare Alley*. New York: Rinehart, 1946.

Gussow, Mel. *Don't Say Yes Until I Finish Talking*: A Biography of Darryl F. Zanuck. Garden City: Doubleday, 1971.

Halliwell, Leslie. *The Filmgoer's Companion*, 3rd Edition, Revised. New York: Hill and Wang, 1970.

Harris, Radie. *Radie's World*: The Memoirs of Radie Harris. New York: Putnam, 1975.

Higham, Charles. *Charles Laughton*: An Intimate Biography. Garden City: Doubleday, 1976.

Higham, Charles and Joel Greenberg. *Hollywood in the Forties*. New York: Paperback Library, 1970.

Knight, Eric. *This Above All*. New York: Harper, 1941.

Lambert, Gavin. *On Cukor*. New York: Putnam, 1972.

Langner, Lawrence. *The Magic Curtain*. New York: Dutton, 1951.

Logan, Joshua. *Josh*: My Up and Down, In and Out Life. New York: Delacorte Press, 1976.

Madsen, Axel. *Billy Wilder*. Bloomington: Indiana University Press, 1969.

———. *William Wyler*. New York: Thomas Y. Crowell, 1973.

Maugham, W. Somerset. *The Razor's Edge*. Garden City: Doubleday, 1944.

McCabe, John. *Charlie Chaplin*. Garden City: Doubleday, 1978.

Merton, Thomas. *The Seven Storey Mountain*. New York: Harcourt, Brace, 1948.

Morella, Joe, and Edward Z. Epstein. *Lana*. New York: Citadel, 1971.

Morgan, Charles. *Sparkenbroke*. New York: Macmillan, 1936.

Moshier, W. Franklyn. *The Alice Faye Movie Book*. Harrisburg: Stackpole, 1974.

Niven, David. *The Moon's a Balloon*. New York: Putnam, 1972.

———. *Bring on the Empty Horses*. New York: Putnam, 1975.

Palmer, Lilli. *Change Lobsters—and Dance*: An Autobiography. New York: Macmillan, 1975.

Parish, James Robert, and Don E. Stanke. *The Swashbucklers*. New Rochelle: Arlington House, 1976.

Parsons, Louella. *Tell It to Louella*. New York: Putnam, 1961.

Powdermaker, Hortense. *Hollywood, the Dream Factory*. Boston: Little, Brown, 1950.

Saint-Exupéry, Antoine de. *The Little Prince*. New York: Harcourt, Brace, 1943.

Selznick, David O. *Memo from Selznick*, edited by Rudy Behlmer. New York: Viking Press, 1972.

Sharpe, Howard. *The Life Story of a Problem Child* (*Photoplay* magazine, issues of July, August, September, 1937.)

Shaw, George Bernard. *Back to Methuselah*, Vol. XVI in "The Collected Works of Bernard Shaw." New York: William Wise & Company, 1930.

Shellabarger, Samuel. *Captain from Castille*. Boston: Little, Brown, 1945.

———. *Prince of Foxes*. Boston: Little, Brown, 1947.

Thomas, Bob. *King Cohn: The Life and Times of Harry Cohn*. New York: Putnam, 1967.

Wolfe, Thomas. *You Can't Go Home Again*. New York: Harper, 1940.

INDEX

361

Glittering lives of famous people!
Bestsellers from Berkley

_____ **DOLLY**   04221-9—$2.50
Alanna Nash

_____ **HITCH: THE LIFE AND TIMES OF**
ALFRED HITCHCOCK   04436-X—$2.75
John Russell Taylor

_____ **LADD: A HOLLYWOOD**
TRAGEDY   04531-5—$2.75
Beverly Linet

_____ **LIVING IT UP**   04352-5—$2.25
George Burns

_____ **MERMAN:**
AN AUTOBIOGRAPHY   04261-8—$2.50
Ethel Merman with George Eells

_____ **MOMMIE DEAREST**   04444-0—$2.75
Christina Crawford

_____ **MOTHER GODDAM**   04119-0—$2.50
Whitney Sune with Bette Davis

_____ **MY WICKED, WICKED WAYS**   04686-9—$2.75
Errol Flynn

_____ **NO BED OF ROSES**   04241-3—$2.50
Joan Fontaine

_____ **SELF-PORTRAIT**   04485-8—$2.75
Gene Tierney, with Mickey Herskowitz

_____ **MISS TALLULAH BANKHEAD**   04574-9—$2.75
Lee Israel

Available at your local bookstore or return this form to:

 Berkley Book Mailing Service
P.O. Box 690
Rockville Centre, NY 11570

Please send me the above titles. I am enclosing $ _____
(Please add 50¢ per copy to cover postage and handling). Send check or money
order—no cash or C.O.D.'s. Allow three weeks for delivery

NAME _____

ADDRESS _____

CITY _____ STATE/ZIP _____ 60